Group Work with Children and Adolescents

A HANDBOOK

of related interest

Communicating with Children and Adolescents
Action for Change
Edited by Anne Bannister and Annie Huntington
ISBN 1 84310 025 8

Meeting the Needs of Ethnic Minority Children
A Handbook for Professionals
Edited by Kedar Nath Dwivedi and Ved P Varma
ISBN 1 85302 294 2

Interventions with Bereaved Children
Susan C Smith and Sister Margaret Pennells
ISBN 1 85302 285 3

Project-Based Group Work Facilitator's Manual
Young People, Youth Workers and Projects
Andy Gibson and Gaynor Clarke
ISBN 1 85302 169 5

How and Why Children Hate
A Study of Conscious and Unconscious Sources
Edited by Ved Varma
ISBN 1 85302 116 4 hb
ISBN 1 85302 185 7 pb

How and Why Children Fail
Edited by Ved Varma
ISBN 1 85302 108 3 hb
ISBN 1 85302 186 5 pb

Chain Reaction
Children and Divorce
Ofra Ayalon and Adina Flasher
ISBN 1 85302 136 9

Parenting Teenagers
Bob Myers
ISBN 1 85302 366 3

Working with Children in Need
Studies in Complexity and Challenge
Edited by Eric Sainsbury
ISBN 1 85302 275 6

Group Work
with Children and Adolescents

A HANDBOOK

Edited by Dr Kedar Nath Dwivedi

Foreword by Robin Skynner

Jessica Kingsley Publishers
London and Philadelphia

First published in the United Kingdom in 1993 by
Jessica Kingsley Publishers
116 Pentonville Road
London N1 9JB, UK
and
400 Market Street, Suite 400
Philadelphia, PA 19106, USA

www.jkp.com

Copyright © 1993 the contributors and the publisher
Foreword Copyright © 1993 Robin Skynner

Second impression 1996
Third impression 1998
Fourth impression 1999
Fifth impression 2003
Sixth impression 2004
Seventh impression 2005
Eighth impression 2006

British Library Cataloguing in Publication Data

Dwivedi, Kedar Nath
Group Work with Children and Adolescents
I. Title
362.7

ISBN-13: 978 185302 157 2
ISBN-10: 1-85302-1571

Printed and Bound in Great Britain by
Athenaeum Press, Gateshead, Tyne and Wear

Contents

To my Teachers,
Mother Sayama and Saya U Chit Tin,
With deepest respect and gratitude

Foreword

It is a particular and very personal pleasure to contribute a foreword to this important book, not least through discovering, on learning about the history through development, that I had the privilege of contributing as an early link to the chain.

While undertaking my training in psychiatry during the mid-1950s at the Maudsley, where S.H. Foulkes was developing and teaching the new form of psychotherapy he called group-analysis, I quickly became impressed by the power of this new method and he kindly accepted me as one of his trainees. He was using the method only with adult patients, but James Anthony, then a consultant in the Children's Department and co-author with Foulkes of the Penguin book *Group Psychotherapy: The Psycho-Analytic Approach,* had experimented a little with groups of children. So when I decided to specialise in child psychiatry, and began experimenting with children's groups myself, I was able to get support and advice from him before he left for the United States to take up his professorship in St. Louis.

From 1958 to 1963, first at the Brixton and then at the Guildford and the Harlow Child Guidance clinics, I became so impressed by the effectiveness of groups for children and adolescents that they became the main mode of treatment; I was soon running about eight a week, while a psychotherapist colleague added to this number. This more than doubled the number of children for whom we were able to provide psychotherapy, and also enabled us to treat effectively many patients who had failed to respond to other methods.

After two years of such work at Guildford, we received the results – based on the accounts of parents, school reports and our own clinical impressions of changes – and concluded that about a third of all treatable cases were best helped through groups, and a third through individual work, while a third could benefit from either method. Thus groups were at least equally effective, and more economical, in two-thirds, making more individual treatment time available for those who most needed it. In this sample the only children who failed to gain at least some benefit from the group psychotherapy (17%) proved to be those with behaviour disorders who were immature and narcissistic, as well as deeply involved with and dominated by mothers who were either psychotic or suffering from other severe psychological problems – children difficult to change by any form of psychotherapy.

Towards the end of this period, in 1962, I began my own first experiments with family therapy, guided by reports that were appearing in the American journals, and a year later moved to Woodberry Down CGC in Hackney where this work became the main focus. Because of constraints of time and lack of the excellent facilities I had enjoyed at Harlow, my experiments with children's groups here came to an end.

Soon after, in 1964, I designed an Introductory Course in Group Work, on behalf of the Group-Analytic Society for the A.P.S.W., run by Dr de Mare and myself but soon expanded to include other mental health professions and course leaders. This developed into the Institute of Group Analysis where it still runs as the introductory 'General Course'. Among the first trainees was Dr Terry Lear, who developed the similar 'Midland Course' based upon it, and who later assisted Dr Dwivedi and his colleagues towards setting up their associated Introductory Course in Groupwork with Children and Adolescents. The latter presents to those who can attend it some of the knowledge this group of pioneering collaborators has gained. But the numbers who can conveniently do so are inevitably limited, and we are fortunate that the present volume now gathers together the authors' rich store of experience and makes it available to us all.

It has long been a source of regret to me that, except for one article, I have not written about my own early work with children's groups. Instead, I am now happy that this team of colleagues has done so, based on a vastly greater range of shared experience and discussion. I congratulate the authors and editor on their achievement, and warmly recommend *Group Work with Children and Adolescents* as vital reading for all those involved in the treatment of children's emotional problems.

Robin Skynner

Preface

In one of the recent Conferences of the Child Psychiatry Section of the Royal College of Psychiatrists, Dr Peter Hardwick from Dorset made a delightful presentation on the topic of a 'stone soup' approach to the creation of his Day Service for mental health problems in children and their families. The story relates to a tramp who carries a stone and goes around telling people about the magical soup-making qualities of the stone. The tramp encourages people to test the qualities of the stone by asking them to start heating a container full of water into which he puts the 'soup stone'. After a while he tests a drop of water on his tongue and declares 'The soup is already coming on nicely, perhaps one or two chopped onions would make it more delicious'. And then, a pinch of salt, some lentils and so forth are suggested, until a truly delicious soup is produced and is consumed by the tramp in addition to serving others.

The situation in Northampton was a bit more fortunate in the 1960s, in that the services of such a 'soup stone' weren't really required in the same way. The Oxford Regional Hospital Board commissioned an In-patient Psychiatric Unit in Northampton, but when the accommodation and staffing became available later Dr Ken Stewart re-examined the needs and opted for a Day Service instead. Thus the Naylands Family Centre opened in 1973. The service consisted of Family Day Programmes utilising the principles derived from Therapeutic Communities, Group Analysis, (Multiple) Family Therapy, Behaviour Therapy and so forth. After his death, the centre was renamed on 27th June 1979, after him, as the Ken Stewart Family Centre.

As the clinical demands on the Child Mental Health Services increased heavily, we started experimenting with group work with children and adolescents, in addition to family day programmes at the Centre. We were greatly inspired by Dr Terry Lear (a close friend of Dr Ken Stewart) who founded the Midland Course in Groupwork and Family Therapy in Northampton and later served as the President of the Group Analytic Society (UK). Thus, most of the staff of the Child and Family Consultation Service have contributed greatly to the development of groupwork with children and adolescents at the Ken Stewart Family Centre. The nursing staff in particular – Sarah Hogan, Mark Hook, Kay McCreadie, Jan Pawlikowski, Paul Sellwood, Susie Towers and Eileen Woolley to name but a few – have devoted most of their time at the centre to the promotion of groupwork.

In association with the Midland Course, we have, since 1990, run an introductory course in groupwork with children and adolescents in Northampton, as we felt that there was an enormous need in this field and there were virtually no training opportunities for those interested. I am very grateful to the committee of the Midland Course, especially Terry Lear, Patrick McGrath, Julie Roberts, Harry Tough and the course secretary Pam Bates. I am also grateful to all the contributors and delegates on the introductory courses on group work with children and adolescents for creating a context for this book and to Leslie Curtress for providing valuable administrative support to the courses.

The course has highlighted the lack of suitable reading materials in the literature. In contrast to the availability of training opportunities, books, journals and papers on groupwork with adults there is really very little available for those interested in group work with children and adolescents. Scheidlinger has repeatedly (1977, 1984) emphasised the pervasive lack of interest coupled with a paucity of trained practitioners in groupwork with children. Abramowitz (1976), reviewing outcome research in this field, noted: 'Published empirical outcome research has been especially rare' (p.321). Bamber (1988) as the Guest Editor of the special issue of Group Analysis on group analysis with children and adolescents remarked: 'In the Journal's twenty one years of publication I can find only three articles and one report of a scientific meeting which deal specifically with children and adolescents' (p.99).

I am very grateful to Peter Harper and Sarah Hogan for their help in planning the structure of the book; to Jessica Kingsley Publishers for their enthusiasm; to Jean Kurecki for her hard work of extensive correspondence; to Andrea Trigg, Christine Greatorex and Carol Weller from the St. Crispin Hospital library for their much appreciated help in obtaining relevant literature; to all the contributors for making such a worthwhile contribution; to Robin Skynner for his foreword; to Jess Gordon, Ved Varma and Patrick McGrath for their constant encouragement; the children, adolescents and their families for giving us the opportunity to work with them and for teaching us so much; and to the readers for taking the trouble to read this book.

I have found this project most enjoyable, especially the support and the experience of working with a large team of direct and indirect contributors.

The heavy clinical demands in our service have meant an enormous pressure on our secretarial staff: Naina Sadarani, Fay Bourne and Sylvia Wilson. The heavy pressure of clinical demands has also meant that I have had to devote most of my weekends and holidays to this project and I am very grateful to my wife, Radha for her unfailing patience. My sons Amitabh and Rajaneesh between themselves have painstakingly typed several drafts of at least eight of my chapters for which I am immensely thankful.

Kedar Nath Dwivedi
Northampton 1992

References

Abramowitz, C.V. (1976) 'The Effectiveness of Group Psychotherapy with Children'. *Archives of General Psychiatry.* 33: 320–326.

Bamber, J.H. (1988) 'Group Analysis with Children and Adolescents'. *Group Analysis.* 21: 99–102.

Scheidlinger, S. (1977) 'Group Therapy for Latency-Age Children: A Bird's Eye View'. *Journal of Clinical Child Psychology.* 4: 40–43.

Scheidlinger, S. (1984) 'Short-Term Group Therapy for Children: An Overview'. *International Journal of Group Psychotherapy.* 34(4): 573–585.

Part 1

Theoretical and Practical Issues

CHAPTER 1

Introduction

Kedar Nath Dwivedi

People can be grouped in a variety of ways: according to their physical characteristics, age, sex, personality, occupation, education and so on. Such groupings, however, are not psychological groupings. The American sociologist, Charles H. Cooley (1864–1929) in his famous work, *Social Organisation* (1909) described society as being made up of primary and secondary groups. Accordingly, primary groups are characterised by intimate face-to-face association and co-operation and are fundamental in forming the social nature and ideals of the individual. In contrast, the relations between the members of secondary groups are 'cool', that is, impersonal, rational, contractual and formal. Membership of a secondary group is simply a means to an end and does not involve whole personalities, but only partial special capacities. The primary group can be an end in itself, providing pleasure or the satisfaction of being together or doing things together in the group (Olmsted 1965). People in a secondary group such as a city, a professional association or trade union are indirectly related, usually with long distance communication. Secondary groups are mainly instrumental while primary groups are usually expressive, with face-to-face interaction. 'The "secondary" group is, in a sense, purely a figment of the imagination' (Sprott 1958 p.16).

'The sense of "self" arises from the social experience of interacting with others' (Hargreaves 1972). Human beings spend most of their waking lives in groups. One may be a member of several groups, thus operating as a family group at home, staff group at work, rugby team whilst playing or attending the meeting of the team, church group, and so on. In addition to such natural or historically rooted groups an extending range of contrived group experiences have also been added to in recent decades with the aim of providing personal growth, expanding emotional sensitivity, offering an experience of group intimacy and of relieving personal distress, problems or psychiatric disturbances (Ryle 1976).

There is an expanding preoccupation with the group as a tool and group techniques are being employed in a variety of settings including industry, media, management, public administration, health, education, personal social services, and government. Slavson (1959) highlighted that '... though we live in a highly scientific and technological era and the threshold of the atomic age, our politics and governments have still many of the characteristics of the horse and buggy period' (p.51). Since most human problems arise in the setting of group life, many can be solved in a group setting. There is a need to find the means to forge the unconscious processes in such a way that human hostilities, aggression and violence towards oneself, other beings and the ecology can be reduced. '... this can be achieved only through groups with their powers to sanction, prohibit, control, accept and reject' (Slavson 1959 p.52).

Slavin (1985) emphasised the importance of co-operative problem solving while working with others in face-to-face situations, from primitive hunting groups to the modern boardroom. One should, therefore, expect an adequate emphasis on co-operative learning and problem solving in schools, families and other institutions that socialise children. In practice, unfortunately, this has been found to be far from the case. 'What seems to have happened in practice is that teachers have taken on board Plowden's views on having children work in groups but have preferred to retain individualisation rather than co-operation in that context' (Bennett 1990 p.7). 'Grouping thus emerged as an organisational device rather than as a means of promoting more effective learning, or perhaps exists for no reason other than that fashion and ideology dictate it' (Alexander 1984 p.40–41).

In a social psychological sense, a group (i.e., a primary group in face-to-face relationship) 'is a plurality of persons who interact with one another in a given context more than they interact with anyone else' (Sprott 1958 p.9). Thus, the criterion of relatively exclusive interaction in a given context is the principle feature of psychological groups. The issues of exclusivity (a boundary phenomenon), dynamicity, interaction and identification are discussed further in the chapter on Conceptual Frameworks in this volume.

Scheidlinger (1982) classifies 'people-helping groups' in four major categories: (1) group psychotherapy, (2) therapeutic groups for clients in mental health settings, (3) human development and training groups and (4) self help and mutual help groups. Group psychotherapy is defined by him as follows: 'a specific field of clinical practice, within the realm of the psychotherapists, a psychological process, wherein an *expert* psychotherapist with special additional group process training, utilises the emotional interactions in small carefully planned groups to "repair" mental ill health, i.e., to effect amelioration of personality dysfunction in individuals specifically selected for this purpose' (p.7). Because of this apparent complexity many clinicians have avoided the use of group work for therapy. Some practitioners also have the feeling 'that the interaction of members will somehow interfere with the achievement of individual goals' (Rose and Edleson 1987 p.3).

An infant's first relationship and interaction are mainly with the mother and the nature of early play in children is, therefore, egocentric (Erickson 1977, Stern 1977). Very young children, for example, at the age of two and three tend to engage in solitary play or with a care giving individual rather than sharing with other children or engaging in co-operative peer group activity, according to nursery observations by Isaacs (1933).

It does take some time for young children to form groups. Occasional groups may appear at four or five, usually in the spirit of hostility towards an outsider, but by the ages of six and seven, if there are opportunities, more stable groups can appear with all the interplay of social learning, sharing, give and take, sense of justice, and so forth. Conflicts may begin to surface between the principles of parental (or adult) authority and standards set by friends. As, during the latency age, children try to master their stage specific developmental tasks, expand the range of their interests (and libidinal objects), and work towards sublimating their Oedipal strivings, they tend to elevate the peer group to a role of primary importance. Thus, the 'peer groups of latency age children unfailingly develop carefully articulated sets of norms and roles that govern how the groups as a whole will function, as well as the kinds of individual relationships that may be constructed within the group's boundaries' (Schamess 1992 p.352).

In recent years there has been a vigorous growth in research on sibling and peer relationships in order to understand their implications for children's well being and adjustment (Dunn and McGuire 1992). Latency age children, as a function of their particular stage in life, are very group oriented. As school children, they spend most of their time in group settings. They are taught in groups and play and eat in groups. For them group work is an effective therapeutic approach, as it recreates the important social aspect of the child's life which occurs among the siblings, with the parents, at school, in the neighbourhood, and so forth.

> 'The group is a particularly effective approach with children because the child is a social being and is generally interested in interaction. Children like to be part of a group and the group can be a most effective process to assist in the learning of developmental tasks... You [the group worker] and the group become a part of a social laboratory in which the child tries new patterns of relating aggression, anger, love, and tests reality'. (Dinkmeyer and Muro 1971 p.213)

> 'The group situation fits in with ease developmentally into children's ordinary lives of school and family. The traditional one to one relationship is an uncommon one for children of school age and

inevitably evokes defences and resistances to the regression implicit in it: this needs exceptional skills to handle and also may restrict individual therapy to certain issues while masking others. The opportunity for the child to see others at different levels of defensive development, in the presence of benign adults who are "holding" the situation in a containing group, will often give him more freedom to examine, drop or restructure maladaptive defences or behaviour patterns'. (Farrell 1984 p.146)

Therapeutic group work with young children was first attempted by Moreno in the early part of the century using psychodrama techniques. In 1934 The Jewish Board of Guardians started group work with children of latency age (8 to 12 years) which later became known as Activity Group Therapy. The main aims were to (i) improve their ego strength and a sense of self worth so often crushed in problem children, (ii) provide substitute love if they were unable to find this in their homes, (iii) offer opportunities for genuine interest in leisure time activities and (iv) rebuild their distorted personalities.

'The members of the group work together: they quarrel, fight – and sometimes strike one another; they argue and haggle, but finally come to some working understanding with one another. Sometimes this process takes six months or more, but once it has been established it becomes a permanent attitude on the part of the individuals involved. We have evidence that these are carried over to the other group relationships in the home, at school and in play'. (Slavson 1940 p.526)

During the 1960s Ginott (1961) popularised therapeutic group work with children. Over the decades this has evolved as an important mode of working with children and adolescents in a variety of settings. In the UK Anthony (1965) and Skynner (1971) promoted group work with children and adolescents. In the form of intermediate treatment it also emerged as a movement using leisure, outward bound, sport, and other activities to cultivate corrective group processes in order to help youngsters in trouble. Group work principles have been utilised in Children's Therapeutic Communities, psychiatric in-patient units, children's homes and other residential institutions along with the use of formal group work sessions. It has also formed the backbone of Youth and Community Work Services. Many schools have already experimented with group work, especially in relation to some selected children and adolescents and in the context of Personal and Social Education. Many Child Mental Health Services (e.g. Child Guidance Clinics and Child Psychiatric Services) not only find group work as economical but also more effective as a tool in their therapeutic work with children and adolescents, although it has to be done in conjunction with family work and other liaison work. Gradually, a substantial amount of literature is beginning to be available regarding the experiences of group work with specific issues and problems, for example, anger, anxiety, sexual abuse, bereavement, delinquency, chronic illnesses, attention deficit hyperactivity disorder, social skills. Many of these are elaborated further elsewhere in this volume.

Most typically, groups have been established either as 'experiential' groups or 'psycho educational' (didactic) groups. In psycho educational or didactic groups, the workers determine most of the agenda and activity by presenting exercises and leading discussions. In an experiential group, the therapeutic aspects of the situation that each child creates within the group are skilfully harnessed (Keepers 1987).

The unstructured experiential groups for children were initially called 'socialisation groups' and these groups used at least some part of their time in special activities such as cooking, painting, collage, drama, as 'activity groups' (Slavson and Schiffer 1975). The idea of diagnostic groups also came in vogue (Anthony 1965, Redl 1944), but these have been difficult to set up (Farrell 1984). A child psychiatrist may not 'always avail himself of the group interview, and may carry away the impression of a pale, sad, inhibited child, looking somewhat "dead", and with very little to say for himself. Should he by chance, place the child in a children's group for a period long enough to let him "warm up" after his clinic experience, he will observe him open out like a Japanese flower in water, suddenly full of colour and spontaneity. A remark often heard in child guidance clinic is that such-and-such a mother had painted her child as a lion, and when he walked into the clinic, he was just like a lamb. Half an hour in a diagnostic group would convince the psychiatrist that a mother knows a lion when she meets one' (Anthony 1965 p.232).

Group work with children and adolescents does differ in certain aspects from group work with adults. Many authors (e.g. Behr 1988, Corder 1987, MacLennan and Felsenfeld 1968, Masterson 1958, Slavson 1953, Sugar 1975) have elaborated on these themes. The reasons for the difference are mainly maturational and developmental. This is why so much space has been devoted in this volume on developmental issues (in Section II). The state of children's cognitive and emotional development determines their ability to conceptualise, cultivate insight, grow out of egocentricity and narcissism, develop empathy and tolerate and utilise feelings. Their modes of communication and capacity for concentration also have important implications for the style of group work.

Slavson (1953) emphasised these differences in relation to ego and superego structures, as the children still derive much of their ego strength from the adults about them. The ego defences are still forming and being organised into definite patterns. The personality is not yet formed but is still evolving. Similarly, the superego is also unformed and derives mainly from the standards set by the adults around.

In group work with children and adolescents there is a tendency towards action. Also, the pace and style of communication is very different from that in adult groups. Themes of conversation may change very rapidly, jumping from topic to topic, often unconnected and in parallel. Moods can be very volatile, with strong emotional expressions. As the conceptual and linguistic abilities of children are still evolving there is a predominance of non-verbal modes of communication and expression. An inability to comprehend fully each other's language can lead to much conflict between a child and adult. Slavson (1953) wrote about a man he knew, whose little girl told him, 'I try to be good, but I can't'. But what she was really trying to convey was, 'I try to be good in a way you want me to be good, but being a child and not an adult, I cannot live up to adult standards' (p.110). Use of play, activity, games, art and drama (detailed elsewhere in this volume), therefore assume special significance in group work with children and adolescents.

Apart from the differences in pace, style and mode of communication, group work with children and adolescents also differs in the quality and quantity of dynamic administration and that of boundary activities or incidents that impinge on the group processes (Behr 1988). Group work with this population requires very insightful and careful advance planning and preparation. '... to operate such groups truly effectively in any institutional setting (clinic, school, children's home and so on), more attention should be paid to the regression, reactions and defences of all staff in the institution whether directly involved in the groups or not' (Farrell 1984 p.154).

Any work with children and adolescents inevitably involves inter-play with their families, family substitutes (e.g. children's homes, foster families), schools and many other agencies and professionals (e.g. doctors, other health workers, social workers, youth workers, and probation officers). Even transport is a major consideration. One has to be constantly aware of the ambience and meaning attached to their attendance in the group. Some family members may feel envious, others may find it cumbersome. There are wider implications of child's dress getting smeared with paint or the timing of sessions being altered even slightly. Many schools and parents find it difficult to tolerate children missing school. They may see the behaviour of the child after the group as unacceptable. Thus, adequate preparation and liaison has to be maintained to protect the group from being sabotaged by a variety of forces. It has to be linked with other therapeutic activities such as family work, marital work, or support to the children's home. However, it also has to be balanced by the maintenance of due confidentiality and trust within the group.

The nature of boundary incidents with implications for limit setting, structuring and control are explored further in the chapter on conceptual frameworks in this volume. Spilling over of the group into the waiting room before and after the session and in fact anywhere in the building or outside is not uncommon. There may be discussions among parents in the waiting room also influencing the entire process. Similarly, the boundaries of the group worker are heavily tested by demands for self-disclosure, physical contact, disciplining and the meeting of physical needs. Bringing parts of the outside world as transitional objects and auxiliary egos is another example of boundary activities in group work with children and adolescents.

A piece of research (Corder *et al.* 1980) that contrasted adolescent groups with those of adults in terms of perceptions of therapists and group functioning highlighted the fact that experienced therapists were more verbally active in adolescent groups and more open in sharing selected personal experience. The groups were more rapid in process, with shorter duration and more abrupt endings. There were fewer extended silences within sessions, with a tendency for the therapists to be more directive and confrontative in their clarifications. 'The therapist of an adolescent group has to work harder than he does in an adult group to disabuse the group of his omnipotent and omniscient role' (Behr 1988 p.131).

Effective group work can enhance social skills, self-esteem and reality testing (Keepers 1987, Arnold and Estricher 1985, Bender 1952). It can also help children to learn delaying gratification, managing feelings, exploring abstractions and values, cultivating creativity and giving of oneself to others. It helps to overcome narcissism and improve the sense of interdependence as well as autonomy.

Many conditions and circumstances (such as encopresis, enuresis, sexual abuse) can induce a sense of shame, embarrassment and isolation. Group experiences can reduce the sense of isolation, normalise responses and mobilise mutual support and acknowledgement of each other's needs and experiences. Rachman (1975) emphasises the positive value of group affiliation and intimate emotional peer contact, where members perceive and support each other in their common goals of discovering themselves as individuals in the successful resolution of basic adolescent identity crisis.

Didato (1974) sets out four therapeutic goals in groupwork with children and adolescents: '(1) to increase capacity to experience powerful affects (positive and negative, without acting them out), (2) to increase capacity for empathy, (3) to strengthen identification with the therapist, (4) to encourage new behavioural patterns in helping the group resolve inter-group conflict through non physical verbal means' (p.747).

Group work has many advantages over other ways of therapeutic working with children and adolescents. It has the dual promise of both interpersonal gain and treatment economy. In this era of 'value for money', 'internal markets' and economical factors driving the public services so clearly, group work becomes the first choice. Although there is not enough research comparing the effect of group work with other therapeutic procedures on children and adolescents, research work on adults has indicated much lower costs for similar results in group work than in individual work, especially in phobia, depressive and stress disorders (Teri and Lewinsohn 1985, Toseland and Siporin 1986). With children and adolescents, however, group work often has to be combined with family work and liaison. In many services an active co-operation of family is essential before any work with children or adolescents can be undertaken. There are many situations which are so problematic that neither individual or group work nor family work in isolation can initiate or sustain a desirable change; however, a combination of several approaches might. It is rather like putting sticks into a bundle that cannot be broken, although each stick could have been broken individually.

In correcting a vicious cycle, one may have to influence at a point which may be most vulnerable to change, rather than the point that may have been most resistant, even though that may be the most pathological. It is not uncommon to find family therapy failing in the face of parental difficulty in initiating change. Sometimes it may be possible for parents to change their behaviours in response to the change in child's behaviour brought about by individual or group work. At other times the chances of producing such changes in parental attitudes and behaviours are so minimal that alternative placements for children are often considered. Such options can be protective in certain respects but can also have damaging consequences. In any case, whether the decision is to proceed or not to proceed with attempting alternative placement, the child or adolescent always needs help with finding ways of coping with various psychological onslaughts.

For most children and adolescents, the small group is a natural and highly attractive setting. Because of its resemblance and kinship with the natural peer group, therapeutic groups more closely simulate the real world for them. In individual therapy settings the huge disparity between the status of the adult therapist and that of the child or the adolescent becomes too obvious. It can also lead to an intense transference, while such transferences become diluted and distributed in a group setting. Similarly, in family therapy sessions there are habitual ways of interactions depending upon the family's particular map of facilitations and inhibitions. A child or adolescent may find it very difficult to convey important feelings lest someone dear and vulnerable gets hurt or becomes assaultative either in the session or outside. Thus, both individual and family therapy sessions can be inhibiting at times. In addition, the group creates the opportunity for the use of many therapeutic procedures, games and exercises that may not be possible in individual or family sessions.

Group work can reach parts that other modes of therapeutic work may not. It creates an atmosphere that is conducive to getting in touch with relevant feelings and issues and sharing them in a group of peers. It also enables children and adolescents to contribute more, work for others and benefit by various identifications. Jointly working on one person's problems has the effect of influencing every one else's in the group. The various interactions in the group trigger perceptions, attitudes and behaviours that have proved to be pathological in one's day to day life. Such materials being enacted live in the group provide opportunities for feedback, experimentation with and practice of alternative perspectives and options. There are frequent and various opportunities for peer reinforcement which are far more powerful than adult reinforcement, as group influences on behaviour can be much stronger than others.

In the cognitive and behavioural therapy approach, such group settings can also provide a chance to learn or to improve one's ability to mediate rewards for others in interactive social situations (with family members, friends, teachers, acquaintances, employees, and so forth). The group worker can construct a situation in which each member has frequent instructions, opportunity and rewards for reinforcing others in the group. 'Offering positive feedback is a highly valued skill in our society; there is good reason to believe that as children learn to reinforce others, they are reciprocally reinforced by others and mutual liking also increases' (Rose and Edleson 1987 p.3).

Thus, a group has many functions discharged simultaneously!

References

Alexander, R.J. (1984) *Primary Teaching.* London: Holt, Rinehart & Winston.

Anthony, E.J. (1965, 2nd Edition) 'Group Analytic Psychotherapy with Children and Adolescents'. In S.H. Foulkes and E.J. Anthony (eds) *Group Psychotherapy: The Psychoanalytic Approach.* London: Maresfield Library. pp.186–232.

Arnold, L.E. and Estricher, D. (1985) 'Parent–Child Group Therapy: Building Self Esteem in a Cognitive Behavioural Group'. Lexington, MA: Lexington Books, D.C. Heath and Co.

Behr, H. (1988) 'Group Analysis with Early Adolescents: Some Clinical Issues'. *Group Analysis.* 21: 119–133.

Bender, L. (1952) *Child Psychiatric Techniques: Diagnostic and Therapeutic Approach to Normal and Abnormal Development through Patterned Expressive and Group Behaviour.* Springfield IL: Charles C. Thomas.

Bennett, N. (1990) Cooperative Learning in Classrooms: Process and Outcomes. 1990 Emmanuel Miller Lecture (Personal Communication).

Cooley, C.H. (1909) *Social Organisation.* New York: Scribners.

Corder, B.F. (1987) 'Planning and Leading Adolescent Therapy Groups'. In P.A. Keller and S.R. Heyman (eds) *Innovations in Clinical Practice 6.* Saratosa: Professional Resources Exchange: 177–196.

Corder, B.F., Haizlip, T. and Walker, P. (1980) 'Critical Areas of Therapist Functioning in Adolescent Group Psychotherapy: A Comparison with Self-Perception of Functioning in Adult Groups'. *Adolescence.* 58: 433–442.

Didato, S.V. (1974) 'Delinquents in Group Therapy'. In C. Sangu and H.S. Kaplan (eds) *Progress in Group and Family Therapy.* New York: Brunner/Mazel.

Dinkmeyer, D.C. and Muro, J.J. (1971) *Group Counselling: Theory and Practice.* Itasca, IL: F.E. Peacock.

Dunn, J. and McGuire, S. (1992) 'Sibling and Peer Relationships in Childhood'. *Journal of Child Psychology and Psychiatry.* 33(1): 67–105.

Erickson, E.H. (1977) *Childhood and Society.* St. Albans: Triad/Paladin.

Farrell, M. (1984) 'Group-Work with Children: The Significance of Setting and Context'. *Group Analysis.* 17(2): 146–155.

Ginott, H.G. (1961) *Group Psychotherapy with Children: The Theory and Practice of Play Therapy.* New York: McGraw-Hill.

Hargreaves, D.H. (1972) *Interpersonal Relations and Education.* London: Routledge and Kegan Paul.

Isaacs, S. (1933) *Social Development in Young Children.* London: Routledge.

Keepers, T.D. (1987) 'Group Treatment of Children: Practical Considerations and Techniques'. In P.A. Keller and S.R. Heyman (eds) *Innovations in Clinical Practice 6:* 165–175. Sarasota: Professional Resources Exchange.

MacLennan, B. and Felsenfeld, N. (1968) *Group Counselling and Psychotherapy with Adolescents.* New York: Columbia University Press.

Masterson, J.F. (1958) 'Psychotherapy of Adolescents Contrasted with Psychotherapy of Adults'. *Journal of Nervous and Mental Diseases.* 127: 517–551.

Olmsted, M.S. (1965) *The Small Group.* New York: Random House.

Rachman, R. (1975) *Identity Group Psychotherapy with Adolescents.* Springfield IL: Charles C. Thomas.

Redl, F. (1944) 'Diagnostic Group Work'. *American Journal of Orthopsychiatry.* 14: 53–67.

Rose, S.D. and Edleson, J.L. (1987) *Working with Children and Adolescents in Groups.* San Francisco: Jossey Boss.

Ryle, A. (1976) 'Group Psychotherapy'. *British Journal of Hospital Medicine.* 15(3): 239–248.

Schamess, G. (1992) 'Reflections on a Developing Body of Group-As-A-Whole Theory for Children's Therapy Groups: An Introduction'. *International Journal of Group Psychotherapy.* 42(3): 351–356.

Scheidlinger, S. (1982) *Focus on Group Psychotherapy.* New York: International Universities Press.

Skynner, A.C.R. (1971) 'Group Therapy with Adolescents Groups'. *Annual Review of the Residential Child Care Association.* 18(16): 16–32.

Slavin, R.E. (1985) 'An Introduction to Co-operative Learning Research'. In R. Slavin, S. Sharon, S. Kagan, R. Hertz-Lazarowitz, C. Webb and R. Schmuck (eds) *Learning to Co-operate and Co-operating to Learn.* London: Plenum (pp.5–15).

Slavson, S.R. (1940) 'Foundations of Group Therapy with Children'. In M. Schiffer (ed) (1979) *Dynamics of Group Psychotherapy.* New York: Jason Aronson. pp.523–537.

Slavson, S.R. (1953) 'Common Sources of Error and Confusion'. In M. Schiffer (ed) (1979) *Dynamics of Group Psychotherapy.* New York: Jason Aronson. pp.85–113.

Slavson, S.R. (1959) 'The Era of Group Psychotherapy'. In M. Schiffer (ed) (1979) *Dynamics of Group Psychotherapy*. New York: Jason Aronson. pp.47–72.

Slavson, S.R. and Schiffer, M. (1975) *Group Psychotherapies for Children*. New York: International Universities Press.

Sprott, W.J.H. (1958) *Human Groups*. London: Penguin.

Stern, D. (1977) *The First Relationship: Infant and Mother*. London: Fontana/Open Books.

Sugar, M. (1975) *The Adolescent in Group and Family Therapy*. New York: Brunner/Mazel.

Teri, L. and Lewinsohn, P.M. (1985) 'Group Intervention for Unipolar Depression'. *Behaviour Therapist*. 8(6): 109–111.

Toseland, R.W. and Siporin, M. (1986) 'When to Recommend Group Treatment: A Review of the Clinical and the Research Literature'. *International Journal of Group Psychotherapy*. 36(2): 171–210.

CHAPTER 2

Structural and
Organisational Aspects

Kedar Nath Dwivedi, Suzanne Lawton
and Sarah Hogan

The structure a groupworker establishes for a group has a profound effect on the interactions within the group and its general dynamics. As group work with children and adolescents can be conducted in a variety of agencies and settings, the groups may vary widely in aims, objectives, structures and styles. The specific organisational and structural aspects of groupwork in specific agencies, for specific problems, and for specific styles are dealt with in other chapters. In this chapter an attempt is made to highlight the value of organisational and structural aspects of group work in general in any agency. These aspects need to be considered before setting up a group, but there is no need to see them as prescriptive.

Venue

The venue where group work is held is very important. It should be a place where there is warmth and comfort, a place where a child or an adolescent can feel at ease and not overawed. Too small a room can force proximity and increase tension, while a very large room can diffuse interaction and increase the risk of its fragmentation. Furniture can block movement and limit the style of interactions, while its absence may lead to discomfort or too much disruptive physical interactions. It is also important to ensure that the group is not interrupted and the room is not used for other purposes during the group time, (e.g. passage way, storage, telephone, office or waiting). The furnishings in the room should create a valuable and warm atmosphere with a feeling of relaxation and also a sense of formality. The chairs in a classroom, for example, may have to be rearranged in a circle before the group meets. The venue should be 'child centred' with evidence of children and young people about, and appropriate artwork, toys or equipment in evidence. Availability of light refreshment may also be desirable. The room should be suitable for the use of resources such as art, play, games and so forth. There may be different rooms for different purposes, for example, activity room, art room, games room, cushion room, or garden. Availability of such specific rooms allows the group to use any of these depending upon the needs of the group at a particular time. However, such an availability can also create distraction, conflicts and tension about what to do next and also the risk of fragmentation of the group.

Recruitment of group members

It is important to decide the minimum and maximum size of the group, which may also be determined by the setting in which the group meets. Large numbers may reduce opportunities for individual participation and increase the risk of disruptive horse play, but may ensure sufficient attendance. Eight is usually considered to be a good size for a small experiential group.

The criteria for selection and referral depend upon the purpose of the group and the nature of the agency. In certain settings such as a school or children's home, children themselves may be able to request participation in a group. If children are referred or nominated by others, they should be thoroughly consulted.

Apart from practical feasibilities, assessment for selection should explore the need, motivation and capacity for engagement. Complete inability to contain any emotional responses, intense impulsivity, somatisation or secretiveness need due consideration as to whether the particular group would be able to deal with this. There may also be strong resistance or ambivalence to group work arising from an intense feeling of, for example, shame, fear, or anger. which may need to be explored before an individual joins the group (Geller 1972).

Individual preparation of the children, their referers and their carers is also very important before a child joins the group. The child's difficulties, expectations and possible outcomes should be noted and the child should have the opportunity to see the venue, meet groupworkers, look at motivations and clarify various practical details before starting. There may be a system of formulating and signing contracts or agreements with the individuals involved and their carers detailing commitments, expectations and aims, and so forth. The child's teachers will need to be consulted if time will be missed from school for attending the group.

Age, sex, ethnicity and other attributes

In group work with children and adolescents, it is beneficial to limit the age spread as closely as possible, as cognitive levels vary with age. However, this can have implications for staffing and group size. Some groupworkers think in terms of group work with preschool, latency, pubertal, young adolescent and older adolescent groups, while others think in terms of two or three year age bands. Sugar (1974) suggests that, in group work with pre-school children, they should be aged within a year or two of each other. At the latency age there may be a three year age spread.

As regards gender, ethnicity or other specific attributes, it is important to keep in mind that there should be enough members of any category present in the group. Thus, just one boy in a group of girls, or just one girl in a group of boys should be avoided. The same applies in terms of ethnicity and any other important attribute, (e.g. disability, being in care, or hyperactivity).

Transport

Transport to and from the group is a very important issue that needs to be given due attention. If not planned and sorted out properly, this may create a great deal of problems in group work. If the parents or relatives are able to bring the child, what would they do while the child is in the group? Timings of transport by Health Service, Education or Social Services may be rather unreliable. Taxi drivers may also find it difficult to control some of the disturbed children.

Groupworkers

As group work with children and adolescents demands a multiplicity of tasks and responsibilities, it is often useful to have a pair of co-workers. In addition to the practical advantages of continuing the group even if one of the groupworkers is on holiday, ill or on leave, there are other advantages as well, such as sharing of tasks, preparation of materials and feedback or liaison meetings, bouncing of ideas, collaborative planning, comparing observations and evaluations and providing varying perspectives during supervision and consultation.

The mechanisms of transference, splitting and projective identification can induce strong feelings in groupworkers but the impact on their relationships can also be used as important indicators and tools for the group processes. Pubescent groups may be more effective if conducted by the groupworkers of the same sex as the members (Kennedy 1989b). The presence of one male groupworker in a group of all females and *vice versa* may create particular difficulties by increasing incestual anxieties and scapegoating. Change of groupworker can also be very disruptive and detrimental to group work. Sadoff *et al.* (1968) provide a detailed account of the impact of such a change in a group with paedophiles.

Groupworkers, particularly the beginners, are bound to have a variety of fears and fantasies regarding the group including, for example, of losing control, group disintegration, unmanageable acting out and resistance, excessive hostility or dependence. The personal emotional needs of the groupworkers can also consciously or unconsciously influence his or her style of groupwork. The need to be liked may make the groupworker over friendly, excessively permissive or of the 'I am one of you' type. The need to be in control may produce an authoritarian atmosphere or a minimisation of all expressions of feelings. The need to avoid self exposure may lead to a withdrawn, underactive, 'sleeper' type of groupworker or an overtalkative textbook-like objective and intellectual 'professor' type commentator.

Length and frequency of sessions

These may vary from setting to setting. For example, in an outpatient setting of a Child Mental Health Service, the group may meet for $1\frac{1}{2}$–2 hours every week. However, in an inpatient setting, or in a therapeutic community or a children's home, the meetings may be held more often and may be of shorter durations. In a school setting it may be confined to a 'period', or may be held after the formal school time table. A school may be able to create a special 'period', or the group may be held in a rolling manner, that is, in different 'periods' thus varying the times and days from week to week, so that no particular subject is sacrificed excessively. In youth service groups, the nature of certain activities may require a much longer time for each session. Being able to meet at the same place and same time at regular intervals does create a kind of rhythm that has its own therapeutic advantages.

The length of each session is also dependent upon the age of the child. Preschool and latency age children may feel fatigue after 45 to 60 minutes, so that a 45 minute session may be sufficient. At a later age a 60 minute session or a bit longer may be more appropriate. It is useful to make sure that these sessions do not interfere with the usual playtime of the children.

Nature and type of group

A clear decision should be made as to whether the group will be a *closed, open* or *slow open* group. In a closed group all members are expected to start and end the group together. Once the group has been set up and started new members are not permitted to join. This is particularly useful in a group that has a *structured* programme and timetable and works in a stepladder fashion, such as psychoeducational groups, or groups using a cognitive behaviour therapy approach. Groupwork for bereaved children (Chapter 14) and sexual abuse (Chapter 16) are examples of such structured groups described in this volume.

Open groups permit members to leave a group when they are ready and for new members to join in as and when there are places available. Such arrivals and departures provide additional opportunities for working through envy, jealousy, rivalry, separation, loss, change of role and so forth. Slow open groups restrict these disruptions to a bare minimum. A group culture has to be established each time a group starts. However, in an open-ended group, it is carried by the experienced members. In an open-ended group, it is also possible to alter the 'mix' of the group as the group continues and a child's length of stay can be linked to the successful completion of his or her individual goals (Keepers 1987). One may also run a group for a certain duration, (e.g. a term), and formally finish that group; but some of the members of that group may be able to join the next group, for example, starting next term (Behr 1988).

With respect to gender, ethnicity, psychosocial circumstances and clinical conditions, the group may be *homogenous* or *heterogenous* depending upon the aims of the group. A homegenous group allows the particular issues to be explored in depth. Heterogenous groups, on the other hand, are relatively unstructured. A heterogenous group enriches with a wide variety of perspectives and can help explore the underlying dynamics behind apparently diverse issues. One should keep in mind that the group should not have only one member of a particular category (e.g. with excessive violence, drug addiction, delinquency, or psychosis). Despite external differences, children and adolescents of a similar age identify with peers as regards normal maturational tasks, needs and conflicts. Kennedy (1989a) presents examples of groups of latency age children, early adolescents, and middle adolescents that included chronically physically ill with physically healthy peers. Such heterogenous groups have demonstrated the potential for aiding their emotional maturation.

Theoretical frame work and the style of the group

This is dependent upon the purpose of the group and the training, experience and orientation of the groupworkers; some of the common theoretical frameworks are outlined in Chapter 3. Some children attending group therapy may also attend family therapy and/or individual therapy. If they experience conflicting approaches in different settings, this may lead to confusion, doubt and lack of confidence in one or the other approach. A group may have a cognitive, behaviouristic, psychodynamic, systemic or some other approach including a combination of the above. However, in group work with children and adolescents there is always an educational component. Some groups may be mainly educational in relation to certain skills (e.g social skills), experiences (e.g. sexual abuse, bereavement, bullying) or management of feelings (e.g. anger management, stress management) and so forth.

'Most typically, groups have been established either as an "experiential" group (Slaveson's Activity Group Therapy) or as a "didactic" group (Children of Divorce Groups). In an experiential group, the effective therapeutic element occurs through the situation each child creates within the group, and in the positive learning experience these situations create either naturally or with the guidance of the therapist. In a didactic group, the therapist determines much of the activity of the group by leading discussion and presenting exercises.' (Keepers 1987 p.168)

If the children are expected to conform to the agenda set by the group-workers, they may find it difficult to bring their own concerns and problems to the group.

Group culture

Some of the group aims (mission statement), and rules may be made more explicit. These may be arrived at by brainstorming in the group and by democratically negotiated processes. In an open group it may not be possible to repeat the above ritual each time a new member joins, but it is essential to communicate to the new member as early as possible. Such rules usually include: refraining from physical violence and refraining from damage to property. Issues of confidentially, the degree of group pressure permitted in relation to self disclosure, need for clarifying behaviours and feelings, co-operation with group activities may, amongst other things, also be included in group rules. Rules about such issues as messing the room, tidying up, smoking, swearing, absences, refreshments, bringing friends, toys or other objects, taking objects away from the group, activity between members outside the group may also need to be considered.

Depending upon the age of the potential members it may be useful to provide an information sheet and sign a 'contract' (Corder 1987). Just setting rules and eliciting everyone's agreement does not mean that the rules will be kept. An important aspect of groupwork is the testing and guarding of these boundaries (Behr 1988). The groupworkers may have to intervene to elicit group processes to guard these boundaries, to explore feelings related to such testing out behaviour and also re-examine the boundaries in case these are too constraining.

Groups differ in styles including such things as the nature of interventions, permissiveness, spontaneity and democratic decision making. The ratio of reflective discussion to the amount of activity, tasks and exercises also differs from group to group depending upon the age, purpose, theoretical orientation and the amount of structuring. Activities and tasks can serve a dual function – participation leads to strengthening of ego, self esteem and relationship capacity. They also provide opportunities for developing insight through feedback, reality confrontation and observations made on interactions, mood, posture and possible motivations. This requires a shift of attitude from being a consumer or performer to being an observer, so that every member becomes a giver and not just a receiver of help.

Having a group conversation while drawing or making something separately or together as a group is also an extremely powerful style. This reduces the exclusive pressure on any one modality and offers more choices for expression of inner states.

Emergence of alliances, pairings and power hierarchies provide opportunities for observations, making sense of and developing insight into various forces involved. In groups of children from the same school, children's home or ward such relationships may already exist before the group starts.

Most groups evolve their own rituals for starting and finishing a session, and for members joining and leaving the group. For example, in one of the groups in our service there was a tradition at the end of each session to choose a chairperson for the next session. During the next session the chairperson would start the proceedings and be responsible for time keeping. The chairperson would also ensure that everyone in the group had an opportunity during the allotted time to share how they were feeling at that time and any important pieces of both good and bad news in the preceding week of their lives. This then leads to discussion and consideration of tasks and exercises relevant to the issues raised in the group. Similarly, there used to be a ritualized break for light refreshment and a ritualized ending of the session with members holding hands in a circle and in turn saying something about the session, goodbye, and their commitment for the next session.

Developmental phases in groups with children and adolescents

Early phase

As with adults in a therapy group, children re-enact the early maternal relationship when joining the group. There is a high dependency level on the group workers and a need for them to provide a structure and help create a group culture.

The children need to feel that the groupworkers can contain their destructive impulses, 'like the good enough mother', and they often test limits to see if the groupworkers can be manipulated. Boundaries and limits are set in the early phase of the group. Sometimes this is achieved through a paper exercise when the group drafts a written contract. The contract then can be brought to and referred to in subsequent meetings. It is important not to set a too permissive culture, allowing the childrens' every need to be met; this would not allow the children to grow emotionally but would leave them regressed and out of touch with reality. Group settings must not be too divorced from everyday life as unnecessary guilt is aroused when the groupworker allows the children to do something that the child knows will not be tolerated elsewhere.

In this phase individual and group interaction patterns are examined as they develop. Disruptive behaviours exhibited at this point are often a way of avoiding belonging to the group. These can include aggressive or impulsive behaviours, attention-seeking/showing off behaviours, chattering and refusing to participate in an activity. Underlying motives and needs (such as fear of being consumed by the group, fear of rejection, unwillingness to trust the group, need to remain separate), based upon their previous experiences of peer groups are often responsible for such disruptive behaviours.

In one of our groups for 11–13-year-old children, during the fifth and sixth sessions of the group, one member (Richy) brought elastic bands to the sessions and throughout chose to flick paper at other group members. Individuals expressed their anger at Richy but his behaviour persisted to the point where Richy became isolated from the group, not sitting around the same table as them and not participating in the same activities. In the sixth session, when asking the group for feedback on Richy's behaviour again, Ben said that he thought Richy did not want to be a part of the group. Following this, Richy was able to share with the group that he had to leave the group as he was moving from living with his natural father, stepmother and six siblings to going back to live with his natural mother. Richy was sad about the change and felt that he was not wanted by his family. Thus, Richy's perceived rejection by his family had forced him to reject the group before they rejected him. Once this was recognised and acknowledged, Richy was able to belong to the group for the short while remaining.

During the early phase the groupworkers help the group to identify and appreciate group norms, for example 'it is okay not to know all the answers', 'it is okay not to get it right', 'everybody has the right to be heard', 'everybody has the right to speak', 'sessions remain confidential', 'you do not have the right to physically hurt anybody', 'you do not have the right to damage any property'.

The nurturing qualities of the groupworkers are summoned by some group members and rejected by others. At times it is not appropriate to interpret such information but just to observe and to recall at a more appropriate occasion. Individuals begin to identify with each other and group roles start to develop. Group exercises may initially be directed at introductions, linking and bridging people together through the sharing of common experiences. This phase enables the development of group identity, adaptation to groupworkers' styles, establishment of group goals and some exploration of intimacy.

Throughout the life of the group dependency on groupworkers is more prevalent in groupwork with children than in adult groups. Similarly, the moves from and into different phases is not as clearly recognisable in children's groups as in adult groups.

Middle phase

By this phase members may have established some role differentiation but there can still be a jostling of relationships between themselves. In the initial phases children and adolescents tend to pair according to their perceived similarities, needs and motives. During the middle phase they realize that these pairings no longer meet their true emotional needs. This leads to regrouping to form different relationships. These may also arise from certain behaviours and disclosures.

By this phase many patterns of behaviours and interactions have become very familiar to the group and many members begin to identify and model themselves upon those they admire. As groupworkers demonstrate their frustration, tolerance, and ability to respond to the varying demands without losing control or undue restrictiveness, punishment or strictness, the possibility of identification is allowed. In this way children experience alternative responses from adults and thus learn more acceptable behaviours on the basis of their responses.

Exercises encouraging sharing of experiences and interchange of feelings about each other in the group are encouraged at this phase and members begin to share intimate details and experience a sense of group cohesion. They are also able to accept more difficult feedback from the group and the groupworkers.

Later phase

By this stage of the group's development it has the potential to be a rich source of warm, honest and intense feelings. There develops a degree of closeness and an improvement in the group members' self-esteem. There is always the potential for any issue from the previous stages to emerge at any given time.

Although they still test out different relationships the group norms and beliefs are firmly established. If the group has functioned as a closed group and members are aware of leaving dates, issues of dependency and individuality will re-appear. If it has been a slow-open group these can be addressed as individuals leave the group. After experiencing the group as so supportive, there is bound to be some difficulty in dealing with the loss of members or addition of new ones. Many children have experienced the loss of a parent through divorce or separation and will have become entangled in the adults' emotional conflicts. Revisiting loss within a positive safe framework is invaluable to children to allow them to perceive responsibilities again. There would also be some positive identification with the discharged group members.

Individuality can be a great cause of anxiety in children and destructive behaviours might re-emerge at this point. Thorough interpretation and giving the child permission to feel like this about the ending will help support them. Modelling honest feelings by the group workers and the ability to contain those feelings will be a great source of encouragement. Each individual will require support to separate from the particular group and continue in their normal social network.

Confidentiality

There has to be an atmosphere of safety and trust in a group, so that the members are able to share their inner feelings and make any self disclosures if they wish to do so, without the fear of people outside the group gossiping about it or abusing such information. However, the groupworkers should be able to share the contents and processes of the group for their supervision with their supervisor and/or their supervision group. Similarly, the groupworker should be able to discuss most of the relevant information with the Family Therapist and/or Individual Therapist in order to ensure effective recycling of clinical gains and the comparison of different perspectives. The groupworker will also be required to participate in any liaison, network, feedback or family meetings where some information in general terms regarding the progress of the individual could be reported without all the details. In case of child abuse issues the more detailed and precise information may need to be communicated with relevant agencies.

Liaison with other agencies and professionals

When a child attends a group, there are many other people who need to know and remain supportive for the group experience to be productive. For example, the child's teacher or school can easily undermine group work by insisting on the child not missing the school lesson. An element of excitement associated with the group session may be perceived jealously, suspiciously or intolerantly by the family, school or the children's home. Different parties responsible for transport have to be in constant communication to ensure there are no misunderstandings or unnecessary delays. Paint stains, misplacement of belongings, illnesses, injuries, and so forth, have implications for a variety of carers and professionals involved with the child (Farrell 1984).

Thus, enabling a child to continue attending the group as long as it is necessary often requires effort, conviction and support from a number of people, who need to be prepared beforehand and to be regularly and promptly communicated with about any relevant information and progress and reminded of the valuable nature of their support and efforts. They should also be consulted at regular intervals for their opinions, observations and evaluations and to discuss any implications for collaboration. This is, therefore, a time-consuming but important aspect of group work with children.

Documentation

As group work is a slow process, proper documentation is essential to discern changes, make sense of events and plan interventions. It is important to write the contents and processes of each session soon after the session as the details tend to be forgotten rapidly. The act of writing down also has a debriefing quality and allows the groupworker to put away certain emotional aspects of the group so that it is not carried over and taken into other activities.

It may be useful to make notes separately for each participant and also for the group as a whole. Similarly, plans for the next group, hypotheses, hunches and observations arising through processes of discussion, consultation and supervision, and also communications arising from liaison and feedback are useful items for documentation.

Video or audiotaping of the group proceedings can be useful not only for later review, reflection and supervision but also for the group to review certain portions for clarification and further insight. Particular care needs to be taken of such materials as regards consent, storage and confidentiality.

In one of the groups in our Service, there were three groupworkers, one of whom took turns to observe the proceedings and take ongoing notes. These notes were found to be extremely useful in comprehending the subtleties of the group processes and were very helpful as learning tools during consultation and supervision sessions.

Planning, briefing, waiting and debriefing

Groupworkers need to set aside regular time to plan and prepare any details for future sessions either together or separately. There also has to be a short period of a few minutes for briefing and reminding each other of the plan just before the group starts. Arrangements need to be made as to what should happen if some of the children arrive early or are picked up late from the group, and the subsequent subgrouping arising from it. Soon after the end of each session the groupworkers also need to get together to share briefly their feelings, experiences and observations and document these as a part of their debriefing exercise. Some groupworkers may be able to arrange for a consultant to be present during such a debriefing exercise as well.

Consultation – supervision

These terms appear to have acquired different meanings in different contexts. Whatever the terminology, there is a need to arrange opportunities for reflection, to make sense of the contents and improve the clarity of vision and perspectives. If possible, a supervision group consisting of a consultant or supervisor and groupworkers running different groups could meet together on a regular basis to reflect upon their groupwork.

As the political, managerial and organisational contexts and structures of the agencies in which the groups are conducted and the significant network of each group member (for example, the family, school, childrens home, doctors, nurses, and social workers) impinge immensely upon the group boundary, enough time and space during consultation or supervision sessions to make sense of it is necessary. Confidentiality, line management, purchasing, providing, case conferences, bureaucracy of procedures, feedback, family therapy, liaison work and so forth, are all potent constituents of boundary phenomena.

Roberts (1990) highlights the phenomenon that some permeability in boundaries does not auger their collapse and that it is possible to allow each part to contribute to and enrich the others. 'The behaviour on the group boundary appears to have exerted a catalytic effect and perhaps brought forward the exploration of conflicts which may otherwise have remained dormant for some time. The therapeutic opportunities which have arisen from these particular events afforded the possibility of integrating in a constructive way the ongoing interactive group processes with the experiences in life outside the immediate treatment situation' (p.21–22).

In recent years both psychodynamic and general systems theory have been used to understand hindrances to collaboration which may arise at the interface between the practitioners, and between the users and the practitioners (Hornby 1989). Thus, organisations can greatly benefit from developmental consultations. Campbell *et al.* (1989) outline a systemic approach for such a purpose. However, according to Maturana (Maturana and Varela 1980) structured changes in an organisation are determined mainly by its own organisational structure rather than by the properties of the outside agents. Maturana coined the term 'autopoiesis' to explain living systems as 'circular self-referring organisations'. Outside agents can only trigger responses. Thus, the concept of instructive interaction is actually an illusion (Leyland 1988).

In many organisations the opportunity for consultation or supervision can be abused to generate a set of binding instructions. The particular attitude or approach to supervision and consultation is influenced mainly by the culture of the organisation. Hawkins and Shohet (1989) describe five types of organisational cultures. In the 'Personal Pathology Culture' all problems of the organisation are seen as located in the personal pathology of individuals. In such a culture supervision may arouse suspicion and paranoid feelings of being watched and of being at risk of being picked on. In the 'bureaucratic culture' there are policies, guidelines, protocols and memos as defences against anxieties to cover various eventualities. Supervision in such an atmosphere can turn into checking up on whether all the tasks have been done correctly.

In a very politicised or highly competitive 'watch-your-back' culture, supervision, therefore, becomes an arena for showing how awful the 'other side' is and presenting a very glossy image of one's own work. In a culture where the organisation is constantly reacting to crisis after crisis, supervision is seldom seen as a priority and is often cancelled or has to be rushed. However, supervision flourishes in a learning and 'developmental culture' as there is an atmosphere of learning and developing throughout the organisation.

According to Houston (1990), clinical supervision is literally an overview, a *Super-vision,* 'so, simply taking the time and trouble to look again, in the presence of a supervisor, at what you and your patient have said and done is a central task' (p.2).

A groupworkers' supervision group can become an excellent opportunity for collaboration and co-operative learning. It is in an atmosphere of safety, openness and trust that the groupworkers' basic assumptions, perceptions and responses can be examined and challenged with a view to change for the better. The process of supervision and consultation is, therefore, a developmental process.

Taibbi (1990) emphasises that 'Reduced anxiety about performance and increased openness in the supervisor-therapist relationship often cause the therapist to drop his or her mask of pseudo-competence or pseudo-helplessness...' (p.546).

Carr (1989) describes a model of clinical supervision in which each of the various dyadic and triadic relationships between the supervisor, supervisee, organisation and the users are perceived to have their own characteristics and exert an influence on the total network. 'The factors involved in each can be on a rational level and also determined by unconscious processes. Each has its own transference and counter transference components; its own combination of ego and shadow, individual and collective, ritualised behaviours; its own set of overt and covert needs, alliances etc.' (p.3).

References

Behr, H. (1988) 'Group Analysis with Early Adolescents: Some Clinical Issues'. *Group Analysis* 21(2): 119–133.

Campbell, D., Draper, R. and Huffington, C. (1989) *A Systemic Approach to Consultation.* London: D.C. Publishing.

Carr, J. (1989) 'A Model of Clinical Supervision'. In *Clinical Supervision: Issues and Techniques.* London: Jungian Training Committee of the British Association of Psychotherapists.

Corder, B.F. (1987) 'Planning and Leading Adolescent Therapy Groups'. In P.A. Keller and S.R. Heyman (eds) *Innovations in Clinical Practice, 6.* Sarasota: Professional Resources Exchange: 177–196.

Farrell, M. (1984) 'Groupwork with Children: The Significance of Setting and Context'. *Group Analysis.* 17(2): 146–155.

Geller, M. (1972) 'Reflection on Selection'. In I.H. Berkovitz (ed) *Adolescents Grow in Groups: Experiences in Adolescent Group Psychotherapy.* New York: Brunner/Mazel. pp.37–48.

Hawkins, P. and Shohet, R. (1989) *Supervision in the Helping Professions.* Milton Keynes: Open University Press.

Hornby. S. (1989) 'A Psychodynamic Approach to the Collaborative Problems of Practitioners Working in the Community'. In *The Application of Psychodynamic*

Understanding to Organisations in the Helping Service. London: Jungian Training Committee of the British Association of Psychotherapists.

Houston, G. (1990) *Supervision and Counselling.* London: Gaie Houston.

Keepers, T.D. (1987) 'Group Treatment of Children: Practical Considerations and Techniques'. In P.A. Keller and S.R. Heyman (eds) *Innovations in Clinical Practice.* 6: 165–175. Sarasota: Professional Resources Exchange.

Kennedy, J.F. (1989a) 'The Heterogenous Group for Chronically Physically Ill and Physically Healthy but Emotionally Disturbed Children and Adolescents'. *International Journal of Group Psychotherapy.* 39(1): 105–125.

Kennedy, J.F. (1989b) 'Therapist Gender and the Same Sex Puberty Age Psychotherapy Group'. *International Journal of Group Psychotherapy.* 39(2): 255–263.

Leyland, M.L. (1988) 'An Introduction to Some of the Ideas of Humberto Maturana'. *Journal of Family Therapy.* 10 (4): 357–374.

Maturana, H.R. and Varela, F.J. (1980) *Autopoiesis and Cognition: The Realization of the Living.* Dordrecht: Reidel.

Roberts, J. (1990) Experiences on the Boundary of a Group: A Clinical Paper for the Qualifying Course of the Institute of Group Analysis (unpublished manuscript).

Sadoff, R.L., Resnick, H.L.P. and Peters, J.J. (1968) 'On Changing Group Therapists'. *Psychiatric Quarterly Supplement.* 42(1): 156–166.

Sugar, M. (1974) 'Interprevive Group Psychotherapy with Latency Children'. *Journal of American Academy of Child Psychiatry.* 13: 648–666.

Taibbi, R. (1990) 'Integrated Family Therapy: A Model for Supervision'. *Families in Society: The Journal of Contemporary Human Services.* 71: 542–549.

CHAPTER 3

Conceptual Frameworks

Kedar Nath Dwivedi

In group work with children and adolescents the problem of control and boundary is a major issue, as dangerous behaviours are frequently encountered. Speers and Lansing (1965), and Slavson and Schiffer (1975) provide vivid descriptions of some of the extremely dangerous behaviours which may create total havoc in the group. Some other examples of disruptive behaviours in groups are quoted below.

'Objects are frequently thrown, snatched and bandied about. Fellow group members are sometimes playfully hit, pinched, stroked, embraced, or displaced from chairs'. (Behr 1988 p.124)

'Our problems with limits included: painting on the walls, throwing and dumping sand far and wide all over the room and at other people, fighting, climbing in and out of windows (a semi-basement room), turning lights on and off, banging things unnecessarily (making verbal communication impossible), running around the building, running down the street, throwing things into a brook (when the group was taken outdoors) and hammering holes in walls. It was often not an easy therapeutic decision as to when the behaviour could be tolerated, "reflected" in terms of feelings of individuals or of the group, or incorporated in an interpretation – as opposed to when it had to be firmly, forcibly, or, alas, even angrily stopped, in order to allow therapy, or even the group as a whole, to continue'. (Farrell 1984 p.150)

'We have described how Carol, when faced with a choice of returning to her CHE or re-absconding, hit and broke a large pane of glass, apparently intent on injuring herself (she could have left the building by a nearby door). The conductors were extremely concerned for her safety, sensing her desperation, and one stood for sometime backed up against the broken pane while the other coaxed and distracted the attention of the distraught girl until she became calmer'. (Dwivedi *et al.* 1992 p.485)

'We went from the usual meeting room to a large cafeteria. The semblance of control I had in the meeting room was lost in the cafeteria where they ran about uncontrollably, stealing food and passing it from the counter line to the others in the dining area'. (Rose and Edleson 1987 p.241)

'Jack, formerly miserable and withdrawn, looked happier and more interested, and showed the others a match trick. The others responded by showing other tricks with matches, and this led up to Dan setting fire to papers in an ashtray. By this time they were all walking about and began to act out freely, whistling at girls through the window, threatening to spit and drop flower-pots on passers-by, with half an eye on the therapist to see how he was reacting' (Skynner 1971 p.22).

It is not unusual to find a conflict between the basic requirements of therapeutic group experiences (for example co-operative interpersonal interaction and tolerance) and the exploitative, antagonistic and antisocial orientation of many children, particularly those with disorders of conduct attending such groups (Schulman 1957). In fact, the very features of the disturbed youngsters that set them apart from the mainstream of life also get in the way of their needed treatment (Willis 1988). The problem of control has also been described in group work with victims of abuse (Dwivedi *et al.* 1992). Hildebrand (1988) found the participants of a group for sexually abused victims restless and extremely noisy, exhibiting raucous and inappropriate behaviour, rushing around and generally severely testing the group worker's capacity to control them.

In psychotherapy, acting out is seen as an incipient attempt to communicate unbearably painful mental contents that cannot reach consciousness (Grinberg 1968). There have, therefore, been many ways to attempt to decode and comprehend such behaviours.

For example, Willock (1983) postulated a link between such dangerous behaviours and experiences in early childhood. During the second year of life the child begins to develop a positive, powerful, protective image of the parents with a sense of admiration and love. However, if the parents do not keep a close enough eye to protect the mobile toddler from getting hurt as the child runs, climbs and explores the environment, such a little one is then faced with a 'jungle' full of dangerously fierce objects. The parents themselves may even be abusive, damaging and hurtful. The child is, therefore, left to rely on his or her own preservative instincts and to call upon the primitive aggressive behaviours to defend from such dangers. As such a child grows up, he or she continues to try to stimulate an anxious concern in the caregivers and thereby derive a perverse satisfaction from the dangerous and risky behaviours. It can, therefore, be seen as a form of attachment behaviour.

Attachment behaviour

The theory of Attachment was originally described by Bowlby (1958, 1969, 1973, 1980) who combined ideas from ethology and psychoanalysis. Bowlby maintained that affectionate ties between young children and their caregivers have a biological basis. As the survival of young children depends on the care they receive from adults, there is a genetic bias among infants to behave in ways that ensures proximity to caregivers and their attention. Babies are, from the beginning, stimulation seeking. Initially, it may be non-specific, but gradually they begin repeatedly to approach particularly stimulating objects and this leads to bonding or attachment. Similarly, there is a genetic bias in adults to behave reciprocally as protectors and providers of security.

Early proximity promoting behaviours such as crying, vocalising, approaching and clinging, gradually become organised into a goal-oriented system focused on specific caregivers, for example, remaining in the same room (a safe and familiar environment with the attachment figure). This also helps to form and maintain a cognitive map of the sensory characteristics of the objects of attachment. During periods of stress there is an intensified need for proximity and body contact with such soothing objects. Thus, when the baby is tired or ill or the environment appears unfamiliar, the goal becomes greater proximity and contact.

Infants use a variety of strategies to manage affective arousal and stress created by separation and reunion with their caregivers. Four patterns of attachment have been identified: Secure, Avoidant, Dependent and Disorganised. Methods for identifying similar patterns of attachment in pre-schoolers, five- to seven-year-olds and adults have also been developed more recently (Goldberg 1991).

Even grownups faced with disasters, loss or stress need to seek proximity with familiar persons or environments, even though that very person may be the cause of the stress. If the attachment figures are either unavailable or rejecting and the intensity of the stress is very distressing, the stimulus seeking behaviour can then become rather generic or indiscriminate. This leads to a pattern of disorganised attachment behaviour that may even appear hostile and violent. The desire to 'reach out and touch someone' could be so intense that it can become disguised, confused, violent, harmful and even fatal (Mawson 1987). Thus, in group work with children and adolescents, confusion may be created by proximity-seeking attachment behaviour manifesting as disruptive, aggressive and violent acting out (Dwivedi 1993).

From indigenous peer culture to therapeutic peer culture

Behaviours that appear to be disruptive, problematic and destructive of group processes in group work with children and adolescents have recently been conceptualised in terms of their need to attach themselves to an Indigenous Peer Culture. The children and adolescents are looking for some way to connect with one another. They may frequently attack each other in order to avoid being attacked themselves, as every other member's pain may be viewed as a threat to their own security. It is only when this indigenous peer culture evolves into a therapeutic peer culture that members begin to moderate their attacks on one another and to talk collectively about their common traumatic experiences. This evolution depends upon the groupworker's ability to find a way of entering the indigenous peer culture as an invited guest and of modifying and expanding this into a therapeutic culture. The groupworker creates a sufficient holding environment for a true dialogue to emerge only by facilitating the cohesion of indigenous peer culture (Spinner 1992).

Thus Pfeifer (1992) proposes that the two complementary peer cultures – indigenous and therapeutic – exist within children's groups. Indigenous culture is strictly of the children's making while therapeutic culture is created by the therapist in collaboration with the members of the group. The groupworker should approach the indigenous culture as an anthropologist would approach another culture with a view to making observations and seeking understanding rather than attempting interventions. Gradually, the groupworker begins to understand and then use the symbols and rules embedded in the children's indigenous peer culture and speak their language in order to 'join in'. It is similar to the initial phase of 'joining in' family therapy. A crucial aspect of this is the groupworker's experience of vulnerability. Eventually, the groupworker may be able to engage the members in collaboratively building a meaning system that is uniquely designed to address their emotional needs.

With the emergence of therapeutic culture the members begin to experience their internalised or real family relationships which are associated with pathogenic and traumatic experiences. Engaging in the therapeutic culture helps to jointly create with the peers a new, symbolic 'family'. Such a constructed corrective family system provides an atmosphere where the needs, wishes and fears of the members influence their responses, including that of the groupworker. Thus with the establishment of a therapeutic culture the group moves into the stage of intimacy, cohesion and differentiation.

Borderline phenomena

There are many features of group work with disturbed children and adolescents that resemble the difficulties in treatment of adult borderline patients (Behr 1988, Dwivedi *et al.* 1992, Lucas 1988). Such difficulties include intense hostile, dependant transferences, severe regressive reactions, self-destructive and violent behaviours and transient lapses into psychosis (Waldinger 1987). An important aspect of borderline pathology is the defective egostructure, due to the lack of soothing introjects because of failure of holding (Buie and Adler 1982). The backbone of any effective treatment of a borderline patient, therefore, is for the therapist to become an 'auxiliary ego' and perform holding functions to help the development of stable mental representations of helpful persons and experiences, before any interpretation can be heard. 'The patient is not interested in the words at all, any more than when the mother picks up the baby, the baby cares which lullaby the mother is singing' (Chessick 1977).

As acting out is also a major problem in the treatment of borderline patients, some of the concepts discerned from the experiences of treating them can be useful in group work with children and adolescents, even if the youngsters are not on their way to borderline pathology. The concepts of holding, auxiliary ego, facilitation of soothing introjects, and so forth are, therefore, very valuable in groupwork with children and adolescents. Providing refreshments during group sessions, celebrations of birthdays and festivals, farewell parties, for example, may facilitate the cultivation of such soothing introjects. The therapeutic value of refreshments in group work with sexually abused victims has already been emphasised by several authors (Blick and Porter 1982, Boatman *et al.* 1981, Hazzard *et al.* 1986).

Other aspects of borderline pathology also include the significance of the use of transitional objects (Arkema 1981, Morris *et al.* 1986) and 'communicative matching' (Masterson 1976). Both help in the successful negotiation of normal processes of separation individuation. A transitional object, for example a blanket, teddy or other cuddly object can serve as a first step in the child's differentiation from the mother (Winnicott 1974). Transitional objects represent the first attempts at forming a mental concept of an object, and exist in a world between reality and illusion.

'Communicative matching' is a kind of 'emotional supply' by the mother to a toddler who in the rapprochement subphase of separation individuation insistently returns to the mother for 'emotional refuelling' after wandering off to explore the 'world'. These 'adventurous pursuits' need to be praised, admired, fussed over and delighted in by the mother. The significance of the use of transitional objects and communicative matching have been highlighted in groupwork with children and adolescents, as in the treatment of borderline patients. It is important genuinely to delight in, fuss over and admire their new-found interests, feelings and pursuits as a form of 'communicative matching' in group work with children and adolescents. Similarly, the appreciation of the fact that they tend to bring various transitional objects to the group is an important aspect of group work with children and adolescents (Behr 1988).

Transitional objects and play are usually reactivated with the spectre of separation in groups with children and adolescents. This may appear in the context of the threat of disconnection – either through bullying, scapegoating and alienation or through possible loss of a member, resource or opportunity.

Sakurai and Abrams (1992) describe how a girl who was being scapegoated introduced a stuffed cat into the group and how, with the emergence of a therapeutic group culture, the group began to play at being cats themselves while struggling with forming alliances.

Another important feature of therapeutic work with borderline patients is the setting of limits and blocking of their acting out behaviours (Waldinger 1987). This again is being recognised as an important concept in group work with children and adolescents.

Permissiveness, structure and control

Sometimes the reason for dyscontrol is attributed to the particular style of group work with children and adolescents. For example, the Activity Groups are based on the principle of reality testing in an accepting and democratic group climate. Thus, central to the concept of Activity Group has been the atmosphere of permissiveness that requires the groupworkers to be consciously passive and to use the minimum of verbal interventions. But a number of reports have highlighted the lightning spread of acting out behaviours in such groups, especially in the context of a few conduct disordered children. According to Epstein and Altman (1972), dedication, warmth, sensitivity, strategy and therapeutic skills become simply irrelevant in such a context. Many children appear to exercise and display power strivings and techniques with a resolute force that is impervious to adult interventions. The idea of their behaviours arising from a sense of powerlessness and inferiority becomes difficult to swallow in such an atmosphere.

> 'The availability of activity posed the risk of defeating attempts at engaging the children in verbal interaction by providing a regressive escape mechanism from discussing uncomfortable material, and the factor of contagion consisting of a chain reaction of boisterous behaviour escalating beyond the therapist's control was a further potential hazard'. (Dannefer *et al.* 1975 p.332)

Thus the combination of craft materials and the permissive atmosphere intended to stimulate internal conflicts, and the presence of some conduct disordered children may work against ego integration and toward the encouragement of random, regressive acting out behaviour (Schulman 1957).

The disillusionment with complete reliance on the permissive approach has led to the introduction of more structuring and more verbal content. It is now recognised that both verbal and non-verbal behaviours are productive mediators of therapeutic understanding and change in children and that children can successfully access, acknowledge and express current and past feelings, can apply secondary processes and have the capacity to borrow ego strength from each other in a group setting (Lockwood 1981).

Limit setting and control (boundary maintenance) therefore, in the alternative model, assumes greater significance. Thus the groupworker encourages ego synthesis and self control by being in control of the group and the activities (Schulman 1957). Such a role requires more intensive intervention in order to establish structure and to serve as a mediating influence. '... secret exchanges, whispering, passing notes, signalling and so on call for immediate exposure and enquiry into the nature of the underlying resistance' (Behr 1988 p.128).

Ginott (1961) devotes an entire chapter to limit setting, listing 54 prohibited behaviours! Furniss *et al.* (1988) in their report of a Sexually Abused Girls Group made it clear that the therapists were prepared to intervene actively if required. They were also prepared to restrain the girls physically in situations of extreme and potentially dangerous acting out.

Evans (1965, 1966) emphasises the need to set firm limits of behaviours to facilitate effective therapy. However, it has to be done in the context of concern, so that the child or the adolescent does not feel rejected to the point of no return. In the absence of such limit setting the extent of acting out in the group could reach such a level that the whole group or many individuals may have to be excluded from group work.

Many youngsters with delinquency and conduct disorders may also have a degree of learning difficulty or learning disability and, in addition to problems of impulse control, there may be considerable limitations in abstract reasoning, use of language and learning potential. A directive approach may rely less on these abilities.

Action and words

In addition to the introduction of structure and control in group work with children and adolescents, there is also a move to encourage them to do less and talk more in the group setting. The idea is to find the ideal mix of doing and talking so that they could talk about as well as play out most of their concerns (Charach, 1983). This mixture of verbal and non-verbal mediators is equally useful in group analytic (or psychodynamic) and cognitive behavioural therapy approaches. Brackelmanns and Berkovitz (1972) also suggest helping adolescents verbalise in group work. In addition, they need to control excessive hostile projections (e.g. on parents) recognising that parents and others are people as well, with faults and feelings.

Total reliance on talking for discussion, observation, confrontation or reflection to the exclusion of any other activity in group work with children and adolescents can be too taxing and difficult to maintain. As the youngsters, particularly those with a degree of disturbance, become bored, excitable, demanding, over-anxious, avoidant, restless or agitated, words alone may be unable to contain the energy of the group. Use of warm-ups, painting, drawing, play, drama, video feedback, and other projects and activities may help to transmute the resistant energy into therapeutic insight. Art has an immense catalytic value with those who just will not interact readily or communicate verbally (Brandes and Moosbrugger 1985). Similarly, music, movement and dance can help experience, express, comprehend and communicate feelings. A musical environment, especially for teenagers, can be more conducive for intimacy and group cohesion (Frances and Schiff 1976). It can stimulate creative fantasy and story making. The use of symbols and metaphors in the form of songs may further enhance the process of understanding feelings, relationships, dilemma and conflicts. Movement and dance provide opportunities for using the body to portray feelings and fantasies that may otherwise be difficult to talk about. Role playing, psychodrama, Gestalt techniques, videotaping and playing back, watching films and so forth, similarly provide alternative perspectives and an increased capacity to focus on relevant matters.

Identity

Group work has an important role to play in issues and problems of identity. The concept of Ego Identity was described in detail by Erikson (1950, 1959, 1968). It has three distinct aspects: an intrapsychic or personal identity; interpersonal or group identity; and an ideological or philosophical identity.

Not only psychological problems but also social conditions can lead to problems of identity. Lack of opportunities for free role experimentation, absence of access to positive and meaningful role models, leadership, history and ideology to identify with can lead to identity confusion. Rachman (1989) has explored the role of group work in identity problems. He describes a process of identity crisis resolution through five phases that follows the development of the necessary emotional and psycho social climate in group work with adolescents.

1. Establishment of a group identity.
2. The identity search.
3. Working on and through identity issues.
4. Resolution of identity conflicts.
5. Leaving the group to continue the identity search.

The significance of racial identity has also been recognised recently.Coward and Dattani, elsewhere in this volume, describe the significance of group work regarding the issues of racial identity.

Transference

Transference in a strict Freudian sense does not take place in pre-school children, as the therapist is also in a 'parental' role with them. However, the transference phenomena can be easily observed in latency age children and in adolescents. In the setting of a group, these phenomena are less well concealed in children than in adults. For example, open sibling and oedipal rivalries can manifest in the choice of seats, activities and sharing of materials (Sugar 1974). These can lead to tremendous pressure on groupworkers as countertransferences, to become punitive, restrictive or overprotective.

In the setting of a group, there can occur, in fact, four-fold transferences: to (i) groupworkers, (ii) group members, (iii) the group as a whole and (iv) the outgroup. In an individual therapy context, a person is, so to speak, the only 'child' of the therapist, while in group psychotherapy everybody is a member of the 'family' (Grotjohn 1972). Thus the reparative processes of group work lead to the establishment of positive transferences, equalisation of relationships and synthesis of different parts.

> 'The psychotherapy group is often portrayed with a maternal image and the conductor who relates to the group frequently has a maternal role. In the experience of group members, merging and separating and associated fears of annihilation resemble those of the mother–child couple in their individuation process'. (Lear 1991 p.441)

Object Relations Theory

> 'Object relations theory presents us with the confounding observation that people live simultaneously in an external and an internal world, and that the relationship between the two ranges from the most fluid intermingling to the most rigid separation'. (Ganzarain 1989 p.10)

Bion applied Kleinian concepts to groups and demonstrated how groups regress to early stages of mental functioning whereby psychotic anxieties and primitive defences are reactivated. Every group, according to Bion, has two groups within it: the 'Work-Group' and the 'Basic Assumption Group'. Basic assumptions (e.g. of dependency, of fight/flight and of pairing) are anonymous and no one wants to own them (Trist 1985; see also the chapter by McGrath in this volume).

Foulkes' (1948) ideas about group dynamics were influenced by Lewin's (1952) field theory and by Anna Freud's (1968) ideas regarding early child development rather than by Kleinian psychoanalytic theories. Foulkes differed from Bion. Foulkes' followers (including, for example, the Institute of Group Analysis in London) therefore do not pay central attention to deep regression, psychotic group anxieties or heightened aggression (Pines, 1985).

In object relations theory, however, there is an emphasis on primitive defence mechanisms such as splitting, projective identification, omnipotent denial, projection and introjection as these are the fundamental mental resources to protect the endangered self and the threatened objects from the fantasised imminent destruction. Projective Identification is described by Ogden (1979) as follows.

> 'In a schematic way, one can think of projective identification as a process involving the following sequence: first, there is the fantasy of

projecting a part of oneself into another person and of that part taking over the person from within, then there is pressure exerted via the interpersonal interaction such that the recipient of the projection experiences pressure to think, feel, and behave in a manner congruent with the projection; finally, the projected feelings, after being "psychologically processed", by the recipient, are reinternalised by the projector...'. (p.358)

'As internal objects are projected onto other individuals in the group, in an attempt to force them into assuming desired roles, they are also projected onto the group entity'. (Ganzarain 1992 p.207)

Trafimow and Pattak (1982), applying the object relations theory to group work with children, highlighted the significance of at least three curative factors: (i) other children serving as multiple objects and objectal alternatives for each other, thus creating and maintaining a loose but strong network of shifting psychological connections, (ii) the group worker serving as auxiliary ego whenever required and (iii) the group as a whole unconsciously symbolising the symbiotic mother by virtue of its benign, nurturant and eternal presence.

According to Ganzarain (1989) the concept of group as 'mother' appeared rather late in the literature. In early psychoanalysis, the emphasis was on the paternal leader as the central figure in group psychology (Freud 1921). Now 'the authoritarian... father seems almost gone. The new tyranny is that of the mother who like the Goddess Kali presents a dual face: the source of love and life and the rival for love and life' (Hearst 1981 p.25). Both the good and bad aspects of the mother, thus, can be present in the group at one and at the same time, 'split' between the group and the groupworker.

Scheidlinger's (1974) concept of 'Mother-Group' or Foulkes' concept of 'Matrix' describes the preoedepal maternal functions of life giving, confirming, sustaining, accepting and fostering trust. Ballas (1987) describes mother as a Transformational Object for the baby. The presence of and contact with the transformational object transforms the entire inner and the external world of an infant. Thus the reparative and healing aspects of group formation (as transformational objects) help to rectify the pathological manifestations as the developmental conflicts in object relations, emotional deprivations, traumas and family pathologies are recapitulated.

Foulkes' concept of Matrix includes 'the network of all individual mental processes, the psychological medium in which they meet, communicate and interact...' (Foulkes and Anthony 1957 p.2). The concept of matrix is also used in physics and unembodied matrix (as opposed to embodied matrix) is described by Bohm (1980) as including a temporality, synchronicity and nonlocality.

'It becomes no longer in keeping with the nature of group phenomena to speak of the inner experience of one individual interacting with that of others, but experience of group persuades us that there is a body of unconscious, shared experience that occurs at the level of the primary process and shows itself in the manifest behaviour and speech of the group'. (Gordon 1989 p.44)

A group, in the nurturant sense, becomes a mental surrogate of mother's breast. Anxieties about losing the loved object can be associated with primitive fears of psychotic proportions. However, the group as a transitional object can also assist in the process of separation individuation. A transitional object is a representation to identify with in passing from the state of being merged with the mother to the state of being separate from the mother (Winnicott 1974). Thus, group work can enhance the work of Early Object Stage leading to the achievement of True Object Stage through separation individuation and establishment of object constancy (Hoffer, 1955; Mahler, 1975; Trafimow and Pattak, 1982).

Winnicott (1974) explained 'There is a direct development from transitional phenomena to playing, and from playing to cultural experiences' (p.60). As the psychotherapy group is a small temporary society with a therapeutic purpose, the experience of the group becomes a cultural experience and the group has also been described as a cultural object (Jacobson 1989).

In contrast to the phenomenon of group as a nurturant 'good mother', the phenomena of 'bad mother group' has also been discussed (Durkin 1964, Glatzer 1969, Ganzarain 1989). Such a group is perceived as over-demanding, non-reciprocal, intrusive and devouring. Private and secret affairs are seen to be enquired into with hostile curiosity and members feel threatened with the loss of their individuality.

Ezriel's (1950, 1952) approach was similar to Bion's, in many ways. He saw the group members relating to the group worker in one way (the Required Relationship) in order to avoid or avert another mode (the Avoided Relationship) which in fantasy was felt to carry some bad consequence (the Calamity) usually in the form of the destruction of the groupworker or the fear of the groupworker counterattacking or abandoning the group.

General Systems Theory

This theory originated in the field of cybernetics by Von-Bertalanffy (1968) as an attempt to unify the natural sciences and social sciences in a single theoretical framework. According to the theory, a 'system' is composed of component parts and their interactions. Nothing exists in isolation but in a hierarchy of systems (that are made up of subsystems) and they are parts of supra systems. Because of such a systemic connectedness, all events are better understood in terms of circular rather than linear causality. Every system, subsystem and supra system has a boundary with characteristic permeability for communication and feedback between different parts.

Thus the psychological functioning of the group as a whole can be seen as a system consisting of dynamically interacting components. These components are held together with the 'glue' of identification (Ganzarain 1989). The subsystem that holds together the components that make up the system is described as a boundary subsystem. It protects the system from environmental stresses through the control of permeability by excluding or permitting entry to various sorts of information, energy and matter (Miller 1975).

The boundary of a group includes the physical as well as the psychological factors that separate relevant regions in its structure (Kaplan and Saddock 1983). A closed door in a room at a specific address at a particular time can symbolise the external boundary that separates the group from the outside world. Internal boundaries may be those between the group workers and the members and between the members. The boundary subsystem of a group is also made up of phenomena including, amongst others, introjections and projections. The processes of mutual projections in a group can get rid of undesirable contents that are perceived to 'poison' the system. Similarly, good, soothing, desirable contents can be introjected internalised and held in. Both lead to fantasies of identification.

The boundary activities (or boundary incidents) appear to impinge very strongly on the group process, particularly in group work with children and adolescents. The boundaries between and among members tend to become highly permeable and the boundary around the group is often assaulted, eroded and extended. Behr (1988) describes a variety of ways in which this happens, for example dropping in and out, late coming, early departure, unexplained absences, wandering around the whole premises, bringing parts of the outside world into the group both animate (as auxiliary ego) and inanimate (as transitional objects). 'Group members frequently stagger in with school cases, carrier bags and assorted containers from which food, drink, books, magazines, cassettes, radios and the paraphernalia of school may appear to be used in a multiplicity of ways to impede and facilitate communication within the group' (p.123).

Cognitive and Behavioural Therapy Approach

The context of group work with children and adolescents is particularly suitable for the use of cognitive and behavioural therapy approaches, mainly because the group provides valuable opportunities for group reinforcement, which for many children is more powerful than individual reinforcement (Woodarski *et al.* 1973). The group also provides human resources and opportunities for role playing, rehearsing, modelling, multiple assessments and feedback. It is a natural laboratory for experimenting with social relationships, brainstorming, discussion and learning.

Cognitive behavioural approaches are by their nature highly structured, at least in the beginning. Later, the structure may be gradually lessened to allow participants to take responsibility for their own pace. The approach consists of continual data gathering and using systematic problem-solving methods. Various component skills such as social and interpersonal skills, recreational and leisure time skills, cognitive coping skills, relaxation skills, self-management skills, problem solving skills can be systematically assessed and improved upon in the setting of the group (Rose and Edleson 1987).

Lack of adequate social skills can often contribute to general discomfort, anxiety, non participation, poor mastery of sexual socialisation and aggression, and to other emotional, behavioural and educational problems. Such social skills as co-operation and sharing, handling competition, winning and losing and the ability to participate in group or individual leisure time activities enhance the quality of their day to day experiences.

Self management skills involve monitoring of environmental cues and one's own feelings, ideation and behaviours and implementing self-instructions, self-evaluation and self-reinforcement. Systematic problem-solving method includes exercising problem-solving strategies in a systematic manner, for example:

1. Determining what the problem is.

2. Brain-storming some of the plans that can be used.

3. Deciding which is the best usable plan.

4. Executing the plan.

5. Evaluating whether the plan worked.

Cognitive coping skills involve the ability to analyse one's own cognitions and to identify and replace self-defeating statements by more appropriate ones. Self-defeating statements may include exaggeration (e.g. giving an insignificant situation more importance than is called for), catastrophisation (e.g. making a tragedy of some trivial event), self put-downs, negative prophecies, over generalisations and thinking in absolute terms (e.g. impossible, never, always).

Improvement in these skills can be achieved through groupwork with overt modelling, rehearsal, coaching and group feedback and reinforcements. Various activities, games, art, craft, storytelling and dramatics can also be used to facilitate the achievement of these therapeutic goals. Group discussion, group exercises, role playing, working in pairs and delegation of group tasks are group procedures that facilitate the process of change. Special subgrouping of children can be created so that the members can work together even outside the group, as generalisation of treatment is very important, so that the desired behavioural changes within the group can extend to situations outside the group and remain stable.

Braswell and Bloomquist (1991) have provided a very detailed description of this approach in group work with children and adolescents with problems of Attention Deficit Hyperactivity Disorder. Several other examples of the approach are also mentioned in this volume, for example by Harrower in the chapter on group work with offenders and by Coppock and Dwivedi in the chapter on group work in school.

References

Arkema, P.H. (1981) 'The Borderline Personality and Transitional Relatedness'. *American Journal of Psychiatry.* 138: 172–7.

Ballas, C. (1987) *The Shadow of The Object: Psychoanalysis of the Unthought Known.* London: Free Association Books.

Behr, H. (1988) 'Group Analysis with Early Adolescents: Some Clinical Issues'. *Group Analysis.* 21: 119–133.

Blick, L.C. and Porter, F.S. (1982) 'Group Therapy with Female Adolescent Incest Victims' In S.M. Sgroi (ed) *Handbook of Clinical Intervention in Child Sexual Abuse.* Chapter 5 (pp.147–75). Lexington, MA: Lexington Books.

Boatman, B., Borkan, E. and Schetky, D. (1981) 'Treatment of Child Victims of Incest'. *American Journal of Family Therapy.* 9: 43–51.

Bohm, D. (1980) *Wholeness and The Implicate Order.* London: Routledge.

Bowlby, J. (1958) 'The Nature of the Child's Tie to his Mother'. *International Journal of Psychoanalysis.* 39: 350–373.

Bowlby, J. (1969) *Attachment and Loss: Attachment.* New York: Basic Books.

Bowlby, J. (1973) *Attachment and Loss: Separation.* New York: Basic Books.

Bowlby, J. (1980) *Attachment and Loss: Loss, Sadness and Depression.* New York: Basic Books.

Brackelmanns, W.E. and Berkovitz, I.H. (1972) 'Younger Adolescents in Group Psychotherapy: A Reparative Superego Experience'. In I.H. Berkowitz (ed) *Adolescents Grow in Groups: Experiences in Adolescent Group Psychotherapy.* New York: Brunner/Mazel (pp.37–48).

Brandes, N.S. and Moosbrugger, L. (1985) 'A 15 Year Clinical Review of Combined Adolescent/Young Adult Group Therapy'. *International Journal of Group Psychotherapy.* 35: 95–107.

Braswell, L. and Bloomquist, M. (1991) *Cognitive Behavioural Therapy and ADHD Children. Child, Family and School Interventions.* New York: The Guilford Press.

Buie, D. and Adler, G. (1982) 'The Definitive Treatment of the Borderline Patient'. *International Journal of Psychoanalytic Psychotherapy.* 9: 51–87.

Charach, R. (1983) 'Brief Interpretive Group Psychotherapy with Early Latency Age Children'. *International Journal of Group Psychotherapy.* 33(3): 349–364.

Chessick, R.D. (1977) *Intensive Psychotherapy of a Borderline Patient.* New York: Jason Aronson.

Dannefer, E., Brown, R. and Epstein, N. (1975) 'Experience in Developing a Combined activity and Verbal Group Therapy Program with Latency Age Boys'. *International Journal of Group Psychotherapy.* 25: 331–337.

Durkin, H. (1964) *The Group in Depth*. New York: International Universities Press.

Dwivedi, K.N. (1993) 'Confusion and Underfunctioning in Children'. In V.P. Varma (ed) *How and Why Children Fail*. London: Jessica Kingsley Publishers.

Dwivedi, K.N., Brayne, E. and Lovett, S. (1992) 'Groupwork with Sexually Abused Adolescent Girls'. *Group Analysis*. 25: 477–489.

Epstein, N. and Altman, S. (1972) 'Experiences in Converting an Activity Group into Verbal Group Therapy with Latency Age Boys'. *International Journal of Group Psychotherapy*. 22: 93–100.

Erikson, E.H. (1950) *Childhood and Society*. New York: W.W. Norton.

Erikson, E.H. (1959) 'Identity and the Life Cycle'. *Psychological Issues*. 1(1), New York: International Universities Press.

Erikson, E.H. (1968) 'Identity, Youth and Crisis'. New York: W.W. Norton.

Evans, J. (1965) 'Inpatient Analytic Group Therapy of Neurotic and Delinquent Adolescents: Some Specific Problems Associated with these Groups'. *Psychotherapy and Psychosomatics*. 13: 265–270.

Evans, J. (1966) 'Analytic Group Therapy with Delinquents'. *Adolescence*. 1: 180–196.

Ezriel, H. (1950) 'A Psychoanalytic Approach to Group Treatment'. *British Journal of Medical Psychology*. 23: 59–74.

Ezriel, H. (1952) 'Notes on Psychoanalytic Group Psychotherapy: II–Interpretation and Research'. *Psychiatry*. 15: 119–126.

Farrell, M. (1984) 'Groupwork with Children: The Significance of Setting and Context'. *Group Analysis*. XVII(2): 146–155.

Foulkes, S.H. (1948) *Introduction to Group Analytic Psychotherapy*. London: L. Heinemann.

Foulkes, S.H. and Anthony, E.J. (1957) *Group Psychotherapy: The Psychoanalytical Approach*. Harmondsorth: Penguin. (Reprinted London: Karnac, 1984).

Frances, A. and Schiff, M. (1976) 'Popular Music as a Catalyst in the Induction of Therapy Groups for Teenagers'. *International Journal of Group Psychotherapy*. 26: 393–398.

Freud, A. (1968) 'Acting Out'. *International Journal of Psycho Analysis*. 49: 165–170.

Freud, S. (1921) *Group Psychology and the Analysis of the Ego*. London: Hogarth Press (1948).

Furniss, T., Bringley Miller, L. and Van Elburg, A. (1988) 'Goal Oriented Group Treatment for Sexually Abused Adolescent Girls'. *British Journal of Psychiatry*. 152: 97–106

Ganzarain, R. (1989) 'A Comprehensive Study of Bion's Concepts about Groups'. In R. Ganzarain (ed) *Object Relations Group Psychotherapy – The Group as an Object and Training Base*. Madison, CT: International Universities Press. Chapter 23 (pp.23–46).

Ganzarain, R. (1992) 'Introduction to Object Relations Group Psychotherapy'. *International Journal of Group Psychotherapy.* 42(2): 205–223.

Ginott, H.G. (1961) *Group Psychotherapy with Children.* New York: McGraw Hill.

Glatzer, H.T. (1969) 'Working Through in Analytic Group Psychotherapy'. *International Journal of Group Psychotherapy.* 29: 292–306.

Goldberg, S. (1991) 'Recent Developments in Attachment Theory and Research'. *Canadian Journal of Psychiatry.* 36(6): 393–400.

Gordon, R. (1989) 'Symbiosis in the Group: Group Therapy for Younger Adolescents'. In F.J.C. Azima and L.H. Richmond (eds) *Adolescent Group Psychotherapy.* Madison: International Universities Press. pp.43–51.

Grinberg, L. (1968) 'On Acting-Out and its Role in the Psychoanalytic Process'. *International Journal of Psychoanalysis.* 49: 171–178.

Grotjohn, M. (1972) 'The Transference Dynamics of the Therapeutic Group Experience'. In I.H. Berkovitz (ed) *Adolescents Grow in Groups.* New York: Brunner/Mazel (p.173–178).

Hazzard, A., King, H.E. and Webb, C. (1986) 'Group Therapy with Sexually abused Adolescent Girls'. *American Journal of Psychotherapy.* 40(2): 213–23.

Hearst, L. (1981) 'The Emergence of the Mother in the Group'. *Group Analysis.* 14: 25–32.

Hildebrand, J. (1988) 'The Use of Groupwork in Treating Child Sexual Abuse'. In A. Bentovim *et al.* (eds) *Child Sexual Abuse Within the Family: Assessment and Treatment.* London: Wright.

Hoffer, W. (1955) *Psychoanalysis: Practical and Research Aspects.* Baltimore, MD: Williams and Wilkins.

Jacobson, L. (1989) 'The Group as an Object in the Cultural Field'. *International Journal of Group Psychotherapy.* 39(4): 475–497.

Kaplan, H.I. and Sadock, B.J. (1983) *Comprehensive Group Psychotherapy (2nd edition).* Baltimore, MD: Williams and Wilkins.

Lear, T.E. (1991) 'Personal Transformations in the Group'. *Group Analysis.* 24(4): 441–454.

Lewin, K. (1952) *Field Theory in Social Science.* London: Tavistock.

Lockwood, J.L. (1981) 'Treatment of Disturbed Children in Verbal and Experiential Group Psychotherapy'. *International Journal of Group Psychotherapy.* 31(3): 355–366.

Lucas, T. (1988) 'Holding and Holding-On: Using Winnicott's Ideas in Group Psychotherapy with Twelve to Thirteen Year Olds'. *Group Analysis.* 21(2): 135–49.

Mahler, M. (1975) *The Psychological Birth of the Human Infant.* New York: Basic Books.

Masterson, J.F. (1976) *Psychotherapy of the Borderline Adult.* New York: Brunner/Mazel.

Mawson, A.R. (1987) *Transient Criminality: A Model of Stress Induced Crime.* New York: Praeger.

Miller, J. (1975) 'General Systems Theory'. In W. Freeman, H.I. Kaplan and B.J. Sadock (eds) *Comprehensive Textbook of Psychiatry, Vol. 2.* New York: Williams and Wilkins. (pp.77–78).

Morris, H., Gunderson, J.G. and Zanarini, M.C. (1986) 'Transitional Object Use and Borderline Psychopathology'. *American Journal of Psychiatry.* 143(12): 1534–8.

Ogden, T.H. (1979) 'On Projective Identification'. *International Journal of Psychoanalysis.* 60: 357–373.

Pfeifer, G. (1992) 'Complementary Cultures in Children's Psychotherapy Groups: Conflict, Coexistence and Convergence in Group Development'. *International Journal of Group Psychotherapy.* 42(3): 357–368.

Pines, M. (1985) (ed) *Bion and Group Psychotherapy.* London: Routledge and Kegan Paul.

Rachman, A.W.M. (1989) 'Identity Group Psychotherapy with Adolescents: A Reformulation'. In F.J.C. Azima and L.H. Richmond (eds) *Adolescent Group Psychotherapy.* Madison: International Universities Press (pp.21–41).

Rose, S.D. and Edleson, J.L. (1987) *Working with Children and Adolescents in Groups.* San Francisco: Jossey–Bass.

Sakurai, M. and Abrams, L. (1992) 'A World Between Realities: An Exploitation of Therapeutic Group Culture and Transitional Phenomena in a Long Term Psychotherapy Group'. *International Journal of Group Psychotherapy.* 42(3): 383–393.

Scheidlinger, S. (1974) 'On the Concept of the Mother-Group'. *International Journal of Group Psychotherapy.* 24: 417–428.

Schulman, I. (1957) 'Modification in Group Psychotherapy with Antisocial Adolescents'. *International Journal of Group Psychotherapy.* 7: 310–317.

Skynner, A.C.R. (1971) 'Group Therapy with Adolescents'. *Groups: Annual Review of the Residential Child Care Association.* 18: 16–32.

Slavson, S.R. and Schiffer, M. (1975) *Group Psychotherapy for Children.* New York: International Universities Press.

Speers, R.W. and Lansing, C. (1965) *Group Therapy in Childhood Psychoses.* Chapel Hill: University of North Carolina Press.

Spinner, D. (1992) 'The Evolution of Culture and Cohesion in the Group Treatment of Ego Impaired Children'. *International Journal of Group Psychotherapy.* 42(3): 369–381.

Sugar, M. (1974) 'Interpretive Group Psychotherapy with Latency Children'. *Journal of American Academy of Child Psychiatrists.* 13: 648–666.

Trafimow, E. and Pattak, S.I. (1982) 'Group Treatment of Primitively Fixated Children'. *International Journal of Group Psychotherapy.* 32(4): 445–452.

Trist, E. (1985) 'Working with Bion in the 1940s: The Group Decade'. In M. Pines (ed) *Bion and Group Psychotherapy*. London: Routledge and Kegan Paul (pp.1–46).

Von Bertalanffy, L. (1968) *General Systems Theory: Foundation, Development, Application*. New York: George Brazillier.

Waldinger, R.J. (1987) 'Intensive Psychodynamic Therapy with Borderline Patients: An Overview'. *American Journal of Psychiatry*. 144(3): 267–74.

Willis, S. (1988) 'Group Analytic Drama: A Therapy for Disturbed Adolescents'. *Group Analysis*. 21: 153–168.

Willock, B. (1983) 'Play Therapy with the Aggressive, Acting Out Child'. In C.E. Schaffer and K.J. O'Connor (eds) *Handbook of Play Therapy*. New York: John Wiley and Sons.

Winnicott, D.W. (1974) *Playing and Reality*. Harmondsworth, U.K.: Penguin.

Woodarski, J.S., Hamblin, R.V., Buckholdt, R.R. and Ferritor, D.E. (1973). 'Individual Contingencies versus Different Shared Consequences Contingent on the Performance of Low Achieving Group Members'. *Journal of Applied Social Psychology*. 2: 276–290.

CHAPTER 4

Evaluation

Kedar Nath Dwivedi and Diddy Mymin

In this chapter we examine the role of evaluation in group work with children and adolescents. Evaluation is of great importance throughout all the various modalities of psychotherapy. With the current emphasis on the effectiveness and efficacy of the health services, evaluation of practices is becoming increasingly important. This is particularly true of mental health, where many practices are poorly evaluated and might, therefore, be of questionable validity. Moreover, evaluation is fundamentally educative in that it enhances the effectiveness of the clinician because the results can serve as valuable, constructive and therefore corrective feedback, reinforcing the good practices and reducing the bad.

There is a great complexity of tasks confronting the clinician interested in evaluating group work. Compared with individual therapy, evaluation of group therapy is far more complex, in so far as each therapy group is unique, by virtue of the interactions of seven or eight idiosyncratic individuals.

This chapter will deal with the evaluation of children and adolescents groups from three perspectives. First, evaluation will be looked at from the research perspective of those interested in the critical evaluation of the practice of group therapy with children and adolescents. As the justification of the efficacy of group treatment as opposed to other modalities of treatment threatens to become an endless debate, this will only be briefly touched upon here. Second, but of greater interest here, is the close evaluation of the group as an ongoing and dynamic element built into the group work programme itself. Third, the more rigorous retrospective evaluation of the group by facilitators, examining the goals for the group as a whole and the individuals in particular, and assessing the outcome of these goals. Clearly, all of these perspectives are closely linked; they have only been separated here for the sake of presentation.

The effectiveness of group work as a treatment model and research considerations

In a brief review of the literature on the evaluation of effectiveness of group psychotherapy in general, Vinogradov and Yalom (1989), noted that multiple outcome studies have tested the efficacy of group treatment for a wide range of psychological problems and behavioural disorders, ranging from neurotic interpersonal behaviour to sociopathy, substance abuse, and chronic mental illness. This large body of research evidence supports the widespread clinical consensus that group psychotherapy is beneficial to its participants. Empirical data on the outcome of specifically children and adolescents' groups, however, is rare. Abramowitz (1976) has pointed out that there are 'almost twice as many case reports or programme descriptions boasting successful use of group therapy with children as articles displaying actual data, listed' (p.321). Case reports and programme descriptions, no matter how optimistic, can never compare with strict empirical evaluation. Specifically reviewing and critically evaluating empirical analyses of group therapy with children, Dies and Reister (1986) and Abramowitz (1976) found the data offered to be lamentably inconclusive and thoroughly frustrating. Dies and Reister did find some reason for greater optimism in that in the decade following Abromowitz's review there was a slight increase in the rate of publication and the presence of several more sophisticated studies. Abromowitz's review of empirical evaluations showed that an approximately equal number of studies yielded generally positive, mixed, and null results.

The positive effect of groups (making use of play, activity, behaviour modification and verbal therapy techniques) on the target problems of immature or problem (disruptive) behaviour, social isolation and withdrawal, poor self-concept and academic underachievement or deficit, may be visible as often as not. Group therapy has been shown to be effective in improving problems of disruptive behaviour (Hinds and Roehlke 1970), in increasing social acceptance (Thombs and Muro 1973), and in enhancing self concept (House 1971) and academic performance (Fisher 1953). But studies by Abraham (1972), McBrien and Nelson (1972), Clement and Milne (1967), Cheatham (1968) and Harper (1978) have weakened the above resolve by failing to demonstrate that group therapy has any impact upon the respective target problems. Although this empirical debate over the value of group therapy with children and adolescents will clearly be a difficult one to resolve in a final way, there is every reason to suspect that it will be resolved favourably. Pevsner's (1982) study showing the effect of group work with children on improving disruptive behaviour and non-compliance, LaGreca and Satogrossi's (1980) and Bierman and Furman's (1984) studies showing the comparative superiority of social skills groups on measures of outcome and generalization, taken together with the general approbation of group therapy of Vinogradov and Yalom (1989) and Abramowitz's (1976) observation that there is little evidence of deterioration as a result of group therapy, all point in the right direction.

The empirical debate over the effect of group therapy with children and adolescents is by no means barren of fruit. Indeed, as Abramowitz emphasises, it indicates ways of improving evaluative technique. There is an urgent need for conceptually broader and methodologically sounder outcome research in group work with this population. It has become apparent that many studies rely on relatively few sessions of treatment and often on novice group workers with very little training and experience in the field. There is also a lack of comparison of various other approaches (and combinations thereof) with group work. Although controls have usually included those attending regular classroom control groups (in school based studies) or individuals from the waiting list (in clinic based studies), there has been no use of placebo-attention control groups. There is a need to explore the impact of group work on pro-social development such as empathy and co-operation. It would also be useful to include measures of possible deleterious consequences of group therapy and to include in the repertoire of evaluation techniques projective devices (e.g. Children's Apperception Test (CAT), sentence completion). In addition, outcome criteria should be relevant to presenting problems and to the goals of the treatment approach under scrutiny. A wider range of outcome domains should also be sampled. There is also a call for more thorough examination of group composition effects. Generally, before arriving at a judgement concerning the worth of therapy, it should be ensured that evaluations have a systematic and rigorously scientific basis.

Recent research findings have appeared indicating the relatively small impact of formal research on clinical practice. Colson and Horowitz (1983) point out that researchers in the various modalities of group therapy are aware of the fact that their studies have seldom become influential in group practice. Dies (1980), surveyed group therapists for their opinions about various training methods. He found that the respondents seldom mentioned the use of research tools (e.g. inventories, rating scales, leader or group assessment techniques) in their training and supervisory practices. It is commonplace for researchers and clinicians to judge group therapy research on the basis of its success or failure cumulatively to provide clear answers, a goal which seems to be unrealistic and guarantees only disappointment. It is more reasonable to expect such research to provide hints, confirm or interrogate clinical hunches, and add to the conceptual background for clinical work.

Evaluation as an ongoing process built into the Group-Work Programme

Group and self evaluation can provide valuable and constructive feedback when built into the group work programme itself. Most outcome research in group work is based upon the group member's evaluation of how helpful they found the group. It is possible, for example, to enquire about certain aspects of growth of a group (e.g. How clear are the goals? How much trust and openness is in the group? How sensitive and perceptive are group members? Is there a sense of belonging and loyalty?) (Douglas, 1976). Ganzarain (1989) cautions that answering such questions can mobilise unexplored negative transference toward the 'bad mother' group. Thus a process of 'vilification' (rather than idealisation) may take place, casting serious doubt upon the efficacy of such evaluative questions.

Vinogradov and Yalom (1989) emphasise the importance of 'self monitoring' in a group. A self monitoring group learns to assume responsibility for its own functioning. At the group's inception the therapist may foster the evaluative function in the participants by means of modelling. For example, she/he, might say at the end of a group session: 'This was an exciting meeting today and everyone shared a lot. I hate to see it end'. The evaluative function may then be shifted onto the participants: 'How is the group going so far today? What's been the most satisfying part?' And finally, the members may be taught that they have the ability to influence the course of a session: 'Things have been slow today. What could we do to make it different?'

For the groupworkers, regular documentation of group processes and contents provides valuable material not only for evaluating the progress of the group but also for making sense of the various group experiences, consultation, supervision, planning and preparation of next steps.

The **Repertory Grid Technique** (Fransella 1970, Watson 1970) is an example of a technique which offers considerable potential in evaluating the subjective experiences of group members, and which is able to inform us about the way in which our system is evolving and about what its limitations and possibilities are. This involves creating a grid of vertical 'constructs' and horizontal 'elements'. A 'group grid', then, may be constructed as follows: a group member constructs a grid in which the 'elements' are the members of the group including the member completing the grid. So from the point of view of a member of a group of eight, say, the 'elements' will be the seven other group members and 'me'. The 'constructs' (which may be thought of as aspects of group perspective) may include relevant attributes such as nervous, hostile, mean, affectionate, defensive, caring, cool, and so forth. The grid is constructed by asking the members to grade or rank order each 'element' with respect to each 'construct'. If this is done both before and after the group's course, the coefficient between the two grids can be measured and taken as a parameter of dynamic change. The resulting series of grids can be analyzed and compared to evaluate changes in group views of individuals and the views of each individual at different times. A 'person perception score' (Fransella 1970) may be derived, because each group member has ranked all the other group members with respect to each of the 'constructs'. Thus, if you want to find out whether, for example, a particular person sees herself as others see her, you simply look at her ranking of herself and compare this with others' rankings of her. A 'background grid' for each member may also be constructed in which the 'elements' could be self and significant others in the member's world. The group grid method not only próvides a wealth of information about changes in the way that group members construe group effects over time (when the grid is administered on a number of occasions), but also makes it possible to derive a score which provides some idea, quantitatively, of how each member sees the others and of how each member perceives 'significant others' in their world.

Thus, grid analyses can provide many psychodynamically relevant measures. The mean 'element' distance of self from others in a grid can be used to derive an Identification Score. Measures of change between occasions indicate how far the member's view of the group have reconstructed and can be quantified by the 'In Group Reconstruction Score'. Similarly, other aspects of group processes such as 'tendency towards consensual construing', 'group involvement', 'seem to have changed', and so forth, can be explored and quantified in this way (Ryle and Lipshitz 1976). Grid techniques are limited in their usage in that they may be inappropriate for younger children whose verbal expressive capacity is limited.

A critical evaluation of group members' progress towards individualized goals

Individual progress in groups can be measured as an evaluation of the members' progress toward individualised goals. A measure of functioning levels using valid rating scales before, during and after group work can provide useful information on behavioural, attitudinal and other psychological changes through the group process.

Ryle (1976) emphasised that an ideal research record of a group should include:

1. A satisfactory categorisation of members in terms of relevant dimensions, of symptomology, social adjustment, psychodynamic status and personality.

2. Members' definitions of their problems, aims and self ratings in terms of these definitions repeated at intervals throughout and after group work.

3. Similarly, definition of the group worker's aims for each member with ratings of achievements at appropriate intervals.

4. An objective account of the group processes and relevant contents.

5. Accumulated subjective accounts of the group experience from the group members.

The focus here will be on objective rating scales which may be used by clinicians to assess severity of disturbance and symptomology of the members. Depending on the goals of the evaluation procedure, the researcher can choose from a variety of scales. These include self evaluative scales, scales completed by significant others in the member's world (e.g. teachers, parents and peers), scales completed by the group facilitator or an independent observer, or a combination of the above.

There are fundamentally two approaches available for measuring and describing psychopathological and social dysfunction in children and adolescents. These are global (unidimensional) measures of severity of disturbance, and multidimensional measures of specific symptoms or symptom groupings.

Global assessment scales

Global scales cannot provide the detailed information that may be obtained from multidimensional scales; however, they appear to be more sensitive to the effects of treatment (McGlashan 1973). The Children's Global Assessment Scale (Shaffer *et al.* 1983), the Global Assessment Scale for Children (Rothman *et al.* 1976, Sorenson *et al.* 1979) and the Case Complexity Scale (Pearce, 1992) are three examples of global scales. Two of these scales may be described as follows. (The following descriptions are by no means exhaustive; they are intended merely to be illustrative.)

> **The Children's Global Assessment Scale (CGAS),** developed by Shaffer *et al.* (1983), is an adaptation of the Global Assessment Scale (GAS) developed by Endicott *et al.* (1976) which was designed for adults. It is a useful measure of overall severity of disturbance. It is designed to reflect the lowest level of a child's or an adolescent's (4- to 16-year-olds) functioning during a specified period of time. The values on the scale range from 1, representing the most functionally impaired child, to 100, representing the healthiest. Scores above 70 on CGAS are supposed to indicate normal functioning.

> **The Case Complexity Scale,** developed by Pearce (1992), takes into account the complexity of a particular case and the demands that it places upon the Health Services. The measures include comorbidity, number of agencies involved, family dysfunction, number of previous failed treatments, social adversity, specifically 'grave' symptoms (e.g. deliberate self harm, illegal activity, child abuse, psychotic symptomology). Such a scale may not be sensitive to changes as a result of group work, but it may provide a useful means with which to measure background resistance and severity. Clearly, other scales more sensitive to change may be used in this context for the evaluation of change due to group work.

Multidimensional scales

The multidimensional scales help to construct a profile of each individual in the framework of factor or cluster analyses. These scales include the Behavioural Problem Checklist of Quay and Peterson (Quay 1977); The Conners Teacher and Parent Rating Scales (Conners 1969, Goyette *et al.* 1978), The Achenbach Child Behaviour Checklist (Achenbach and Edelbrock 1983), The Rutter Scales (Rutter 1967, Rutter *et al.* 1970), The Bristol Social Adjustment Guides (Stott 1974), The Devereux Adolescent Behaviour Rating Scale (Spivack *et al.* 1967). Again, the following descriptions merely illustrate briefly some of the scales included above and by no means represent a comprehensive list of available scales.

> **The Behaviour Problem Checklist of Quay and Peterson** (Quay 1977) is a three point rating scale for 55 relatively frequently occurring problem behaviour traits in children and adolescents. The problem behaviour dimensions measured by the Checklist are those of Conduct Disorder (psychopathy, unsocialised aggression), personality disorder (neuroticism, anxious–withdrawn) inadequacy–immaturity, and subcultural (socialised) delinquency.

> **The Bristol Social Adjustment Guides for Children** (5–16 yrs) are available separately for the child in school, in the family and in residential care. A list of phrases under various headings and subheadings are listed and the carers are requested to underline the phrases that describe the child's behaviour and attitudes over the past month. Some of the headings include parent–child relationship, interaction with teacher, school work, games and play, attitudes to other children, personal ways, physique, school achievement, attitudes to residential care staff. The scales include unforthcomingness, withdrawal, depression, inconsequence, peer group deviance, hostility, overdependance, and so forth.

> **The Rutter Scales** (Rutter *et al.* 1970) are completed by parents (scale A2) and teachers (scale B2) on the basis of the child's behaviour over the past 12 months. Each item (31 items in A2 and 26 items in B2) is rated on a graded 3 point scale (e.g. doesn't apply, applies somewhat and certainly applies). This scale first identifies children who have a high number of reported problem behaviours and then provides scores on neurotic and antisocial subscales.

> **The Child Behaviour Checklist** (Achenbach and Edelbrock 1983) relies on the report of parents for the assessment of problem behaviour and social competence in children between the ages of 4 and 16 years. The CBL consists of a social competence scale and a behavioural problem scale. The Behaviour Problem Scale consists of 118 items and includes a wide range of problem behaviours (e.g. 'Acts too young for

his/her age'). Statements are endorsed on a three point scale, (ranging from very true to not true).

Self report questionnaires

Self report questionnaires can be used in conjunction with any of the above.

The **California Test of Personality** (Thorpe *et al.* 1953) consists of a series of five questionnaires for successive developmental levels measuring various components of personal and social adjustment. It is a forced choice self report questionnaire requiring 'yes' or 'no' answer to questions like 'Do you often think that nobody likes you?' or 'Do you believe that you have more bad dreams than most of the boys and girls?'

The **Personal Adjustment Inventory** (Rogers 1961) is intended for use with children of 9–13 years. Separate forms are administered to girls and boys. Questions cover a wide area of a child's life in which maladjustment can occur. From the responses one can derive the following: a Personal Inferiority Score, a Social Maladjustment Score, a Family Maladjustment Score and a Day Dreaming Score.

Children's Depression Scale (Lang and Tisher 1978) is a two part scale which determines the nature and extent of childhood depression by the use of 48 depressive and 18 positive statements which the respondent sorts into five categories ranging from 'very right' to 'very wrong'. The scale can also be administered to the child's parents through the use of an adapted parent's questionnaire. As well as positive and depressive scores the CDS yields subscales as follows: affective response; social problems; self esteem; preoccupation with own sickness and death; guilt; pleasure and enjoyment. It gives a useful indication of the particular focus of a child's depression via the sub-scales.

The Brief Symptom Inventory (BSI) The BSI is essentially the brief form of the SCL-90-R, a self report inventory that was developed by Derogatis and Melisaratos (1983). Each item of the BSI is rated on a 5-point scale of distress (0–4), ranging from 'not-at-all' to 'extremely'. The BSI, like its parent instrument, the SCL-90-R, is constructed to measure nine primary symptom dimensions or constructs. These include somatization, obsessive–compulsive, interpersonal sensitivity, anxiety, hostility, phobic anxiety, paranoid ideation and psychoticism. In addition to the nine primary symptom dimensions, there are three global indices of distress associated with the BSI: the General Severity Index (GSI), the Positive Symptom Distress Index (PSDI), and the Positive Symptom Total (PST). The function of each of these global measures is to communicate in a single score the level or depth of symptomatic distress currently experienced by the individual. The GSI combines information on the number of symptoms and the intensity of perceived distress. The PSDI functions very much as a measure of response style, and the PST is simply a count of the symptoms which the client reports having experienced to any degree.

The Multidimensional Anger Inventory (MAI). This self report questionnaire includes 38 items which measure the following dimensions of anger: frequency, duration, magnitude, range of anger rousing situations, mode of expression and hostile outlook (Siegel 1987). The MAI is distinguished from other anger inventories by its simultaneous assessment of multiple dimensions of anger as well as by its reliability. It has been administered to children from eleven years old and up.

Self help questionnaires are particularly helpful in assessing self image. When an individual is assigned a task of evaluating himself, whatever the method of his evaluation, he inevitably makes reference to a system of central meanings that he has about himself and his relations to the world about him, which we call the self concept. Self image is an efficient measurement to evaluate personality. It is a criterion of the quality of personality functioning (Fitts 1973). In many studies it has been found that this measure can discriminate between adjusted and maladjusted people who were tested on the basis of behavioral criteria or different personality tests (Fitts 1973). Self image is a central concept in all theories of personality ranging from the dynamic approach, which perceives the self as an efficient organizer and preserver of the balance between the dynamic energy systems that are active in the individual, through the humanistic approach, which emphasizes the influence of the environment on personal growth, to the cognitive social approach, which focuses on the cognitive aspects of the self.

There are numerous instruments available to measure self esteem. These include the following, briefly described. The **Adjective Checklist** (Gough and Heilbrun 1965) consists of 300 adjectives in an alphabetical list (e.g. absent minded, cruel, gentle, immature, kind). Subjects are required to check those adjectives which they consider would describe them. The **Self Esteem Inventory** (Coopersmith 1967) is a 58-item scale intended for use with children from 10 to 16 years. The **Adjective Rating Scale** (Lipsitt 1958) is a 22-item scale for children from 9 to 15 years. The **Children's Self Concept Scale** (Piers and Harris 1969) has 80 items and is designed for the age group 8 to 16 years. Children are asked to register 'yes' or 'no' in response to such statements as 'I am shy', 'I have good ideas'. The items were drawn originally from Jersild's (1952) survey. **Self Esteem Scale** (Rosenberg 1965) and **LAWSEQ** (Lawrence 1981) are relatively short scales of 16 and 10 items respectively. The **Canadian**

Self Esteem Inventory for Children (Battle 1976) has, on the other hand, 60 items and 5 subscales. It is intended for use with 8- to 11-year-old children and also contains a lie subscale. The scale measures an individual's perception in areas of self, peers, parents and school. The items have also been selected from the Adjective Checklist (Gough and Heilbrun 1965) and the Coopersmith's (1967) Self Esteem Scale. The items include both high and low self esteem and the individual checks each as 'yes' or 'no'. For example, 'I am as happy as most boys and girls', 'I am a failure at school'.

There are also a number of academic self esteem measures available. For example, The **Aberdeen Academic Motivation Inventory** (Entwistle and Welsh 1969) is a 24-item self rating inventory for the assessment of academic motivation (e.g. 'Is it important to you to do well at school?' or 'Do you like to leave your homework to the last minute?').

References

Abraham, K.A. (1972) 'The Effectiveness of Structured Socio-Drama in Altering Classroom Behaviour of Fifth-Grade Students'. *Dissertation Abstracts International* 32a:3677–3678.

Abramowitz, C.V. (1976) 'The Effectiveness of Group Psychotherapy with Children'. *Archives of General Psychiatry* 33:320–326.

Achenbach, T.M. and Edelbrock, C.S. (1983) *Manual for the Child Behaviour Checklist and Revised Child Behaviour Profile.* Burlington: Department of Psychiatry, University of Vermont.

Battle, J. (1976) 'Test-Retest Reliability of the Canadian Self Esteem Inventory for Children'. *Psychological Reports* 38:1343–1345.

Bierman, K.L. and Furman, W. (1984) 'The Effects of Social Skill Training and Peer Involvement on The Social Adjustment of Preadolescents'. *Child Development* 55:151–162.

Cheatham, R.B. (1968) 'A Study of the Effects of Group Counselling on the Self Concept and on the Reading Efficiency of Low Achieving Readers in a Public Intermediate School'. *Dissertation Abstracts International* 29b:2200.

Clement, P.W. and Milne, D.O. (1967) 'Group Play Therapy and Tangible Reinforcers Used to Modify the Behaviour of 8-Year-Olds'. *Behavioural Research Therapy* 5:301–312.

Colson, D. and Horowitz, L. (1983) 'Research in Group Psychotherapy'. In H. Kaplan and B. Sadock (eds) *Comprehensive Group Psychotherapy.* Baltimore: Williams and Wilkins.

Conners, C.K. (1969) 'A Teacher Rating Scale for Use in Drug Studies with Children'. *American Journal of Psychiatry* 126:884–888.

Coopersmith, S. (1967) *The Antecedents of Self Esteem.* San Francisco: Freeman.

Derogatis, L. and Melisaratos, N. (1983) 'The Brief Symptom Inventory: An Introductory Report'. *Psychological Medicine* 13:595–605.

Dies, R.R. (1980) 'Group Psychotherapy: Reflections on 3 Decades of Research'. *Journal of Applied Behavioural Science* 15:361.

Dies, R.R. and Riester, A.E. (1986) 'Research on Child Group Psychotherapy: Present Status and Future Directions'. In: A.E. Riester and I.A. Kraft (eds) *Monograph 3, American Group Psychotherapy Association Monograph Series* 173–220. Madison: International Universities Press.

Douglas, T. (1976) *Group Work Practice.* London: Tavistock Publications.

Endicott, J., Spitzer, R.L. and Fleiss, F.L. (1976) 'The Global Assessment Scale: A Procedure for Measuring Overall Severity of Psychiatric Disturbance'. *Archives of General Psychiatry* 33:766–771.

Entwistle, N.J. and Welsh, J. (1969) 'Correlates of School Attainment at Different Ability Levels'. *British Journal of Educational Psychology* 39:57–63.

Fisher, B. (1953) 'Group Therapy with Retarded Readers'. *Journal of Educational Psychology* 6:354–360.

Fitts, W.H. (1973) *The Self Concept and Behaviour: Overview and Supplement.* Nashville, TN: Counsellor Recording and Tests.

Fransella, F. (1970) '... And Then There Was One'. In D. Bannister, (ed) *Perspectives in Personal Construct Theory.* London: Academic Press.

Fransella, F. and Bannister, D. (1977) *A Manual for Repertory Grid Technique.* London: Academic Press.

Ganzarain, R. (1989) 'The "Bad Mother" Group'. In R. Ganzarain (ed) *Object Relations Group Psychotherapy.* Madison: International Universities Press. Ch. 4:67–87.

Gough, H.G. and Heilbrun, A.B. (1965) *The Adjective Check List Manual.* Palo Alto: Consulting Psychologists Press.

Goyette, C.H., Conners, C.K. and Ulrich, R.F. (1978) 'Normative Data on Revised Conners' Parent and Teacher Rating Scales'. *Journal of Abnormal Child Psychology* 6:221–236.

Harper, P.B. (1978) 'Self Concept and Scholastic Achievement'. M.A. Thesis Submitted to the University of Capetown. (Unpublished).

Hinds, W. and Roehlke, H. (1970) 'A Learning Theory Approach to Group Counselling with Elementary School Children'. *Journal of Counselling Psychology* 17:49–55.

House, R.M. (1971) 'The Effects of Non-Directive Group Play Therapy upon the Sociometric Status and Self Concept of Selected Second Grade Children'. *Dissertation Abstracts International* 31a:2684.

Jersild, A.T. (1952) *In Search of Self.* New York: Teachers College, Columbia University.

LaGreca, A.M. and Santogrossi, D.A. (1980) 'Social Skill Training With Elementary and School Students: A Behavioural Group Approach'. *Journal of Consulting and Clinical Psychology* 48:220–227.

Lang, M. and Tisher, M. (1978) *Children's Depression Scale.* Victoria: Australian Council For Educational Research.

Lawrence, D. (1981) 'The Development of a Self Esteem Questionnaire'. *British Journal of Educational Psychology* 51:245–251.

Lipsitt, L.P. (1958) 'A Self Concept Scale for Children and its Relationship to the Childrens Form of the Manifest Anxiety Scale'. *Child Development* 29:463–471.

McBrien, R. and Nelson, R. (1972) 'Experimental Group Strategies with Primary Grade Children'. *Elementary School Guidance and Counseling* 6:170–174.

McGlashan, T. (ed) (1973) *The Documentation of Clinical Psychotropic Drug Trials.* Rockville, MD: National Institute of Mental Health.

Pearce, J. (1992) Case Complexity Scale. (Personal communication).

Pevsner, R. (1982) 'Group Parent Training versus Individual Family Therapy: An Outcome Study'. *Journal of Behaviour Therapy and Experimental Psychiatry* 13(2):119–122.

Piers, E.V. and Harris, D.B. (1969) *Manual for the Piers Harris Children's Self Concept Scale.* Nashville: Counsellor Recordings and Tests.

Quay, H.C. (1977) 'Measuring Dimensions of Deviant Behaviour: The Behaviour Problem Check List'. *Journal of Abnormal Child Psychology* 5:277–288.

Rogers, C.R. (1961) *On Becoming a Person.* Boston: Houghton Mifflin.

Rosenberg, M. (1965) *Society and the Adolescent Self Image.* Princeton, NJ: Princeton University.

Rothman, D., Sorrells, J. and Heldman, P. (1976) *A Global Assessment Scale for Children.* Oakland, Ca: Alameda County Mental Health Services.

Rutter, M. (1967) 'A Children's Behavioural Questionnaire for Completion by Teachers: Preliminary Findings'. *Journal of Child Psychology and Psychiatry* 8:1–11.

Rutter, M., Tizard, J. and Whitmore, K. (1970) *Education Health and Behaviour.* London: Longman.

Ryle, A. (1976) Group Psychotherapy. *British Journal of Hospital Medicine* 15(3):239–248.

Ryle, A. and Lipshitz, S. (1976) 'An Intensive Case Study of a Therapeutic Group'. *British Journal of Psychiatry* 128:581–587.

Shaffer, D., Gould, M., Brasie, J., Ambrosini, P., Fisher, P., Bird, H. and Aluwahlia, S. (1983) 'A Children's Global Assessment Scale (CGAS)'. *Archives of General Psychiatry* 40:1228–1231.

Siegel, J.M. (1987) 'The Multidimensional Anger Inventory'. In P.A. Keller and S.R Heyman (eds) *Innovations in Clinical Practice* 6:279–287, Sarasota: Professional Resources Exchange.

Sorensen, J.L., Hargreaves, W.A. and Le Blane. (1979) 'Comparison of Impairment Scales for Children'. *Program Evaluation Series.* San Francisco: Langley Porter Neuropsychiatric Institute, University of California.

Spivack, G., Spotts, J. and Haimes, P. (1967) *Devereux Adolescent Behaviour Rating Scale.* Devon, PA: The Devereux Foundation.

Stott, D.H. (1974) *The Bristol Social Adjustment Guides Manual: The Social Adjustment of Children.* London: Hodder and Stoughton.

Thombs, M.R. and Muro, J.J. (1973) 'Group Counselling and the Sociometric Status of Second Grade Children'. *Elementary School Guidance and Counselling* 7:194–197.

Thorpe, L.P., Clarke, W.W. and Tieges, E. (1953) *California Test of Personality.* Monterey, Ca: CTB/McGraw Hill.

Vinogradov, S. and Yalom, I. (1989) *Group Psychotherapy.* Washington: American Psychiatric Press.

Watson, J.P. (1970) 'A Repertory Grid Method of Studying Groups'. *British Journal of Psychiatry* 117:309.

Part 2

Developmental Perspectives

CHAPTER 5

Developmental Considerations in Therapeutic Planning

Peter Harper

Development is a lifespan process involving physical, behavioural, cognitive and emotional changes over time (Nash *et al.* 1990). Understanding the processes involved in development facilitates the postulation of models from which predictions about behaviour and emotional functioning can be made. Where behaviour is aberrant and emotional functioning immature, developmental models provide a useful baseline from which deviations can be understood, the central issues in the developmental process identified, and treatment planned.

Psychological literature is permeated with models of development, representing the varied perspectives of numerous theorists. However, common to the models is the consensus that:

1. development is an interactive, creative, ever changing and dynamic process;

2. the parent is not the exclusive (or even the primary) source of the growing child's construction of reality or development of coping strategies; and

3. significant growth and change can occur at any stage of life.

An understanding of the behavioural changes occurring during development is perhaps initially best achieved by a review of the underlying general processes. Observational studies have provided the content from which the following processes have been derived:

1. All organisms, and humans are no exception, are subject to ongoing change and adaptation to a range of complex environmental demands, with a resultant shift from immature to more mature behaviours.

2. Biological determinants and social influences are powerful forces which bring about changes in behaviour in the progression from primitive undeveloped behaviour to highly complex, structured behaviour. Relatively recent literature (Stern 1985) has highlighted the complexity of the human infant and its interactive capacity in the development of a wide range of successively more varied and complex behaviours, with a Sense of Self emerging very early on in life.

3. Behavioural observations have paved the way for various theorists to infer a number of different mediating structures in development. Bowlby, Freud, Piaget and Maslow, to name but a few, have all postulated the existence of various mental structures, reflecting the infant's increasing functional efficiency and adaptability (CRM 1975). Over time these structures become more complex and differentiated.

4. There is a considerable body of knowledge which emphasises the basic patterns along which behavioural change occurs. Thus is it assumed that development proceeds along definite and predictable lines, building sequentially on preceding stages, with the occurrence of some events being critically important if the resolution of the various developmental conflicts is to be achieved.

5. The goal of development is ultimately the attainment of the capacity to direct behaviour independently, and to be free of the often automatic responses that the developing person has to internal and external stimuli.

It is not the intention of this review to offer a summary of the numerous theories of development. Instead, drawing on a variety of models, on obser-vational studies, and clinical experience, a considered integration of the characteristics, needs and tasks, parental styles and behavioural outcomes will be provided in an attempt to provide an overview against which clinicians will be able to target their psychotherapeutic provision more accurately and effec-tively.

In offering this outline the author acknowledges the influence of Schaeffer (1981), Pine (1985) and Levin-Landheer (1982). Pine argues that the phase concept in many theories of development does not properly refer to the totality of the child's experience, but rather to certain affectively central moments of the child's day – these are moments in the child's day when the issues of the various phases are active, and these critical events are often short-lived, occurring around moments of intense internal need and satisfaction. Innumerable formative moments are centred around different phenomena which themselves occur against a background of ongoing and important but perhaps low-key circumstances which facilitate experiences such as those of self-continuity, competence and self-esteem in the life of every developing child. Each developmental achievement therefore contributes to the child's personal psychology of them-self, and all experiences are inevitably organised around this construction of self (Magner 1992). This experience-based developmental framework permits the integration of numerous theoretical viewpoints.

Levin-Landheer (1982) highlights the shared pattern of growth, with common themes, issues, and the physical and emotional changes typical of each stage, which stand free of issues of race, colour, class, background, gender and circumstance. Erikson (1964) postulated a similar formulation in which each stage has particular developmental tasks to which the individual will return in the resolution of life's ongoing primal theatre. 'Each one is a scene of action during which we respond to certain specific needs, using methods and techniques which may or may not be satisfying. We experience conflicts, deal with issues and hopefully develop the inner resources which will carry us on to the next stage successfully' (Levin-Landheer 1982, p.129). She acknowledges the fundamental experiences and interchanges required in relationships if the individual is to develop the resources to negotiate the tasks at hand successfully. These transactions are stage specific and 'provide the essential nutrients for healthy growth' (p.130).

Let us now proceed to an integrated review of the central characteristics of the developmentally important moments in the lives of all people:

Stage 1: Birth to six months

During the initial stage of life sensory-motor functioning is central and is characterised by the infant's total vulnerability and healthy dependence on the parent caretaker (most commonly the mother). The infant experiences itself as being merged with the mother (or mother substitute), experiencing maternal vicissitudes as its own. Thus if the mother feels tense, the child too will experience tension. The young infant is largely ego-centric, likes rhythms (such as feeding and sleeping) and will protest vigorously at the internal discomfort it experiences when they are disrupted. Crying is the signal with which the infant will indicate any internal discomfort from which it seeks release.

The young infant's psychological needs centre on being cared for, nurturance, warmth, physical closeness and touch. Healthy emotional bonding takes place in contexts in which parents are genuinely pleased at the arrival of the newborn, expressing their joy in gentle confidence, 'giving' as much as is needed. Physical holding, too, plays an important role. However, it is also important that the infant not be overstimulated. When the infant has its needs adequately fulfilled a sense of belonging and security, trust in self, and an optimism about life (expressed in unrestricted curiosity and creativity), results. On the other hand, overfeeding, anticipating and responding before the infant signals a need, being unresponsive, punitive or tense, effectively conveys prohibitory messages to the infant about its existence, its feelings and its needs, which are incorporated by the infant.

Inappropriate meeting of infant needs (or not fulfilling them) may, in childhood, result in a variety of problems. These may include such conditions as marasmus, anaclitic depression, (Spitz 1946), passivity, feeding and sleeping problems, failure to thrive, continuous crying, autistic-like conditions, developmental regression, bowel problems and a rejection of closeness. Problems presenting in adulthood which may have their origins in this initial developmental phase include anorexia, obesity, addictions, psychotic conditions and suicidal and homicidal tendencies, a sense of scarcity, fears of separation and change, and difficulty in relying on others in the satisfaction of needs. Clinicians need to be sensitive to a range of different clues which may be suggestive of unresolved difficulties arising from infancy. Themes relating to dependency and supply are most suggestive and may be manifest in wanting to eat frequently, an inability to concentrate and think coherently, and either wanting to be dependent on others or totally rejecting emotional proximity. The therapeutic needs of individuals facing conflicts of this nature centre around the provision of a nutritious emotional diet of warm, intimate and pleasurable contact, in the unconditional acceptance of the individual. Facilitating the meeting of the client's needs without them having to suffer is important, as is the provision of rhythmic experiences symbolic of the early eating/sleeping rhythms. In general terms, helpful therapeutic interventions will be responsive to the client's need for confirmation that 'being' and having feelings and needs is a core human experience.

Stage 2: Six months to eighteen months

Development through the first eighteen months of life proceeds at an unprecedented rate. After the first six months of life the infant rapidly develops a whole range of new skills, which enable it to move away from the mother and exercise its curiosity in the exploration of the world around it. This is the stage during which the infant becomes increasingly physically mobile and is therefore able to initiate exploration, starts to feed itself, and may start to identify its own needs. Most exciting for many parents is the emergence of speech. Environmental provision of consistency and predictability are fundamental to the confirmation for the growing infant that there are people in the world who are trustworthy and caring. This is the stage at which infants will explore and 'do', using sensory exploration as the primary mode through which they meet the world. Healthy development is facilitated by a parenting style which allows active exploration to take place simultaneous with the continuation of supportive and loving relationships.

Physical safety is imperative for the exploring youngster who needs interesting and varied opportunities to expand an inquiring mind. Restrictive parenting in which statements of the nature of 'No don't do that...' is contraindicated, as is a focus on the setting of inappropriate developmental goals such as toilet training and independent feeding. Patient parenting, which allows the child to initiate getting attention and separating and returning, facilitates a vital sense of continuity. Parental enthusiasm for the initiation of action on the part of the child should not underestimate the ongoing need for nurturance. Although children at this stage may require appropriate limit setting they do not warrant punishment and discipline.

The child who is deprived of constructive and positive parenting in this stage of his development may become passive, withdrawn and dependent. He is unlikely to initiate exploratory activity and his anxious attachment is most frequently seen in his crying easily. An absence of stimulatory experience may result in developmental delay and slow learning in a child who may harm himself easily and display hyperactive behaviour which appears goalless.

In later life individuals whose needs have not been adequately met in the six to eighteen months period tend to endure extreme discomfort before taking care of themselves. Frequently injuries are a feature and such an individual tends to lack a coherent awareness of their body or feelings. Motivational problems and boredom are common as difficulty is encountered in goal setting, and the individual may experience a pervading sense of listlessness and lifelessness. Pleasure is frequently absent from the life of such individuals, who respond to difficulties with either inappropriately frenzied activity or by engaging the fight-flight response. Themes of curiosity or intuitiveness may predominate and there is a tendency to engage in pleasure seeking activities which provide a variety of stimulation and in exploratory activities without forethought of the consequences. Immobility is a common dread.

Effective therapeutic endeavours with the individual with a developmental lesion at this stage are most fruitful when they promote the individual's sense of exploration and achievement within a context of reasonable expectations. Particular attention should be paid to issues of safety during exploration, with this being most effectively facilitated by the giving of clear information about the world. Promotion of an awareness of bodily sensations is often helpful, particularly within a regime of close physical nurturance and stroking. Enthusiasm about creativity and help in making sense of different feelings by 'checking out' is most conducive to psychological growth.

Stage 3: Eighteen months to three years
Most commonly referred to in the psychoanalytic literature as the anal stage, this is also the stage of preoperational thinking in the Piagetian frame. It is the

stage during which the toddler develops an acute sense of their separateness and is often characterised by expressions of intense rage. The toddler is no longer the centre of all attention, as is most frequently the case in preceding stages, and the toddler effectively loses the previously close structuring of his life. Control is a central issue here and this stage is often referred to as the 'Terrible Twos' because of the toddler's strong tendency to be oppositional, negative and resistant to parental requests. 'No!' is a frequent utterance as the toddler strives to achieve a degree of autonomy. The presence of language may facilitate problem-solving more easily. The toddler develops a new ability to think, although the characteristic thought process at this early stage is linear cause-effect thinking.

A primary developmental task is that of socialisation, the establishment of appropriate independence, and the rudiments of a sexual identity. The provision of encouragement of the individual's capabilities is made easy for parents by the toddler's thirst for information. However, the primary focus in the parent–child relationship is around limits. The toddler resists limits, and yet requires firm but gently imposed reasonable limits which allow separation from the previously healthy symbiosis whilst introducing opportunities for reality testing. The provision of clear information, reasons for actions, and the continuation of nurturance and fun augur well for psychological well being. This is the age during which toilet training is most effectively first introduced, but, as with all issues of discipline, the primary emphasis should be on caring.

Toddlers need challenges and opportunities to succeed in their problem solving attempts. Inappropriately high or low expectations or solving problems for children, without giving them the opportunity to have an attempt to do so themselves, is likely to promote resistance and exacerbate the intensity and frequency of temper tantrums. A sense of security is facilitated in cases in which parents refrain from competitive engagement with their children and where they allow the expression of anger without letting the child lose. Healthy self control, respect for others and a propensity for effective thinking in the context of a clearly developing sense of identity emerge when parenting has been facilitative.

The alternative picture is characterised by displays of excessive temper, in which the child is excessively demanding, loses control, and may hit and bite in an attempt to secure its dysfunctional ends. Conflicts over bowel functioning are not uncommon, though alternate responses may be to develop excessive shyness, passivity and anxiety in an individual who avoids engaging others, and who prefers to withdraw. Night terrors and a pervading sense of fearfulness are also not uncommon.

The oppositional–negative style may persist in later life as the growing individual is preoccupied with issues of control. Obsessional behaviour and acute competitiveness may also characterise the life of such individuals. Somatic tension manifests most frequently in sphincter tightness and intestinal problems.

Rebelliousness and the expression of anger (or its angry denial) may be the clearest indication of difficulties at this stage of development.

Treatment planning for individuals with difficulty at this stage of development is most effective when they acknowledge and actively promote the individual's ability to think for themselves and be effective in problem resolution without having to be perfect. Opportunities to make mistakes without catastrophic consequences are helpful. The provision of clear boundaries and the acceptance of negativity without it being harmful to the individual or others promotes health. Anger should be separated from the experience of other emotions and the individual encouraged to think effectively whilst simultaneously experiencing the full range of emotions appropriate to the situation in which they find themselves. Reciprocity and the development of thinking which takes both self and others into account is central to the individual's striving to separate healthily from the relationships of early infancy.

Stage 4: Three years to six years

In the Piagetian frame, preoperational thinking is further developed during this stage of development, although in the psychoanalytic frame the central concern is with Oedipal issues. Sexual exploration is a core feature of the child of this age. An awareness of sexual differences emerges and the child characteristically engages in fantasy and imaginative play. The opposition of the preceding stage gives way to co-operation and an ability to understand the rudiments of concepts of time, rules and sharing. An awareness of consequences develops and the child is actively able to effect different outcomes by initiating strategies of change.

Experimentation, particularly in social relationships takes place as the individual tests out his newly developed sense of control and power, and learns what it means to be male or female in society. Exploration of the larger world takes place as the child is exposed initially to play groups and later to nursery and formal schooling opportunities. Support and encouragement of this process ensures the establishment of a core sense of initiative.

A parenting style which facilitates the successful negotiation of the demands of this developmental stage again requires consistency and patience. Children need help and modelling in the separation of fantasy from reality and in the comfortable development of their sexual identity. It is most helpful to teach conversational skills and to allow the child to develop prowess and pride in their ability to think, feel and do. Where children are made to feel responsible for their parents' feelings and behaviour, where they are taught to forego their own needs in the exclusive service of others, or where parents withdraw nurturing and are overly seductive, children are likely to display a range of different problems. Phobic responses and rituals around food, excessive anxiety, bedwetting, soiling and hyperactivity are possible dysfunctional outcomes. Alternatively, difficulties in relationships may be manifest in withdrawal into fantasy and magical thinking or threatening and bullying behaviour, as the child acts out internal discomfort.

In later life it is not uncommon for individuals with difficulties at this stage to engage in almost perpetual wishful thinking. The use of seductive overtones in the manipulation of others into taking responsibility is also a common feature. Sexual/gender identity problems too may occur, as may sexual acting out. With a propensity to think, (magically at times), emotional material and needs are often denied.

The clinician may be alerted to difficulties in this phase of development when issues are presented at the polarities of a number of different continua – for example fantasy and reality; creativity and destructiveness, sanity and madness, masculinity and femininity, and so forth.

The development of constructive assertion in establishing a clear identity is an important therapeutic goal when working with such individuals. A major therapeutic task is to learn that it is possible for the individual to have a coherent view of the world whilst remaining true to themselves and being powerful. Magical thinking should be confronted and the individual learn that it is possible to have one's needs met without having to resort to states of confusion, fear or even insanity.

Stage 5: Six years to twelve years

This, the psychoanalytic Latency Period, sees the development of concrete operational thought. Children of these ages cluster in same sex groups and tend to exclude members of the opposite sex from their activities. An orientation to achievement and competitiveness may result in a tendency to be argumentative, particularly in the family context. The child's value system is frequently augmented from sources outside the family, and teachers and peers begin to play an increasingly prominent role.

Accomplishments and a sense of 'industriousness' are the central tasks of this age group of children. Stimulating experiences and challenges make for growth. Failures should be accepted as learning opportunities and the inevitable disagreements accepted as characteristic of this phase. Children in this age group have access to a developing sense of humour and this often paves the way for the successful integration of success, failure and the awareness that there are a multitude of different ways in which outcomes can be achieved. 'Doing experiences', the opportunity to argue constructively, and the taking of responsibility are important growth experiences. Unhelpful parental behaviours include situations in which parents become competitive with their offspring, or those in which they are either dogmatic and authoritarian or permissive and overly relaxed.

Successful negotiation of the developmental tasks results in a sense of pride at accomplishments, with a concomitant sense of the individual's capability and personal adequacy. The fundamental technology of the culture is firmly established during this stage.

Difficulties in negotiation of the developmental tasks may be reflected in a preoccupation with issues of competition and anxieties over performance. Lying, cheating and stealing may result. Difficulties at school and school phobias may also appear, or behaviour problems become manifest. Not completing tasks and 'giving up', or excessive rebellion are indicators that there are difficulties in the negotiation of the developmental tasks. Somatic symptoms most frequently include headaches and a 'nervous stomach'. Depressive equivalents may be noticed and the child may be excessively self critical.

The young person or adult experiencing difficulties which originate in this stage, presents as rigid and inflexible. They frequently do not complete tasks in spite of a harried, perfectionistic style. Performance takes place without forethought, and self criticism and self deprecation are commonplace. Problems are frequently made overt when there is a necessity to deal with authority figures or when new skills are being learned.

Remediation of these difficulties takes place when interventions facilitate a sense of wellbeing in achieving according to one's own unique style, without having to suffer, argue, discontinue or engage in irresponsible behaviour in an attempt to get one's needs met. The clarification of value structures, too, can be most helpful.

Stage 6: The teenage years

Increased cognitive capacity, and the ability to hypothesize and to use abstract thinking processes heralds in the teenage years. The psychoanalytic schools refer to this stage as the Genital Phase, and the entry into adolescence is certainly characterised by rapid physical growth and change, particularly in the individual's secondary sexual characteristics. The moodiness of the adolescent is a common parental complaint! From having excluded members of the opposite sex in their earlier years, the adolescent begins to develop an increasing interest in such members. Peer relationships become increasingly important while the adolescent–parent relationship is probably most accurately referred to as being 'hostile–dependent'.

The central developmental task of the young person is emancipation from parents. Issues of identity re-emerge and value structures are refined, as the lifestyle of the individual becomes increasingly established. Parental acceptance of the process of separation with the simultaneous provision of information regarding physical changes and sexual behaviour, support and confrontation regarding responsibility and behaviour, and the gradual loosening of parental control as the young person emerges as a peer, are all conducive to congruent development. Adolescents may portray a veneer of total independence, but they nonetheless need appropriate parental nurturance, friendship and fun. The removal of healthy guidelines at too early a stage, or seductive parenting will preclude the development of personal identity and a healthy internalised value structure.

As a result, depressive reactions with suicidal features may appear. Alternatively, where nurturance has been withdrawn, sex is often used as a means of securing nurturance. Inner controls are not established and rebellion, poor hygiene, avoidance behaviours or the development of dependencies on others, sex or substances may be noted. Psychiatric problems may include anorexia nervosa. In later life these behavioural patterns may be seen to continue, with a concomitant failure to establish intimate relationships by the use of a self centred, one-up-man-ship type style.

Therapeutic provision should address the parental style and identity issues core to adolescence. Honesty, unconditional acceptance and the simultaneous confrontation of behaviours which avoid due attention to needs, thinking and feeling, are crucial in the promotion of mental health in young people.

Conclusions

In planning for the therapeutic needs of children and adolescents (as well as adults), the clinician with a developmental perspective is well placed to offer appropriately targeted and therefore effective interventions. A knowledge of the expected range of behaviours 'normally' manifested by children and adolescents, of the life's issues they face, and of the experiences which scupper healthy development, facilitates easy planning for the provision of therapeutic experiences in the group setting. Therapeutic provision may target specific deficits in childhood developmental experiences and/or it may address the conflicts and confusions arising from the range of life experiences of the developing person – (usually mediated by worrying or problem behaviour). The provision of experiences and responses which address developmental imbalances are the cornerstones of effective group treatments. The overview which is provided in this chapter provides a general framework from which the clinician can distil either the wholesome experiences the group member lacks, or the issues around which conflicts are clustered.

A real challenge lies in the provision of therapeutic experiences which address developmental lesions and the individual's level of cognitive functioning, in age appropriate words, actions and activities. The creation of a safe, predictable and consistent environment for an eight-year-old (whose reasoning ability is likely to be at the Piagetian concrete operations stage) would be articulated by very different therapeutic responses from those which would be used with an adolescent with similar life's issues, but capable of using abstract thought processes.

Prior to commencing groupwork, a thorough assessment of the potential group member's emotional, cognitive, and social functioning is vital if provision is to be accurately targeted. For some, such an assessment will highlight the need to facilitate learning emotional literacy, whereas for others the provision of opportunities to socialise within clearly articulated limits may be sufficient provision. For each member, thorough consideration of developmental issues is paramount. In this context it is important to consider whether or not groupwork is contraindicated for children and adolescents with 'primary' relationship deficits. Clinical experience favours the provision of individual therapy as the treatment of choice. Once an ability to bond and relate is established, use of group treatment resources may then be possible and more appropriate.

References

CRM Books (1975) *Developmental Psychology Today.* New York: Random House.

Erikson, E.H. (1964) *Childhood and Society.* New York: Norton.

Levin-Landheer, P. (1982) 'The Cycle of Development'. *Transactional Analysis Journal.* 12,(2) 129–139.

Magner, V. (1985) Developmental Chart. London: Metanoia Psychotherapy Training Institute.

Magner, V. (1992) Personal Communication on Developmental Theory.

Nash, E.S., Stoch, M.B. and Harper, G.D. (1990) *Human Behaviour.* Cape Town: Juta.

Pine, F. (1985) *Developmental Theory and Clinical Practice.* London: Yale University Press.

Schaeffer, B. (1981) *Corrective Parenting Chart.* Minneapolis, MN.: Self-Published.

Stern, D.N. (1985) *The Interpersonal World of the Infant.* New York: Basic Books.

Spitz, R. (1946)*The Psychoanalytic Study of the Child.* Vol.2. New York: International Universities Press. pp.113–117.

CHAPTER 6

Emotional Development

Kedar Nath Dwivedi

Bridges (1930), using earlier ideas by Watson (1919) and Dashiel (1928), observed that 'visceral' pattern reactions appear to undergo differentiation during human development, just like any other form of behaviour. She pointed out that at birth there is a reaction of excitement or general disturbance, 'It is difficult to tell whether a baby is frightened, angry, or even pleasantly excited... This general excitement, within a short time – perhaps days and perhaps only hours – becomes differentiated into two general types of emotion' (p.517), that is, delight and distress.

There are at least three patterns of affect that can be observed in infancy: (i) the states of well being, contentment or tranquillity, (ii) the states of distress and (iii) the cataleptic response. The cataleptic response consists of the baby suddenly lying motionless with nonconverging staring eyes and a sleep-like respiration. This type of response is induced in situations of danger and is seen in the young of all known species. In human babies, however, it disappears after two months (Papousek and Papousek 1975). This state may have elements that are common with later hypnotic phenomena, 'frozen watchfulness', catatonic states, and depressive stupor (Dorpat 1977).

Thus, the emotional states of delight and distress are the two precursors of a huge variety of specific emotions that evolve in the course of maturation. For example, the infantile state of well being gradually differentiates into emotions such as tenderness, pride, joy, security, contentment, love, and so forth, and that of distress into feelings of pain, anger, jealousy, anxiety, shame, guilt, disgust, humiliation, embarrassment, and so forth. The specific contents of differentiation also depend on the psycholinguistic aspects of the particular culture.

Every phase of psychosexual development provides an occasion for emotional maturation; however, the latency period tends to induce maximum growth in the acquisition of various skills related to emotional maturation.

Emotional maturation has several aspects, such as emotional differentiation, desomatisation, the ability to tolerate emotions and to utilise emotions as signals to oneself. Just like the skills of walking, talking and sphincter control, the development of emotional skills also requires appropriate help from parents.

The capacity to tolerate one's emotions comes with the ability to self-regulate them. This capacity develops through identification with the caring persons and their active encouragement of the child to self-regulate. A skilful parent allows the baby to experience emotions, but if the emotion begins to exceed the baby's tolerance in terms of intensity or duration, the parent intervenes to protect the baby from being overwhelmed. Such intervention may include the mere presence of the parent, various distractions, compensations (e.g. feed or dummy) and rituals that enable the baby to employ self-soothing functions. As they grow, they can identify with the parenting person and initiate such interventions themselves, as soon as their emotions begin to go beyond their limits of tolerance.

Some parents, however, discourage or even punish any self-soothing or autoerotic activity in the child. They may have a general aversion to physical contact or have jealousy of any other object – even a transitional object. If the parent is unable to convey to the child the feeling that it is all right to assume some possession of the automatically controlled parts of themselves, there may follow a sense of inaccessibility to one's affect regulatory functions leading to such serious difficulties as psychosomatic illness, substance abuse, or total dependence upon one's partner for sexual arousal (Krystal 1988).

If the parents are unable to protect the baby from an overwhelming intense emotion, a state of psychic trauma can develop, threatening to disorganise or even destroy all psychic functions. In adults, this can even lead to psychogenic death, but in children this is usually aborted by the use of defence mechanisms. However, such emotions are subsequently perceived as particularly dangerous. This leads to a dread of being flooded with such feelings (e.g. abandonment, hurt, etc.) and subsequently the employment of various strategies (e.g. inducing altered states of consciousness, substance abuse, soothing and distracting rituals) to defend oneself against the slightest possibility of such feelings emerging into one's consciousness.

Another aspect of emotional maturation is that of desomatisation. Through symbolic and linguistic development of awareness and of identification of one's feelings, formulation of observations and experience, and verbalisation of feelings and demands, there is a reduction in massive somatic responses. In the beginning, emotional behaviour is the only means of communication between the baby and others but gradually symbolic and linguistic communication begin to take over. However, if the parents continue to respond only to very intense emotions, the child is forced to continue to use emotions to communicate or control others. This may also interfere with the maturational aspect of desomatisation and may lead to the development of a histrionic communication style. Similarly, an increased cultural emphasis on internal responses to stress may lead to the conversion of chronic affective states into psychosomatic patterns.

Emotional maturation also means the development of the capacity to utilise emotions as signals to oneself. One begins to learn that all emotions are transient in nature and if one is not angry or frightened of one's emotions, they usually run their course and can be utilised to one's advantage. Emotions play a very important role in all our mental events; motivation, memory, and various aspects of cognitive and information processing functions. Normally these are preconscious or subliminal and we become aware of them when they become intense and break into our consciousness. There is, therefore, no state of emotionlessness, just as there is no state of weatherlessness. However, this fact has been comprehended only recently in Western psychology and psychiatry; Freud's theorisations in terms of catharsis and discharge of emotions had misled the science for a long time.

In the Eastern psychologies of several thousand years, on the other hand, there has been an emphasis on the transitoriness of emotions and the absence of emotionlessness (Atwood and Maltin 1991, Dwivedi 1990). According to Eastern wisdom, the best way to handle feelings is through expanding one's consciousness to get in touch with one's feelings, to recognise them and to accept them. Being aware of the physiological aspects of the feelings and discerning their transitory nature, without getting stuck with the mental objects that trigger them, can help to transmute their energy. The development of skills in harnessing the emotional energy to one's advantage is described as 'Taming the Tiger' in Eastern psychology (Rinpoche 1987).

Cognitive development and emotion

The thinking and understanding of children in relation to their feelings and motivations are also influenced by the limitations of their cognitive development, as outlined in the previous chapter. Pre-operational children are, for example, unable to acknowledge mixed feelings. For a young child, it is difficult to realise that people can hide their inner or true feelings or can put their feelings out of their own awareness. It is only during adolescence that one begins to understand that feelings can also be unconscious.

Because of egocentric thinking, young children tend to project the cause of their own emotions onto others. If a child gets upset by losing a toy or because of not being able to watch a particular television programme, they may think that the same must be true of their parents as well (Harter 1983).

Because of the magical type of thinking, young children confuse their fantasies with reality. They may feel that things in their environment have happened because they have wished, feared or thought about them. Many children, therefore, feel totally responsible for parental break-ups, accidents, losses, disasters, and so forth. Young children can also feel responsible for other's emotions. Feelings of responsibility, for example, for parental anger, is extremely common between the ages of 4 and 11 years. It is only later that children realise that their parents and significant others have an emotional life outside their own.

At times some adults responsible for children are unable to appreciate the cognitive, emotional and behavioural limitations of children or the differences in the assumptive worlds of adults and that of children. Thus, adults may make demands upon children that may be beyond the child's cognitive, emotional and behavioural capacity (Dwivedi 1993a). This may be due to their own pathological upbringing. They may see in their children certain characters from their own childhood – a sibling, parent, or grandparent – and unconsciously project a kind of power into the child that is unrealistic and unhelpful. Being overburdened with responsibilities beyond one's emotional capacity or the experience of neglect and abuse by the very parental figures on whom one depends for emotional growth can have seriously emotionally-damaging consequences (Dwivedi 1984, 1993b, Dwivedi et al. 1992).

During periods of stress there is an intensified need to obtain proximity and soothing body contact with attachment figures. Even adults faced with the stress of loss, or disaster, seek the proximity of familiar persons or environments. Even though that very person may be the cause of the stress, the need for a soothing response from such an attachment object does not diminish. If the attachment figure becomes rejecting, or is physically or emotionally unavailable and the degree and duration of distress is too intense in a vulnerable individual, the attachment behaviours can then become indiscriminate, disguised or disorganised. This leads to a state of emotional confusion, where the desire to 'reach out and touch someone' can become so intense that it can become aggressive, violent, hurtful, harmful and even fatal (Mawson 1987).

In states of high emotional arousal there is often an impairment of cognitive functions. Thus, it becomes easy to misjudge things and not think clearly. The inability to remember things that one knows so well is often experienced in states of anxiety during interviews, examinations, stage performances, addressing an audience and so forth. Misattribution is also not uncommon and the wrong people can get blamed during states of emotional arousal.

As the labelling of one's emotions is a product of the learning process, familiarity with some types of emotions and unfamiliarity with certain others may be due to the frequency with which they are experienced. Some children may not have consciously experienced affection and love, so as to know it when they get it. Thus, one can easily misunderstand excitement as anger, desire as fear and so forth.

Our responses to stimuli have three components: (1) cognitive (Experiential labelling), (2) psychophysiological and excitatory (e.g. heart rate, breathing, temperature) and (3) motor (behavioural). When the stimuli change (e.g. from anger-provoking to desire-provoking), our responses also change. However, the speed of adjustment of the three components mentioned above are rather different. Motor adjustment may be rapid but the excitatory adjustments are usually slow and incomplete. Thus, one emotional state carries over into the other. An example of this phenomenon of emotional transfer, fusion or confusion can be found in some sex offenders where sexual and aggressive feelings augment each other (Zillman 1984).

Thus, cognitive processes, psychoeducational aspects and cultural values have important influences on emotional maturation. In Western cultures, the excessive emphasis on self expression and independence appears to be creating a breeding ground for Narcissistic Disorders (Lasch 1980). The Narcissistic family systems are characterised by intense Narcissistic rage and shame (Jacobs 1991). However, some of the Eastern child-rearing practices enabling children to transcend narcissism, appreciate interdependence and cultivate empathy, could have a great deal to contribute to help overcome the current rising tide of Narcissistic Disorders (Dwivedi 1993c, Roland 1980).

References

Atwood, J.D. and Maltin, L. (1991) 'Putting Eastern Philosophies into Western Psychotherapies'. *American Journal of Psychotherapy.* XLV(3): 368–382.

Bridges, K.M.B. (1930) 'A Genetic Theory of Emotions'. *Journal of General Psychology.* 37: 517–527.

Dashiel, J.F. (1928) 'Are There Any Negative Emotions?'. *Psychological Review.* 35: 319–327.

Dorpart, T.L. (1977) 'Depressive affect.' *The Psychoanalytic Study of the Child.* 32: 3–27. New Haven: Yale University Press.

Dwivedi, K.N. (1984) 'Mother–Baby Psychotherapy'. *Health Visitor.* 57(10): 306–307.

Dwivedi, K.N. (1990) 'Purification of Mind by Vipassana Meditation'. In J. Crook and D. Fontana (eds) *Space in Mind: East-West Psychology and contemporary Buddhism.* Shaftesbury: Element Books.

Dwivedi, K.N. (1993a) 'Confusion and Underfunctioning in Children'. In V.P. Varma (ed) *How and Why Children Fail.* London: Jessica Kingsley Publishers.

Dwivedi, K.N. (1993b) 'Child Abuse and Hatred'. In V.P. Varma (ed) *How and Why Children Hate.* London: Jessica Kingsley Publishers.

Dwivedi, K.N. (1993c) 'Coping with Unhappy Children who are fromEthnic Minorities'. In V.P. Varma (ed) *Coping with Unhappy Children.* London: Cassell (in press).

Dwivedi, K.N., Brayne, E. and Lovett, S. (1992) 'Group Work with Sexually Abused Adolescent Girls'. *Group Analysis.* 25: 477–489.

Harter, S. (1983) 'Cognitive Developmental Considerations in the Conduct of Play Therapy'. In C.E. Schaffer and K.J. O'Connor (eds) *Handbook of Play Therapy.* New York: John Wiley and Son.

Jacobs, E.H. (1991) 'Self Psychology and Family Therapy'. *American Journal of Psychotherapy*. XLV(4): 483–498.

Krystal, H. (1988) *Integration and Self-Healing*. Hillsdale, New Jersey: The Analytic Press.

Lasch, C. (1980) *The Culture of Narcissism: American Life in an age of Diminishing Expectations*. London: Abacus.

Mawson, A.R. (1987) *Transient Criminality: A Model of Stress Induced Crime*. New York: Praeger.

Papousek, H. and Papousek, M. (1975) *Parent–Infant interaction*. New York: Associated Science.

Rinpoche, D.A. (1987) *Taming the Tiger*. Eskdalemuir: Dzalendara Publishing.

Roland, A. (1980) 'Psychoanalytic Perspectives on Personality Development in India'. *International Review of Psychoanalysis*. 1: 73–87.

Watson, J.B. (1919) *Psychology from the Standpoint of a Behaviourist*. Philadelphia: Lippincott.

Zillman, D. (1984) *Connections Between Sex and Aggression*. London: Lawrence Erlbaum Associates.

CHAPTER 7

Empathy and Prosocial Development

Malcolm Walley

Introduction

In 1967, the Ryder Cup, one of golf's most prestigious tournaments, came to a dramatic and memorable conclusion. Probably the greatest golfer of that era, USA's Jack Nicklaus, holed his final putt and knew his team had at least drawn the match. Nicklaus then deliberately picked up his opponent's (Tony Jacklin) ball marker to ensure that Jacklin could not lose the game with his next shot. Afterwards, Nicklaus stated that he did not want his opponent to lose knowing what that would mean to Jacklin's team and support in the nation.

He *felt* their potential disappointment which motivated an action to prevent such an outcome. Nicklaus's *empathy* (some current researchers now prefer the term *sympathy*) led to *altruistic* (prosocial) behaviour.

It is the intention of this chapter to overview the current status of research into the nature of empathy and its relationship with prosocial behaviour, and to discuss the implications of these findings for those who work with young people.

To be born human is not necessarily to be born humane. Our capacity to identify with and psychologically embrace the inner worlds and experiences of our fellows would seem to be a defining characteristic of our species. It is at the core of our humanity. Yet we might seriously question its universality.

Empathy, 'sharing the perceived emotion of another – feeling with another' (Eisenberg and Strayer 1987 p.5), has been closely linked to altruism and prosocial behaviour or helping (Thompson 1987, Eisenberg and Miller 1987a). Indeed, as Argyle (1991) and others have pointed out, helping behaviour is significantly dependent upon the process of empathy. The term 'empathy', rather surprisingly, is of relatively recent origin. In 1909, the psychologist

Titchener devised the term as a translation of the German word 'Einfuhling', which referred to the projection of personal feelings onto an object of art or aesthetics. Similarly, 'altruism' has been attributed to Comte, the nineteenth century founder of sociology, to mean 'an unselfish regard for the welfare of others' (Wispe 1978).

Empathy and prosocial behaviour

Whilst empathy has sometimes been construed as a prosocial response in and of itself, more frequently it has been considered a mediator of other interpersonal responses (Barnett 1987), notably prosocial behaviour.

The idea of empathy or sympathy as major determinants of prosocial or altruistic behaviour is quite deeply rooted in contemporary developmental and social psychology (Feshbach 1978, Eisenberg and Miller 1987a). Greater interest has therefore been focused upon whether empathy might be primarily innate or learned, and in understanding those circumstances whereby links between empathy and altruism are most likely to occur. However, an earlier review by Feshbach (1978) of the few studies available at that time found that, whilst a negative relation pertained between aggression and empathy in children, there was no firm conclusion with regard to pro-social behaviour and empathy.

In their attempts to measure empathy, psychologists have devised a range of measures. These include the picture story method whereby a child is shown slides of another whilst being told a story and then asked how s/he felt; questionnaires which ask directly about being affected by others' emotional experiences; non-verbal reactions may be observed while subjects watch videotapes; and physiological responses, to instances of others in distress, for example, may also be recorded.

As we will find, however, the results found by researchers are shaped by the measures of behaviour which they use – a fact given little emphasis outside of the specialist literature.

Underwood and Moore's (1982) review, mainly of studies on children using the picture/story indices of empathy, found no statistically significant association between emotional empathy and altruism – although they did concede stronger indications of a relationship between empathy and altruism where non-verbal measures were used.

Eisenberg (1982) in her review of the increased research literature, however, *did* find a significant positive correlation between empathy and prosocial behaviour in adults, together with some positive indications for children. More recently, Eisenberg and Miller (1987b), undertook a meta-analysis of previous studies according to the method of measuring empathy used, and found low to moderate positive correlations between empathy and both prosocial behaviour and cooperative/socially competent behaviour. Nearly all of the measures used by the researchers, with the exception of the picture story method, were found to be associated with empathy.

This expansion of research has led to a refinement of the concepts under investigation. Eisenberg and Miller (1987) define *empathy* as 'an affective state that stems from the apprehension of another's emotional state or condition, and that is congruent with it'; whereas *sympathy* is 'an emotional response stemming from another's emotional state or condition that is not identical to the other's emotion, but consists of feelings of sorrow or concern for another's welfare'. It is important that in neither definition is there a focus upon the self, which contrasts with researchers' use of the term *personal distress* as 'the motivation merely to alleviate one's own aversive emotional state' (Eisenberg *et al.* 1991).

Eisenberg and her colleagues (1991) point out there is now considerable evidence which points to a differential relationship between sympathy/empathy and personal distress with respect to altruism and prosocial behaviour, particularly amongst adults. However, it is worth bearing in mind that empathy may not always give rise to prosocial behaviour, especially with respect to young children. Barnett (1987) points out that children may react to the discomfort produced by witnessing another's upset by escaping from the situation or even attacking the victim.

Empathy in relation to other aspects of human behaviour
Argyle (1991) has proposed that empathy is closely linked to cooperation as well as helping, and cites a study by Marcus *et al.* (1985) on pre-school children to support this.

Bryant (1987) has found that levels of empathy are linked to mental health. She investigated empathy and social perspective taking (being able to take the perspective of another) in 7- and 11-year-olds, who were later tested at 10 and 14 years, respectively. Bryant discovered that empathy was strongly related to various measures of mental health, whereas social perspective taking showed little if any relationship with mental health.

Bryant contrasted her findings with our traditional view of maturity as implying self-sufficiency and detached autonomy, along with the assumption that emotional attachments and interpersonal involvement are better underplayed. Indeed, adolescents may be at risk psychologically when so detached, thereby linking with current research into stress-buffering. There is further discussion of Bryant's research below. Somewhat correspondingly, Totman (1990) proposed that social connectedness was predictive of wellbeing, in contrast with the stresses incurred through disconnection from social engagement.

Finally, the extent to which empathy and its association with altruism and aggression might be genetically linked is of interest. Rushton *et al.* (1986) studied 573 adult twin pairs of males and females in the UK. His findings suggested that approximately 50 per cent of variance on measures of empathy, altruism and aggressiveness were due to genetic factors, whereas the common environments of twins were apparently found to contribute little to altruism and aggressiveness.

At each age women had higher altruism and lower aggressiveness scores than men, and over the lifespan altruism increased progressively from 19 to 60 years, whereas aggressiveness decreased. Also, altruism and aggressiveness were negatively related, which might have implications for working with young people. For example, empathy and prosocial behaviour might be enhanced indirectly through facilitating a reduction in aggression, and *vice versa*.

Our work with young people might be enhanced if we understand more thoroughly the roots of human empathy and altruism, not only the genetic aspects, but the place of empathy and altruism in human evolution. To this we now turn.

Evolution, empathy and altruism

At first sight there would appear to be a contradiction between the idea of individual 'fitness', in natural selection terms (whereby an individual's genes are passed on to succeeding generations), and the self-sacrificial aspects of altruistic behaviour – that (in Darwinian terms) to be altruistic is to reduce one's biological fitness.

This contradiction has been effectively addressed by Hamilton (1964, 1975) who devised the concept of 'inclusive fitness' which is the sum of fitness deriving from selfish behaviour and fitness owing to altruistic behaviour towards relatives (since relatives will be carrying a proportion of the same genes as oneself). However, Alexander (1979) refers to this behaviour as 'nepotism'; namely, selfish behaviour having the appearance of altruism since it benefits relatives as well as one's own concerns. He would argue that biologically the case for 'true' altruism, in terms of intention or motivation, does not exist.

Widely accepted, though, is Trivers' (1971) concept of reciprocal altruism, whereby assistance rendered to an individual by another is returned via an appropriate interaction, usually at a later date and not necessarily involving individuals who are genetically related. He proposes that this behaviour will spread in a group where the net benefits to the 'reciprocists' exceed that to the non-altruists. Apparently, such reciprocal altruism has been observed in certain baboon groups (Packer 1977). The possibility of 'cheating' or exploitation of altruists would be inhibited in the long term – and Crook (1980) suggests that the universality of sanctions against such antisocial behaviour in human groups is long standing.

Trivers (1985) proposed that 'reciprocal altruism' would be most likely to develop under conditions of long life span, small and stable groups, low dispersal, little hierarchy, and, significantly, the ability to recognise other individuals – conditions which apparently prevailed amongst primitive peoples.

Also, human cheating is restrained by the formation of friendships – mutually facilitating helping and liking. The emotional rewards of friendship would also enhance helping and cooperation. Axelrod and Hamilton (1984) suggest that a further inhibition upon cheating (and its consequent initial payoff) in early human groups might occur where victims are kinsfolk, thereby generating a partial interest in the outcomes for the other person. The balance between nepotism and reciprocal altruism gives rise to the development of a motivational system which both initiates and supports reciprocation, detects cheating, and protects against exploitation.

Boyd and Richerson (1985) propose that group cooperation, particularly amongst non-kinship individuals, is fostered through cultural rather than genetic selection. Such cooperation confers advantages such as enhanced defence against predators, protection of young and so forth. It is the cooperative and more altruistic groups which may be most effective in defence against real or assumed threat (Argyle 1991). Some remote Amazonian tribes may be fierce to outsiders but gentle and tender towards insiders, particularly the young.

Of interest to youth workers would be the perspective which suggests that it is males who are more likely to form groups, particularly groups which are task-oriented and hierarchical, as echoed in sports teams, work and social groups and so forth (Argyle 1991), along with the global phenomenon of teenage gangs. Within the groups there are aspects of cooperative and prosocial behaviour, as well as competition.

It is important to appreciate how human interaction depends upon an ability to empathise, to feel oneself as another, in order to evaluate where an individual stands emotionally during an on-going transaction. Much of human life involves the formation and dissolution of partnerships. Since a partner can exploit another by deceit, individuals monitor their relationships for reciprocity. The evolution of subtle empathic abilities which underlies independent action, requires a competence in distinguishing one's own state of mind from those empathised to be present in the other.

In short, there are reasonable indicators that altruism is a valuable part of human heritage and that a capacity for empathy is vital for effective human interaction. From this basis we can ask how empathy tends to emerge in the early years of life and what are the factors which may enable it to flourish?

How does empathy develop?
If empathy and altruism are indeed a part of human evolution, the presence of empathy and helping behaviours, at least in embryonic form, in very young children would be anticipated. There is some evidence to support this. Thompson (1987) reports that two-day-old infants are capable of responding to the cries of a child, although this may be a form of social facilitation or behavioural contagion (a sort of reflex reaction).

From an early age individual differences are apparent, which tend to be consistent over time. Infants and toddlers are therefore extremely responsive to the social and emotional responses of others, and are not merely egocentric, indifferent, or incapable of understanding the emotional experiences of others. This is an important contribution to our perception and understanding of young children.

By the middle of the second year, toddlers have become more sophisticated in reacting to others' emotional experiences and will often show verbal expressions of sympathy. There is individual variation also, which may be in part the result of the behaviour of parents or others (see below), although the *capacity* for empathy seems to have developed by the middle of the second year.

In their 1987 review, Lennon and Eisenberg point out that there has been relatively little research into the influence of age upon empathy or sympathy. From the range of measures used, however, there are some pointers to a progressive emergence of empathy with age. For example, using picture/story scenarios, children's empathic responses to others typically increase with age up to mid-elementary school and then appear to level off. Questionnaire measures also show an increase in empathic responses in the early school years, at least in response to similar persons, whereas no consistent pattern of age-related change is apparent for children older than approximately the age of 11.

Some studies have used teacher ratings of empathy. For example, Sawin *et al.* (1981) asked teachers to rate first and third grade children in terms of their sensitivity to others' emotions and these also were positively related with age. Referring to Bryant's (1987) study, with regard to age changes in empathy, she found that empathy tends not to increase from 7 to 10 but does so from 10 to 14.

Following another line of enquiry, Thomas and Chess (1977) and Bates (1987) found that 7-year-old children low in distractibility (i.e., not easily soothed when upset, or not easily deterred from one's present emotional focus) were more empathic. Interestingly, being able to focus upon feeling without being distracted at the age of 7 could be an antecedent to the development of empathic experience in later childhood. It may be that low distractibility helps to facilitate a tolerance for experiencing unpleasant emotion in others as well. Such an intensity of response, however, was more strongly related to high levels of empathy in girls rather than boys.

Paternal and older sibling ability to read a child's feelings at the age of 7 was positively related to empathy at the age of 10. Also, Strayer (1983) found that parents judged empathic children as easier to get along with; and teachers judged them as independent. Bryant also found that early emotional expressiveness towards fathers and siblings relates positively to later empathy. A similar relationship did not hold for mothers. Early emotional connectedness to fathers and older siblings affects later emotional connectedness to others during middle childhood.

Hoffman (1982) has proposed a developmental model of empathy which assumes that age-related changes in the experience of empathy reflect underlying changes in the individual's evolving cognitive sense of the other. There does seem to be some developmental consistency among young children between their emotional sensitivity and responsiveness to the needs of others. For example, 1- to 1.5-year-old children often respond to another's distress by orienting to the other, showing distress, and perhaps seeking out their own caretaker; the two-year-old is much more likely to attempt to intervene effectively on behalf of the victim of distress (Radke-Yarrow and Zahn-Waxler 1984, Zahn-Waxler and Radke-Yarrow 1982).

Once the child imbues emotional expressions (facial, vocal and so forth) with emotional meaning, during the second half of the first year, a capacity to respond vicariously to the emotions of others seems to follow soon afterward.

Certainly some modes of empathic arousal, such as those requiring advanced associative and perspective-taking skills are beyond the capabilities of the very young child. Older children have been found more likely than younger to respond to abstract kinds of distress and subtle cues from others.

Marked individual differences have been found in the extent to which children spontaneously match their own facial expressions to those of sad characters depicted in affect-laden slide or film presentations (Buck 1975). Zahn-Waxler and Radke-Yarrow (1982) have reported stable and patterned individual differences in empathic responding among one- and two-year-olds as well as individual continuity to the age of seven in the child's intensity, complexity, and mode of response to others' emotions.

Some childrens' prosocial behaviour was more emotional, whereas others reacted to children's distress unemotionally and analytically (e.g. inspecting, exploring, asking questions), in an aggressive manner (e.g. hitting a person who made a baby cry) or in an anxious and avoidant manner which suggested an intolerance of the emotional needs of others (e.g. turning and running away). About two-thirds of children reported showing a pattern of responding at seven years of age that was similar to the pattern displayed at two years.

If such distinctive individual differences in responding to another's distress are already present at such an early age, then the childhood years may be a particularly important time for parents and other socialising agents to attempt either to strengthen or modify the child's existing behaviour.

It may be that personal distress reactions, because they could be related to self-protection and survival, may appear earlier in life than sympathy or empathy. This suggests possible differential biological bases for such reactions. This point has been taken up by the more recent research by Eisenberg and her associates (1991), discussed below.

Gender differences in empathy

There is a widely held view that females are more empathic than males and a range of theories have been developed which support this view (e.g. Freud 1925, Deutsch 1944).

Using both the child (Bryant 1982) and adult (Mehrabian and Epstein 1972) scales of empathy, sex rather than age has been associated with empathic arousal. Females of all ages have scored higher on empathy than males – apart from Strayer's (1983) study which found no sex differences in six-year-olds. However, Lennon and Eisenberg (1987) emphasise that surprisingly little research has been carried out into the socialisation of gender differences in sympathy or empathy.

Interestingly, the research reviews by Block (1976) and Maccoby and Jacklin (1974) found *no* consistent gender differences. However, Hoffman (1977) in his review of 11 studies, mostly conducted on young children and using a single measure of empathy, found that females universally scored higher on empathy, although statistical significance was only attained in six.

Perhaps more crucially, Eisenberg and Lennon (1983), in their more comprehensive and statistically careful review, found that gender differences in empathy were substantially dependent upon how empathy was actually being operationalised and measured. With some measures of empathy (e.g. paper and pencil self reports) they found large gender differences; for other measures (e.g. picture/story indices) they found small differences; and for others (e.g. facial/gestural and physiological measures) they found no gender differences.

In their later (1987) review, Lennon and Eisenberg suggest that gender differences favouring females may be due in part to biases in the self-reports, in that females are possibly expected to be more concerned for others, and be more emotional than males. Both males and females may respond in sex-stereotypical ways when asked to report on sex-typed characteristics. Differences in patterns of socialization may result in females being more likely to respond sympathetically or to experience personal distress/emotional contagion than boys. Also, researchers have probably not controlled for the demand characteristics of self-report questionnaires, nor have they adequately differentiated between the various possible emotional responses to other's distress.

In summary, reports of gender differences in empathy may be artifacts of the method of measurement.

Where demand characteristics are high and participants have conscious control of their responses, gender differences may be expected to be large; where demand characteristics are less manifest, gender differences are likely to be less. When demand characteristics are low and subjects have less conscious control over their responses (e.g. physiological and somatic measures), no gender differences are apparent.

Measures less likely to assess emotional contagion or personal distress (e.g. reflexive crying, picture/story techniques, facial/gestural measures, physiological measures) reveal small gender differences in empathy. However, where sympathetic responding is the likely process under investigation (e.g. self-reports in simulated situations) females appear to be more emotionally reactive than males. Eisenberg *et al.* (1991) found that women are more empathically aroused to films of people in distress. It may be relevant in this context that a meta-analysis of helping and prosocial behaviour by Eagley and Crowley (1986), covering 37,000 subjects in various studies, found that overall men helped more, especially on occasions which fitted the traditional male 'chivalrous' role (i.e. where the helped are women; onlookers are present; and some risk, strength and related skills are appropriate).

Some guard against over-emphasising the importance of socialization and contextual cues is provided by Rushton *et al.* (1986) whose genetic studies, mentioned earlier, suggest that we are dealing also with heritable differences both across and within gender.

Factors affecting empathy: implications for groupwork

Having outlined the development of empathy, it is now appropriate to consider those factors which might nurture its progress, with implications for groupwork with young people.

Secure early attachment

The importance of early attachment experiences for subsequent psychological development is well known (e.g. Bowlby 1970). Sullivan (1940, 1953) also proposed that empathic responsiveness in children is related to their involvement with the emotional life of the mother.

The particular significance of positive and secure early attachment experiences for empathic development appears to be mediated by enhanced attention to others. Mussen and Eisenberg-Berg (1977) propose that securely attached children would be less preoccupied with satisfying their own needs and more responsive to the feelings and needs of others less securely attached children. However, there has been little research as to how early attachment might affect development of responsiveness and sensitivity to others.

Some indications of the importance of secure attachment comes from Main (1977), who reported that infants early characterised as securely attached to their mothers at around 12–15 months of age, and showed more interest in/ were rated as more sympathetic to adults and other children several months later than less securely attached children. The researchers have suggested that the degree of parental responsiveness to the child's cry and other expressions of distress, may be highly relevant to the development of empathy.

Parental affection and emotional expression

Hoffman (1982) suggested that parental affection, by satisfying the child's own emotional needs, also plays an important part in the development of empathy. Eisenberg-Berg and Mussen (1978) found that mothers of highly empathic adolescent sons were reported as being more affectionate than were mothers of less empathic boys, and it is possible that a similar relationship holds for girls also.

Barnett *et al.* (1980) found that highly empathic undergraduates characterised their parents as having been more affectionate with them in their childhood than did relatively less empathic undergraduates. However, Koestner *et al.* (1990), in their extremely interesting 26-year longitudinal study into empathy, whilst finding that parental behaviour strongly predicted empathic levels in their offspring when adult, did *not* find a relationship with the level of parental affection toward the child, contrary to what had been predicted.

Also, perhaps somewhat surprisingly, Bryant (1987) found that parental support was not related to children's empathic development and social perspective taking, although paternal support predicted the development of social perspective taking during middle childhood but not adolescence.

Emotional expression in the family

Eisenberg *et al.* (1991), in their study of personality and socialization variables in adults' vicarious emotional responses to scenarios of distress in others (i.e., vicarious emotional responding), found (1) a relationship between emotional expressivity in the home and self-reported emotional reactions (which held for women but not for men); and (2) family cohesiveness which was consistent with the notion that supportive, sympathetic families rear empathic children (Barnett 1987). Family cohesion was positively related to self-reported sadness and sympathy. Staub (1986) has argued that empathy and sympathy are more likely if one is emotionally connected to others and that emotional connectedness may require a positive self concept, a well developed sense of other people, and the positive evaluation of human beings in general. Similarly, Kesterbaum *et al.* (1989) have argued (and have provided data to support their assertions) that the quality of the parent–child attachment affects children's interpersonal closeness and emotional sharing and that caring families provide other-oriented prototypic models of self, others and relationships. Perceived family support and warmth not only influence children's tendencies to attend to others' emotional states but also exerts an effect into adulthood.

Eisenberg *et al.* (1991) found that women's vicarious responding when shown two films (one about a child with spina bifida – intended to evoke sympathy/empathy; the other about a homicidal driver – intended to evoke personal distress) was associated with being raised in families where positive emotions and submissive negative emotions (but not aggressive, non-reconcili-atory negative dominant emotions) were perceived to be frequently expressed.

Dunn *et al.* (1987) suggests that being reared in an expressive family may increase offsprings' awareness of their own emotional responses. Eisenberg *et al.* (1991) also propose that reported gender differences might be understood in terms of emotional expressiveness being regarded as a feminine trait, while boys and men, even in expressive families, tend not to be encouraged to express their feelings.

In support, Tomkins (1963) has indicated that emotionally expressive parents who respond with sympathy and concern to their child's feelings of helplessness and distress are teaching their child to express distress without shame and to respond sympathetically to the distress of others. Also, Zahn-Waxler *et al.* (1979) found that children whose mothers were rated high in empathic care-giving were found to be more emotionally responsive and helpful to persons in distress than were children of less empathic mothers.

Barnett *et al.* (1980) found heightened empathy in 4–6-year-old girls was associated with that of their mothers and an absence of such a relationship for boys was interpreted in terms of sex-typing, whereby typically, in the families studied, fathers showed less empathy than mothers. Similarly, Strayer (1983) reported that mothers' but not fathers' empathy scores were significantly correlated with those of their children (this time both boys and girls).

It is noteworthy that most studies have tended to focus upon the mother's contribution rather than that of the father, and Barnett (1987) has speculated that the apparent increased involvement by fathers in the care of children is worthy of study.

Koestner *et al.* (1990) in their investigation of parental behaviour towards their children when aged five years, and the level of empathy indicated 25 years later (when aged 31 years), found the single most influential parental dimension to be the level of paternal involvement. This seems to support the work of Rutherford and Mussen (1968) who found that prosocial behaviours such as altruism and generosity were related to active involvement in child care by fathers. Koestner *et al.* (1990) also found that important maternal variables included (1) maternal tolerance of dependent behaviour in their children; (2) maternal inhibition of child's aggression and (3) maternal satisfaction with the role of mother.

Bryant (1987) reported how the role of mothers in the development of empathy seems to be more one of stress buffering in the form of acknow-ledging and possibly legitimising the sustained focus on the child's own feelings of distress. Bryant found it was the mother's rather than father's reported expressiveness in response to children's stress that appeared to facilitate the development of empathy. This was particularly so for girls at the ages of seven and ten. Mothers' reported expressive responses to children's stressful experi-ences at the age of ten predicted both boys' and girls' subsequent high empathy at 14. Why paternal reports of expressiveness was not predictive of empathy is not clear. Bryant raises the possibility that self-reports of father's expressiveness were not valid and that observation of actual behaviours may be more effective. She also suggests it is the sustained attention on emotional states, either internally or externally which fosters empathic growth.

Discussions with the same sex parent seem useful for both social perspective taking and empathy development during middle childhood. However, intimate discussions with the opposite sex parent seem to be beneficial over time rather than immediately, at least for boys. Bryant suggests discussion of feelings with mothers during middle childhood positively affects empathy development of both boys and girls during adolescence.

On another tack, Hoffman (1975) has proposed that empathy may be fostered around events which involve various aspects of discipline. Where a child's actions have harmed another individual, Hoffman contends that parental use of the inductive disciplinary technique, which calls attention to the victim's distress and encourages the child to imagine him/herself in the victim's place, is likely to arouse the child's empathic potential and promote prosocial behaviour. Parents who employ an inductive style of discipline have been found to have children who score higher on indices of generosity and consideration for others, compared with parents who practice a predominantly power-assertive disciplinary style (Dlugokinski and Firestone 1974, Hoffman and Saltzstein 1967).

In support of the above, Bryant (1987) found that parental indulgence of 7-year-olds predicted poorer empathy at the age of ten. Fathers involvement in limit setting, at the ages of seven and ten, was predictive of high empathy in boys and girls, and that paternal non indulgence at the age seven was related to enhanced empathy among boys and girls at the age of ten, and boys up to the age of 14. Parental disciplinary distress towards a child's wrongdoings, by encouraging the child to think about the consequences of his/her actions, appears to be effective for the development of empathy up to the age of ten for both sexes, and up to the age of 14 for boys.

In addition, research by Zahn-Waxler *et al.* (1979) showed how heightened emotional responsiveness and prosocial behaviour in 1.5- to 2.5-year-old children was found to be associated with mothers who:

1. conveyed a clear cognitive message to the child (explanation or demonstration) of the consequences of his or her behaviour for the victim, and

2. reinforced this message with a display of intense emotion and statements of principles and expectations for the child's behaviour.

Interestingly, merely encouraging an awareness of the affective state of another person through the use of a calm and well-reasoned explanation was found to be insufficient to elicit the child's emotions and attempts to help. It seemed quite likely that the intensity of the mother's emotional reaction conveyed the importance of the event to the child as modelling emotional responsiveness to distress in another.

Overall, though, the highest levels of empathy were found in those adults who as children had parents who both spent a lot of time with, and enjoyed being with their children.

Involvement with the extended family network

The nature of children's involvement with the parents' generation was predictive of both concurrent and longitudinally assessed empathy and social perspective taking.

Bryant (1987) reported that neither peer nor sibling involvement predicted empathy. However, involvement with grandparents at the ages of seven and ten predicted children's current empathy levels. Whilst involvement at the age of seven with grandparents predicted later empathy at the age of ten, similar involvement at the age of ten with grandparents and other adults was *not* predictive of children's subsequent empathy during adolescence.

Involvement with pets, including 'intimate talks' correlated with current expressions of empathy at age seven and ten, though, was not predictive of later development. Similarly, 'intimate talks' with grandparents or similar were positively related to expressions of empathy among seven- and ten-year-olds. Also, the emotional importance of grandparents was positively related to a girl's later empathy, but not to empathy during childhood.

It is possible that the stress-buffering and non-judgemental aspects of relationships with grandparents, pets and so forth, may foster the development of empathy by providing opportunities for the expression and recognition of feelings in self and others.

Other models

A range of studies have shown how exposure to other sensitive and caring models may affect empathic development in children, in that children have been found to emulate television characters who display prosocial actions such as offering sympathy and assistance to needy others (see reviews in Mussen and Eisenberg-Berg 1977, Rushton 1979, 1981, Staub 1979). For example, Coates *et al.* (1976) found that nursery school children who watched segments of 'Mr Rogers Neighbourhood' showed more affectionate physical contact, sympathy and emotional support for peers than did children who had watched segments of a programme which showed less prosocial content. However, Radke-Yarrow *et al.* (1983) consider there to be insufficient evidence from this research as yet.

Encouragement of the perception of similarity to others

Children have been found to respond more empathetically to those who are perceived as similar to the self than to those who are perceived as dissimilar. This appears to be the case when the similarity is defined in terms of a shared characteristic such as race or sex (Bryant 1982, Feshback and Roe 1968, Klein 1971). Additionally, shared personal experience (Barnett 1984, 1987) may also prove influential.

Therefore, to encourage a child to perceive others as similar to self may contribute to the development and expression of empathy. Further to this, Radke-Yarrow et al. (1983) propose that parents' perceptions of others in relation to the family should be important for children's prosocial behaviour and influence their feelings of empathy.

A range of methods developed in other contexts might be effectively applied in working with perceptions of similarity and empathy in children and young adults. For example, empathy exercises used in counselling training might be adapted for groupwork (e.g. Nelson-Jones 1983, 1989). Also, meditational techniques, traditionally developed to develop compassion, might also be applied within a group setting. Typically, such exercises focus upon emphasising similarity of feelings and expectations in oneself and others, which leads to an appreciation as to how the lives and experiences of others may not be so different from our own. A discussion of how traditional Buddhist training exercises may be applied to a modern therapeutic context can be found in Welwood (1979) and Walley (1987, 1990).

Discouragement of excessive interpersonal competition

Encouragement of a highly competitive interpersonal orientation may generate heightened self-concern within a child and interfere with his or her inclination to respond to another's needs. Feshbach (1975) reported that a paternal emphasis on competition was associated with low levels of empathy in sons (but not daughters).

Highly competitive boys have been found to be less generous (Rutherford and Mussen 1968) and less empathic (Barnett et al. 1979) than less competitive peers. Competitive environments tend to be associated with lower levels of sharing and comforting than cooperative ones (Barnett and Bryan 1974, Bryan and London 1970). Argyle (1991) in his review of cultural differences in cooperation, has found that individualistic societies tend to show greater competition, lower social support and poorer health (especially with respect to incidence of heart disease). It can be useful to be reminded that there are or have been other cultures far less competitive than our own. For example, in Tibet, prior to the Chinese occupation, non-competitive sporting events and displays were held, invariably accompanied by good humour rather than by a 'winner-take-all' mentality.

Encouragement of a positive self-concept

Children who are encouraged to feel good about themselves may be more inclined to empathise with others than children who are preoccupied with personal inadequacies and other concerns about the self.

Strayer (1983) found empathy in six-year-old children to be associated with a positive self concept. Feshbach (1982) reported how empathy in girls was positively correlated with maternal tolerance and permissiveness and negatively correlated with maternal conflict, rejection, punitiveness, and excessive control.

Barnett *et al.* (1985) has discussed how perception of oneself as an independent and competent helper may facilitate the development of empathy. Children who are given encouragement and opportunities to gain helping skills may be more inclined to empathise with needy others, which, according to Hoffman (1976) will provide the child with opportunities for developing 'sympathetic distress and awareness of the other's perspective'. Whiting and Whiting (1975) reported how assigning children specific care-giving responsibilities for their younger brothers and sisters increased the levels of sensitive care-giving.

Conversely, children who are treated in a harsh and unloving way may demonstrate less empathy. Camras *et al.* (1983) observed that abused 3–6-year-old children were consistently less accurate in identifying facial expressions of emotion. Also, Main and George (1985), in their study of 1–3-year-olds, reported that non-abused children responded frequently with concern, empathy, and sadness to the distress they witnessed, whereas not one abused child showed any of these reactions. Rather, abused children tended to react with physical attacks, threats or anger.

By way of summary, Barnett (1987) proposes the development of empathy and related responses would appear to thrive in an environment that:

1. satisfies the child's own emotional needs and discourages excessive self concern, thereby enabling the needs and emotions of others to become more salient.

2. encourages the child to identify, experience, and express a broad range of emotions.

3. provides numerous opportunities for the child to observe and interact with others who, through their words and actions, encourage emotional sensitivity and responsiveness to others.

4. provides peers who, because of similarity, may play a vital part in the development of empathy and related responses. An intimate friendship in childhood in particular helps an individual to develop a sense of humanity (Sullivan 1953).

An additional resource for working in this area comes from the exercises and role plays used in the development of self-acceptance and self-regard from a

Rogerian counselling perspective (Nelson–Jones 1989). A central principle in Rogerian counselling training is that self-acceptance and self-understanding facilitates understanding and acceptance of others.

Various techniques and perspectives are available. Visualisation exercises may be used which rehearse feelings of warmth and acceptance towards an image of oneself (alongside others) (see Walley 1987). Indeed, for example, a building block of Buddhist psychological development and training, proven over many centuries, has been to make friends with oneself. Without such a foundation, however aquired, affection and empathy towards others may well become distorted and blocked.

Concluding remarks on applications of empathy research to groupwork

Systematic empirical research into empathy and prosocial behaviour, then, is perhaps surprisingly recent. However, despite limitations in measurement and methodology, research to date has pointed out some areas of understanding and agreement.

First, that a propensity for empathic and altruistic behaviour is deeply ingrained in human nature (thereby countering any perspective which views mankind primarily as an aggressive animal). Second, that indicators of empathic responding are present from an early age. Third, that empathic development may be facilitated by parental behaviour and other areas of social interaction.

Also, the expression of distress from early childhood is also associated with enhanced empathy (e.g. Lenrow 1965), although subsequent socialization may differentially affect empathic development in males and females.

Whilst both parents can play a crucial role in the empathic growth of their children, the work of Koestner and others would suggest that paternal influence may be more significant than was generally thought. Koestner suggests that this can contribute to our understanding of the psychological consequences of divorce upon children, particularly as there is often a likelihood of divorced fathers losing at least some contact with their children.

High levels of empathy are also associated with mental health and prosocial behaviour. Indeed, empathy may mediate these behaviours, providing a useful focus in working with young people. Research has quite effectively demonstrated the importance of emotional expression in empathic development. Therefore, to encourage emotional expression, particularly with respect to the occurrence of distress in others, would be valuable groupwork. Exploration of this area of experience, particularly with young males, could focus upon the distinction between sympathetic and personal distress responses. The aversive and self-protective aspect of personal distress could be examined, which contrasts with the more empathic-sympathetic reaction with its movement towards and support for the person in distress. There may be a gender based differentiation here which might be fruitfully explored further.

It is possible that some young males, whilst being emotionally affected by distress in others, are somewhat uncomfortable with a compassionate and tender approach. As noted earlier (Eagly and Crowley 1986), males *are* comfortable with a 'chivalrous/heroic' role, particularly in relation to females.

The use of role models for empathy training may be utilised. Quite frequently celebrities, (e.g. sports stars) are actively involved in deserving causes. Also, the 'getting into a character' work now widespread in history education, as well as dramatic training could be attempted in a group setting. Perception of others as similar to oneself also enhances empathy. Along with emotional expression and identification with the needs and situation of others, close friendship and intimacy are also valuable sources of empathic development, leading to the stress-buffering benefits of feeling socially connected and belonging.

Hoffman's (1976, 1982) proposal to parents that they allow their children to be exposed to a wide range of experiences and emotions so as to foster their sensitivity to the feelings of others, could also be generalised to work with adolescents.

A valuable resource for empathy work and group sharing arises from Feshbach's (1982) suggestion that empathic responsiveness and helpfulness may be enhanced by having weathered a dysphoric experience, such as a serious familial illness or a loss.

A young person's perception of similarity to others may also be enhanced through the encouragement of universalistic beliefs and values that emphasise the connectedness of all people. Reference has already been made to the potential for groupwork of Rogerian-type counselling skills and along with those self–awareness/meditational techniques derived from spiritual traditions such as Buddhism and other perspectives. It is worth bearing in mind how some cultures view human nature as more fundamentally positive and wholesome than is perhaps the case in western tradition, which might facilitate contact with feelings of self-worth. Also, modern scientific and ecological knowledge may be utilised to develop feelings and perceptions of relatedness and interdepend-ence. These facts and fundamentals of modern living might help to foster feelings of belonging and connectedness along with their stress-buffering attributes.

Where similarity and connectedness are accompanied with feelings of self-worth, conditions are set for nourishing empathy, wellbeing and prosocial behaviour – in short, personal responsibility. The human has become humane.

References

Alexander, R.D. (1979) *Darwinism and Human Affairs.* Seattle: University of Washington Press.

Argyle, M. (1991) *Cooperation: the Basis of Sociability.* London: Routledge.

Axelrod, R. and Hamilton, W.D. (1984) 'The Evolution of Cooperation in Biological Systems'. In R. Axelrod (ed) *The Evolution of Cooperation.* New York: Basic Books.

Barnett, M. (1987) 'Empathy and Related Responses in Children'. In N. Eisenberg and J. Strayer (eds) *Empathy and its Development.* Cambridge: Cambridge University Press.

Barnett, M.A. (1984) 'Similarity of Experience and Empathy in Preschoolers'. *Journal of Genetic Psychology,* 145: 241–250.

Barnett, M.A. and Bryan, J.H. (1974) 'Effects of Competition with Outcome Feedback on Children's Helping Behaviour'. *Developmental Psychology,* 10: 838–842.

Barnett, M.A., Matthews, K.A. and Howard, K.A. (1979) 'Relationship Between Competitiveness and Empathy in 6- and 7-year olds'. *Developmental Psychology,* 15: 221–222.

Barnett, M.A., King, L.M., Howard J.A. and Dino, G.A. (1980) 'Empathy in Young Children: Relation to Parents' Empathy, Affection, and Emphasis on the Feelings of Others'. *Developmental Psychology,* 16: 243–244.

Barnett, M.A., Thompson, M.A. and Pfeiffer, J.R. (1985) 'Perceived Competence to Help and the Arousal of Empathy'. *Journal of Social Psychology,* 125: 679–680.

Bates, J.E. (1987) 'Temperament in Infancy'. In J.D. Osofsky (ed) *Handbook of Infant Development* (2nd.ed.) New York: Wiley.

Block, J.H. (1976) 'Assessing Sex-Differences: Issues, Problems and Pitfalls'. *Merrill-Palmer Quarterly,* 22: 283–308.

Bowlby, J. (1969) *Attachment and Loss: Vol.1. Attachment.* London: Hogarth.

Boyd, R. and Richerson, P.J. (1985) *Culture and the Evolutionary Process.* Chicago: University of Chicago Press.

Bryan, J.H. and London, P. (1970) 'Altruistic Behaviour By Children'. *Psychological Bulletin,* 73: 200–211.

Bryant, B.K. (1982) 'An Index of Empathy for Children and Adolescents'. *Child Development,* 53: 413–425.

Bryant, B.K. (1987) 'Mental Health, Temperament, Family, and Friends: Perspectives on Children's Empathy and Social Perspective Taking'. In N. Eisenberg and J. Strayer (eds) *Empathy and its Development.* Cambridge: Cambridge University Press.

Buck, R.W. (1975) 'Non-Verbal Communication of Affect in Children'. *Journal of Personality and Social Psychology,* 31: 644–653.

Camras, L.A., Grow, J.G. and Ribordy, S.C. (1983) 'Recognition of Emotional Expression by Abused Children'. *Journal of Clinical Child Psychology*, 12: 325–328.

Coates, B., Pusser, H.E. and Goodman, I. (1976) 'The Influence of "Sesame Street" and "Mister Rogers' Neighbourhood" on Children's Social Behaviour in Pre-School'. *Child Development*, 47: 138–144.

Crook, J. (1980) *Evolution of Human Consciousness.* Oxford: Oxford University Press.

Deutsch, H. (1944) *The Psychology of Women: A Psychoanalytic Interpretation.* New York: Grune and Stratton.

Dlugokinski, E.L. and Firestone, I.J. (1974) 'Other Centredness and Susceptibility to cHaritable Appeals: Effects of Perceived Discipline'. *Developmental Psychology*, 10: 21–28.

Dunn, J., Bretherton, I. and Munn, P. (1987) 'Conversations about Feeling States Between Mothers and their Young Children'. *Developmental Psychology*, 23: 132–139.

Eagley, A.H. and Crowley, M. (1986) 'Gender and Helping Behaviour: A Meta-Analytic Review of the Social Psychological Literature'. *Psychological Bulletin*, 100: 283–308.

Eisenberg, N. (1982) (ed) *The Development of Prosocial Behaviour.* New York: Academic Press.

Eisenberg, N. and Lennon, R. (1983) 'Sex Differences in Empathy and Related Capacities'. *Psychological Bulletin*, 94: 100–131.

Eisenberg, N. and Miller, P. (1987a) 'Empathy, Sympathy, and Altruism: Empirical and Conceptual Links'. In N. Eisenberg, and J. Strayer (eds) *Empathy and its Development.* Cambridge: Cambridge University Press.

Eisenberg, N. and Miller, P.A. (1987b) 'The Relation of Empathy to Prosocial and Related Behaviours'. *Psychological Bulletin*, 101(1): 91–119.

Eisenberg, N. and Strayer, J. (1987) *Empathy and its Development.* Cambridge: Cambridge University Press.

Eisenberg, N. *et al.* (1991) 'Personality and Socialization Correlates of Vicarious Emotional Responding'. *Journal of Personality and Social Psychology*, 61(3): 459–470.

Eisenberg-Berg, N. and Mussen, P. (1978) 'Empathy and Moral Development in Adolescence'. *Developmental Psychology*, 14: 185–186.

Feshbach, N.D. (1975) 'Empathy in Children: Some Theoretical and Empirical Considerations'. *The Counselling Psychologist*, 4: 25–30.

Feshbach, N.D. (1978) 'Studies of Empathic Behaviour in Children'. *Progress in Experimental Personality Research*, 8: 1–47.

Feshbach, N.D. (1982) 'Sex Differences in Empathy and Social Behaviour in Children'. In N. Eisenberg (ed) *The Development of Prosocial Behaviour.* New York: Academic Press.

Feshbach, N.D. and Roe, K. (1968) 'Empathy in Six- and Seven-Year-Olds'. *Child Development*, 39: 133–145.

Freud, S. (1925) 'Some Psychological Consequences of the Anatomical Distinction Between the Sexes'. In J. Strachey (ed) *Sigmund Freud: Collected Papers* (vol 5, pp.86–197) London: Hogarth Press 1950.

Hamilton, W.D. (1964) 'The Evolution of Social Behaviour'. *Journal of Theoretical Biology* 7: 1–52.

Hamilton, W.D. (1975) 'Innate Social Aptitude of Man: An Approach from Evolutionary Genetics'. In R. Fox (ed) *Biosocial Anthropology*. New York: Wiley.

Hoffman, M.L. (1975) 'Moral Internalisation, Parental Power, and the Nature of Parent–Child Interaction'. *Developmental Psychology*, 11: 228–239.

Hoffman, M.L. (1976) 'Empathy, Role Taking, Guilt, and Development of Altruistic Motives'. In T. Lickona (ed) *Moral Development and Behaviour: Theory, Research and Social Issues*. New York: Holt, Rinehart and Winston.

Hoffman, M.L. (1977) 'Personality and Social Development'. *Annual Review of Psychology*, 28: 295–321.

Hoffman, M.L. (1982) 'Development of Prosocial Motivation: Empathy and Guilt'. In N. Eisenberg (ed) *The Development of Prosocial Behaviour* (pp.281–313) New York: Academic Press.

Hoffman, M.L. and Saltzstein, H.D. (1967) 'Parent Discipline and the Child's Moral Development'. *Journal of Personality and Social Psychology*, 5: 45–57.

Kesterbaum, R., Farber, E.A. and Sroufe, L.A. (1989) 'Individual Differences in Empathy Among Preschoolers: Relation to Attachment History'. In N. Eisenberg (ed) *New Directions for Child Development: Vol.44. Empathy and related emotional responses* (pp.51–64) San Francisco: Jossey-Bass.

Klein, R.S. (1971) 'Some Factors Influencing Empathy in Six-and Seven-Year-Old Children Varying in Ethnic Background' (Doctoral dissertation, University of California: Los Angeles, 1970).

Koestner, R., Frans, C. and Weinberger (1990) 'The Family Origins of Empathic Concern: A 26-Year Longitudinal Study'. *Journal of Personality and Social Psychology*, 58(4): 709–717.

Lennon, R. and Eisenberg, N. (1987) 'Gender and Age Differences in Empathy and Sympathy'. In N. Eisenberg and J. Strayer (eds) op.cit.

Lenrow, P.B. (1965) 'Studies in Empathy'. In S.S. Tomkins and C.E. Izard (eds) *Affect, Cognition and Personality: Empirical Studies*. New York: Springer.

Maccoby, E.E. and Jacklin, C.N. (1974) *The Psychology of Sex Differences*. Stanford: Stanford University Press.

Main, M. (1977) 'Analysis of a Peculiar Form of Reunion Behaviour Seen in Some Young Daycare Children'. In R.A. Webb (ed) *Social Development in Daycare*. Baltimore, MD: Johns Hopkins University Press.

Main, M. and George, C. (1985) 'Responses of Abused and Disadvantages Toddlers to Distress in Age-Mates: A Study in a Day Care Setting'. *Developmental Psychology*, 21: 407–412.

Marcus, R.F., Roke, E.J. and Bruner, C. (1985) 'Verbal and Nonverbal Empathy and Prediction of Social Behaviour of Children'. *Perceptual and Motor Skills*, 60: 299–309.

Mehrabian, A. and Epstein, N. (1972) 'A Measure of Emotional Empathy'. *Journal of Personality*, 40(4): 525–543.

Mussen, P. and Eisenberg-Berg, N. (1977) *Roots of Caring, Sharing, and Helping: The Development of Prosocial Behaviour in Children*. San Francisco: W.H. Freeman.

Nelson-Jones, R. (1983) *Practical Counselling Skills*. London: Holt, Rinehart and Winston.

Nelson-Jones, R. (1989) *The Theory and Practice of Counselling Psychology*. London: Cassell.

Packer, C. (1977) 'Reciprocal Altruism in Olive Baboons'. *Nature* 265: 441–3.

Radke-Yarrow, M., Zahn-Wexler, C. and Chapman, M. (1983) 'Children's Prosocial Dispositions and Behaviour'. In P.H. Mussen (ed) *Handbook of Child Psychology*. New York: Wiley.

Radker-Yarrow, M. and Zahn-Waxler, C. (1984) 'Roots, Motives and Patterns in Children's Prosocial Behaviour'. In E. Staub (ed) *Development and Maintenance of Prosocial Behaviour: International Perspectives on Positive Behaviour* (pp.81–99). New York: Plenum Press.

Rushton, J.P. (1979) 'Effects of Prosocial Television and Film Material on the Behaviour of Viewers'. In L. Berkowitz (ed) *Advances in Experimental Social Psychology* (Vol.12) New York: Academic Press.

Rushton, J.P. (1981) 'Television as a Socialiser'. In J.P. Rushton and R.M. Sorrentino (eds) *Altruism and Helping Behaviour: Social, Personality, and Developmental Perspectives*. Hillsdale, NJ: Erlbaum.

Rushton, J.P., Fulker, D.W., Neale, M.C., Nias, D.I.C.B. and Eysenck, H.J. (1986) 'Altruism and Aggression: The Heritability of Individual Differences'. *Journal of Personality and Social Psychology*, 50: (6)1192–1198.

Rutherford, E. and Mussen, P.H. (1968) 'Generosity in Nursery School Boys'. *Child Development*, 39: 755–765.

Sawin, D.B., Underwood, B., Weaver, J. and Moslyn, M. (1981) 'Empathy and Altruism' (Unpublished manuscript, University of Texas, Austin).

Staub, E. (1979) *Positive Social Behaviour and Morality: Socialization and Development* (Vol.2) New York: Academic Press.

Staub, E. (1986) 'A Conception of the Determinants and Development of Altruism and Aggression: Motives, the Self, and the Environment'. In C. Zahn-Waxler (ed) *Altruism and Aggression: Biological and Social Origins* (pp.135–164). Cambridge: Cambridge University Press.

Strayer, J. (1983) 'Affective and Cognitive Components of Children's Empathy'. Paper presented at the biennial meetings of the Society for Research in Child Development, Detroit, Michigan.

Sullivan, H.S. (1940) *Conceptions of Modern Psychiatry*. London: Tavistock Press.

Sullivan, H.S. (1953) *The Interpersonal Theory of Psychiatry*. New York: Norton.

Thomas, A. and Chess, S. (1977) *Temperament and Development*. New York: Brunner/Mazel.

Thompson, R.A. (1987) 'Empathy and Emotional Understanding: the Early Development of Empathy'. In N. Eisenberg and J. Strayer (eds) *Empathy and its Development*. Cambridge: Cambridge University Press.

Tomkins, S.S. (1963) *Affect, Imagery and Consciousness, Vol.2; The Negative Effects*. New York: Springer.

Totman, R. (1990) *Mind, Stress and Health*. London: Souvenir Press.

Trivers, R.L. (1971) 'The Evolution of Reciprocal Altruism'. *Quarterly Review of Biology* 46: 35–37.

Trivers, R.L. (1985) *Social Evolution*. Menlos Park, California: Benjamin Cummings.

Underwood, B. and Moore, B. (1982) 'Perspective-Taking and Altruism'. *Psychological Bulletin,* 91: 143–173.

Walley, M.R. (1987) 'Buddhism and Mental Health Care'. In G. Claxton (ed) *Beyond Therapy*. London: Wisdom Books.

Walley, M.R. (1990) 'Tibetan Buddhist Mind-Training'. In J. Crook and D. Fontana (eds) *Space in Mind*. Shaftsbury: Element Books.

Welwood, J. (1979) *Meeting of the Ways*. New York: Schocken Books.

Whiting, B.B. and Whiting, J.W.M. (1975) *Children of Six Cultures*. Cambridge: Harvard University Press.

Wispe, L. (1978) *Altruism, Sympathy, and Helping*. London: Academic Press.

Zahn-Waxler, C., Radke-Yarrow, M. and King, R.A. (1979) 'Child Rearing and Children's Prosocial Initiations Towards Victims of Distress'. *Child Development,* 50: 319–330.

Zahn-Waxler, C. and Radke-Yarrow, M. (1982) 'The Development of Altruism: Alternative Research Strategies'. In N. Eisenberg (ed) *The Development of Prosocial Behaviour* (pp.109–137). New York: Academic Press.

CHAPTER 8

Historical Development of Group Psychotherapy

Patrick McGrath

From a study of the literature, it is clear that group psychotherapy has been influenced by many persons and philosophies, both American and European. It is being gradually, indeed grudgingly, admitted that Americans are the main contributors and innovators in this field. However, it does emerge with striking clarity that in both America and Europe, many people were grappling with similar problems and developing similar ideas around the same time.

American influences

Dr Joseph A. Pratt

Even though groups had been used in primitive miracle treatment, and group hypnotism and hysteria were employed by shamans and medicine men from time immemorial, Dr Joseph Pratt, who was not a psychiatrist but an internist, has been credited with initiating the practice of group psychotherapy. In July 1905 Pratt, working in Boston, organised his first group, which consisted of 20–30 tuberculosis patients. His method was called his 'class method' rather than 'group', and included lectures about the disease of tuberculosis and the method of cure. In 1930 he transferred this technique to psychiatric patients and found to his delight that, as with tuberculosis patients, it was the sick person he was treating rather than the disease.

Pratt's meetings began with a roll call and he then addressed the group of up to 30 people as if talking to one person. Each person was given a slip of paper on which to state whether or not he was improved and those who had not improved were given an individual interview. People attended between 25 and 100 meetings, or more. Despite all his success, it is not clear that Dr Pratt was fully aware of the group as a factor in his 'class method'.

L. Cody Marsh

In 1919 Marsh, who was both a psychiatrist and a minister, and was familiar with Pratt's work, began to apply the 'class method' to institutionalised mental patients. His classes consisted of about 16 people, which included patients, relatives, teachers, nurses, and clergymen. All were referred to as students and had to sign a psychiatric pledge to co-operate and to be punctual and regular in their attendances. Students attended weekly lectures given by Marsh on a variety of topics pertaining to the origins and manifestations of mental illness. The accent was on education – on teaching rather than treatment, as outside reading was assigned, written papers were required and graded examinations were given. If a student did not do well, he would be required to repeat the course. The possibility of being assigned a personal tutor who would work with the student privately was always there. Marsh treated all sorts of psychiatric disturbance, psychotics, stammerers and various psychosomatic and organic disorders. Stammerers in particular did well. The classes included people of various levels of intelligence and social class, and lectures were presented in simple, clear, jargon-free language.

E. W. Lazell

At the same time, the psychiatrist E. W. Lazell was also working with institutionalised patients. His approach consisted also of didactic lectures to schizophrenic patients about their disease. He would describe the signs and symptoms of the disease and aspects of Freudian theory. Once again the accent was on education and teaching rather than on treatment. He realised that the factor which accounted for the positive changes he observed was patients getting to know one another. He also realised that much of the lecture material was retained by the patients. Sharing information and the comparison of symptoms among them, whether during the lecture or afterwards, was the beginning of interaction. Lazell was one of the first to theorise about the group method of treatment. Lazell followed a psychoanalytical orientation in his explanation of psychological phenomena, even though he used the didactic technique.

Marsh and Lazell both worked with psychotic patients within institutional settings. Group methods were at this time also being applied outside institutions to neurotic disorders.

Trigant Burrow

Trigant Burrow was born in Norfolk, Virginia, in September 1875. His parents were cultured and sensitive. His father was a pharmacist and his mother a devout Roman Catholic. She influenced Burrow's decision to study at Fordham University in New York City where most of the staff were Jesuits. On graduation from Fordham, he entered the University of Virginia Medical School. After receiving his medical degree, he studied obstetrics in Munich for a time and then continued studies in Vienna. He took courses in psychiatry while in Vienna. When he returned to the USA, he continued his medical studies at the John Hopkins Medical School. In 1909 Burrow obtained his PhD in experimental psychology and moved to New York. He was introduced to Freud and Jung during Freud's trip to Clark University to deliver his now famous lectures. Burrow was encouraged to study psychoanalysis and went to Switzerland to enter analysis with Carl Jung. In 1910 he returned to the USA and began the active practice of psychoanalysis and became one of the founders of the American Psychoanalytic Association. His interest in the individual's relationship to the social forces of which he is a part soon led to his using the group setting as a vehicle for psychoanalytic treatment. Between 1923 and 1932 Burrow embarked on a new era of group behavioural exploration which he called group analysis and later psychoanalysis. He was beginning to experience difficulty in having his work published in the psychoanalytic literature and was being shunned by his colleagues, since his continued emphasis on group treatment estranged the growing psychoanalytic community in the United States. In 1933 he was denied membership of the American Psychoanalytic Association, of which he was a founder. He much wanted Freud's approval but never gained it. In group sessions the patients would speak frankly to one another about their thoughts and feelings. He believed there should be no secret about emotional illness or about how persons react to one another.

> 'Burrow saw the real problem of neurosis as the inward sense of separativeness which dominates everyone – the dim yearning for togetherness which he called the pre-conscious state. It is society that is sick and suffers from social neurosis so that adjustment of the individual involves compulsion to conform to a social image which renders him incapable of making full and individual responses to the real biological moment thus rendering him neurotic'. (De Mare 1972 p.63)

While it cannot be denied that Burrow was a talented and original pioneer, his emphasis was upon the individual's interaction and the spontaneous group tensions that inevitably arise in the course of a daily intimate living in close proximity. His patients lived together with the doctors and they did work through their attitudes and conflicts towards one another, undoubtedly with great benefit; however, the group was not used as a consciously planned instrument of psychotherapy.

Louis Wender

Wender also employed the didactic technique and adopted a psychoanalytically oriented approach. In 1930, at the Hastings Hillside Hospital, Wender employed a formal lecture type of setting with six to eight patients. He introduced lecture material and leading questions followed by discussion. There was little interchange between the patients themselves. The meetings lasted one hour, and took place two or three times a week. He also encouraged the continuance of individual treatment. Wender's explanations to patients were of psychic phenoména and their difficulties were derived from Freudian psychology.

Paul Schilder

Schilder was the first psychiatrist who used a small group of adult patients for deep analytical treatment. He began his work at the Bellvue Hospital in New York City in 1937. He worked with small groups of eight to ten psychotic and neurotic patients who had individually been under his treatment. He used the technique of free association and pointed out that the thoughts and feelings of one member stimulated associated thoughts and feelings in another. His focus was the socialising effect of the group upon its members and dream analysis played a significant part. He specified the value of group treatment for patients suffering from social anxiety (e.g. shyness, or blushing) and from obsessional neuroses, and believed that the patients realised that the thoughts and feelings that seemed to isolate them are in reality common to all.

Samuel Slavson

Slavson was very much a pioneer in group psychotherapy, and his contributions to this specialised modality of treatment over more than four decades are difficult to assess in their entirety. Slavson began as an engineer and became a school teacher, interested in psychoanalysis. Slavson states that, based on a hunch derived from the work he was doing as a teacher in 1911, in classrooms and other settings, he introduced in 1934 the concept of the small group in therapy consisting of five to eight children. The group leader is permissive and accepting and children are allowed to act spontaneously. As a result, conflicts are acted out and can be examined. He called it Activity Group Therapy.

All of Slavson's endeavours are rooted in his firm belief in man's innate gregariousness. He coined the terms 'groupism' and 'social hunger' to describe the uncompromising need of man for the company of man. There is an unmistakable thread of continuity linking Slavson's work with individuals in groups – his basic regard for the needs of individuals, his recognition of the creative potentialities of every human, given the opportunities for their actualisation, and an overriding conviction that troubled individuals can derive sustenance in constructive group participation.

Slavson was a pioneer in analytical group psychotherapy. He was the originator of tested group treatment modalities for carefully selected patients, the founder of the American Group Psychotherapy Association, and its first President. He was founder of the Association's official publication *The Interna-*

tional Journal of Group Psychotherapy and its editor for many years, and was the initiator of what became the International Association of Group Psychotherapy.

One of the amazing facts is that this man, whose only professional training was as a civil engineer, was entirely self-trained in the wide gamut of all his various group endeavours and in human relations. Years before he heard of Freud, he was actively involved with individuals and social problems as well as in creative pursuits. Decades passed before he learned the nature and meanings of psychoanalytical psychology. It was two personal analyses by a former trainee of Freud that illuminated for Slavson the deeper unconscious motivants of the human psyche. It was after his discovery of Activity Group Therapy and the other methods of treatment he later formulated that the relevance of psycho-analytical precepts became clear to him (Schiffer 1979 p.xxiii).

There seems to be much in the precise training and discipline of engineering that served him well through the years of explorations in clinical procedures. This precision is exemplified in both the quality of his work and in his numerous publications, which are models of clarity and succinctness, and also in the rigorous standards he set for study and experimentation.

> 'Slavson can be numbered among the select group of explorers who, acting as their own guides, were capable of discovering entirely new dimensions. Implicit in his personal conviction that the propelling force behind his lifetime's creative output is the enduring belief in the pervasive influence of social forces in the lives of men and his unremitting faith in the essentiality of truth. The group is the milieu from which men's health and unhealthy flow'. (Schiffer 1979 p.xiv)

Alexander Wolf

Wolf began practising groups in his private practice in New York in 1938, although he did not publish his findings until 1949. He undertook what he called 'psychoanalysis in groups' and applied the principles of psychoanalysis based on Freudian theory to the group setting. He used the four basic tenets of psychoanalysis: dream interpretation, free association, analysis of resistance and transference. Each member is encouraged to see the role of the analyst in the psychoanalytic sense. Wolf emphasised the individual patient. Despite his very considerable emphasis on the group as such, Wolf appears to have failed to recognise the possibility that psychotherapy in a group setting can be primarily conceived as going beyond analytic concepts. He does not deny group dynamics but does not give it the significance it deserves. The emphasis is on depth analysis rather than the impact of group support and interaction.

> 'The group *qua* group cannot become the means by which its members resolve intrapsychic difficulty. The need for such differentiation led us to change our concepts of the psychoanalysis of groups to that of psychoanalysis in groups. We do not treat a group. We must still analyse

the individual in interaction with other individuals'. (Wolf and Schwartz 1962 p.241)

In 1938 Wolf introduced the alternate session as a vital part of the group therapeutic process. This is a situation where the group members meet regularly without the therapist. Of this innovation Wolf says

> 'We are convinced that the alternate session is a happy historic addition to psychoanalysis in groups, as a better way of relating the therapeutic process to the realities of living. The alternate session must not be considered only in terms of unconscious persistences or the utilisation of it for pathologic purposes on the part of therapists or patients. It provides opportunities for freer interaction among the peers. A more rapid and effective working through of hierarchical problems can be accomplished where security and an interchange among members on their own are encouraged. The alternate meeting is a clinical therapeutic measure contributing significantly to an enlarged view of the nature of healthy human relations. Therapy is facilitated in intensity, direction and time by the proper utilisation of the alternate session as part of the therapeutic procedure of psychoanalysis in groups'. (Wolf and Schwartz 1962)

European influences

While Pratt was working with tuberculosis patients in America in 1905, Moreno was using group techniques with a variety of patient populations in Vienna.

Jacob L. Moreno

Moreno, a psychiatrist, is associated mostly with the technique of psychodrama. He was also one of the European pioneers of group psychotherapy. In 1911 Moreno developed a technique of puppetry and drama in a child guidance clinic in Vienna which he called 'psychodrama'. In 1921 he developed the idea further, to the extent of opening a 'spontaneity' theatre for adults which came to be used in the treatment of mental patients. In 1925 he brought psychodrama to the United States. The origins of psychodrama date to the early decades of the twentieth century, to around 1915 when Dr Karl Joergensen of Sweden introduced his Stegrieftheater or spontaneity theatre. Back and Illing (19??) have, however, traced the origins of the Stegrieftheater to George Simmel who, in the 1890s, led the theoretical foundation for sociometry as well as psychodrama. Dr Moreno modified and embellished Dr Joergensen's method in America to accord more with psychiatric concepts. From the foundations of Simmel, Moreno designed a technique for measuring interaction. It consisted of mapping out on a sociogram the significant attraction–repulsion relationships, the likes, dislikes, and the indifferences between various members of a group. He identified clusters or social atoms in groups in which the individuals are held together by tele, the feeling of individuals for one another, the cement which holds groups together. It was Moreno who first used the term 'group therapy'.

Sigmund Freud

In 1921, with the publication of *Group Psychology and the Analysis of the Ego,* Freud speculated on how individual psychology was transformed into group psychology.

> 'Group psychology is therefore concerned with the individual man as a member of a race, of a nation, of a caste, of a profession, of an institution, or as a component part of a crowd of people who have been organised into a group at some particular time for some definite purpose'. (Kaplan and Sadock 1971 p.3)

Freud based his deductions on group psychology and group behaviour upon the studies of Le Bon, McDougall and Trotter. Le Bon and McDougall's studies dealt with large groups rather than small groups, the latter were more the concern of Trotter. Freud was quite aware of the difference in the dynamics in small groups, in crowds and in masses, but nevertheless treated these types as one in his discussions and applied observations of one to the other. Freud concluded that the 'group is similar to the primal Lorde'.

> 'The psychology of such a group, the dwindling of the conscious individual personality, the focusing of thoughts in a common direction, the predominance of the affective side of the mind and of the unconscious psychical life, the tendency to the immediate carrying out of intentions as they emerge – all this corresponds to a state of regression to a primitive mental activity of just such a sort as we should be inclined to ascribe to the primal Lorde'. (Ruitenbeck 1969 p.30)

Freud emphasised the importance of the leader in group formation and group functioning but he differentiated the leaderless group, a mob capable of great excesses, from a leader centred group, an agent potentially capable of reducing anxiety and neurosis. 'Where a powerful impetus has been given to group formation, neurosis may diminish and at all events temporarily disappear. Justifiable attempts have also been made to turn this antagonism between neuroses and group formation to therapeutic account' (Ruitenbeck 1969 p.37).

Freud developed his concept of identification in Group Psychology and the Analysis of the Ego and put forward three types of identification: 'Firstly the original form of emotional tie with an object; secondly introjection of the object into the ego; and thirdly perception of a common quality shared with some other person' (Ruitenbeck 1969 p.32). It must be clear to anyone interested in groups, working with groups or conducting psychotherapy groups that all of these aspects of identification mentioned by Freud are operative. 'It must be admitted that Freud's insights into group formation and the transferences that exist between the members and the leader, form much of the basis for present day psychoanalytical oriented group psychotherapy' (Kaplan and Sadock 1971 p.4). Although Freud did not practice group therapy, group psychotherapists owe him a great debt of gratitude.

Alfred Adler

Like Freud, Adler was Jewish and spent much of his early life in Vienna. Born in 1870, he joined Freud's seminar where from the beginning he regarded himself as a junior colleague rather than disciple.

Adler perceived man as a social being primarily and exclusively and was the first to emphasise that human behaviour is goal directed, purposive. He contended that all human actions have a purpose and that the purpose is primarily of a social nature. Since man's problems and conflicts are recognised in their social nature, the group is ideally suited not only to highlight and reveal the nature of a person's conflicts and maladjustments, but to offer corrective influences. The group is a value-forming agent and it influences the convictions and beliefs of its members.

Adler and his co-worker used a group approach in their child guidance centres in Vienna in 1921. The characteristic dynamics of group psychology in Adler's psychology had the following four phases:

1. The establishment and maintenance of the proper therapeutic relationship.

2. The exploration of the dynamics operating in the patient.

3. Communicating to the patient an understanding of himself.

4. A re-orientation.

The Adlerian psychologists who developed the group approaches always considered man as a social being and as socially motivated. They observed the difficult child together with parents and siblings and always treated the whole family. For them the group was always the natural setting.

Adler died suddenly during a lecture tour in Scotland in 1937. With the exception of Freud, it is doubtful whether any single writer has had a greater influence upon the thought and practice of others.

Karen Horney

Horney practised as an analyst in Berlin where for over 15 years she was an orthodox Freudian, teaching at the Berlin Psychoanalytic Institute. Moving to the United States, she became Associate Director of the Chicago Institute and lecturer at the New School for Social Research, but it was as a staff member of the New York Psychoanalytic Institute that she began to stress the part played by social factors in neurosis and to challenge the biological assumptions of the orthodox Freudians. Ultimately, her views had departed so far in the social direction that she left the main body and, on the eve of her death in 1952, she was Dean of the new American Institute for Psychoanalysis. It is not surprising that she was interested in group psychotherapy and two years before her death she encouraged several psychoanalysts to begin work with groups.

> 'Group analysis is valuable not only socially but also for the promise it holds out as short-term therapy. It is not only a way of reaching more people but it is a peculiar kind of therapy with problems of its own. It is apparent that group analysis is of great value, how great remains to be seen. It is of such high promise that it should be continued not only for adults but also for younger people such as adolescents'. (Ruitenbeck 1969 p.101–2)

Kurt Lewin

Any work on the history of group psychotherapy must include the influence of Kurt Lewin. Lewin was a German Jew born in Posen in 1890, who experienced anti-semitism in his early years. He was finally forced to flee from the Nazis in 1933 and went to America. He was a psychologist by training but had also studied philosophy under Ernst Cassirer. He was greatly influenced by the emerging Gestalt psychology. For Lewin, the group was more than the sum of its parts. It is an entity in its own right with particular and unique qualities which are different from those of the individuals who constitute it. He contended that the acts of any individual can only be explained on the basis of the social forces, the field to which he is exposed. He coined the term 'group dynamics' in 1939. According to Lewin, each individual exists in a psychological field of forces that for him determines and limits his behaviour. This psychological field surrounds each individual and Lewin called it 'the life space'. It is a highly subjective 'space', dealing with the world as the individual sees it.

Lewin also defined the concept of group pressure, whereby influence is brought to bear on a group member so that his behaviour changes. The group member in turn influences the group and together they join a gestalt or whole. The group, although composed of different individuals, does function as a unit, having a life of its own and group standards, group ethics and goals emerge that are unique to a particular group.

Freud the clinician and Lewin the experimentalist – these are the two men whose names will stand out before all others in the history of our psychological era. For it is their contrasting but complementary insights which first made psychology a science applicable to real human beings and to real human society.

British influences

Wilfred Bion

It could be argued that the most original theory of group behaviour was developed by Bion and who, together with Freud, Lewin and Foulkes, has provided a major source of theoretical influence. He is best known for his concept of the group as a whole having a separate mental life with its own dynamics and structure. He carried out most of his work as a member of the Tavistock Institute of Human Relations and led Dicks to write, 'Most of us in the Tavistock circle would assign pride of place to Wilfred Bion's massive conceptual contribution to the theory and practice of group relations'. (De Board 1978 p.35)

Bion was a psychoanalyst of the Kleinian school. Central to Klein's theories is the concept of projective identification and the way adult behaviour can regress to infantile mechanisms. Bion used these concepts to underpin his theory of groups, seeing them not only as individual but also as group phenomena. Bion believed that without the aid of these theories, it would not have been possible to make any advance in the study of group phenomena. In 1961, first at Northfield and later at the Tavistock, Bion made some original observations about the way in which groups collectively may avoid working. He referred to these phenomena as the basic assumptions, of which there are three:

> BaD, i.e., dependency
>
> BaP, i.e., pairing
>
> BaF, i.e., fight/flight.

The individual contains certain innate patterns which become apparent in the unorganised group. These patterns or basic assumptions band the group together, creating a sense of security and unity, but are opposed to the work group which is aimed at carrying out its allotted, consciously decided upon task.

In the work groups, organisation and structure result from the co-operation of members but the basic assumption group is not organised. Bion used the term 'valency' to describe the way in which individuals are compelled to behave according to the prevalent basic assumption and calculated that, despite the influence of the basic assumption, it is the work group that triumphs in the end.

Bion describes the individual as a 'group animal at war' and suggests that the organisation inherent in the work group removes the psychological disadvantages of group formation. He makes no reference, however, to any process of group maturation as conceived by Foulkes in his concept of the group matrix. Bion's contribution is immense and an essential study for anyone interested in groups.

Henry Ezriel

Ezriel was also a member of the Tavistock Institute of Human Relations. He continued to treat the group as a whole as if all its contributors were the product of one patient – as if the group had a mind which he and his followers proceeded to analyse. Bion had termed it 'the group mentality' and Ezriel described something similar in his common group tension which is the common denominator of the members' shared preoccupations. He proceeds, once this has shown itself, to analyse the role that each member adopts in relation to it, pointing out on the one hand the desired relationship and on the other the avoided relationship contingent upon the calamity that would ensue. For Ezriel, interpretation was the only role of the therapist.

S. H. Foulkes

Foulkes has been one of the main organisers of the group therapy movement in Great Britain. His influence and his contribution has been immense. He bridged the gap between the here and now and the there and then. The central plank of his approach is that man is a social animal, born and brought up in a social situation through and within which personality develops.

He was born in 1898 in Karlsruhe, then the capital of the Great Duchy of Baden. He was the youngest son of a comfortably-off Jewish family. In 1919 he decided to study medicine and at university he read Freud. Elizabeth Foulkes (1980) records 'This was in 1919 and ever since Freud and his work have been the greatest influence in my professional life and remain so at the present time. From then on I knew exactly what it was I wanted to be, namely a psychoanalyst' (p.7). When he moved to Frankfurt for post-graduate studies, he came under the influence of Kurt Goldstein. The holistic approach of Goldstein was central to his thinking and underpinned the development of group analysis. The analogy of likening the individual person in his group to a model point in a network of resources also stems from the time spent with Goldstein. He had contact with gestalt psychology and this influence is reflected in his view of the individual and the group as a figure/ground constellation. He also attended seminars given by Schilder. In April 1933 Foulkes, his wife and three children, left Germany and came to settle in London. By 1942 Foulkes had amassed considerable experience and knowledge of groups and their functioning. This knowledge was further enhanced through his experience at the military neurosis centre at Northfield, near Birmingham.

Foulkes developed a technique of analysis by groups in which the group itself becomes the apparatus for undertaking its own therapy. In an article published as early as 1942, Foulkes states that the 'group has some specific therapeutic factors' of which he singles out:

1. The sharing, socialising effect;

2. The mirror reaction;

3. The activating of the collective unconsciousness, the stimulating effect of the group situation;

4. The exchange and information elements;

5. The form that communication took, namely that of group association modelled on free association, of free-floating discussion developed to its full extent.

Foulkes studied the transference situation of members to the therapist conductor, and was among the first to describe the transference that existed between the members themselves and the group as a whole. He diverges from Bion and Ezriel in believing that interpretations from other members of the group can be as potent, if not more so, than interpretations from the conductor. After the war, a circle of colleagues interested in furthering their understanding of groups and how to apply group psychotherapy met regularly with Foulkes. He died suddenly on 8th July 1976 at the age of 77, in London, while conducting a group seminar with colleagues. The flame lit by Foulkes has been carried on by Pines, Skynner, De Mare, Kreeger and others. Group analysis has flourished not only in Great Britain but in Europe and further afield. In 1971 the Institute of Group Analysis was set up. It is now one of the leading training institutes in the world.

Group work with children and adolescents

There is no denying that psychotherapeutic groups with children and adolescents are anything but easy to handle when compared with the usual adult out-patient group. Behr (1988) says adolescent groups 'call for a highly structured setting with an emphasis on containment, support and positive regard at the expense of interpretation. The therapist of an adolescent group has to work harder than he does in an adult group to disabuse the group of his omnipotent and omniscient role' (p.131). Scheidlinger (1985) has found it useful to subdivide group treatment of adolescents with four separate types:

1. Group psychotherapy, which uses the emotional interaction of the group to enable a youngster to obtain relief from distress and modify his or her pathological mode of functioning.

2. Therapeutic groups, which include all the group approaches other than group psychotherapy, that is counselling, therapeutic community meetings, occupational therapy, rehabilitation, art and dance therapy, groups held to reduce adolescent anxieties and resistance to hospital procedure, and milieu or behaviour modification groups.

3. Human development and training groups, which have the basic aims of countering social isolation and making relationships more authentic,

spontaneous and meaningful, and helping people to become more sensitive to their feelings and their bodies.

4. Self-help groups.

In relation to children, Slavson (1979) states 'psychotherapy with children is less difficult, less protracted and the outcomes more basic and more lasting than with adults... because the neurotic engrams have not been as yet crystallised, they can be altered more easily' (p.559).

Peck and Bellsmith (1954) state:

> 'A properly selected group will expose the patient's characteristic distortions as they appear in the interaction between himself and certain members of the group. Since he is also capable of entering into relatively healthy relationships with certain other members of the group, he is able to more easily examine and work through his relationship distortion, because he is supported by the reassuring reality of his healthy social ties within the group'. (p.154)

I would like to conclude this section by quoting Terry Bruce (1988):

> 'Although there is now quite an extensive literature on adolescent psychiatric groups, it is extremely useful to read of other people's experience in attempting to conduct them. I suspect that there is still quite a number of consultant child and adolescent psychiatrists who have not had the experience of running such groups. In my opinion the experience of running an adolescent group should form part of every child and adolescent psychiatric senior registrar's training. Such groups provide first hand experience of having to confront and contain disturbed adolescent behaviour. They also provide psychiatrists with an opportunity to observe and to begin to try to understand the adolescent process. In addition they can give the adolescent psychiatrist an insight into the problems of control and discipline which secondary school teachers are coping with every day'. (p.131)

Recent developments

In recent times there have been significant imported developments in four areas:

1. Short-term group therapy.

2. T groups.

3. The human potential movement.

4. Self-help groups.

Other developments are taking place which give cause for some concern, and group therapists are emerging after weekend courses interested in doing good and healing the sick mind, forgetting that the structures of the mind were not built in a day and cannot be reconstituted over a weekend. Anthony (1971) described them thus:

> 'Within recent times a cascade of experimental approaches has inundated the group arena, so that the more conventional procedures have been transiently swamped by fresh waves of novel and largely untried techniques to which the public has oriented itself because of the novelty, the implicit seductiveness and the promise of quick change'. (p.4)

References

Anthony, E.J. (1971) 'The History of Group Psychotherapy'. In H.I. Kaplan and B.J. Sadock (eds) *Comprehensive Group Psychotherapy*. Baltimore: Williams and Wilkins.

Aveline, M. and Dryden, P. (1988) *Group Therapy in Britain*. Milton Keynes: Open University Press.

Behr, H. (1988) 'Group Analysis with Early Adolescents'. *Group Analysis*. 21(2): 119–131.

de Board, (1978) *The Psychoanalysis of Organisations*. London: Tavistock Publications.

Brown, J.A.C. (1961) *Freud and the Post Freudian*. London: Pelican.

Bruce, T. (1988) 'Discussion on Paper by Harold Behr'. *Group Analysis*. 21(2): 131–133.

Foulkes, E. (1980) *S H Foulkes – Selected Papers*. London: Karnac.

Foulkes, S.H. (1983) *Introduction to Group Analytic Psychotherapy*. London: Maresfield Reprints.

Freud, S. (1960) *Group Psychology and the Analysis of the Ego*. New York: Bantam Books Inc.

Jennings, S. (1975) *Creative Therapy*. London: Pitman and Sons.

Kaplan, H.T. and Sadock, B.J. (1971) *Comprehensive Group Psychotherapy*. Baltimore: Williams and Wilkins.

de Mare, P.B. (1972) *Perspectives in Group Psychotherapy*. London: Cox and Wyman.

Morrow, A.J. (1969) *The Practical Therapist: The Life and Work of Kurt Lewin*. New York: Basic Books Inc.

Peck, H.B. and Bellsmith, V. (1954) *Treatment of the Delinquent Adolescent*. New York: Family Service Association of America.

Pines, M. (1983) *The Evolution of Group Analysis*. London: Routledge and Kegan Paul.

Pines, M. and Roberts, J. (1991) *The Practice of Group Analysis*. London: Tavistock/Routledge.

Ruitenbeck, H. M. (1969) *Group Therapy Today*. Chicago: Aldine Publishing Company.

Scheidlinger, S. (1985) 'Group Treatment of Adolescents – An Overview'. *American Journal of Orthopsychiatry*. 55(1): 102–111.

Schiffer, M. (1979) (ed) *Dynamics of Group Psychotherapy* by S.R. Slavson. New York: Jason Aronson.

Slavson, S.R. (1979) *Dynamics of Group Psychotherapy*. New York. Jason Aronson.

Wolf, A. and Schwartz, E. K. (1962) *Psychoanalysis in Groups*. New York: Grune and Stratton.

Part 3

Tools and Techniques

CHAPTER 9

Play, Activities, Exercises and Games

Kedar Nath Dwivedi

The most significant mode of communication in children is often non-verbal and is usually loaded heavily with feelings and actions, unlike that of adults who tend to transform these into language and concepts. The predominant means of communication in children also varies with their age. Young children tend to express their feelings through play, children in their latency period through constructive or destructive activity, although play and activity are usually accompanied by language as well. Older children, adolescents and adults tend to use language as the main channel for communicating feelings. Group work with children has consequently to rely more upon play, activities, games and exercises in their living and relational contexts than on mentation and concepts. Slavson (1945), therefore, recommended different therapeutic settings for group work with children of different ages.

Play

Young children need to express their fantasies through tangible objects. Toys such as dolls, animals and various characters, and materials such as sand, plasticine, or water, can be easily used to project their fantasies and conflicts. Such materials are also very attractive to young children and help to hold their interest in the group.

In young children, play is considered to be the therapeutic equivalent of 'free association' in adults. Although children can also free associate and generate fantasies, these can be too anxiety provoking and difficult to tolerate. Moreover, due to their cognitive limitations, they may find it difficult to apply logical processing to treat these materials merely as internal objects. Thus, instead of free association, play has been seen to be an effective medium of expressing inner feelings and conflicts. Through play children are able to project thoughts, feelings and conflicts onto the play characters. This also helps in immediate tension release and in mastering emotional conflicts (Harter 1983).

In the initial stages of group work using play, children tend to go for solitary, exploratory play. Some may flit from one activity to another in an overactive way, moving around the room like a whirlwind. Such exploratory playing and experimenting with things such as bubble blowing, or playing with water, clay, or sand, from a tactile point of view help children to feel secure in the setting of the playroom (Hellersberg 1955). Preoccupation with food and cooking and their incorporation in play can be linked to the oral stage of development. Demands for immediate attention, affection and gratification of needs, and explosion of rage if the demands are not immediately met, recapitulate the Narcissistic elements of play (Peller 1955).

Gradually, children are able to move from egocentric, solitary, exploratory motor (playground type), oral (cooking, and so forth) and anal (messy) levels of play to more social, representational and constructive play, expressing through the medium of play their conscious and unconscious needs, fantasies, ideas, thoughts, feelings and conflicts. Various characters, toys, dolls, animals, and so forth become endowed with feelings, intentions and relationships representing those from the world of the child. Social play allows the children to experiment with new ways of relating, with improved ego strength, attitudes and insight gained during the work of the group.

It is important that the children are able to choose their representational materials from puppets, doll houses, or other objects and are enabled to create dialogues as well. Emotional linking and interpretative ideas can also be introduced indirectly through these characters and dialogues. In the context of acceptance and emotional nurturance, play provides a means of enacting and working through difficult fantasies and life events. In one of our groups a boy kept playing (dangerously) with the window of the group room (on the first floor). In his real life he had been rescued through a first floor window when he was very young as his mother had set fire to the bedroom while he and his brother were in bed. Soo (1985) gave an example of a boy playing 'vampire' in a group. In his actual life he had experienced premature weaning due to blood in his mother's milk. Hickin (1971), describing play therapy groups in a large children's home, highlights the problem of sharing. 'So far, the group experience seems to offer to deprived children the opportunity to come to terms with their intolerable greed and unsatisfied feelings as long as the therapist is willing to join them in their painful search' (p.39).

Thus, all therapies for children have a common reference in the early process of play therapy – which corresponded to psychoanalysis in adults – where unconscious material was expressed in play rather than through verbalised thoughts (Lockwood 1981). However, the recognition of the need to include in the focus various aspects of interactions between individuals in a group setting (Yalom 1970) led to the concept of Activity Groups without diminishing the emphasis on play.

Activity

In activity, action is to a varying degree aim-directed, while in play, action may be an end in itself. However, the main purpose of using play or activity in group work with children is to generate interaction between them so that the games and the materials may serve to stimulate the unconscious strivings towards a resolution. Children of latency age with a degree of individuation in their ego development can use tools, materials and games of a nature that suggest more practical outcomes (e.g. making a 'peacock' by sticking together pieces of paper cut in the shape of their hands).

Activity groups involve emotional re-education based upon social interaction of group members around the use of play, material and food rather than from the primary method of interpretation, group discussion or reflection. The settings and responses are supposed to have to a child the same meanings as words and concepts have for adults (Slavson and Schiffer 1975). A permissive atmosphere allows the children to regress to a primary narcissistic state, that is, being busy in solitary activities; talking without listening to each other, and so forth before attempting more mature object relations.

As children have limited life experiences and have limitations in cognitive and emotional maturation, with a tendency to narcissistic and animistic perception of reality, the group environment also provides various opportunities for testing out reality. The groupworkers and the group, by reflecting upon the wishes, thoughts, feelings and demands of individuals and the group, convey the fact that the meanings of their actions have been understood. Thus, in an atmosphere of security, curiosity, interest and care, children may be able to correct their defective sense of reality.

These activities provide a setting for socialisation, as children are encouraged to engage in a selective variety of craft activities that serve as a springboard for eliciting feelings and encouraging peer interactions. There has also been a belief in the activity-oriented group, in that when children are given the opportunity to express feelings in and through activity, the resultant catharsis results in a breakthrough of repressed impulses and feelings with subsequent changes in behaviour, and that peer interactions lead to corrective changes in interpersonal relationships and modes of behaviours (Epstein and Altman 1972).

As young children have egocentric, animistic and narcissistic preoccupations and perceptions, people, objects, things and toys become their extension and targets for love and hate. The things a child does to toys, pets and siblings reflect what he or she would like to do to the 'parents'. If the child is restrained from such actions, other objects are then created in fantasy to meet such needs. However, by the latency period such substitutional fantasies may dissolve and others are perceived as entities in themselves and not just an extension of oneself.

Identification is facilitated by the group worker being permissive rather than restrictive or negative. The essence of reality testing is, therefore, the kindliness and interest of the groupworker and the group and their acceptance. However, lack of boundaries and controls can overload the ego strengths of the children and make them feel both anxious and unwanted.

Exercises and games

The issue of control is a major component of group work with children and adolescents and is discussed in detail elsewhere in this volume. Activity Groups, due both to the exciting nature of the activities and the permissive atmosphere, can augment this problem. At times there is a need for more structuring and control by the group workers, especially when members are anxious and unsafe. With participants in revolt, however, it may become necessary to install impersonal controls. The rules inherent in games, therefore, provide valuable additional sources of control. Thus, the locus of control can be shifted to suit the needs of the group and can vary between personal and impersonal control and between group workers and group members with the ultimate aim of self regulated independent control. However, the timing of such shifts are very important (Rose and Edleson 1987).

As games vary in their level of prescriptiveness, they can be selected in such a way as to suit the ability of the group to handle regulations. If the group has difficulty in submitting to control of any kind, games with low levels of prescription may be more useful (e.g. storytelling, various tag games, hide and seek). As the group's ability to handle rules begins to improve, games with higher levels of prescriptiveness can then be introduced.

Rules of games can be changed to convert games from being competitive to being co-operative, or *vice versa*. The complexity of rules can also be titrated to the particular needs of the group at the particular time and place. Not only do games provide opportunities for exercising creativity and imagination, but games can be transformed in various creative and imaginative ways to meet particular needs.

As activities and games are often great sources of fun, play and enjoyment, these can help in creating interest and improving motivation. These increase the attraction of the group and provide opportunities for experiencing the group members and workers in a pleasantly playful context. As already highlighted in the chapter on conceptual frameworks in this volume, it is important for the group workers to 'join in' the indigenous peer culture before it can be transformed into a therapeutic peer culture. Unless children or adolescents are engaged in the group, it is difficult to proceed further. Even in the object relations therapy approach, the phase of engagement is the basic foundation of any treatment. It is only then that the projective identifications begin to surface (see also the chapter on interpretation). However, 'Many adults have forgotten how to play. This is not meant as an insult, rather it is stating the obvious' (Dearling and Armstrong 1980 p.7).

Group exercises and games provide a rich opportunity for indirect observation of interactions under different levels of stress and situations. They reveal various resources, coping skills, deficiencies and needs and offer possibilities for learning and practising new roles, relationships and skills, with an immense impact on the self image and self esteem of the participants.

As highlighted in the chapter on emotional development (in this volume) emotions are a crucial resource rather than something to be got rid of (discharged) or controlled (pushed down) as dangerous. But, 'the young person's unwillingness to experience their own rage or grief, possibly out of fear that if they did they would become a whirlwind of destruction, leaves them feeling cut off, tense, or stressed lest they lose their grip on their "armour"' (Loftus 1988 p.219). As feelings are embodied resources, Action Groups facilitate people in experiencing their emotions in a safe setting and in moving on through their distress.

The elements of ritual provide a way of supporting and containing strong emotions (Scheff 1979). The active parts of certain rituals (e.g. repetitions, multiple symbols, dance, music) according to d'Aquili *et al.* (1979), can induce positive limbic discharges in the brain leading to increased contact between people and social cohesion. The combination of both digital and analogue information (e.g. through stories and symbols) in rituals and games is conducive for the two main brain hemispheres to spill over into each other, sometimes experienced as a 'shiver down the back' (Ornstein and Thompson 1984, Roberts 1988).

The true effects of messages and learning in ritualised contexts are powerful in penetrating the depths of the unconscious. Therapists are finding that crucial changes are initiated when carefully designed rituals are enacted (O'Connor and Hoorwitz 1988). New meanings, behaviours and actions can occur through the transformation of what is already known, familiar and repetitive, as rituals provide a framework for expectancy (Douglas 1966).

It is important to be careful in selecting games and exercises for the group and in planning and preparing various aspects before hand. Factors such as the children's level of competence, their concentration span, the stage of the group, relevant emotional and interactional issues and themes, and the availability of space, time, materials and equipment should all be taken into consideration. For example, should the group aim at increasing or decreasing physical movement at this stage? If there is restlessness and agitation due to long discussion in the room, it may be possible to reduce at least some of it by moving to different parts of the room from time to time. Better still, by planning ahead in this way, it may be possible to prevent such restlessness.

The different features of various games, activities and exercises can be categorised into dimensions (e.g. physical field, activity behaviours, constituent behaviours and level of prescriptiveness) that are useful in planning, preparing, implementing and evaluating programmes – and their potentials (Gump and Sutton-Smith 1965, Rose 1972, Vinter 1974, Ross and Bernstein 1976, Garvin 1981, Rose and Edleson 1987). Games are useful for a variety of purposes. They can help to relax and can act as catalysts for developing self-expression, new identity, interpersonal relationships, co-operation, communication, emotional sensitivity, feedback and insight.

In the literature now, there is no dirth of detailed descriptions of games, exercises and activities that can be used or adapted to suit needs of the particular groups. Some examples are: Bond (1986), Boyd (1973), Brandes (1982), Brandes and Phillips (1978), Butler and Allison (1978), Celano (1990), Corder *et al.* (1977), Davidson and Gordon (1978), Dearling and Armstrong (1980), De Mille (1967), The Diagram Group (1977), Fluegelman (1976), Gardner (1973), Girl Scouts of the USA (1969), Harlow (1977), Heitzmann (1974), Howard (1970), James and Jongeward (1975), Jeffs (1982), Johnson (1989), Lennox (1982), Lewis and Streitfield (1973), Orlick (1978), Panmure House (1978), Phillips (1960), Schaefer (1987), Taylor (1976), Zakich (1975).

Readers are recommended to refer to such sources rather than depend upon this chapter for detailed descriptions of useful exercises or games in groups. The problem is not so much the finding of such games and their detailed instructions but of selecting them for their compatibility with the desired goals of the group. Here we look into some ways of classifying such games, activities and exercises, as there can be numerous classifications, for example (1) according to the phase of the group, (2) theoretical approaches, (3) themes and (4) materials and activities employed.

Games and exercises for particular phases of the group

Introductory exercises and games

By providing opportunities for members to get to know each other quickly and/or welcome newcomers, such games can help the group to relax. By adding fun to the process of introduction, the element of inhibition may be reduced. However, it has to be kept in mind that introductions can, at times, increase tensions within the group by making participants more aware of strangers or of being watched. Any element of coercion, therefore, should be avoided, otherwise the participants, especially newcomers, feel that they have to 'perform' in order to be accepted by the group.

There are a large number of exercises and games that one can devise or choose from. For example:

- Splitting in pairs to find out the biographical details of the partner and then getting together in the group to introduce the said partner to the group.

- Sitting in a circle and talking (or shouting) one's name in turn, or including all the previous names told in the circle, adding adjectives or other items (e.g. aims for attending the group, talents, likes, hobbies, feelings, news). This can be done at the individual's own pace or to a rhythm (e.g. of clapping or some other movement). Gestures or mimes depicting one's own feelings and mood can also be added.

- Passing objects to different members of the group while calling their names, such objects could be real (e.g. cushion, ball) or imaginary. Thus, a variety of name games can be constructed and played.

- Participants miming an activity they enjoy or something that is very important to them.

- A Treasure Hunt type of game involving milling around, meeting and talking to participants in turn in order to list, chart and act upon instructions provided for by the treasure hunt, (e.g. finding someone who has been on a long trip; with whom one may have a lot in common; who wears glasses; who has a similar nose or socks).

Loosening up, energising, warming up exercises and games

Some very simple games and exercises can quickly warm up a group, shifting their attention from outside preoccupations to the matters within the group. These can also help the participants by focusing on more awareness and self-disclosure. Some examples are:

- Rhythmic clapping.

- Milling around and changing the level of interaction.

- Splitting in pairs and mirroring the partner's gestures, postures, movements, expressions, and so forth.

- Sitting in a circle and passing imaginary (mimed) objects, masks, whispers, or other objects, round the circle.

- Group story making, group singing, tug of war, and so forth.

- Breaking in and breaking out of the tightly held circle of the group (see below).

- Various card games (see below).

More exploratory or healing exercises and games

More personal and deeper issues can be explored and worked through as a session progresses or as the group moves to a more engaged and ready state of development in its career. Various role plays, scripts and drama can be devised to access, mobilise and restructure habitual, emotional, intimate and complex relationship matters. The chapter on the use of drama (in this volume) explores this further. Various board games (see below) can be helpful in facilitating different levels of self disclosure, interpersonal feedback and enactments in a playful atmosphere where members respond to the instructions on cards or squares of the board game. Some of the theme-specific games and exercises are also mentioned below.

Ending games and exercises

These can help to facilitate encapsulation of learning that has taken place during the session, during the life of the group or during the period of a member's attendance. Each person in turn may be asked to give a summary, to anything they wanted to say but didn't say, to say what things they liked or disliked most, and so forth. The rituals involving affectionate and non-verbal behaviours (e.g. shaking or holding hands), blessings, future projection, and commitments, help to handle the process of loss while creating a moving and positive experiences for the group.

Corder (1987) describes the value of 'Legacy Tape' and 'Memory Book' linked to a member departing from the group. The Legacy Tape is prepared by the departing member outside the group and is played for the group during the first session of his or her absence. The tape includes the departing member's feelings and advice about the group. The Memory Book is made up by each member of the group contributing a page. This is presented to the departing member at his or her last session. It includes things the authors promise to remember about the departing member and things the author would like the departing member to remember about the author, about the group and about himself or herself.

Theoretical approaches

Transactional Analysis

In Transactional Analysis, the word 'game' (used in a technical sense) includes dishonesty and ulterior motivation. Eric Berne's (1964) definition of 'game' is, therefore, as follows:

> 'A GAME is an ongoing series of complementary ulterior transactions progressing to a well defined, predictable outcome. Descriptively it is a recurring set of transactions, often repetitious, superficially plausible, with a concealed motivation; or, more colloquially, a series of moves with a snare, or a 'gimmick'. Games are clearly differentiated from

procedures, rituals, and pastimes by two chief characteristics: (1) their ulterior quality and (2) the pay off. Procedures may be successful, rituals effective, and pastimes profitable, but all of them are by definition candid; they may involve contest, but not conflict, and the ending may be sensational, but it is not dramatic. Every game, on the other hand, is basically dishonest, and the outcome has a dramatic, as distinct from merely exciting, quality'. (p.44)

Transactional Analysis (TA) has a language of its own, but once the language and concepts are understood, observing, identifying and exploring various relationship phenomena in TA terms become real fun. Also, there are manuals for explaining TA to children and adolescents (Freed 1973, 1976, Freed and Freed 1977). Lennox (1982) has described a number of exercises based upon TA principles that are specifically suited to children and adolescents, especially in residential institutions. Some of the themes included in her exercises are: winning and losing, identifications of ego states and transactions, Warm Fuzzies and Cold Pricklies (positive and negative strokes), collecting and trading 'stamps' (one's favourite feelings, e.g. rejection, anger, or suspicion, are saved up to cash, i.e., to justify a piece of negative behaviour, e.g. self mutilation). There are also exercises to play TA games (e.g. the 'Yes, But Game' where the player responds to any solution offered, by starting the sentence with 'Yes, but...'), explore TA scripts (e.g. by examining stereotypes, family trees, family sayings, etc.) and commitment for change.

Davis *et al.* (1988) describes the use of genograms (family trees) in a group for latency age children. It 'focused the group's manifest communication on changing family roles and relationships, both as they had occurred in reality and as they were symbolically re-enacted within the group process. Feelings of shame, guilt, anger and loss were markedly ameliorated as the group members studied the structure of their extended families within an environment which encouraged normative peer interaction and progressive emotional development' (p.189).

Humanistic approaches to groups

The Humanistic Psychology movement or the Human Potential Growth Movement has led to the mushrooming of various Growth centres in the West that aim to enable ordinary people come to terms with deep seated fears, prejudices and hostilities. These feelings may not prevent them from carrying out their daily lives but do obstruct them from developing their fullest potentials. Fritz Perls, for example, was closely identified with the work of the Esalen Institute at Big Sur, California, which became a centre for promoting encounter groups, Gestalt therapy, Rogerian psychotherapy, bioenergetics, Zen, yoga and other existentialist philosophies. Thus, these exercises have included ideas from a number of therapeutic schools, enabling individuals to get in touch with their true selves by stripping off their habitual defences.

According to Gestalt therapy, awareness precedes change and Perls *et al.* (1973) describe a number of experiments for sensing opposing forces; expanding, sharpening and integrating awareness; experiencing the continuity of emotion; changing anxiety into excitement; discovering projections, and so forth. Awareness of the different roles one plays helps to attack the defence system. Thus unfinished business can be allowed to pour out in a safe way (e.g. in the form of pounding on a cushion). Similarly, bioenergetic exercises are designed to identify and thereby reduce muscle tension, which dulls feelings. According to bioenergetics, individuals spend a great deal of time tensing up as a defence against painful, distressing or uncomfortable emotional experiences. Eventually, this forms a chronic barrier against feeling anything.

The encounter groups utilise various techniques from humanistic psychology movement and there are, therefore, a number of encounter group models. For example, Perls' (1974) model may focus more on 'unfinished business', Moreno's (1948) on resolution of role conflict and Rogers' (1973), emphasis on the context of unconditional positive regard, empathy, safety, trust, intimacy, and so forth. The core of an individual's interactional behaviours is an attempt to deal with the existential problems (Schulz 1973); inclusion (belonging); control (influence); and affection (emotional interdependence).

Lennox (1982) describes a number of games and exercises derived from encounter group practice that can be useful in group work with children and adolescents. These include various exercises and games for increasing the physical and emotional awareness continuum; verbal, (both spoken and written) and non verbal communications; increasing creativity and spontaneity; role playing, psychodrama, positive and negative feedback; co-operative problem solving; and breaking down barriers, building up trust, facilitating group cohesion, exploring fantasy and having fun.

Cognitive and Behaviour Therapy approaches

In cognitive and behaviour therapy approaches too, fun and games are seen as essential media for learning prosocial behaviours. These provide an opportunity for practising such behaviours and for improving the recreational skills which become tools for building better relationships and better quality of life.

> 'Games provide an opportunity for the child to learn the consequences of his actions without having to suffer them. In a game mistakes and exposure of ignorance are more tolerated. Games, usually encourage laughing and joking, which can be instrumental in relieving anxiety and facilitating involvement'. (Cartledge and Milburn 1981 p.100)

There are a number of board games to choose from, or one can design one's own game with the help of the group, which can add variety to the typical social skill routines of modelling, coaching, rehearsal and feedback. Heitzmann (1974) provides useful guidelines for designing, selecting or evaluating such games.

Social Skill Board Games (Rose and Edleson 1987) are played by rolling a dice and moving to various squares that instruct to pick 'role play cards' (e.g. responding to a bully demanding money), 'think cards' (e.g. when was the last time that you were upset), or 'fun card' (e.g. tell a joke) piled in separate decks. Other squares provide instructions for movement (e.g. go back three spaces) or for obtaining treats.

A variety of problem-solving exercises involving identification of the problem, brainstorming options, and selecting, implementing and evaluating the implementation of the most appropriate option can usually be done in the form of enactments and games. Role playing is a useful technique for rehearsing problem solving. Members may also be encouraged to reverse roles or stance (e.g. playing the part of their own parent in a disciplinary conflict) and then discuss their perception of other's reaction to their behaviour. The game of 'Rack' or 'Hair Cut' is played by participants taking turns to undergo a minute or two of intense verbal criticism (or 'slagging') by the group without cracking up.

In the cognitive and behaviour therapy approach, tasks involving diaries, charts and practices for homework are often the most essential ingredients. However, such evaluatory exercises and games can also be used during the session itself. We ran a group of seven- to ten-year-old children who started pestering the group workers by wanting to assist in fetching the refreshments at the end of the group. In order to decide who should get that opportunity at the end of each group, a plan of scoring each participant's efforts during group was devised and implemented, with enormous effects.

Games and exercises for different themes

Aspects of group work around particular issues, themes and problems, such as bereavement, anger management, social skills, delinquency, encopresis, or sexual abuse have been elaborated elsewhere in many chapters in this volume, along with some possible exercises, activities and games. Similarly, various games and exercises can be found in the literature or devised to explore further specific problems such as teenage pregnancy, substance abuse, conduct disorder, school refusal, eating disorder, chronic or terminal illnesses, separation, or divorce. Feelings of shame, embarrassment, jealousy, envy, loss, anger, anxiety, fear, and so forth can also be explored much more deeply in the safety of structured exercises and games (e.g. the game of miming such feelings trigger-ing further in-depth personal exploration of dealings with feelings). Issues around assertiveness, violence, prejudice, persecution, victimisation, rescue, and other themes can be explored by devising role plays, as teams of animals (meek, aggressive, assertive), tribes, passengers on a train, situations at school and so on.

Inclusion

Feelings around belonging, inclusion or exclusion can be contacted by games like 'breaking in' and 'breaking out'. The group stands in a circle with tightly linked arms and the volunteer either in the middle or outside the group. The game involves the volunteer breaking out or entering into the circle while the group tries to prevent it.

Trust

There are a number of games to explore and build trust in a group, for example:

- Splitting into pairs and walking around with one's eyes closed following the verbal or tactile directions of the partner.

- The group stands in a fairly tight circle with arms outstretched and the volunteer in the middle with feet together, body rigid and arms by the sides. The volunteer then leans backwards until the balance is lost and is caught by the outstretched arms of the circle and gently pushed in different directions.

- The group is organised into two rows facing each other with closed arms and holding hands with the person immediately opposite, thus creating a chain along which the volunteer can be passed with a rocking motion.

Self awareness, self disclosure and self esteem

Exercises and games involving designing coat of arms, sentence completions (e.g. 'I am proud of...'), writing one's own epitaph, preparing advertisements, drawing oneself as a tree, plant, animal, bird, playing magic shops and survival games, and so forth can be very useful. The 'Coat of Arms' could include (1) my best points, (2) my worst points, (3) what I would like to do next year and (4) what I would like to be in ten years' time. The advertisements to sell oneself may be as a friend, a pupil, a sibling, an offspring, a boyfriend or girlfriend, and so forth. Johari's (Indian Jeweller's) window has four panes, i.e., (1) things that others know about me, (2) things that others know about me but I don't, (3) things that I know about me which others don't know and (4) things that no-one knows about me. Participants can draw and fill in these panes of their Johari's Window with examples.

The 'survival' game may involve pretending to have gathered together in an imaginary nuclear shelter to stay until radiation levels outside drop to safe levels. Unfortunately someone has to leave so that enough air and food is left for the survival of the rest of the group. This calls for debate on the value of various personal attributes and roles. The scenario can be varied, (e.g. to a life boat).

The 'magic shop' involves individuals trading or swapping a bit of personal quality one has a lot of (e.g. being cool) for a bit of something one is lacking (e.g. being sensitive). It facilitates individuals to identify their strengths and weaknesses. It is important that the participants should feel safe from the risk of being scapegoated by the group as a consequence of their disclosures. They can also be provided with the opportunity for trying out (act out) their newly gained qualities in the group.

Communication

An interesting game of 'rumour clinic' involves the demonstration of how messages get distorted as they are passed from person to person. This can be done by passing a message by whispering to the next person in turn, or by calling in one member at a time from outside who is given the message by the person who received it the last. In this way the message in the beginning and at the end can also be audio taped and replayed to appreciate the distorting influences.

Co-operative teamwork

Various aspects of teamwork including leadership, communication, division of labour, and co-operation can be explored by a variety of problem solving, puzzles and lego tower building type of exercises. For example, the game of 'pyramid' involves five volunteers who are requested to arrange themselves together in such a way that there are only four feet (or two feet and two hands) on the ground. A similar game of untying the knot involves dividing the group in two teams. One team is sent outside the room while the other team stands in a circle holding hands and then tangling themselves up (still holding hands) by stepping over linked arms and crawling between legs to get fully 'knotted'. The team from outside the room is then invited to work out a way to untie the 'knot' without disconnecting the hands.

Empathy

One of the games involves participants milling around with a card stuck on their forehead. The person himself or herself doesn't know the contents of his or her own card and can't read it but others can and are not allowed to tell. The cards have instructions like 'I talk too much, get me to listen'; 'I am lonely, help me find a friend'; 'mirror my posture, gesture and expressions as we talk'. Each instruction is on two cards. As people read each other's cards (but not aloud), they subtly react to what the cards say. The aim is also to find the person who has the same card and share the feelings aroused by the other people's responses.

Exercises and games according to different materials and activities

Another way of classifying exercises and games would be in relation to the type of materials and activities involved, such as (1) major athletic games, (2) group action games, (3) paper and pencil exercises, (4) art, (5) drama, (6) sculpting, (7) story telling, (8) group fantasy, (9) card games, (10) board games, and so on.

Major athletic sports often have a rather high status in peer circles and many children or adolescents attending groups may have had little success in these, or may have experienced derogatory remarks about their lack of skills. Unfortunately, it is difficult to incorporate such sports in a short session of group work, as most require equipment, skills, space and time that may not be available. However, there are many sports such as Judo and Kabaddi (traditionally played in India, requires no special equipment and involves prolonging one's breath, touching and/or holding one's opponents and tactically negotiating boundaries). These can also have immense psychological significance and can be adapted to the particular physical constraints of a group. Group action games such as various tags (e.g. hopping tag, three legged tag, blindfold tag, 'stuck-in-the-mud'), slow races and relays (carrying a spoonful of water for example) involve movement, balancing, and co-operation and are also useful as energisers and warm ups.

Some paper pencil exercises such as Johari's window and coat of arms have already been mentioned. Other chapters in this volume offer ideas for art, drama, sculpting, visualisation, story telling and group fantasies. The story of Warm Fuzzies and Cold Pricklies (Steiner 1974) can be told to the group to set out the significance of strokes in TA terms. Bettelheim (1975) makes us acutely aware of the irreplaceable importance of fairy tales, revealing the true contents of many such stories. Children make use of these to cope with their baffling feelings of helplessness, smallness, anxieties about the strangers and mysteries of the outside world. Telling an appropriate story in a group or making up a story involving the group can facilitate projection and the working through of a number of significant issues. The group may be sitting or lying down in a circle. Someone starts to tell a story and stops whenever he or she likes, for the next person to continue the story. This continues round the group, making up a story.

One of the sculpting exercises may involve picking a card (but not telling the group what is written on it) and choosing people from the group and moulding them into the scenario stipulated on the card. Another type of sculpting exercise may involve a member of the group making a sculpture by putting all the group members in position in relation to each other. The position of each member in the sculpture (thereby in the group as seen by the sculptor) provides a context for further exploration and expression of feelings.

One of the most amusing and fascinating games of this kind involves working in pairs which use their bodies to design different moving parts of a human machine, (e.g. a lawn mower). Pairs then join together to make bigger parts until all members of the group are involved in making the machine.

A game of cards involves participants picking up one card at a time in turn and giving it to the most appropriate person in the group. The cards have to be prepared beforehand by the group worker and the items can be varied to suit the stage of the group. Some examples might be: the most honest person; the person with the nicest hair; the kindest person; the easiest person to talk to; the happiest person. In the beginning stages of the group one should avoid including cards with any negative items (e.g. the person who eats the most, the person who often gets it wrong).

Board games

The Social Skills Board Games have already been mentioned. 'Pathways' is a similar board game with gold and silver discs and stars (Nelson 1992). The 'Learning Life Game' (Corder 1977, 1987, Corder *et al*. 1977, Kraft 1989) includes squares labelled to correspond with item cards of three categories: (1) knowing yourself, (2) understanding each other and (3) problem solving. Each item card reflects a discussion question or task for the group. These include five different levels of intimacy or expectations for disclosure or group cohesion required by the task. Examples of items are: 'what is the best and worst thing about the school you go to? Ask the person on your right the same question' (Level A of Knowing Yourself); 'what was the meanest thing you ever did to someone? What made you do it? How do you feel about it now? Would you handle it differently now? How? Have the person on your right answer this question for himself/herself' (Level E of Knowing Yourself). There is also room for 'learning cards' dealing with Transactional Analysis concepts which can be interwoven.

The Gardner's (1973) 'Talking, Feeling and Doing Game' can be used with children aged from four to mid-teens (Gardner 1983, 1986, Celano 1990). The players earn chips by responding to cards which are designed to tap cognitive, affective and behavioural aspects of a broad range of human experiences. Examples include What things come into your mind when you can't fall asleep? (a talking card); A girl was very angry at her father and wished that he would be hit by a car. Later that day he was hit by a car. How did she feel? What did she think? (a feeling card); Make believe you're opening up a letter that you've just received from someone. What does the letter say? (a doing card).

The 'Rainbow Game' (Rainbow House 1989) includes board games specifically designed to work with sexually abused children and adolescents. The Rainbow Game also includes cards which offer opportunities for story telling, free association and other instructed responses (e.g. one word cards such as judge, trick).

The use of a video camera and its playback can also be a very useful tool for the group to facilitate focusing on certain issues and mobilising feedback and confrontation. Mallery and Navas (1982), using this tool in a group with preadolescent boys, highlighted the role of the video system in defining the physical and psychological boundaries of the group. The video system is treated by the group members as if it were a peer, another member, and it can even evoke transference reactions (e.g. Hi, Dad! to the camera).

References

d'Aquili, E.G., Laughlin, C.D. and McManus, J. (1979) *The Spectrum of Ritual: A Bioenergetic Structural Analysis.* New York: Columbia University Press.

Berne, E. (1964) *Games People Play.* Harmondsworth: Penguin.

Bettelheim, B. (1975) *The Uses of Enchantment. The Meaning and Importance of Fairy Tales.* Harmondsworth: Penguin.

Bond, T. (1986) *Games for Social and Life Skills.* Cheltenham: Stanley Thornes.

Boyd, N.L. (1973) *Handbook of Recreational Games.* New York: Dover Publications.

Brandes, D. (1982) *Gamester's Handbook Two.* London: Hutchinson.

Brandes, D. and Phillips, H. (1978) *The Gamester's Handbook.* London: Hutchinson.

Butler, L. and Allison, L. (1978) *Games, Games.* Playspace.

Cartledge, G. and Milburn, J.F. (1981) *Teaching Social Skills to Children.* Elmsford, N.Y.: Pergamon Press.

Celano, M.P. (1990) 'Activities and Games for Group Psychotherapy With Sexually Abused Children'. *International Journal of Group Psychotherapy.* 40(4): 419–429.

Corder, B.F. (1977) *The Life Game.* Chapel Hill: University of North Carolina Press.

Corder, B.F. (1987) 'Planning and Leading Adolescent Therapy Groups'. In P.A. Keller and S.R. Heyman (eds) *Innovations in Clinical Practice, 6.* Sarasota: Professional Resources Exchange (pp.177–196).

Corder, B.F., Whiteside, R. and Vogel, M. (1977) 'A Therapeutic Game for Structuring and Facilitating Group Psychotherapy with Adolescents'. *Adolescence.* 46: 261–268.

Davis, L., Geikie, G. and Schamess, G. (1988) 'The Use of Genograms in a Group for Latency Age Children'. *International Journal of Group Psychotherapy.* 38 (1): 189–210.

Davison, A. and Gordon, P. (1978) *Games and Simulations in Action.* London: Woburn Press.

De Mille, R. (1967) *Put Your Mother on the Ceiling: Children's Imagination Games.* New York: Walker.

Dearling, A. and Armstrong, H. (1980) *The Youth Games Book.* Bridge of Weir (Renfrewshire): Intermediate Treatment Resource Centre.

Diagram Group (1977) *The Way to Play: The Illustrated Encyclopaedia of the Games of the World.* Bantam.

Douglas, M. (1966) *Purity and Danger: An Analysis of Concepts of Pollution and Taboo*. New York: Praeger.

Epstein, N. and Altman, S. (1972) 'Experiences in Converting an Activity Group into Verbal Group Therapy with Latency-Age Boys'. *International Journal of Group Psychotherapy*. 22: 93–100.

Fluegelman, A. (1976) *The New Games Book*. Garden City, N.Y.: Dolphin Books/Double day.

Freed, A.M. (1973) *T.A. for Tots*. Sacramento, California: Jalmar Press.

Freed, A.M. (1976) *T.A. for Teens*. Sacramento, California: Jalmar Press.

Freed, A.M. and Freed, M. (1977) *T.A. for Kids*. Sacramento, California: Jalmar Press.

Gardner, R.A. (1973) *The Talking, Feeling and Doing Game*. Cresskill, N.J.: Creative Therapeutics.

Gardner, R.A. (1983) 'The Talking, Feeling and Doing Game'. In C.E. Schaffer and K.J. O'Connor (eds) *Handbook of Play Therapy*. New York: John Wiley and Sons. Chapter 14: 259–273.

Gardner, R.A. (1986) 'The Talking, Feeling and Doing Game'. In C.E. Schaffer and S.E. Reid (eds) *Game Play: Therapeutic Use of Childhood Games*. New York: John Wiley and Sons.

Garvin, C.D. (1981) *Contemporary Group Work*. Englewood Cliffs, N.J.: Prentice-Hall.

Girl Scouts of the USA (1969) *Games for The Girl Scouts*. New York: Girl Scouts of The USA.

Gump, P. and Sutton-Smith, B. (1965) 'Therapeutic Play Techniques'. In P. Gump and B. Sutton-Smith (eds) *Conflict in the Classroom*. Belmont, California: Wandsworth.

Harlow, E. (1977) *101 Instant Games*. London: MacDonald.

Harter, S. (1983) 'Cognitive-Developmental Considerations in the Conduct of Play Therapy'. In C.E. Schaffer and K.J. O'Connor (eds) *Handbook of Play Therapy*. New York: John Wiley and Sons. Chapter 5 (pp.95–127).

Heitzmann, W.R. (1974) *Educational Games and Simulations*. Washington, D.C.: National Education Association.

Hellersberg, E.F. (1955) Child's Growth in Playtherapy. *American Journal of Psychotherapy*. 9: 484–502.

Hickin, S. (1971) Play Therapy Groups. *Groups: Annual Review of the Residential Child Care Association*. 18:33–39.

Howard, J. (1970) *Please Touch*. New York: McGraw Hill.

James, M. and Jongeward, D. (1975) *The People Book*. Menlo Park, California: Addison-Wesley.

Jeffs, M. (1982) *Manual for Action*. London: Action Resources Group.

Johnson, T.C. (1989) *Let's Talk About Touching.* Philadelphia: Child's word/Child's play, Centre for Applied Psychology.

Kraft, I.A. (1989) 'A Selective Overview'. In F.J.C. Azima and L.H. Richmond (eds) *Adolescent Group Psychotherapy Monograph 4.* American Group Psychotherapy Association Madison: International Universities Press.

Lennox, D. (1982) *Residential Group Therapy for Children.* London: Tavistock Publications.

Lewis, H.R. and Streitfeld, H.S. (1973) *Growth Games.* London: Sphere.

Lockwood, J.L. (1981) 'Treatment of Disturbed Children in Verbal and Experiential Group Psychotherapy'. *International Journal of Group Psychotherapy.* 31(3): 355–366.

Loftus, M. (1988) 'Moving to Change: Action Groups in an Out-Patient Setting'. *Journal of Adolescence.* 11: 217–229.

Mallery, B. and Navas, M. (1982) 'Engagement of Preadolescent Boys in Group Therapy: Video Tape as a Tool'. *International Journal of Group Psychotherapy.* 32(4): 453–467.

Moreno, J.L. (1948) *Psychodrama.* New York: Beacon House.

Nelson, D. (1992) Pathways. (Personal Communication).

O'Connor, J.J. and Hoorwitz, A.N. (1988) 'Imitative and Contagious Magic in the Therapeutic Use of Rituals with Children'. In E., Imber-Black, J. Roberts and R. Whiting (eds) *Rituals in Families and Family Therapy.* New York: W.W. Norton and Co. pp.(135–157).

Orlick, T.D. (1978) *The Co-operative Sports and Games Book.* New York: Pantheon Books.

Ornstein, R. and Thompson, R.F (1984) *The Amazing Brain.* Boston: Houghton Mifflin.

Panmure House (1978) *So You Think You Can Play Games?* A Handbook of Group Games and Techniques. Panmure House.

Peller, L.E. (1955) 'Libidinal Development as Reflected in Play'. *Psychoanalysis.* 3(3): 3–11.

Perls, F.S. (1974) *Gestalt Therapy Integrated.* New York: Vintage Books.

Perls, F.S., Hefferline, R.F. and Goodman, P. (1973) *Gestalt Therapy.* Harmondsworth: Penguin.

Phillips, H. (1960) *Pan Book of Card Games.* London: Pan Books.

Rainbow House (1989) *The Rainbow Game.* Warner Robins, GA: Rainbow House Children's Resource Centre.

Roberts, J. (1988) 'Setting the Frame: Definition, Functions and Typology of Rituals'. In E., Imber-Black, J. Roberts and R. Whiting (eds) *Rituals in Families and Family Therapy.* New York: W.W. Norton and Co. pp.3–46.

Rogers, C. (1973) *Encounter Groups.* London: Pelican–Penguin.

Rose, S.D. (1972) *Treating Children in Groups.* San Francisco: Jossey-Bass.

Rose, S.D. and Edleson, J.L. (1987) *Working with Children and Adolescents in Groups*. San Francisco: Jossey-Bass.

Ross, A.L. and Bernstein, N.B. (1976) 'A Framework for the Therapeutic Use of Group Activities'. *Child Welfare*. 56: 776–786.

Schaefer, C. (1987) *Therapeutic Uses of Childhood Games*. New York: John Wiley and Sons.

Scheff, T.J. (1979) *Catharsis in Healing, Ritual and Drama*. Berkeley and Los Angeles: University of California Press.

Schulz, W. (1973) *Here Comes Everybody*. London: Penguin.

Slavson, S.R. (1945) 'Differential Methods in Relation to Age Levels'. In: M. Schiffer (ed) (1979) *Dynamics of Group Psychotherapy*. New York: Jason Aronson. pp.567–583.

Slavson, S.R. and Schiffer, M. (1975) *Group Psychotherapies for Children: A Textbook*. New York: International Universities Press.

Soo, E.S. (1985) 'Applications of Object Relations Concepts to Children's Group Psychotherapy'. *International Journal of Group Psychotherapy*. 35(1): 37–47.

Steiner, C. (1974) *Scripts People Live: Transactional Analysis of Life Scripts*. New York: Grove Press.

Taylor, A. (1976) *Pub Games*. London: Mayflower Books.

Vinter, R. (1974) 'Program Activities: An Analysis of Their Effects on Participant Behaviour'. In P., Glasser, R. Sarri and R. Vinter (eds) *Individual Change Through Small Groups*. New York: Free Press.

Yalom, E. (1970) *The Theory and Practice of Group Psychotherapy*. New York: Basic Books.

Zakich, R. (1975) *The Ungame*. Anaheim: The Ungame Company.

CHAPTER 10

Art Psychotherapy Groups

Tessa Dalley

In this chapter it is my intention to explore the theoretical and practical issues that arise when working with groups of children using art materials. By describing first my own professional orientation and approach and the setting in which I work, the scene will be set for some discussion around the issues that are raised in the description of clinical case material and group process which might, I hope, stimulate further debate and discussion.

Introduction

Art therapy is now an established profession and is gaining recognition of its importance in work with children. The images or art objects made in the session provide the means through which the children in therapy can begin to communicate and make sense of their feelings and experience, within the safe confines of the relationship with the therapist. Most children have some difficulty in articulating verbally their feelings, thoughts and concerns, as their command of language might not be as sophisticated as that of an adult. Using images in therapy offers a non-verbal 'language' for those children whose difficult behaviour might be an indication of some distress or unhappiness. Most art therapists work within a psychodynamic framework using transference and counter transference, both in the understanding of the relationship to the therapist and in terms of the image produced (Dalley 1984, Dalley *et al.* 1987, Case and Dalley 1992, Schaverien 1992).

Some recent literature documents clearly the work of art therapists working with individual clients and the use of art materials as a central focus for the therapeutic process (Case and Dalley 1990, Simon 1992). Working in art therapy groups, and the different models that have been established in art therapy practice, have been explored extensively in the literature (Waller 1992, Case 1990, McNeilly 1984, 1987, Liebmann 1986). In particular, the literature has focused on the debate within the profession as to the merits of directive or non directive ways of working. McNeilly (1984) using a group analytic model argues strongly for the conductor to allow the theme to emerge through the group images, whereas others such as Liebmann (1986) prefer to offer a more structured framework in which themes are provided for the group to work with. For the full discussion of this argument see Case and Dalley (1992) and Waller (1993).

In a recent publication Waller (1993) examines in depth many different ways of working in art therapy groups and outlines the theoretical orientation for the work. She makes the point, however, that most of the literature about working with children is concerned with individual work and that the work that is currently in process with children in groups is less well documented. 'Art Therapy would seem to offer an excellent opportunity for interaction as children readily use materials, and do so spontaneously, except in rare cases where they are very withdrawn and inhibited and need special encouragement. Interestingly, the most recent book about art therapy and children in Britain; *Working with Children in Art Therapy* (1990) focuses almost entirely on individual art therapy sessions' (Waller 1993). She goes on to refer to an account of an art group with dyslexic children in a school for children with learning difficulties (Fielden 1990).

That there is a lack of information on group work with children is a useful point and it is hoped that this publication, devoted to group work with children and adolescents, will go some way to rectify this. Some documentation of art therapy group work with children in schools can be found and has been established for some years (Dalley *et al.* 1987, Case and Dalley 1992) but this approach has been slower to develop in other settings. The origins of group work in schools is easy to understand as children can often be readily identified as needing help because of disruptive, aggressive and other types of anti-social behaviour within their peer group at school. To work in a small therapeutic group situation enables them to reflect and think about their responses to each other and provides a structure to help to work through these problems. Using art materials and making things either together or separately in the group gives the children an opportunity to explore aspects of competition, leadership, and dominance in a group and also their feelings of anger, envy, rivalry that this intense interaction brings to the surface.

Waller (1993) suggests that the reasons for having a group with children and adolescents are much the same as for having a group with adults. 'It is a very different experience from being in the classroom'. Foulkes and Anthony (1965 p.190) make the point that age and natural group formation to some extent dictate the therapeutic techniques used with children and it is essential, they argue, that therapists familiarise themselves with the developmental phases of childhood and the sequential changes that occur in the child's intellectual, emotional, social, moral and linguistic spheres. The importance of this will become clear in the examples given later in the chapter.

Theoretical framework of Art Psychotherapy groups

Before looking at the detailed clinical material, it might be helpful to think about the theoretical framework in which these groups operate. As Waller (1992) suggests, most groups are based on the assumption that, if we accept that patterns of behaviour are learned, it is possible to unlearn or relearn more effective or rewarding ways of being. There is much to be learned from interpersonal interaction within the boundaries of a group. Bloch and Crouch (1987) state 'there is a fundamental therapeutic factor which is a direct consequence of interaction, variously labelled as interpersonal learning and learning from interpersonal action. As these labels imply, we are concerned with a learning process in which the emphasis is on learning from actual experience; more specifically from new efforts – tantamount to experimentation – at relating to others' (p.68).

Two important aspects of groups are identified by Yalom (1975). One is that of the group as a social microcosm which resembles customary everyday functioning in which patients tend to behave in their usual maladaptive way. It is by observing and drawing attention to these behaviour patterns in the group that the therapist and other group members can have a 'corrective emotional experience', thus helping each other to change. Bloch and Crouch (1987) summarise this process 'The patient takes the risk emboldened by the group's supportive structure of expressing some strong emotions to one or more group members, including, perhaps the therapist. Within the context of the here and now, the protagonist is able to reflect on the emotional experience he had undergone and to become aware, with the aid of fellow members how appropriate his actions were. This awareness paves the way for an improvement in interpersonal relating' (p.77).

Before describing the use of art therapy groups in particular, it is worth summarising the list of curative factors outlined by Waller which relates to most interactive groups. These are giving and sharing of information, installation of hope and seeing how others have benefited; the members of the group help each other and they discover that others have the same problems, anxieties and fears. The small group acts as a reconstruction of the family and members can use each other to work out feelings about family members with a multiplicity of transference relationships. Catharsis can occur when a member confesses to a state of mind which they had previously hidden, to desires and fantasies they had been deeply ashamed of, or relives a traumatic event in the group, which might bring great relief. Members can learn how they interact with others and have some feedback about this, and the group is valued by its members as a safe place where deepest feelings can be shared without fear or retribution and where confidence is kept and trust established. The group provides an opportunity for the past to be re-played in the present with the opportunity for feedback and change. All these features can be seen in the following case material.

Art Psychotherapy groups

If the overall aim of group therapy is for children to uncover unconscious feelings and understand how these affect their lives in the here and now, we need now to look at how the presence of images in the group can greatly enhance the work of a group. Maclagan (1985) makes the basic assumption that art therapy is a kind of net for images and that the images have meaning and value not only for the person who created them but also for the group. The images do not have to be aesthetically pleasing; they may, in fact, be chaotic, aggressive, unstable or impersonal, or contain, 'psychotic' features. The image has to be looked at and accepted for what it is, first by the person who made it. The structure of the art therapy group provides a frame within which feelings, and fantasies, can be discovered and communicated without being depersonalised.

What makes an art therapy group essentially different from a verbal group is that at some point each member becomes 'separated' from the group to work individually on the process of art making. As Case and Dalley (1992) point out, 'this has a profound shaping on the group dynamics and on the art object formed' (p.196). They continue 'All groups express a tension between dependence, the desire to merge into a group identity, and separation, a wish to express individual difference. Art therapy groups uniquely differ from verbal groups in having a structure which can give time and space for each side of this tension to be explored' (p.196).

Case and Dalley (1992) explore in some depth the different types of children's groups by giving illustrated case materials indicating various possibilities of working. They first describe working with individuals within a group in which the art therapist will be working with the group, but informed by individual psychological theory rather than group theory. They also describe working with the individual, and the group process in which there is more emphasis on the group process, and feel that both these ways of working are best suited to the needs of pre-latency and latency children. By keeping to the boundaries of time and space, and consistent behaviour, the group will come to build up a trust in this symbolic space for them to explore feelings and anxieties and the developing relationships in the group. The art therapist is working analytically with transference phenomena, both interpersonally and through the pictures. The history and development of each art object and the general atmosphere in the group can be understood in terms of group dynamics by observing the children's working processes. How the children place themselves in the room in relation to the therapist, and to each other, is an important factor in the communication to the therapist about transference phenomena.

There is a special quality in painting with others, as it is an experience that offers time alone while being in the presence of others. It offers opportunity for transferences to early relationships through memories of playing in the presence of an adult. While making art objects, individuals withdraw internally to express themselves in the space of their choice; there is also opportunity for physical interaction with other children in the group.

In this way, the child is able to express and maintain individuality while still identifying and working with the group. Children in art therapy groups are more able to control how much they are active and to which part they actively contribute. They can participate with a 'speaking picture' without actually speaking. They may actively help the other members to explore their images while their own has no time for attention that week. Working with a concrete medium in a group means that everyone will have been seen even if they do not speak. When the paintings are discussed there will be an immediate 'here and now' reaction to the painting receiving the focus. Part of this will be an 'aesthetic' response. This is complex, because an individual painting will be seen in the field of other art objects, all influencing each other visually, and each child's perception of them. Each person in the group will be reacting interpersonally as well as interpictorially. Pictures may be attracting or repelling them. They will also be projecting into them as well as into other group members (Case and Dalley 1992). Once the group is established, the group can be open to explore the images in depth and allow both a personal and a group meaning. The group culture is based on the way that the images are formed and worked with and how this is facilitated by the therapist. Meanings can be understood in terms of group process. The therapist will comment on this and also on how the images contain these group dynamics both in terms of the individuals and the group as a whole.

Illustrated examples of Art Psychotherapy groups for children

These groups are called 'Art Psychotherapy groups' because of the use of art within a group psychotherapeutic framework. As I have had experience of running groups with children in schools along the lines described by Case and Case (1990), I decided to introduce a similar resource into the setting of the Child and Parent department within a clinic which is a consultation and therapy centre for both children and adults. As the art therapist working within a multi-disciplinary team, my work involves both individual and group work in art therapy, as well as working alongside colleagues for assessment and family work.

At the moment two separate groups are running concurrently, and the work is undertaken with a co-therapist, one of whom is a child psychotherapist, the other an art therapy trainee. Both groups have been running for two years using the same model and it has been very useful to be able to compare them when thinking about parallels of themes, developmental stages and other similar features that have emerged over time. On several occasions, similar themes and issues have arisen for both groups and this will be explored here in some detail. The groups are held regularly, at the same time each week for one hour in the school term. The membership is four children who are between the ages of five and eleven. Group members are not matched according to age or sex as the age range tends to set up a sibling type of relationship as if in the family. For example, one child who is eleven and might be the 'baby' of his family can experience being the 'oldest' and being looked up to in the group by the younger members. Similarly, a six-year-old who is the eldest of a large number of younger siblings can benefit greatly from being seen as the youngest, or the baby, and these 'baby' needs are given some special attention as a result. It is very interesting how, during intense moments in the group's interaction, sibling relationships are unconsciously re-enacted, even to the extent of using the sibling's name by mistake. This is very useful material for the group and jealous, competitive, rivalrous feelings can be explored openly.

Referrals for the group are received through the normal channels of the clinic and are often from educational psychologists, social workers and GPs. It might be that the clinic gets a referral and the team feels it might be appropriate for the group and, in this case, the referral would be discussed with the referrer and then the parents and child concerned. All new referrals are met (with their parents) by the therapists to discuss the group, and whether they feel it is appropriate treatment for their child's difficulties, and general concerns are explored fully at this initial stage.

We have found that children who can most benefit from these groups tend to display problems with peer relationships, aggressive or disruptive behaviour in class or in the playground and, generally, difficulties with anti-social behaviour when in groups. Often these children are able to show that they can behave and function well with the individual attention of an adult, either with mother, a special teacher or a close one-to-one relationship. The problems arise when the adult's back is turned or they are for some reason unavailable; the child finds himself in difficulty and gets into trouble at these unattended moments. Treatment within a group is therefore more appropriate than individual therapy, as the actual interactions of the children can be observed and noted by the group as a whole, which helps the child come to some understanding by being able to reflect on those responses which occur at times when they feel uncontained. Interpretations by the therapists on the group dynamics and individual processes help to build a foundation for looking, but also for change.

The children are asked to make a commitment to the group for a year and this is regularly reviewed on a termly basis. Parents or people in the most immediate care of the child meet together with the therapists once a term to share thoughts about how the group is going and in this sense are required to support the treatment. As the space is confidential, content of the work is not disclosed but general process and developments in the child's behaviour are thought about. Regular network meetings with the school, the head teacher and class teacher, helps an understanding of progress in terms of relationships in class and in the playground. It is often the case that these children have emotional difficulties which are expressed by these behavioural problems, which in turn prevent them functioning well at school and achieving at an age appropriate level. This leads to all sorts of negative stereotypes within the child's mind and sometimes within the peer group. Frequent discussions with the school, to which the parent will be invited, help to consider all these various difficulties of the child together. We have found it essential that the support structure is maintained outside the immediate area of the group experience, as this helps the child integrate what he takes from the group into his wider experience of his life at home and at school.

Support for the child in the group is also maintained by a commitment from parent or guardian to take responsibility for transport to and from the group. This reinforces the sense of containment and it is helpful for both child and parent to support the treatment in this way. We encourage the children to communicate with the group if for any reason they cannot attend. Regular attendance is expected as it is the commitment to the group over time that creates the group identity, builds cohesion, feelings of belonging and safety for the child so that the full effect of the group process can take place. The groups are held in the art therapy room, in which a wide range of art materials are available to enable the children in the group to communicate together and facilitate some degree of understanding by reflecting on this interaction. By looking at the dynamics of the group and how it evolves from week to week, the children can think about their experience, behaviour, feelings and the effect these have on each other. They can even discover they are not alone in their situation and their responses; problems can be shared and attempts are made to work these through rather than the more common experience of school or family, where a child might be disciplined by sending them away from the original scene in which the problem arose. The group is, therefore, helping each child with their individual responses to situations but also allowing them the opportunity to develop and consolidate their relationship with peers. This involves trust, openness and at times quite complicated emotions, which can be addressed.

The group becomes a safe space in which the children feel they belong and can express their deepest difficulties and anxieties. For this to happen, it is essential to establish strong boundaries for the group to function as a good enough container for these difficult feelings. The group starts and finishes on time, there are strict rules about not hurting each other and not damaging anything in the room. There has to be respect for the room and the materials, in that the room has to be cleaned by the group for other people's use.

During the hour, the children arrive and usually immediately begin to play, paint or make things within the room. There is no set theme or subject and the children are free to work with whatever art materials they choose. As they are aware of the group rules about their use they are quick to point out to each other if there is some misuse of the room or materials. During this time the children freely interact and the group workers comment either on individual process or a group dynamic which addresses the behaviour in the group at the time. After three quarters of an hour, there is thinking time for ten minutes, during which the children are asked to think about what they have made and share their images, together. There is five minutes allocated for clearing up before the end of the group. Within this structure, themes and issues emerge which are either pertinent to the individual or the group as a whole and so we try and work with both, indicating how each connects with the other. The images made in the group always stay in the group room and under no circumstances can any aspect of the materials or the objects made be taken away. This is to reinforce the sense of safe keeping by the therapists and this particular group boundary is often the one which is tested the most. They can look at them from week to week but nothing comes into the room and nothing leaves it. This is a fundamental limit that should be made at all times when working with art materials in therapy.

Case examples

As the content of the on-going group remains confidential, one way of describing what happens is to discuss process and themes that have emerged over the two years the groups have been running. Group A is a group of three boys and one girl. Two of the boys have been in the group for two years and so feel that they are the 'older' ones, which in fact they are chronologically. They are eleven and nine – the 'newcomers' are seven and five. The arrival of a girl in the group caused great anticipation on behalf of the older boys and her arrival caused a change in their behaviour within the group, as they began some overt sexual display in their fight for her attention. The competition between the group members tends to be expressed in terms of their anxieties about their sexuality and the approaching onset of puberty. They played mating games with the toy animals, which were paired together with a lot of giggling and embarrassment. In their play together, there was an element of horseplay in showing off for her and in this sexual anxieties and preoccupations were expressed. They wanted to talk about it, but they didn't and this ambivalence is expressed in many of the drawings, painting and clay figures which they associate with their genitals. On example of this occurred when the youngest boy was making a clay object and the oldest said loudly to him 'that looks like your willy'. The younger boy, not yet ready to explore his sexuality so openly, immediately changed the shape of his model. Here we have one child moving into latency and the other just emerging into his pre-adolescent state and gives an example of how the different ages and stages in the group can work together.

Meanwhile, the girl remained silent and strong and manipulated the boys so that she had what she wanted. After her arrival, squirting paint onto paper became a new activity in the group. This was initially co-operative when they played a game of folding the paper and together they felt the paint through it. One of the boys explored intimate feelings of 'finding himself in the womb' as his picture reminded him of the womb and brought up feelings of being inside. For him the experience of being an only child was explored, as well as being 'the only' child which seems to be the root cause of his attention seeking and demanding disruptive behaviour. Sharing the attention of the group leaders is hard for him to bear and yet he does not know how to take it for himself. For the girl and the older boy, this led to the exploration of their sibling relationships – the girl has an older brother and the boy a younger sister and this was pointed out in the process of this interaction. The younger boy, who joined most recently, met with an intensely hostile response from the two older boys to which he responded by physically attacking them back. There followed what felt like uncontrollable chaos and at its height the group workers found it impossible to be heard, and so they spoke to each other across the group about what they thought was going on. This had the immediate effect of stopping the children as if they were listening to parents. The dispute seemed to be rooted in the deep anxiety and threat of a new sibling/baby in the family, and the need for reassurance that this had not separated the couple/parents, as when this link was made there was the feeling of tangible relief.

Talking to each other rather than to the children was a response by the group workers in an attempt to hold the situation together. Many times in the group, there has been near deterioration into 'anarchy' as the limits are tested and the boundaries have to be held firm by the group workers. As these strong emotions are felt and expressed in the group, it is not surprising that these kind of responses are made by the children, but in the heat of the moment it is hard to make these rationalisations as the therapists experience it as emotional battering. The strain of holding this together has led to some disagreements between the two therapists about strategy, management, and approach, as if we were two parents fighting about the management of their family. The under-lying dynamic is that the therapists are taking on a lot of the children's fury with their own parents. Once this was made conscious we became aware that this split in fact was what the children most desired but yet most feared. Three out of the four children have only one parent and so their experience of 'two parents' in the group is a difficulty with which they struggle and their unconscious response to it is to attempt to recreate the split. It has been their early experience that conflict, which usually involves them, has the effect of destroying the relationship between two adults, and the group provides the forum for the re-enactment and renegotiation of this fundamental issue. It is noticeable that the absence of one therapist – with illness, for example – tends to make the group more co-operative and less anxious on one level, as this is their 'normal' experience of one parent relating. But at a deeper level, the anxiety is very high, with questions concerning the whereabouts of the other therapist – have they made her ill or driven her away as is the case with their own family situation, about which they feel guilty and to some extent responsible. These painful issues therefore surface and are explored.

As the children usually lack male role models, this manifests itself in the group by attempts to disregard limits, particularly at the beginning of the group, and the continual need to test them out. This is compounded by the difficulties of managing their aggressive feelings. This has the effect of throwing up a 'father' figure between the two therapists, who tends to take on the role of setting the limits and being the 'policeman' or the 'superego' figure. This is continually talked through and addressed in the group and also within the therapists' own supervision. It needs to be clearly thought about in terms of why this polarity or split takes place in the group and the unconscious expression of the need for 'absent' father. Connected with this, the two younger children who joined the group last were persistently late, as if they were trying to find their place in the group, and it was felt that they were coupled together in this to defend against the impact of the group tension. This led to a continual dynamic of coupling and, where two members would pair up, this would be followed by an episode that attempted to disrupt this. For example, with the two who had similar sibling relationships, this was disrupted by the older boy and when this was commented on by the therapist, he attempted to couple with the younger boy to defend against the pain of the couple. As an only child himself, with a close relationship with mother, to experience couples is very painful for him and so he disrupts them, but then attempts to couple with the other member to defend against this pain. At the end of one particular session, he became so disruptive that he had to be excluded from the group (exclusion means standing outside the door until he feels ready to join the group in a calm manner, a strategy that is resorted to in times of unmanageable behaviour on the part of any member of the group and this is understood by all members). This was understood as his need to defend against his intense anxiety about the known absence due to holiday of one of the therapists the following week. The pain of one parent, or lack of couple and the sense of desperately missing father was uncontainable.

There is always the need to help the children reflect on their behaviour and the painful feelings that it is necessary to think about if some progress to be made. The older two children have a greater capacity to articulate their feelings verbally and so they tend to dominate the space in the group. This makes it more difficult for the others to be able to express their particular concerns and difficulties. As a result, the younger two members tend to make use of their picture-making more; both have a rich imagination and use the painting, colouring and clay work to 'speak' for them. If they do take space and seek attention, it is hard for the older ones to allow them to do this and there are great efforts made to help them look at their envious attacks – the fact that they so badly need 'mother's' attention (which has never been enough for them) that they cannot tolerate others having it. This is intensified as the breaks approach and the last but one session culminated in one of these older children weeping painfully about his father and the other disrupting this so severely that he had to be excluded while the other was allowed to take the space in the group. However, this was felt to be unsatisfactory as the feelings must be literally and metaphorically contained in the room, and so exclusion was a compromise and did not allow the excluded child the possibility of being able to take in exactly how unbearable it was for him to hear this particular problem that was so connected to his own experience. One child was articulating the problem for the whole group, in a sense, and yet to hear it is so difficult that disruptive behaviour is the response, as a way of getting out of it. This sets up the real difficulty in terms of managing the group – does one allow the space to be disrupted, giving no one the opportunity to express real concerns, or does the disruptive child have to be removed to allow one child the space? These dilemmas are constantly addressed in these groups.

During this episode, however, the younger child made a fascinating image out of clay which he had worked on over several weeks. He finished this during the last group before Christmas, saying it was a Christmas cake with a cherry on top (Figure 10.1). The likeness to a breast is striking and it was discussed

Figure 10.1

in terms of needing to maintain links during the holiday period – connections to mummy, the group and holding the group together. A most important statement for the group which was experiencing such difficulty in feeling nurtured and cared for, and needed to disrupt things and break things for the attention. For the child himself, this could be an expression of needing to be fed, or feeding the group, and this is one example of many that can be seen to be an image which has personal meaning for the child but is also an expression of the group unconscious process.

One aspect of the management is how to work with the child who is taking on the disruptive role for the group. If one child is taking on the disturbance for the group this is usually demonstrated in his behaviour in the group, through his use of materials, spilling, messing, not clearing up and so on. What has to be understood is how the other children might be channelling their own aggression through this child and he is taking this on and acting it out for the group. In the example just given, the disruptive child might be taking on the aggressive, disruptive aspects for the boy who was then able, calmly and sensibly, to construct such a nurturing image. This is very common among groups and we try to help the child taking on this role, who is often quite vulnerable inside, to enable him to distinguish between his own anger and what is other people's. Fights in the playground are often about children taking on the fight for others, feeding into their own aggression, which is then inappropriately displaced and acted out.

In discussion between the therapists in the supervision, it has been suggested that the group as a whole should be asked how to manage this. That is, they should be consulted and drawn into thinking for the group by addressing the problem facing the group. If the therapist is always seeming to be taking on the task of interpretation, then the group does not take on any responsibility for itself as a whole, or the individual feelings that are being expressed. To share the feelings is a way of owning them for themselves and we have found this to be a valuable way of working. This was seen to be useful particularly for one of the older boys, who is now much more able to think for the group, think about the other children's experience and empathise with them, and anticipate the therapists' comments, so that he is taking that role on for himself and the group. His newly developed capacity to do this has changed his behaviour within the group substantially, and in discussion with school and mother, it seems things have improved a great deal. From being one of the most out of control, disruptive, attention seeking members of the group, he is beginning to be able to take in and internalise the group model of relating and acceptance of difference and can negotiate his relationships so that he can function more appropriately within a group setting, both in our group and in the classroom. We will be working towards his leaving after one more term.

This demonstration of being able to work within a group of peers is tangible evidence of internal shifts made by the child so that he feels able to function in a group without the need to disrupt or seek attention, and generally can bear the attention of one adult being shared among others. The approach of the group concentrates mainly on the unconscious processes that are surfacing for the individual and the group, and such processes as projection, mirroring, splitting and projective identification can all be seen to be operating and are commented on by the therapists where appropriate. This psychoanalytic approach and intensive exploration of internal feelings, fantasies and fears can sometimes be placed in balance by reference to outer world phenomena which helps place the group in context for the child in his outer world. For example, one child persists in copying pictures from magazines, as he feels his inner world to be so empty and devoid of interest that he cannot 'do' anything else. When another child offers the explanation of imagination, it becomes clear to this child that the paucity of his image mirrors his empty life experience, devoid of love and care, which is a painful situation to come to terms with. Acceptance of this, however, can be therapeutic. This same child, whose clumsiness and physical uncoordination is symptomatic of his sense of neglect, once knocked a picture of the wall in the room and the glass smashed on the floor. We looked at his and the group's response but we also tried to explore with him what his

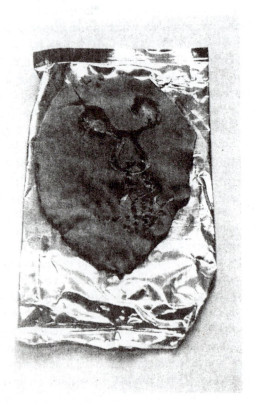

Figure 10.2

expected response was – that is, what would mother have said if this incident had happened at home. This helps the child look internally, work within the group but also think about outside and links to home.

Running two unconnected groups has brought up an interesting similarity in the themes and issues that arise. In both groups, sweets and money were brought in as a way of testing what can be brought to the group. These were put on a shelf until the end of the group and the point is made that the children feel the need to bring these as security, something of their own, feeling the need to feel powerful or have more than the others. Both groups develop either interactive or group projects, or some children find space for their own process and work separately on their own for most of the session and talk about their work by sharing it with the group at the end. One such child in Group B, which is made up of four boys all aged between seven and nine, feels the need to think about his father, and his experience of several tragic accidents that have happened to himself and his close family. Like the other boys in this group, he has no available father and so feels that the lack of this parent acutely relates to his problems of self confidence and uncontrollable outburst of aggression, particularly towards himself. He spends a long time drawing on his own, thinking about death and ghosts – which is how he experiences his father,

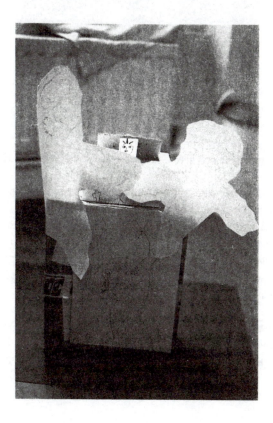

Figure 10.3

Figure 10.4

although he knows he still lives – it was other close relatives that were killed (Figure 10.2).

As a general theme, ghosts have reappeared several times in different ways, through models, life size drawings, cut outs from paper and the enactment of putting a towel over the head and making ghostly noises around the room. This can either be understood to be about an absent member of the group, if someone is away that week, but more generally perhaps expresses a deeper sense of absence or loss in their experience with the lack of parent or absent, inconsistent caring. (Figures 10.3 and 10.4)

We can see, therefore, that this image is expressing something for the group as well as something very important for the individual child. Within the group dynamic, however, this child's perceived withdrawal into his own world sometimes makes it difficult for him to be seen as part of the group. He is not often invited into their play, but as a result sometimes finds the others overdominant and intimidating. It is part of the group's work to allow him to feel acceptable to the group and yet able to disclose such painful material to them. How can he be seen as 'butch' masculine and strong, which is the image he wants to portray and is the reason for his aggressive behaviour, and at the same time express vulnerabilities and sadness in what is predominantly a 'macho culture' of the group. This tension was clearly expressed in his island that he made out of clay – with animals on it to protect him, but marooned and isolated and in danger of falling off to their death (Figure 10.5). It is equally important to look at this personal work within the group interaction, as others from the group can learn from his capacity to express and articulate his difficulties. This really helps the others in the group as they come to respect him for his openness and for risking his vulnerability to the group. Conversely, when the group enters into a group game as they frequently do from week to week (in this case it was a base made out of the furniture, turning round the chairs, and an army base changed into a place where sex happened, to a hiding place for them) the continuation of this game enabled this child to participate and experience group interaction. The absent father (this child's father was a soldier) again sets up difficulties about dominance and competitiveness, and they also explored what it is like to be a father, have sex and babies, all of which was discussed in this base.

Figure 10.5

In both groups these themes are frequently around, and in various ways the phallus shapes appear in the work and can be looked at in these terms. The boys feel relief to have their struggles recognised and understood and this gives way to a deeper anxiety about their own sexuality and capacity to be a man and their own sense of potency and virility. With unpredictable, often aggressive models of fathering, their concerns are around how to manage this and relate to it without copying it (Figure 10.6).

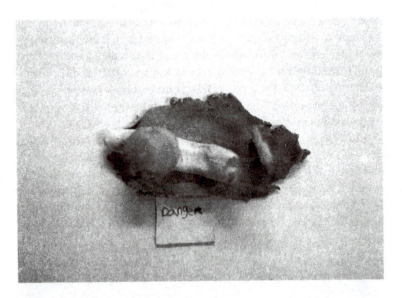

Figure 10.6

Another expression of this was a group activity that started as Christmas decorations as the boys, excited about Christmas and also anxious about the break, needed to leave their mark in the room. On the understanding that it would be taken down at the end of the session, they spent the whole time in negotiation how to do this, with the most dominant child taking control as usual. His potency in the group is a threat to others and they react in different ways. One is compliant, helpful and follows him; the child struggling with his vulnerability tends to switch off and do his own thing, usually playing with the easel as if a machine gun/phallic symbol; and the other, a withdrawn child who has difficulty with his self image because of his overweight, joins in, but in his own way. As can be seen by the photograph (which was taken with permission of the whole group as a way of 'preserving' the image) the balls are hanging down but the long thin shapes in the background have this child's name on – as if to state he has his own penis and he will make it show just as much as the others, without making the noise and the need for domination of the group that the others are involved with. This was useful for him and the whole group to think about, and is a good example of how the group theme emerges and can involve individual processes within it (see Figure 10.7).

Another activity that emerged for both groups was the need to make a web within the group room. This involved yards of string and sellotape stretching from wall to wall and the whole group joined into the activity with relish. In one group this culminated in tying one of the therapists to her chair as if ensnared by the web. In both situations, connections were made to making it safe, to using the whole room as container and finding the limits of the room, and ensnaring and catching the therapists as a spider would a fly. Both groups felt the need to stick to the therapists, which would enable them never to be separate.

Figure 10.7

Other sorts of enactment, which are more subtle interactions, occur – such as emulation of one member by another. The child just described, who used the sessions more for his own process, is working towards connecting to the others, playing with them and communicating with them within the group. This image shows a tentative gesture towards copying another. The image is not so complete and was heavily criticised by the group for not being finished or 'so good', until it was pointed out what was going on. This child was taking a big risk in trying to get closer, physically painting closely to him on the floor, and it was pointed out that he can't be the same but that he was trying to get close. The child he was trying to connect with also found this an uncomfortable experience. He was an only child, a natural follower and complied generally with the dominant force in the group. When others in the group made a move towards him, he tended to move away, as he found it difficult to share both in play and in emotional space. He would find solace in his own activity. So to find himself the focus of someone else's attention was uncomfortable, but he could not move away from it, as he had been copied in a concrete way in the image. The image was a record of this and an important experience for both of them. For one, that some one can look up to him as an individual and want to be like him was a new experience, and for the other to be able to survive this without ridicule

Figure 10.8

Figure 10.9

and obscurity and blending into others' worlds was very useful for both of them. (Figures 10.8 and 10.9)

Figure 10.10

Other pertinent examples are shown in Figures 10.10, 10.11 and 10.12. Figure 10 is one boy's experience of himself of being stuck together like a lot of different pieces into one big blob. He is small, very overweight and gets teased ruthlessly at school. However, his experience as a very small baby was of a series of serious operations which were life saving, but the result of this medical preoccupation has left little space for his real sense of identity to develop. This is a powerful statement of how he feels, placed on a box that says 'spare people'. Likewise, another more confident, dominant child makes the clay heads, again to explore his identity – who is he and how can he begin to explore his real feelings of insecurity and vulnerability when he presents these 'macho' masks to the outside world (Figure 10.11) The group acknowledges this and helps him explore it.

Figure 10.12 was made by the same child and, to look at it, it might make sense to think that he is trying to convey the same difficulties. How can he look inside his head if it is empty? However, the actual process that took place was as follows. Another child came to the group with a balloon, and after much pleading from this child, he was given it to make papier-mâché. He made it lovingly over two weeks, burst the balloon and made these two masks by breaking open the heads. It emerged in the discussion that he had witnessed his father head-butting his mother and this was a direct expression of it,

Figure 10.11

Figure 10.12

although unconscious at the time. It was the most containing experience for him to be able to express his traumatic experiences in the here and now and feel heard and understood through the use of his images.

Conclusion

These examples, I hope, illustrate the complexity and intensity of these groups. Unconscious material surfaces through images and words, actions and behaviour and it is the therapist's task to try and help the children make sense of this. Generally, the need to set strong limits makes the group a safe experience for intense and powerful feelings to be expressed and worked through. The groups are sometimes chaotic, disruptive, and full of aggression, or are reflective, sharing and empathetic experiences. The commitment to them by the children is striking and is well supported by the parent and the school. It is exhausting but rewarding work and it is to be hoped that more children will have the benefit of these groups in the future. The length of the waiting list, growing by the day, indicates that there is a great need for this kind of work. It can enable the child to learn how to be in groups and have a therapeutic experience that can easily translate to their normal living situation and also equip them for the many small and large groups in which they will have to cope in future life.

References

Bloch, S. and Crouch, E. (1987) *Therapeutic Factors in Group Psychotherapy.* Oxford: Oxford University Press.

Case, C. (1990) 'Reflections and Shadows: an Exploration of the World of the Rejected Girl'. In C. Case and T. Dalley (eds) *Working with Children in Art Therapy.* London: Tavistock/Routledge.

Case, C. and Dalley, T. (eds) (1990) *Working with Children in Art Therapy.* London: Tavistock/Routledge.

Case, C. and Dalley, T. (1992) *The Handbook of Art Therapy.* London: Routledge.

Dalley, T. (1984) *Art as Therapy: An Introduction to Art as a Therapeutic Technique.* London: Tavistock.

Dalley, T., Case, C., Schaverien, J., Weir, F., Halliday, D., Nowell Hall, P. and Waller, D. (1987) *Images of Art Therapy.* London: Tavistock.

Fielden, T. (1990) 'Art Therapy as Part of the World of Dyslexic Children'. In Liebmann, M. (ed) *Art Therapy in Practice.* London: Jessica Kingsley Publishers.

Foulkes and Anthony (1965) *Group Psychotherapy.* London: Penguin.

Liebmann, M. (1986) *Art Therapy for Groups.* London: Croom Helm.

Maclagan, D. (1985) 'Art Therapy in a Therapeutic Community'. *Inscape: Journal of Art Therapy* (Late edition): 7–8.

Acknowledgements

I would like to thank the clinical team in their continuing support for my work and particularly Rosalie Kerbekian and Bobby Lloyd who, as therapists, have informed my thinking and developed the work considerably.

McNeilly, G. (1984) 'Directive and Non-Directive Approaches in Art Therapy'. *The Arts in Psychotherapy.* 10(4): 211–219. (Reprinted in *Inscape*, December).

McNeilly, G. (1987) 'Further Contributions to Group Analytic Art Therapy'. *Inscape. Journal of Art Therapy.* (Summer): 8–11.

Schaverien, J. (1992) *The Revealing Image. Analytical Art Psychotherapy.* London: Routledge.

Simon, R. (1992) *Symbolism of Style.* London: Routledge.

Waller, D. (1993) *Group Interactive Art Therapy.* London: Routledge.

Yalom, I. (1975) *The Theory and Practice of Group Psychotherapy.* New York: Basic Books.

CHAPTER 11

Relaxation, Visualization and Nourishment

Fredi Harrison

Relaxation, visualization and nourishment are the methods I use to help people with high levels of anxiety and low levels of self-esteem. Anxiety and poor self-esteem often seem to go hand in hand, so that whilst people can learn to relax quite successfully, the benefits will usually be short-lived unless there is a programme of confidence-building running alongside.

I have begun to look at the methods I use now as anxiety replacement. I believe that anxiety is addictive and can be treated in much the same way as other addictions. I have been asked over and over again by my clients 'if I don't have anxiety, what will I have?'.

The fear of getting better can be quite crippling to the process and much work needs to be done to identify what anxiety can do *for* a person rather than *to* him. All of us have normal levels of anxiety which can be very useful in producing just enough adrenalin to spur us into action when we need to act. We need to run when endangered or dodge when something is about to fall and hit us. We need to steel ourselves to sing in a concert, or act in a play or go for an interview or, in my case write this chapter!

That rush of anxiety and excitement gives us a useful edge to our perform-ance and without it we may well appear too lackadaisical and casual. The people who come to me for help are experiencing that degree of colly-wobbles *all the time*. They don't feel relief when an event is over. The feeling may not be connected with an event at all. It is just there and it is exhausting. Exhaustion, though, does not bring sleep. In order to sleep peacefully one needs to be relaxed and one cannot relax when exhausted and so it goes on. The cycle begins and my job is to break into that pattern and to change it. This is where the difficulty lies.

I have noticed that people get 'hooked' on a 'stress buzz'. The feeling is so habitual that to take it away is like taking alcohol from an alcoholic or tobacco from a habitual smoker. The slow process of discovering what may be left is the meat of our therapy groups.

Learning to live with healthy levels of stress can be daunting. As soon as there is a common stress reaction in a person who has been the victim of crippling stress, he will immediately read that as a sign that he is going backwards to the horrifying state that was so familiar. But being so familiar, it may be almost more comfortable than the even keel and he may scrabble back to that state of fear. The sufferer may put himself into situations where he knows he will feel anxious in order to get the 'buzz'.

One of the best examples I had of this was Kevin, who was a roofer. He came for therapy because of general anxiety and panic attacks. His worst fear was heights. He had been given sick-leave from work because of his illness and did not have to climb any ladders in the normal course of that sick-leave. But every day he went to the site and climbed the ladder. He called it 'testing'. Sometimes, though, the panic attack stultified him and he could not go up. Then he went through so much self-disgust and withdrawal that he would feel suicidal.

I have noticed that when clients are experiencing stress at a peak they rarely think about killing themselves. They may cut themselves, bang their heads or pace or hop from foot to foot. Sometimes they will hug themselves and rock or clench their teeth and muscles. But when they start to feel less anxious and the withdrawal produces feelings of depression and worthlessness, they may feel like killing themselves and so as a helper I am watchful and vigilant at this time. Hence, there is a need for substitution for the anxiety state. The methods which I shall describe are all ways of looking after oneself without the anxiety drug.

I started this work in a family centre with a group of women, all of whom were experiencing a reactive form of anxiety – that is, anxiety following a particular incident. Some came because of problems in their relationships with children or partners. Some came because the day-to-day stress of having small children around had built up to screaming pitch. Most of them had skeletons in their cupboards from their childhoods and their coping mechanisms were framed by their early experiences.

I discovered that a mixture of relaxation and talking therapy seemed good for these women and so I devised a programme of yoga-type exercises with breathing, stretching, warming and deep relaxation. We did that for forty-five minutes each time and then we would sit up, drink tea and talk for a further forty-five minutes.

Because the immediate feelings of panic and fear had subsided, due to the relaxation, the talking took on a deep, pertinent, unhysterical note and people's voice tone was lowered as the body language became unthreatened and unthreatening. The deepest, most intimate secrets emerged and were talked about lovingly and carefully whilst the group grew closer together.

I had to run the group on a twelve week cycle which meant opening it up for new membership each time. There were the common problems of people not wanting to leave the group and so it became rather large at one point, but we never made anyone drop out and it found its own natural, safe level.

I believe, and do still, that we were treating the whole person with this method and when I have done body-work since, the response has always been immediate. Women who have had babies, especially, can feel bad about their bodies and this group was about acceptance, non-judging and hope. Many of the women were in their teens and were fairly traumatised by the physical and mental effects of having a baby. I worked with a colleague in the centre and trained her so that she was able to take on the group when I left the job. The group exists to this day (four years on) and membership remains high.

Since that time I have been running groups for anxiety release and stress management in a mental health unit. The unit is residential with day care facilities and is a half-way house. Some people there have been in hospital and are not ready to go back into the community and some are working hard to stay out of hospital.

The groups are made up of mixed ages and sex. The youngest member is seventeen and the oldest is nearly sixty. My experience to date has not included working in this way with groups of adolescents or children only. I have worked with very small children and their parents in a relaxation group and have taught baby massage as a form of anxiety release in a mother and baby clinic. I am certain that my methods would be applicable to groups of adolescents with very few adaptations. The timing of each section of the session may need to be shortened. The yoga-type exercises could be replaced with short bursts of more strenuous exercise for the release of excess energy before a controlled 'coming-down' and relaxation. The visualization and nourishment exercises would stay the same. I can only guess that a therapist using body-work with a group of adolescents will need to be prepared for much discussion about sex and sexuality. It just happens that the context for my work is one of groups of anxious people which includes older adolescents, young adults, middle-years and elderly. There are real benefits in 'family-type' age groups – not least, issues of identification and role-modelling.

The first group started as part of a whole programme for people living in or day visiting the unit. Clients were referred to the group by their key workers. They may have been attending other groups as well, such as art and craft, cookery, music making or community meetings and some people attended groups every day whilst others came for my group only.

I had about ten people to begin with and very little idea of what to expect, as I had asked not to be informed by the workers as to the nature of their clients' problems, having decided that I wanted to work with these people uninfluenced by other peoples' opinions or diagnoses. I started in a similar way to that in which I had worked in the family centre – relaxation followed by talking – but quickly realized that I was dealing with a much more varied and stressed group. As we talked, they told me and each other of their illnesses and treatments, their medication and their addictions. I had in any one group alcoholics, anorexics, bulimics, psychotics, schizophrenics – and these were just the conditions which they identified to me. I assumed (and I think rightly) that they would be the experts to teach me all about their conditions and so a two-way teaching process began. I taught them how to recognise and deal with their fears (real or fantasy) and they taught me how those fears came about and how the effects of medication and hospitalization could help or hinder some of the coping strategies I was advocating.

Between us we developed a new and more effective form of relaxation which involved visualization as part of the whole. We worked on the talking therapy as well – it was known as 'the talkie bit' – and found ways of dealing with specific issues through a series of what we called 'nourishment exercises'. I shall describe some of these in detail later (along with some visualizations and relaxations) but for now I shall describe them as alternative ways to nourish and nurture without recourse to food, drink, pills, spending money, cigarettes or any of the other methods which my group members had been using.

Sometimes people would find it hard to lie down on the floor or to have someone else lying next to them. One or two had special places in the room – near the door, near the window or near me. I would never insist that anyone lay down or, indeed, did anything they did not want to. There were two rules only, the first being absolute confidentiality. They promised each other that they would not talk about the group outside the group. All the business was done within the group and even though there were regular post-group tea-drinking sessions they were confined to general chat. Occasionally, someone might say that they had heard another member being somewhat free with their answer to 'well, what happens up there in that room?' but when it was brought to the group it was dealt with there.

The second rule was 'You may not hurt yourself or another person'. People were encouraged to describe the feelings of wanting to hit or kill another person or to hurt themselves rather than actually to do it and for some, expressing the feeling was a first. Much of the work was about having permission to experience a feeling and finding ways of appropriate expression.

Awareness of bodies and sensations became central to the work. One of my first observations about people in an acute anxiety state was how unaware of their bodies they seemed and how un-coordinated they were. People would often fall over, be wobbly, yawn uncontrollably or shake. They would be unaware that their shoulders were up by their ears and their fists tightly clenched. They would not pay attention to hunger or thirst and sometimes I would see a tongue cleave to the roof of a mouth. When we looked at the eating or drinking done by the person, only then would he become aware of not having drunk anything for a day or two.

So it was body work I started with and the tried and tested methods produced the expected results. When people are allowed to experience their bodies without shame, they open their minds to new thoughts and feelings as well. Gradually the group took on a life and grew. There was such a mix of people, with enormous spans between their stages of illness, that for a while the 'almost better' people seemed to help and encourage the fragile new referrals. In fact we reached a stage where I was able to rely on nine group members to look after themselves whilst I dealt with the tenth who was hospitalized immediately following the session.

Alice had stayed in hospital several times over the years and was making her way towards another crisis. I consider that she was one of the few people whom the group was unable to help. When she was well there were benefits for her in the group, but when she was very ill the group was detrimental to her and may have speeded up her progress towards breakdown. Her thoughts were by now so bizarre that any visualization I might do with the group was open to extreme and violent interpretation by Alice. When she finally went into rocking, wetting, shaking and moaning during a session, I was able to contain and hold her whilst asking the others to go down and make tea and to meet back in the group room in fifteen minutes. This they did and because they were able to use the rest of the session to explore their own fears of 'losing it like Alice did', the whole experience was one of learning and universality. One of the things I learnt was that I needed a co-worker!

There were no experienced groupworkers in the unit (on the staff) and so I agreed to train one of the key workers. I have had trainee co-workers ever since and have found that the link between them on the inside and me as a sessional worker has been useful.

The first group grew and changed. I was seeing clear signs that new, nervous people were finding it more difficult to come into a group of people who must have seemed perfectly well to them. We had crossed the bridge between experience being a help, to it becoming a barrier. The very poorly ones were slowing the progress of the nearly well ones as I always had to work at the level of the most anxious. We decided to split the group into 'oldies' and more recent comers.

The second group started in a similar way to the first but with a trainee co-worker from the start. This group was hard work. These people were unable to come straight into a room and lie down for relaxation. They needed an 'off-loading' session before anything else could happen.

Every week they would come in and together we would clear the chairs out of the room (the other group always did this automatically and without me). We would then talk about how much light to have in the room, depending on what they felt that day. After careful negotiations about positions and space for sitting or lying we would then do 'baggage', each person telling the group what was 'up top'. Having expressed their immediate anxieties and fears, they then managed to lie down and give in to my voice giving them permission to let go. Again, my visualizations were open to massive variations in interpretation by each person and the resonances fed back by them were fascinating. A whole sequence could be ruined for an individual if I invited them to take a drink of tea during an imaginary journey, when that person only ever drinks coffee! I learnt to adapt my language. I recognised people's inability to adjust, even in their heads, and I realized how desperately important was order and routine in the life of an anxious person. Casualness comes with calm and confidence. When all one's reference points seem topsy-turvy with the onset of stress, then accuracy and specifics assume an enormous importance. So now there is either tea or coffee offered in my visualization!

The difference in the kind of talk at the beginning of a session and that which comes after exercise and relaxation continues to astound and gratify me. When it works it really works. We have noticed that the immediate benefits are short term to start with, which is why I call the group 'anxiety release'. For one and a half hours per week each person will experience a change in his habitual feeling of tension. If the benefits are to last, the new sensation needs to become the habit and that takes time and practice. It also takes a great deal of catharsis and talking therapy to understand and cope with the guilt, trauma, life-scripting and despair that most anxiety sufferers carry about with them. These areas are where the major changes need to occur and unless they are worked with, there will be no long-term benefits form relaxation, visualization and nourishment.

Each person latches on to a particular part of a method and uses that part over and over again. Ray has panic attacks, mostly when he is driving his car. He has told me that he imagines me sitting on his shoulder telling him how to slow his breathing and how to make a 'body circuit' by joining the thumb and first finger. He can drive right through an attack now but knows that it is safest to stop the car whilst he deals with it.

I talk to the group about my giving them a bag of tools. There may be some which they never or rarely need to use. Those ones stay in the bag. Other tools will be taken out and used daily, and the more they are used the more faithful, trusty and familiar they become. Rosa frequently uses a strong, visual image involving removing the bricks in a wall, one by one when she feels stuck. Trish talks about climbing her own mountain until she reaches her summit and not attempting to climb other people's for them. All these images and techniques have developed within the group and then get passed around for other people.

Relaxation – Setting the scene

I shall attempt to describe my methods of teaching relaxation in such a way that it may be possible for other therapists to use them.

It is essential that you choose a room which is not a right of way to another, which has a closeable door with a sign on it to indicate that there must be no entry for the duration of the group, and which has a warm, comfortable surface on the floor. There should be no pictures or notices on the walls, no clock and as little noise as possible. You will need windows with curtains or blinds and enough floor space for people to lie down without touching another person and for each one to be able to stretch without touching the wall.

The room should be emptied of any furniture but small cushions should be available for head or back support if necessary. The environment must be taken seriously. The colour of a room can make tremendous differences to the response. My group room is a soft, warm pink. This is an ideal colour for relaxation. Warmth is a must and attention should be paid to heating and light.

As people enter the room there may be some general greeting and chat for a few minutes. If you are using the 'baggage exchange' method which I described earlier, then you would invite people to sit on the floor in a circle and would introduce the session with ground rules, timing, and any business which needs to be done before inviting the sharing process to begin. You may need to address each person by name and take turns, but as the group becomes more experienced you will find that someone just launches in and the exercise takes off by itself. After this you would ask the people to lie down for relaxation and they would make a wheel shape on the floor, each person being a spoke of the wheel with feet to the middle. It is interesting to ask people to make the wheel with heads towards the centre from time to time and report back their sensations afterwards.

If you are going straight into relaxation at the very beginning of the session, the only talk would be a negotiation about warmth, light levels and space. Otherwise you would invite group members to lie down immediately and then you may remind them of group rules, timing and the session plan.

Here are the words I use for relaxation. 'I want you to lie down on your back with your head in line with your feet so that your body is straight. Turn the backs of your hands to the floor with the palms uppermost and the fingers gently curling. Move your arms a little way from your body. By doing that you are opening your chest and allowing more air into your lungs. Tuck in your chin and make a long neck at the back, imagining someone pulling a hair at the crown of your head. Close your eyes if you feel safe but open them and have a look at the room if you need to.

Notice how much of your body touches the floor and then wriggle and shake your spine and hips so that more of your body touches. Feel your body weight on the floor. The muscles are softening, loosening and spreading over the carpet. The solid floor will hold and contain you. You cannot fall or be pushed, you are quite safe. Think of your body as if it had no bones. Imagine the body made of warm wax, melting and spreading. Breathe evenly, do not try to change your breathing.

Now, transfer your attention to listening to the sounds. Tune in to the sounds of your own body. Be aware of the other sounds in the room – other people breathing, tummies rumbling, my voice. Then listen to the sounds outside of this room and outside of the building. Do not resist the sounds. Learn to accept a certain amount of noise if it is inevitable. Much of relaxation is about accepting that which cannot be changed as well as changing that which is unacceptable.

Re-focus your attention towards your breathing. Notice your own slow breath in and out. With each breath in, think of renewal, strength, vitality. With every breath out, let go of the toxins, the worry, the bits you do not want. Yawn if you feel like it, yawning exaggerates the breath.

Take your attention back to your body weight. Notice how much of your body is touching the floor now. Bring your feet together, turn your toes up towards the ceiling, push through your heels. Feel the tension in your feet, just your feet. Hold it – and let go. Allow the feet to fall outwards again, floppy, like a rag-doll. Now do that with both legs. Tighten the muscles in your legs – your calves, thighs and around your knees tighten – then release. Let your legs fall outwards, heavy, and loose. Tighten your buttocks and suck in your tummy until it feels hollow, slowly, slowly release the muscles and feel them softening and spreading again. Rock and wriggle your hips from side to side, loosening and lowering the base of the spine. Do not push the spine into the floor, just let it fall naturally.

Think about your shoulders now and push the shoulder blades back and down into the floor. Feel your chest rising as you do that. Release them forward again and wriggle your shoulders down, away from your ears. Make a fist with both hands and tighten and straighten your arms. Lift them a little way off the floor and tense them until they shake. Let them go with a plop as they hit the floor and turn the backs to the carpet. Allow the fingers to curl again. Now spread the fingers as wide as you can as if you were stretching an octave on a piano. Think of each finger separately and really stretch the skin between each one. Very slowly allow the fingers to relax and curl again. You will feel a good tingling in your hands. Once again, tuck in your chin, straighten and wriggle your body, allow your feet and legs to fall outwards and then screw up your face, squeeze the muscles around your eyes, forehead, cheeks, chin and ears. Slowly relax the face. Imagine cool fingers massaging and smoothing the skin across the cheekbones and forehead.

Have a check around your body. If any part still needs your attention, take control of that by tensing and releasing. Otherwise, just lie still, enjoying the feeling of being totally relaxed.'

These words are spoken slowly, with long pauses when appropriate and with a very low voice tone.

Visualization

I use three types of visualization and each has a different application.

The first is really descriptive story telling. I provide all the detail. I ask the group to imagine that they are in a particular place, which I describe. I give them smells, temperature, colours, textures, sounds, sights, sensations and directions. I tend to choose real places and experiences that I have had so that my detail is accurate and there is a definite image of a real place and time. I may ask them to become children or even infants in their journeys and may invite them to take another person with them.

Of course the whole experience will be open to each person's interpretation, depending on their own life experiences and I do not believe for one moment that they see what I see in my head. This does not matter. In fact the free exchange of images and pictures which follows a descriptive visualization is stimulating, interesting and sometimes funny. I should point out here that the groups, although highly-charged and very serious in their aims, can be hilariously funny. We laugh a lot and much is changed through free and genuine laughter. This needs separating out from 'Gallows' laughter which is used frequently as a defence.

This fully descriptive story telling session comes at the end of every total relaxation and takes fifteen minutes, followed by time to talk afterwards.

The second form of visualization is less detailed and is truly fantastical, in that I provide a framework for a mythical/mystical journey and each member supplies his own colours, smells, atmosphere and people. Here are the words 'Imagine a large empty place and put yourself there. You are alone. As you gaze into the distance you see a person coming towards you. The person gets nearer. This person is your wise person and has a gift for you. You take the gift. The person leaves.

Now you are walking towards a hill. You climb that hill and at the top you find a well. There are steps down the side of the well and you start to climb down them. When you reach the bottom you notice a door. You open the door. You are outside in another large space.

There is a building in the distance, you walk towards it. As you approach, you wrap yourself in a cloak which makes you invisible. You go inside the building and there are people there. They cannot see you. You watch them.

Now you explore the building inside and outside. When you have seen everything you come out to the space. You take off the cloak. There is a hand stretching down from the sky. You are being invited to hold it and go with it upwards. You may or may not.

When you have done whatever you decided to do, you start your journey back. You find the door, you go through it. You climb the stairs in the well. You emerge onto the hill top. You climb down the hill, back to the large empty place. You are alone. You have your gift.'

At this point I would ask the group to sit up wordlessly and to paint what each one saw. This would be done in total silence except for necessary negotiations about paints, paper and brushes. Felt-tips may be used of course.

Then I would ask each person to pair with another (not the therapist or co-worker) and to talk through the picture. I should then invite the group to re-convene and to share anything at all.

This visualization takes a whole session and is really useful for catharsis, movement and realization. It is a journey of discovery and people love it.

My final favourite is one called 'polarities'. This is useful when the group seems to be in a state of flux or transition and cohesion or conclusions are illusive.

Here are the words. 'Think of two absolute opposites, stand between them with each one an equal distance from you. Go to one of them and study it from all angles. Move away and go to the other. Study it from all angles. Go back to the middle and allow them to move inwards a little. Stop. Go to the first. Study it from all angles. Go back to the middle'.

Now you repeat and repeat until you have taken the polarities to a point where they are really close to the person in the middle and then you would say 'step back and away from the opposites. From this new position, allow them to merge, to combine, to fuse'.

I should now invite group members to describe their feelings rather than what they saw. This can be an uncomfortable time of reckoning. It does induce deep, careful thought and needs good skills in containment from the therapist.

There must be ample time for reflection and sharing and 'polarities' should not be used with a group which is not yet safe and well established.

Nourishment

This is a term I use for describing how alternatives to anxiety may be discovered. One of the most effective nourishment exercises goes as follows. Ask the group to work in pairs. Each pair sits on the floor facing each other and almost touching.

Here are the words. 'Decide who is A and who is B. A talks to B using the sentence "I nourish myself by..." (here, supply an example like "having a bath by candlelight") Keep talking until there are no more nourishments left. If nothing comes to mind simply repeat the sentence "I nourish myself". Use this sentence for each new nourishment. After three minutes I shall ask you to stop and swap so that B will talk to A for three minutes. When you have each had a turn I want you to talk in those pairs about the exercise and your experience of it.'

There is a second part of this exercise which you may need to use depending on how people respond. If there is a good and positive feeling around the group, you may want to hold on to that and go into a relaxation. If there is some uncertainty and discomfort then use these words. 'Once again work in pairs A and B. A now talks to B using the sentence "I ignore my needs by..." (here supply another example like "not eating when I am hungry"). Repeat the sentence with each addition and if nothing comes just say "I ignore my needs"; and leave it there'. Again, you would stop them and ask them to swap after three minutes and then to talk.

This exercise is particularly good for pointing up ways in which we do not allow ourselves comfort except that which can be damaging (like smoking, drinking, drugs, over-eating and over spending) or it may be used simply as an exchange of new ideas for self-help.

A stress and anxiety group is never boring, always hopeful and invariably well-attended. Unfortunately I know I shall have work like this for as long as I want it. Stress can be crippling but is never untreatable.

CHAPTER 12

Use of Drama

Cherry Stephenson

What is drama?

The word 'drama' comes from the Greek 'Drao' meaning 'I do', or 'I struggle'. It also means 'action'. When people talk about drama they often confuse it with theatre; although some of the elements of theatre are present in that it portrays, through vocal and physical enactments, the predicaments of life, drama in the educational or therapeutic setting has its roots in *playing* rather than the play.

There are a number of theories on playing or child play and several of these suggest that it is a crucial aspect of childhood which enables the individual to cope with the present and prepare for adulthood. Peter Slade (1963) wrote that play is an essential aspect of young life through which the child thinks, relates, works, remembers, tests, creates and develops concentration. Ian Petrie (1974) endorsed this view when he concluded that play is 'a medium through which children may internalise experiences and come to terms with their world; and through play children may practise skills' (p.6). This is only a step away from educational, or child-centred drama, which provides a base for therapeutic drama.

Child-centred drama is essentially play guided by the teacher along specific lines to provide learning experiences in such areas as decision making, language development, imaginative creativity, co-operation with others and the acquisition of personal and social skills. It builds on the child's own experience of life to, as Wagner (1979) puts it, 'literally bring out what children already know, but don't yet know they know' (p.13). Retaining the ability to play is crucial in adulthood, since it keeps us in touch with our spontaneity; as Howard Blatner (1973), a disciple of Moreno (the inventor of Psychodrama), says:

'It is essential that we learn to recognise the vitality which can only grow within the context of play, and to cultivate and refine play so that we can preserve the spirit in our adult lives'. (p.2)

Drama has often been demeaned as a teaching method, perhaps because it is such a palatable approach for its recipients. Petrie (1974) puts his finger on this: 'It might be thought that if an activity is enjoyed, it is sufficient and good reason, in most cases, for encouraging it. In education, perhaps because of an element of Puritism, we have tended not to fully realise the intrinsic value of enjoyment' (p.8).

What drama gives is the unique opportunity for experiencing rather than simply discussing and theorising; for living through a situation, rather than hearing about it secondhand. This is true for both educational drama and drama therapy. It is, as an ancient Chinese proverb says:

'I hear: I forget.

I see: I remember.

I do: I understand.'

Both classroom drama and drama therapy seek to enable people to have a greater understanding of themselves and the world around them; to develop self confidence and mutual respect. Where educational drama and drama therapy differ is that in education the aim is to provide a global view, whereas therapy focusses on the interpersonal problems of the individual and assists in the working through of these problems.

My approach to group work with adolescents has been influenced by a wide range of people from both educational and therapeutic worlds, most of whom I have had the fortune to meet and with several of whom I have worked. They include Dorothy Heathcote (1985), Moreno (1946), John Hodgson (1966), Sue Jennings (1973, 1975, 1986) Carl Rogers (1961, 1977, 1983), Donna Brandes (1977), Marcia Karp (1991) and Ken Sprague (1991). With such a varied group of mentors at my elbow, it is inevitable that I have developed an eclectic style.

The main principles which guide my work are that participants should be given opportunities for self discovery within an atmosphere of mutual trust and toleration; that staff members should participate fully; that positive regard, self discipline and the growth of self esteem should be actively encouraged.

These are all very laudable; just the sort of phrases you would expect to see in a book of this nature. But how can such a climate be created? Is it possible, particularly when the majority of the group is undergoing examination or treatment for exhibiting signs of disruption, disturbance and anti-social behaviour? These are surely the last people from whom to expect co-operation, trust and toleration. That is the first key. You cannot *expect* it, you can only encourage and foster it. It is not a miracle process. In some sessions there is a spirit of collaboration and energy; at other times there is disunity or disruption, as in the rest of life. The main strength that drama therapy has is that it necessitates active participation and allows scenarios to be *experienced* from different viewpoints by the same individual, in a safe setting, where a range of approaches can be tried out, or rehearsed, without the consequences which would accrue in a real life situation.

What, then, is the framework for developing trust? First, there has to be a sense of security for both staff and young people that there won't be any unexpected interruptions. Building up a climate where people are going to express and explore their feelings needs a safe environment. This means selecting a room which isn't overlooked, covering any glass panel in the door with sugar paper and ensuring that support staff do not attend the session and respect that there should be no interruptions. It is also important that staff who do not attend are kept informed of what happens in drama sessions to avoid the growth of mistrust which surrounds something which appears exclusive and secret. In one unit where I worked this took the form of a hand-over meeting immediately following the drama session. If it can be part of the policy of the unit that each staff member, whether doctor, nurse, social worker or teacher attends and takes part in a series of sessions, then there are the dual benefits of breaking down barriers between different disciplines, as well as staff and young people, and demystifying what happens behind closed doors.

Security also comes from setting out clear expectations at the start of the sessions. These may sometimes have to be reinforced when the clientele is changing quite frequently. These expectations may be at the practical level of the group members ensuring, with the group leader, that the room is cleared of unnecessary furniture *before* the start of a session and that the sessions begin and end at the times stated. Because of the nature of some activities, particularly in the warm up period, it is often advisable for everyone to remove their shoes and put them well out of the way. Some final points about the type of room which is most suitable: it is helpful if the floor is wooden or of a similarly suitable surface which is pleasant to sit on. It is an advantage to have a carpet in it that is large enough for the whole group to sit on in a circle and it is also important that it is warm and that the windows can be opened if it gets too warm. Chairs can be useful and a small table to represent an office or dining table, but it is better to have two or three chairs only rather than one for each person. Some cushions, particularly floor cushions, are also useful for channelling aggression, or creating safe barriers or nests.

It goes almost without saying that the collective awareness which the staff has of individuals should guide the range and depth of the approaches used. Sometimes emotions can be triggered unexpectedly and it is important that the leader has the guidance and support of other staff who are clinically trained.

The start of a session is a tricky time. The individual participants will arrive with their own preoccupations, perhaps reluctant to attend, bringing in strong feelings from incidents unconnected with people in the room, or wishing to air and pursue resentments that have recently taken place with peers. Sometimes they can become the focus of the session and sometimes they may be a distraction. The group leader puts out his or her antennae at this stage, whilst maintaining equilibrium and must be prepared to abandon any pre-planning, however detailed, if he or she senses that the group has different needs from those previously chosen. This awareness needs to be maintained throughout the session; there is no room for the leader to allow their thoughts to move outside the room where they are working.

The way I start a session is to sit on the floor and wait for the rest of the group to join me in a seated circle. Once it has been explained, in the first week, I sit, looking down without any sense of impatience until everyone has gathered. This encourages self-discipline and it also sets up a non-verbal contract. As each person joins the ring they are making a commitment to taking part in the session. When everyone has gathered and is silent, the first activity is set up. This may be a physical or verbal warm-up, depending on the mood of the group and the aims of the session.

Each session shares a clear framework, although what takes place within it varies enormously, since it is a creative process. It includes the warm-up; the main activity, which will tend to be interactive; and finally a closing, when people can express how they felt about what has happened. Underpinning all of these is an approach which encourages positive comment and discourages destructive attacks on individuals. This does not mean an avoidance of looking at inappropriate behaviour, interpersonal problems and so on, but establishes ways of looking at the difficulties we encounter in life without apportioning blame or scape-goating any group member.

In the early days of the group meeting, different warm-ups and endings are introduced. As the group gets used to working together, opportunities are given for the group to decide on what happens within the set framework, to propose exercises, activities or themes and decide as a group which they will use. Sometimes, individuals are given the opportunity to choose a part of the session, as a reward for the contribution they have made, or to give the right finishing note when someone has been deeply touched by the experience they have explored and shared. This is a standard stage in psychodrama as we shall see later. These strategies provide further aids towards the development of group discipline and autonomy.

It is a mistake to think of each session simply as a collection of exercises strung together. The experiential, 'playing' nature of the activities puts them in touch with their imaginative, artistic side and enables the group to reach deeper awareness collectively, through the medium of their own unique creativity and creation.

It is perhaps helpful for people who are setting up groups to consider the various approaches which can be drawn upon. The main techniques which seem to be effective with young people include gestalt, psychodrama, sociodrama, trust and encounter exercises. There is considerable overlap between them and sometimes it is hard to decide which category they come under. I don't think it matters. What does matter is being able to incorporate them appropriately within a session. Here follows a brief description of each of them. A fuller picture can be found by reading the books mentioned at the end of this chapter, but the best way to learn how to use any drama therapy technique is to experience it in a session with an experienced leader.

Gestalt

Fritz Perls (1969), the originator of Gestalt Therapy, called it the psychology of the obvious. It is concerned with the 'here and now' which Perls saw as the means to discovering the ways we can most effectively handle the world. By looking more closely at what is of importance to us from moment to moment he believed we can learn about ourselves. The focus is on HOW things happen, not WHY. It means letting go of intellectual understanding and developing greater awareness through all the senses. As Perls put it. 'Lose your heads and come to your senses!'

Psychodrama

Psychodrama was invented by Jacob Levy Moreno. It is a creative technique which involves the acting out of problems, conflicts, relationships in the past, present or future in a group setting with a dramatic format and theatrical terms. The person who provides the focus and chooses to work on a problem is called the Protagonist and it is through their individual struggles that the universal nature of the human condition is recognised, culminating in a deep, releasing expression of emotion, a cathartic experience. The protagonist is facilitated by the Director, or therapist, who works in collaboration with the protagonist and the rest of the group. The prospect of gaining insights and catharsis may be as great for the other group members as it is for the protagonist. At times the rest of the group may take on roles to assist the protagonist in replaying a life situation. These are called Auxiliary Egos. Often fantasy is used, so the creativity of the group is tapped by representing whatever is needed to enable the protagonist to explore their personal problems. It might be by representing different aspects of the personality, or conflicting values that are causing pain, by providing a desired or feared environment and so on. When not playing a role the other group members form the Audience where they actively participate in and support the central action. The space where the enactments take place is the Stage, whether it be a raised platform with rostra or an area in a room. There are three essential phases to a psychodrama session; the warm-up, the enactment and the group sharing. A key factor is utilising the spontaneity in all participants; in Moreno's words '... Conscious evolution through training of spontaneity opens a new vista for the development of the human race' (Moreno 1934 cited in Moreno 1946 p.47), to achieve greater understanding and give cathartic release.

Psychodrama is a powerful tool, perhaps *the* tool, and although I only touch on it here, I believe it offers profound learning opportunities and insights. It is not something that can be learnt from books, however, but experientially, from a recognised practitioner.

Sociodrama

Sociodrama also owes its origins to Moreno. It shares the same theatrical mode but is more concerned with collective issues rather than the problems of an individual. Again, it offers catharsis and insight and concentrates on role training (Sternberg and Garcia 1989 p.24). Through a group action approach, mutually agreed social situations are enacted to discover responses and solutions to difficulties. With young people the themes will be those particularly relevant, although not exclusively related, to adolescence. They may include issues concerned with AIDS; abortion; social acceptability or parental conflict; unemployment or drug addiction. A group of victims of bullying may explore the common problems of their situation, as may young people from an ethnic minority group who have been subjected to racial discrimination. The Sociodrama will focus on those aspects which are relevant to the group by enacting a hypothetical situation, rather than becoming personalised as in a psychodrama.

Trust exercises and encounter games

The purpose of these is to raise our awareness about ourselves so we can begin to break down the personal barriers which we all erect and respond to each other in a more open and spontaneous way. They take the form of highly structured exercises designed to challenge our preconceived ideas, prejudices and assumptions about ourselves and others and provide opportunities for people to take risks and build trust. They may take the form of physical exercises where one partner entrusts themselves to another, as in closing their eyes and allowing themselves to be led around obstacles or an unfamiliar building; or, on a more intimate level, of taking turns to feel the surfaces of a partner's hands or face. They may be concerned with revealing fears, anxieties or aspirations to a partner or the group or with hearing personal feedback from an individual or the group. In all such activities the rules are very explicit, with emphasis on the positive. It is vital that the leader keeps in tune with the appropriateness of such exercises and introduces them when the group is able to handle them with commitment. There may be signs that people feel threatened by grinning, giggling or withdrawal, but this often passes if the leader ignores it and helps everyone to concentrate on the task by their own example.

In the early stages of group work, (particularly if the leader is lacking in confidence), if there is strong resistance, which may take the form of mockery, uncontrolled giggling or strong hostility, it is better to change activities swiftly, as one dominant group member can quickly affect the rest. Sometimes, it is useful to take time out and as a group look at the different reactions that were triggered off and put forward views on how individuals felt. It is imperative that the leader refrains from commenting on how she would have wanted people to behave. In fact, if the leader is able to stay quiet, generally the group reaches a consensus of what they perceive to be constructive use of the time which will closely match the leader's own aims. When the leader has gained experience, these resistances can provide a useful focus for whole group work.

Two excellent resource books for encounter games and trust exercises are, *Gamesters' Handbook* (Brandes and Howard 1977) and *Creative Drama in Group-Work* (Jennings 1986).

Case studies

To put these methods in context I shall outline sessions taken at different times during the academic year in one unit for disturbed adolescents. It catered for young people between the ages of eleven and eighteen with symptoms including depression, anorexia nervosa, elective mutism and obsessional behaviours.

Session 1

This was an initial session with a group of ten participants, aged between eleven and seventeen. Four staff also took part and these included a psychiatrist, a nurse, a teacher and myself. A few days before this session we met and discussed what we might do. We had decided that our aims for the term were:

1. To develop group trust

2. To introduce psychodrama and related techniques 'through which problems could be aired, shared and reviewed in a sympathetic climate'

After clearing the room of furniture with the students and having taken off our shoes I sat down on the floor and asked the others to join me. When everyone was quiet they were asked to partner someone next to them and spend three minutes listening to their partner telling their life story. The listener was then asked to tell her/his life story. It was explained that they were to select what they wanted to say. There was no compulsion to reveal anything they did not wish to divulge. Each person then introduced their partner to the rest of the group, placing a hand on their shoulder and speaking in the first person as if they were that person: 'My name is Jane and I don't know what to say'... When they had been introduced, each person had the opportunity to add or amend anything before going on to the next pair. When everyone had been introduced, people were asked to describe in a word or a sentence how it felt being introduced and introducing another person to the group.

The next activity was Sculpting. Each person takes it in turn to enter the circle where they are placed in any posture or attitude by the person to their left. This is demonstrated first so people understand that they need to allow others to move their limbs and retain that shape without resisting. The sculptor has to ensure that they don't place their partner in an impossible pose that can't be maintained and must watch that they handle others with care.

To give an additional dimension, when each sculpture was finished I placed my hand on their shoulder and 'egoed' them, that is, spoke aloud a possible thought the statue might be having at that moment, such as 'I'm reaching out as far as I can', or 'This makes me feel silly', and so on.

We then moved into a group sculpture which was arranged by one group member, whom I picked. The instruction was to arrange the group in relation to each other and to end by placing herself in the group. When everyone had been placed, they had the opportunity to say how they felt about the position they had been put in and to move if they wished. As with all such discussions, only one person could speak at a time.

To bring the session to an conclusion we sat in a circle. Each person was asked to make a statement about what they had liked least about the session. This was to be listened to, but not commented upon by everyone else. Finally, everyone was asked to say what they liked most about the session and again no comments were allowed.

The staff felt this had been a successful first session since concentration and involvement had been high and people were already beginning to take risks in the comments they made.

Session 2

This followed a week later, building on some of the exercises introduced in the first week. The staff chose the theme of Boredom, since this is a recurring feeling that young people complain about and the aim was to assist people in identifying it and to increase self-awareness.

In a circle, the first activity was a warm-up to stimulate and raise energy and aid concentration. This took the form of a clapping game. The leader claps a simple rhythm which everyone repeats, then each person inserts their first name in turn in the pause in the clapping. (Sometimes, instead of using names it can be making a facial expression or sound to express how each person is feeling at that moment).

The next activity was Clay. This is an extension of the sculpting introduced the previous week, where each pair spends longer, one allowing the other to move him or her into a shape or series of shapes, the last of which has to be sustained for some time whilst the rest of the group is added in to form one giant sculpture, joined together at different places, but without distorting the shapes people have been put into. When everyone was in place, I suggested that the mass changed into wax and slowly melted into a great heap. After disentangling themselves, but still sitting or lying on the floor, the theme of Boredom was introduced. Everyone was asked to take up a stance that they often adopt when they are bored. It was suggested that they might like to close their eyes to aid concentration whilst the following suggestions were made in the manner of Gestalt therapy, to encourage greater attention to detail:

What does you face feel like when you're bored?

How do your limbs feel?

The inside of your mouth?

What colours do you picture?

What smells?

What tastes?

Are you at rest or active?

Is it pleasant or unpleasant?

How do you feel in your stomach when you're bored?

What has to happen to bring you to this state of boredom?

What do you feel about yourself when you're bored?

The group then put forward their observations about boredom and the situations in which it occurred. Some people felt confident enough to demonstrate how they behaved in this state which then meant that the psychodramatic technique of *doubling* could be taught. This is a useful device where someone who feels empathetic to the protagonist copies their body posture and accompanies it with a verbal description of how they are feeling. If they are accurately reflecting how the protagonist feels this will be endorsed by him or her, as any comments which are off target will be rejected. Often the person doubling is able to say what the protagonist cannot allow themselves to speak and helps in the recognition that what is most distressing and painful to the individual is painful and distressing universally. The protagonist can often build on what the person doubling offers to explore and identify problems more deeply.

In this particular session a boy of thirteen, called Alan, put himself forward. He said he was in a permanent state of boredom. He was doubled by different group members and had a conversation as if with himself in which he questioned his constant headaches, his reluctance to make friends and his feelings of low self-esteem. The session closed on an optimistic note when another boy offered to play games with him in the future and a girl commented on how open Alan had been.

Session 3 theme: Aggression

The warm-up began with the exercise where everyone finds a partner, two lines are formed, standing facing each other, each partner on opposite sides of a central line placing their hands on each other's shoulders. The aim is to pull the partner over the line. It works best on an uncarpeted floor. The leader needs to check that people do not use unscrupulous means to win, such as digging their nails in or squeezing hard.

This moved into an exploration of how pairs could use the same energy in a co-operative mode, by asking each pair to discover as many symmetrical ways as possible to form a mutually supporting bridge with their partner; thigh to thigh, nose to nose, bottom to bottom, hand to hand and so on.

Next we tried the following exercise: partners face each other and place their palms together, at shoulder height, with just a slight pressure. Keeping the palms together each pair slowly raises and lowers their arms. The object is to catch your partner off-balance by suddenly removing your hands.

Finally we played 'Breaking in and Breaking out', which became one of the most popular warm-ups for the group. The whole group, except for one volunteer, forms a strong circle, arms linked, tightly held together. The volunteer can use any method to get into the centre of the ring from outside as long as it doesn't cause physical harm. Once inside the circle, the aim is to get out. Before commencing the group is reminded: 'Look after yourself. Look after everyone else as you want to be looked after'.

Then we discussed the feelings these different exercises had aroused, starting by asking for people to say one word to describe how they felt about a particular aspect of the session. Discussion was mainly around the feelings of frustration and aggression which the last exercise aroused. Most people seemed to find breaking in easier than breaking out. The approaches included taking a run and throwing themselves bodily at the wall of people, tickling a friend, pleading or squirming in. Breaking out was harder as it wasn't so easy to take the group by surprise. Sarah tried walking round in the circle saying, 'I wonder, I wonder where should I break out?' Then suddenly turned and burst between two unprepared people.

This led to talking about life situations which trigger these feelings, and some conjecture whether we deal with problems in the way we break in or out. Then we moved into the re-enactment of one of them, in the psychodrama mode.

Barry frequently finds himself in conflict situations at school because, as it emerged by his enactment of a playground incident, he takes on the Robin Hood role. He chose another boy, Alan, to represent him and was able to see an alternative way of operating. As with all psychodynamic situations, the work ended where Barry replaced Alan as himself in a successful encounter, where he avoided the temptation to become embroiled in yet another rescue/conflict situation.

The session ended with a sharing of resentments and appreciations. In my notes I recorded that: 'There are signs of more openness in people's general ability to express their feelings and challenge each other. We ended with an atmosphere of warmth and achievement'.

Other approaches
The approaches to drama therapy are infinite. Sometimes the group can benefit from the use of masks or artifacts which give another dimension to the work.

One particular group enjoyed artwork and so they made gypsona half-masks on each other, a trust exercise in itself. These were then built up with exaggerated features and painted to represent a significant adult in each person's life. As with the other activities, staff made masks alongside students. It turned out that everyone had made a mask to represent either their mother or father so we used them in drama sessions in different ways. The first time they were used as a parents' gathering.

The session started in front of mirrors, looking at the mask and adopting the gestures and body movements that person tended to use. Then everyone walked to the drama room in the manner of their parent and began to circulate. At first they were asked to ignore everyone else, but concentrate on thinking about their son or daughter, avoiding eye-contact with others and making no attempt to speak to anyone. Once concentration had been built up people were asked to repeat to themselves a key phrases or phrases that they had heard that parent use to describe them. Next they went to each member of the group in turn, introducing themselves, 'I'm Mrs Jones, Pam's mum. She's such a worry to me'. As confidence developed they were able to expand and talk at more length about their 'child' as they felt they were perceived by their parent. This led into a psychodrama session with one group member exploring the frustra-tions and conflicts of her home situation, assisted by others in the group. In the final part of the session the rest of the group shared the ways in which different aspects of the psychodrama had struck echoes in their own lives. The girl who had taken on the protagonist role was asked by me how she would like the session to end. She had gone from a state of tension and aggression, through tears of cathartic release, to calm, as the psychodrama concluded, and requested to be hugged by the group. This we did, first individually and then as a whole group with her in the midst of us; quietly; newly aware of the struggles which we all go through in life, and respectful of her generosity in allowing us to share more closely things that are often kept private and guarded.

In such a session the masks are not necessary, but with young people they provide a physical shield which can help those who have inhibitions initially about speaking.

There are certain games or exercises which have been particularly enjoyed and requested by different groups. I have mentioned 'Breaking in and Breaking Out': another popular exercise is 'Some-one said of You'... A volunteer leaves the room and the group selects three positive statements about that person. They are called back in to hear each one in turn, which the spokesperson prefixes with 'Someone said of you that'... The subject has one guess as to who made the comment. If she or he is wrong, the statement originator must immediately own up. It is common for the group to 'volunteer' staff members for this and is a clear indicator to the leader that the group is applying the appropriate controls.

Another heavily requested exercise is 'Rocking'. This is a trust activity which cannot be introduced until there is a certain level of cooperation and physical control in the group. It is often used in the closing phase of a psychodrama. The volunteer lies on the ground, eyes closed, ankles uncrossed, arms at sides, in a relaxed position. The other group members spread themselves round, designating particular people to look after the head, shoulders and so on with the minimum of speech. Everyone places their hands under the body to make a supporting cradle at the same time. Slowly the body is raised and rocked. This may be accompanied by quiet humming or singing. This continues as long as the group can maintain it, then the person is gently lowered to the ground. Everyone remains close to the volunteer until they begin to come out of their relaxed state.

As a final point, it has helped me to remember, especially when I first began, that it is best to say 'Stop!' when it seems things are going beyond one's experience and control, and to lead the group back to more familiar territory.

Conclusion

It seems to me that working in this field with young people is challenging, occasionally terrifying and very rewarding. In setting up a creative climate which encourages young people to gain insights and begin to come to terms with the frustrations and pain of living, there is a built-in bonus that the leader also is exposed to those same opportunities for developing self-awareness. Therapy is not something that the leader gives the group; it is the shared outcome of people working seriously and playfully together.

References

Blatner, H. (1973) *Acting-In: Practical Applications of Psychodramatic Methods*. New York: Springer Publishing Company.

Brandes, D. and Howard, P. (1977) *Gamsters' Handbook*. London: Hutchinson.

Heathcote, D. and Herbert, P. (1985) 'A Drama of Learning: Mantle of the Expert', *Theory into Practice*, 24 (3) 173–180.

Hodgson, J. and Richards, E.(1966) *Improvisation*. London: Methuen and Co. Ltd.

Jennings, S. (1973) *Remedial Drama*. London: Pitman Ltd.

Jennings, S. (1975) (ed) *Creative Therapy*. London: Pitman Ltd.

Jennings, S. (1986) *Creative Drama in Groupwork.* Bicester, Oxon: Winslow Press.

Karp, M. and Holmes, P. (1991) (eds) *Psychodrama Inspiration and Technique.* London: Tavistock/Routledge.

Moreno, J.L. (1934) *Who shall Survive?* New York: Beacon House.

Moreno, J.L. (1946) *Psychodrama Vol. 1* New York: Beacon House.

Perls, F. (1969) *Gestalt Therapy Verbatim.* Moab, Utah: Real People Press.

Petrie, I. (1974) *Drama and Handicapped Children.* Birmingham: Educational Drama Association, Rodway Drew and Hopwood Ltd.

Rogers, C.R. (1961) *On Becoming a Person.* Boston: Houghton Mifflin.

Rogers, C.R. (1977 Reprint) *Encounter Groups.* London: Pelican Books.

Rogers, C.R. (1983) *Freedom to learn for the Eighties.* Columbus, Ohio: Charles E. Merrill.

Slade, P. (1963) 'Drama with Handicapped Children'. *Creative Drama.* 3: 83–89.

Sprague, K. (1991) 'Everybody's a Somebody: Action Methods for Young People with Severe Learning Difficulties'. In P. Holmes and M. Karp (eds) *Psychodrama Inspiration and Technique.* London: Tavistock/Routledge. pp.33 – 51.

Sternberg, P. and Garcia, A. (1989) *Sociodrama: Who's In Your Shoes?* New York: Praeger.

Wagner, B.J. (1979) *Dorothy Heathcote: Drama as a Learning Medium.* London: Hutchinson.

Additional Reading

Houston, G. (1990) *The Red Book of Gestalt.* Aylsham, Norfolk: F.C. Barnwell.

James, M. and Jongeward, D. (1976) *Born to Win: Transactional Analysis with Gestalt Experiments.* Reading, Massachusetts/Menlo Park, California: Addison Wesley.

Perls, F.S., Hefferline, R.F. and Goodman, P. (1973) *Gestalt Therapy.* London: Pelican.

CHAPTER 13

Use of Interpretation

Kedar Nath Dwivedi

The setting for an interpretative group work requires to be conducive to production of fantasy without promoting embarrassment, anxiety or guilt. At the beginning of a group there is often an intense initial anxiety that needs to be dealt with. This anxiety is often associated with anticipatory fear of rejection, isolation, disappointment, difficulties in meeting demands and resulting humiliation, embarrassment and shame. Because of the intensity of this initial anxiety children may behave in a stand-offish way, shy, non assertive and refraining from asking or talking to each other. Some may keep playing the same games repeatedly and trying to obtain security from familiarity of the game.

As the experiences right from the beginning of life remain with us in the depths of our minds throughout our lives, these may be revoked in situations that resemble the past in some way. Thus joining a group may feel like coming in contact with a 'transformational object', an object (like mother's breast) that can transform all the suffering, craving and pain into a state of fulfilment, happiness and delight. It may be wished like being a 'foetus inside the mother's womb' so that simply by being present and just sitting passively one partakes of all emotional nutrients via an 'umbilical cord'. However, joining a strange group can also feel like being pushed out at birth from a familiar environment into one that is strange, cold and terrifying. Coming new to a group may evoke feelings of ignorance, bewilderment, confusion, anxiety, isolation, loss of control, embarrassment of being late or different. One might feel ashamed even to reveal how frightening these thoughts and fantasies could be – for example the thought of being cut open like in an operation (Salzeberger-Wittenberg *et al.* 1983). However, after a while, new members usually discover that their anticipatory fears were rather unjustified. It is this sense of relief that helps the participants to become further interested in the group.

Brackelmanns and Berkovitz (1972) describe four stages that a therapeutic group of youngsters go through: (1) The Fragmented Stage, (2) Preworking Stage, (3) Working Stage and (4) Termination Stage. During the Fragmented Stage there are several discussions taking place at the same time without allowing members to finish what they were saying and there are frequent interruptions with matters apparently irrelevant to the current conversation. This creates a disjointed, chaotic and disruptive atmosphere which is often due to the feeling that nobody would be interested in what they have to say. There is a resistance to any in-depth discussion and the group workers feel like being traffic police, redirecting discussions and pointing at what is happening.

During the Preworking Stage, a degree of commitment is observable and the group workers are able to introduce important themes, observations and comments. The Working Stage comprises of verbal and non-verbal activities, mainly focused on the discussion and resolution of problems and feelings with a considerable degree of self disclosure. During the Termination Stage, the feelings, experiences and thoughts are openly expressed and various conflicts with parents, peers, siblings, authority figures, and so forth are dealt with. There is also a sense of personal achievement and success during this stage.

Schwartz (1960) has emphasised the need to inform youngsters at every opportunity that, if they could talk and understand what they felt inside, there would be no need to act these feelings out and this could also help them control their lives better.

Interpretative group work can take place along with play and activities that facilitate the demonstration of conflicts and fantasies. This interpretative work involves the understanding of children's symbolic or representational behaviours. The group workers need not become better parents and directly gratify all the emotional needs of the children. There is also no need to be centrally involved in the play and games in the group, since then the group workers could lose the perspective of being observers of the whole group and could also arouse 'sibling rivalries'. However, they must remain friendly and informative.

Everything that children demonstrate need not be reflected upon, commented or interpreted. In the beginning, attention should be paid to the superficial and conscious aspects of resistance before focusing on unconscious matters. Sometimes an enthusiastic running commentary on various group activities can induce a reflective atmosphere in the group.

There is a tendency for children and adolescents to present their 'Consumer' and/or 'Performer' selves in groups. From the consumer point of view, any material, activity, game, suggestion or decision by the workers or the group can be turned into likable, dislikable, gratifying, repulsive or boring, and so on. As the groupworkers attempt to please these 'consumers' it begins to escalate into a vicious cycle. Similarly, even the simplest demands (e.g. for painting, drawing, commenting, sharing news and other tasks or activities) can be perceived by the participants as sources of performance anxiety interfering with their spontaneous co-operation.

Mutual influences in a group setting also intensify the sense of being consumers and performers. Although difficult, it is therefore important to steer away from escalating such feelings and to attempt to engage the 'observer' parts of the participants. A running commentary on group activity, in this sense, helps to engage this part of the group. Someone may be invited to guess what may be troubling someone else in the group. The following excerpt from one of our groups illustrates the various levels of fantasy, projection and disclosure that such an invitation can lead to.

Groupworker:	'Ken, Why do you think Philipa may be feeling sad?'
Ken to Philipa:	'Are you sad because your Dad didn't give you any presents?'
Philipa:	'No, he gave me a very nice present'.
Ken:	'I didn't get any presents from my Dad. I don't even know where he lives now. I don't care!'
Philipa:	'No, I live with my Dad and Stepmum. My Dad likes my Stepmum's daughter more than he likes me because my Mum died'.

As already emphasised elsewhere in this volume, a degree of emotional nurturance and acceptance allow the group to become a symbolically idealised 'good mother' for the members. Developmental deficits become reflected in the process of establishing the 'pecking order' and splitting in the group. Hostile scapegoating and bullying are exhibited by those with a history of identification with the aggressor. Various games that spontaneously emerge in such a group can serve as a means of enacting fantasies and traumatic life events for their working through. Soo (1985) described a youngster who devised a hide and seek game in his group. He became a 'vampire' and captured his victim in a darkened room with the announcement 'I love to suck blood!' In his real life he had experienced premature weaning because of blood in his mother's milk.

Sugar (1974) gave an example of a child who complained with a feeling of rivalry that the groupworker was helping another child in a game of checkers. The worker pointed out in a gradual manner about the way different children used their thinking. He explained that he was helping one child to use his thinking properly because this child was in the habit of using his thinking only to get angry with his parents. Another child's thinking, according to him, tended to become jumbled up in situations of hopelessness; yet another child avoided thinking as he was afraid of thinking about feeling hurt and, therefore, tended to act like a clown.

While joining in a representational or projective play, it may be useful to seek the assistance of children in creating dialogues and thus to step back from providing a response oneself too quickly. For example, a child speaking for the 'Mother Doll' may say to the 'Brother Doll' 'You better stop watching telly and go to bed, otherwise you will be late again for school tomorrow'. If the group worker needs to give voice to the 'Brother Doll', the child or children could be requested to suggest an appropriate response. Thus, the groupworker may ask the children (perhaps whispering), 'what should we have the "Brother Doll" say now?' and then repeat what was suggested by the children (loudly) as a response from the 'Brother Doll', 'I am scared of going upstairs'. However, when the time is right, an emotional linking or interpretative idea can be introduced by the group worker through one of the characters, say the 'Sister Doll': 'Just like some of the kids in this room, you also fear that your parents might hurt each other when you go to bed'.

In group work with children and adolescents, dealing with boundary phenomena involves much greater time and energy. Testing of group boundaries may be manifest in a variety of ways (e.g. extending the group boundary to the entire building or campus, wandering in and out, bringing various animate and inanimate objects). The door of the group room, thus, also assumes a great symbolic significance. Repeatedly passing through the door can be highlighted as practising leaving and then coming back in order to get in touch with the feelings of what it will be like when the group breaks for holidays, or ends.

Willock (1990) has highlighted the hidden play element in many defiant behaviours in children. Through a developmental line of play (e.g. Peek-a-boo, object tossing, being chased, bye-bye gestures and words, hide and seek), children develop a capacity to cope with feelings of loss and separation anxiety (Kleeman 1967, 1973). When such a line of development is distorted, the need for such interactive play influences their behaviours to the extent that these appear inappropriate, defiant, and disruptive. Sexual and aggressive themes also tend to surface more quickly in group work than in individual work with children. But excessive acting out and sexual horseplay may subside when the hidden motives are identified – 'Here, it will be all right to talk about...'

The group work approach developed at the Tavistock Centre (Ezriel 1950, 1952) emphasises the value of interpreting the current here and now behaviours in terms of wishes (or unconscious motives), fear of catastrophic consequences of acting on such wishes and the current group interactions and behaviours as defences against such consequences. Evans (1965, 1966) applied a similar approach in group work with adolescents by focusing on their here and now behaviours, enabling them to explore underlying motives, anxieties, conflicts and alternative but more appropriate solutions, and to improve their capacity to tolerate frustrations and anxieties.

Brackelmanns and Berkovitz (1972) point out that most adolescents referred for treatment feel powerless, inadequate and incompetent. They deal with these feelings in self-destructive ways by exerting themselves against their parents. As parents overreact and feel themselves helpless in turn, this allows the child to deny his or her own feelings of helplessness and to obtain gratification without acknowledging the dependency needs.

The style and pace of communication in group work with youngsters reflect that of the membership – 'rapidly changing themes, volatile moods, evanescent thinking and a tendency towards action' (Behr 1988, p.120). Bad language, slang and joke telling can be very common in such groups, but these are also clues to the nature of underlying anxieties. Thus risky subjects such as sexual, racial or cultural prejudices may be first peddled in the form of jokes and provide an opportunity for opening further discussion and exploration. Similarly, an attempt can be made to help the group understand the meaning of bad language in the context of a particular group conversation. News, reports and stories from television, video and films and so forth, are also very common topics for conversation in these groups and can be related to personal fantasies and experiences, just like working with dreams in adult groups (Behr 1988).

Spontaneously occurring here and now events can trigger deep and meaningful group processes conducive to reflection and insight. Phelan (1972) described the impact of a sudden explosive shout, an event that crystallised the emergence of the group as an entity. The whole group was electrified, 'what was that – a shot?' triggering a flurry of free and jumbled associations, for example 'It sounded like my mother and father fighting at night'.

Azima (1989) highlights the value of a triad of empathy, confrontation and interpretation as important clinical tools. However, their effectiveness depends greatly upon their timing, sequencing, blending and the art of delivery. Empathy and confrontation have to be adequately juxtaposed. A demanding, narcissistic, acting out or histrionic person may appear to need confrontation but would be better engaged with empathy first. A shy, withdrawn and fragile individual may arouse natural empathy but could be better served with active initial confrontation. The word 'confrontation' conjures up a political, hostile or negative connotation, but it is simply a description of events within the memory of the group offered when the occasion is 'ripe', so that the possibility of denial is diminished.

In working with offenders (including sex offenders) who show excessive denial, confrontation becomes an important ingredient of group work. Rachman and Raubolt (1983) have identified the confrontations often used in group work with delinquents: (1) 'The Showdown' session when the delinquent behaviour creates an emergency situation where an immediate and dramatic action is necessary, (2) Intensive Confrontation when a situation is considered very serious (approaching an emergency) and a persistent therapeutic pressure is needed to face the compulsive delinquent behaviour and (3) Gradual Confrontation geared to the individual's capacity to integrate interventions.

Depressed, withdrawn, passive, dependent and often drug-abusing youngsters may offer serious resistance to consistent confrontation and attempts at understanding their behaviours. They require more provocative techniques to stimulate communication (Slagle and Silver 1972). In a group session, when members appear emotionally inert, passive and understimulated, Behr (1988) suggests warming up techniques that may stimulate communication, for example questions designed to provoke fantasy thinking or observations on each other's moods and behaviours.

Empathy is putting oneself in the same experiential mode as the individual evoking the response. It builds caring, trust and compassion. The proportion of empathy and confrontation may vary from situation to situation, but the right blend of 'empathic confrontation' is one of the most therapeutic forms of communication and paves the way for interpretation.

Interpretation is an attempt to explore the underlying and even the unconscious meaning behind repeatedly identified behaviours, feelings and conflicts. Although it is the groupworker who initially demonstrates the interpretative style, both the groupworkers and the individual group members should be able to make interpretations, either to a specific individual, to the group as a whole, or about themselves. The skill lies in allowing the interpretation to unfold gradually without being hasty, overclose, invasive or scholarly. 'It should never be used as a means for the therapist to use therapeutic insight in order to give the child information which he or she is not yet ready to receive. To do so would leave the child-patient feeling persecuted and intruded upon by the therapist' (Dale 1990, p.109).

The Object Relations Therapy approach can be divided into four stages (Cashdan 1988): (1) Engagement, (2) Projective Identification, (3) Confrontation and (4) Termination. Demonstrating interest, joining in their conversation and activities and emotionally linking their comments help to enhance engagement. When the members discover that modes of expression which were normally reserved for the peer group are acceptable to the current group, it often paves the way for release of traumatic and vivid material into the group. Members often tell story after story of dreadful personal and family events. 'Very little so called "analysis" is necessary during this phase of group activity. The earnest recounting of a story to a group of peers ever ready to respond spontaneously with anecdotes of their own or to express genuine sympathy, horror or indignation is sufficient to relieve tension, create an atmosphere of trust and allow the group to move on to a more confrontative or interpretative mode of communication' (Behr 1988, p.126).

Such an emotional linking and genuine interest gradually creates an atmosphere of care, concern, connectedness and involvement and going beyond the feeling of 'just a bunch of kids' or 'just another professional'. This then paves the way for the surfacing of 'Projective Identifications'. Projective Identifications are patterns of interpersonal behaviours that induce others to behave in a certain way (see also chapter 3). These may arise from pathological feelings of helplessness (due to unmet dependency needs), of control (due to parentification), of eroticism (due to sexual exploitation) or of self sacrifice (due to ingratiation). These in turn induce feelings of excessive caretaking, incompetence, arousal and inappropriate appreciation, respectively, as countertransference reactions in the group workers and others. During this stage of Object Relations Therapy it is important to bring the operation of these pressures into the open and to highlight them.

During the third stage of Confrontation there is a firm and consistent refusal to conform to the pressure of these projective identifications (or meta-communications) but in a very caring and concerned way, for example 'you don't have to be in control of everything in the group to be liked by the group', 'you can survive without depending upon me totally', 'the group could continue to like you without you having to use your body'. Such confrontations have to continue until the projective identifications are dropped and the individuals begin to feel comfortable without them.

During the last stage, that of Termination, it may then be appropriate to link group members' projective identifications with their past experiences (e.g. 'as a little child you may have been afraid that if you weren't.., you might have been put away'). The capacity to operate in the future without the destructive object relations is consolidated and further developed during this stage.

Shapiro and Dominiak (1990) outline the common psychological defences, as seen in the treatment of sexually abused adolescents. Although there is a tendency to recreate components of the abuse experience, there may also be denial, distortion, displacement, splitting, projection, acting out and projective identification. Denial invalidates any exploration, and overcoming denial is typically a slow and painful process. Distortion leads to skewing of reality of interpersonal events and interactions such as exaggerated self-blaming, scalding devaluation of others or idealisation of parental figures or peers. Displacement allows the individuals to be distracted and to focus attention elsewhere.

Splitting helps to create a distance from unwanted feelings and memories. A true self/false self dichotomy, for example, may lead someone to appear very compliant while feeling enraged or helpless internally (Ganzarain and Buchele 1988). Through projection one can place both conscious and unconscious feelings (e.g. of worthlessness, self blame) onto others. Acting out allows the expression of unconscious impulses and wishes in such a way that one is able to avoid being conscious of the accompanying feelings (Vaillant 1977). 'Holding' is, therefore, considered to be an important therapeutic task, so that the experiences which an individual cannot consciously 'own' or acknowledge can be 'held' and contained for, by the group workers and the group. It is similar to a mother 'taking on board' the baby's distress. 'In so doing, she acts in the first instance as a "dustbin" or "nappy" into which the baby can dump or evacuate experiences which it cannot process or integrate. However, she does more than this. She also metabolises or detoxifies those overwhelming emotions and sensations which are beyond the baby's capacity to digest or assimilate' (Dale 1990 p.109).

In group work with adolescents with a history of sexual abuse, because of the various defences, it is difficult for them to get in touch with their true feelings and make sense. It is the process of projective identification that often helps the group workers to learn about the member's affective experiences. Schacht *et al.* (1990) describe their experience of group work with abused boys. It seemed that the boys believed that they must be the abuser in the group in order not to be abused. Some had experienced early repeated sexual abuse at a preverbal stage of development and, therefore, had difficulty putting feelings into words (Segal 1974, O'Shaughnessey 1983). Instead they would act out and behave in a manner that elicited their own feelings in others. This process of projective identification thus provided a clue to their internal world of feelings. Their behaviours made the group workers feel sad, frightened, hopeless, helpless, and so forth. As the groupworkers began to share these feelings aroused in them, the boys started joining in likewise.

Gadpaille (1959) describes a sequence of resistance in group work with delinquents: (1) Open defiance, in the form of distrust of the group worker's interests and motives, (2) Testing by telling 'dirty' stories, use of obscene language, expressions of resentment and hatred and acting out, and (3) Silence.

Willis (1988) highlights the difficulties in engaging youngsters in group work as they (1) get easily bored and need a lot of stimulation, (2) are over excitable and have difficulties with anxiety, (3) can be very demanding, like a baby (4) have difficulty in channelling energy, (5) are frightened of too much disclosure, (6) fear being singled out and also being excluded and (7) exhibit extreme acting out behaviour. In the light of the above she has evolved an eclectic, non-action, non-directive method of group work called *group-analytic drama* by combining the fundamental techniques and approaches derived principally from the fields of group analysis, psychodrama and sociodrama.

References

Azima, F.J.C. (1989) 'Confrontation, Empathy and Interpretation: Issues in Adolescent Group Psychotherapy'. In F.J.C. Azima and L.H. Richmond (eds) *Adolescent Group Psychotherapy*. Madison: International Universities Press (pp.3–18).

Behr, H. (1988) 'Group Analysis with Early Adolescents: Some Clinical Issues'. *Group Analysis*. 21: 119–133.

Brackelmanns, W.E. and Berkovitz, I.H. (1972) 'Younger Adolescents in Group Psychotherapy: A Reparative Superego Experience'. In I.H. Berkovitz (ed)

Adolescents Grow in Groups: Experiences in Adolescent Group Psychotherapy. New York: Brunner/Mazel (pp.37–48).

Cashdan, S. (1988) *Object Relations Therapy: Using the Relationship.* New York: Norton.

Dale, F.M. (1990) 'The Psychoanalytic Psychotherapy of Children with Emotional and Behavioural Difficulties'. In V.P. Varma (ed) *The Management of Children with Emotional and Behavioural Difficulties.* London: Routledge (pp.96–114).

Evans, J. (1965) 'In Patient Analytic Group Therapy of Neurotic and Delinquent Adolescents: Some Specific Problems Associated with these Groups'. *Psychotherapy and Psychosomatics.* 13: 265–270.

Evans, J. (1966) 'Analytic Group Therapy with Delinquents'. *Adolescence.* 1: 180–196.

Ezriel, H. (1950) 'A Psychoanalytic Approach to Group Treatment'. *British Journal of Medical Psychology.* 23: 59–74.

Ezriel, H. (1952) 'Notes on Psychoanalytic Group Psychotherapy: II Interpretation and Research'. *Psychiatry.* 15: 119–126.

Gadpaille, W.J. (1959) 'Observations on the Sequence of Resistances in Groups of Adolescent Delinquents'. *International Journal of Group Psychotherapy.* 9: 275–286.

Ganzarain, R.C. and Buchele, B.J. (1988) *Fugitives of Incest.* Madison CT: International Universities Press.

Kleeman, J.A. (1967) 'The Peek-a-Boo Game: Part I: Its Origins, Meanings and Related Phenomena in the First Year'. *Psychoanalytic Study of Child.* 22: 239–273.

Kleeman, J.A. (1973) 'The Peek-a-Boo Game: Its Evolution and Associated Behaviours, especially Bye-Bye and Shame Expression During the Second Year'. *Journal of American Academy of Child Psychiatrists.* 12: 1–23.

O'Shaughnessey, E.C. (1983) 'Words and Working Through'. *International Journal of Psychoanalysis.* 64: 281–289.

Phelan, J.R.M. (1972) 'A Psychoanalytic Approach to Group Therapy with Older Teenagers in Private Practice'. In I.H. Berkovitz (ed) *Adolescents Grow in Groups: Experiences in Adolescent Group Psychotherapy.* New York: Brunner/Mazel (pp.63–79).

Rachman, A.W. and Raubolt, R. (1983) 'The Clinical Practice of Group Therapy with Adolescent Substance Abusers'. In T.E. Bratter (ed) *Current Treatment of Substance Abuse and Alcoholism.* New York: Free Press.

Salzberger-Wittenberg, I., Henry, G. and Osborne, E. (1983) *The Emotional Experience of Learning and Teaching.* London: Routledge and Kegan Paul.

Schacht, A.J., Kerlinsky, D. and Carlson, C. (1990) 'Group Therapy with Sexually Abused Boys: Leadership, Projective Identification and Countertransference Issues'. *International Journal of Group Psychotherapy.* 40(4): 401–417.

Schwartz, M. (1960) 'Analytic Group Psychotherapy'. *International Journal of Group Psychotherapy.* 10: 195–212.

Segal, H. (1974) *Introduction to the Work of Melanie Klein.* New York: Basic Books.

Shapiro, S. and Dominiak, G. (1990) 'Common Psychological Defenses seen in the Treatment of Sexually Abused Adolescents'. *American Journal of Psychotherapy.* XLIV (1): 68–74.

Slagle, P.A. and Silver, D.S. (1972) 'Turning on the Turned Off: Active Techniques with Depressed Drug Users in a County Free Clinic'. In I.H. Berkovitz (ed) *Adolescents Grow in Groups: Experiences in Adolescent Group Psychotherapy.* New York: Brunner/Mazel (pp.108–121).

Soo, E.S. (1985) 'Applications of Object Relations Concepts to Children's Group Psychotherapy'. *International Journal of Group Psychotherapy.* 35(1): 37–47.

Sugar, M. (1974) 'Interpretive Group Psychotherapy with Latency Children'. *Journal of American Academy of Child Psychiatrists.* 13: 648–666.

Vaillant, G.E. (1977) *Adaptation to Life.* Boston: Little, Brown and Co.

Willis, S. (1988)' Group Analytic Drama: A Therapy for Disturbed Adolescents'. *Group Analysis.* 21: 153–168.

Willock, B. (1990) 'From Acting Out to Interactive Play'. *International Journal of Psychoanalysis.* 71: 321–334.

Part 4

Subjects and Themes

CHAPTER 14

Bereaved Children and Adolescents

Susan C. Smith and
Sister Margaret Pennells

Do children grieve? Some adults are not sure if or how children grieve, and children themselves can react in so many different ways that adults become confused about how a child feels. A child may feel angry because of the death and misplace that anger onto others; they can be sad one minute, and happily out playing the next. The complexity of childrens' responses to death, and the fact that adults can sometimes misinterpret childrens' reactions has often led to many of their needs not being fully met. Some professionals have been able to help bereaved children through a family therapy approach or individual counselling. We feel, however, that for some children, especially those who feel isolated and need peer group support, a group work approach can be efficacious (Pennells and Kitchener 1990). There appears to have been little group work undertaken in this country with bereaved children although some attempts have been made based on the 'drop-in' model. In this chapter we will outline the structured group work approach which we have developed, the various thera-peutic methods we have used and our effort to evaluate our work.

Bereavement in children and adolescents

It is our experience that children's reactions to bereavement fall into three broad categories: behavioural, emotional and physical, and encompass problems experienced both inside and outside the family.

Some reactions of children and adolescents in grief are similar to those of adults: rejection, guilt, shame, anger, blame and so on. Some comments made by them in our groups have been:

'If I had helped her more, I would have saved her'.

'I didn't know how to tell my friends that my Dad had committed suicide because I didn't know what they would think about me'.

'If I could find the milkman who ran Peter over, I'd kill him'.

Most grief reactions in children are largely dictated by a child's developmental stage. Pre-school children often appear to ignore death; they do not understand its finality, thinking that it is just sleeping. Between five and eight years old they become intrigued with death and are concerned with fantasies and ghosts and monsters that can be frightening. This is also the age of magical thinking where one's wishes can come true – maybe they wished the person would die, and they did. At nine plus children begin to grasp the permanency of death and are more able to express their sorrow as adults do. Some children may become withdrawn, hostile or angry. Some may also appear unaffected or callous regarding the death of someone close to them, leaving adults feeling confused or angry.

Adults are likewise going through their own grieving process and therefore may find it difficult to understand what the children are going through, or be able to help them. They may emotionally withdraw from the children, over-protect them or exclude them.

Children have many other problems to face: they may not be told the truth about the death, they may not be included in bereavement rituals, children at school may be cruel to them, and they may have to cope with changes in their family situation, resulting in their feeling very confused and very alone.

Children and adolescents may feel angry and may express this through violence and aggression towards other children or adults. Others can become withdrawn or anxious about the changes that are occurring around them and may have eating and sleeping problems or become clinging and tearful. Adolescents may show signs of depression and even make suicide attempts. Some children experience physical and health problems following a bereavement, for example they may develop asthma, stomach aches, headaches and some may even imitate the symptoms of the person who has died. They can become very anxious and insecure about their own health and that of other family members and wonder if they too might die. Some of these problems can lead to nightmares and fantasies which completely overtake their normal functioning and can inhibit their social and emotional development.

They need the opportunity to explore what has happened to their family as a result of the bereavement and to understand the feelings they are experiencing. If they have not been told the truth about the death, or have been excluded from the bereavement rituals, they need help to come to terms with this and have their questions answered. They often need an adult outside their situation with whom to share their experiences, which will help them work through their grieving process. Such children are often helped by professionals through family work or individual counselling.

A group work approach

Family work or individual counselling are valid means of helping bereaved children, but we feel that these methods do not specifically address a child's isolation in grief or give them peer group support. Knowing the benefits that other groups have achieved (e.g. groups for sexually abused children, social skills groups), we decided to apply a group work approach to bereaved children (Kitchener and Pennells 1990). Despite extensive reading and trying to contact other services, we could not find anyone else who was using a group work approach for this purpose. With this information in mind, one might wonder why we would attempt to use group work at all. However, when the group work approach is studied as a whole, the benefits that can be gained make it a worthwhile method to consider.

Aims of a group work approach

Our main aim is to create a space for children to be able to share with peers and this fosters a sense of mutual identity which helps to stabilise relationships outside of the group. Most of the children referred to our groups are exhibiting behaviours which are unacceptable and tend to isolate them. This increases their drive to gain attention, which in turn affects their behaviour, and so on, in a downward negative spiral. Some of the goals that can be achieved in group work are the alleviation of isolation, increase in self esteem, reassurance and support and the reduction of powerlessness and stigma (Stock-Whitaker 1985, Preston-Shoot 1987). It therefore seemed that group work may be the ideal medium to tackle some of these problems. 'The basic idea of group work is that members may help both themselves and others by – exchanging ideas, suggestions and solutions, by sharing feelings and information, by comparing attitudes and experiences and by developing relationships with one another' (Heap 1985). Over all we aim to help children express their fears and sorrows and to complete some of the unfinished business with the deceased, as it is the inability or lack of opportunity to do so that seems to influence their behaviour.

Many of the children who come to our group have also experienced major life changes as a result of their bereavement and because of this have become very 'different' from their peers (e.g. Reception into care, removed from their home, change of custodial parent). For many of them, they have been the first amongst their peers to experience a death; this again serves to make them different, an object of curiosity and ridicule. The group is a chance to 'normalise' their situation, to mix them with others who have had similar experiences so that they feel less isolated and 'different', a mutual aid system sharing with others and being able to hear possible solutions and ideas. To achieve our aims we try to reach a series of specific goals, these are:

1. Help to express the effect of the loss. (Expression of feeling.)

2. To increase the reality of the loss.

3. To provide opportunity to voice fears and concerns.

4. Create opportunities to acquire knowledge.

5. Encourage healthy withdrawal from the deceased.

6. Re-adjustment after loss – to seek new relationships, adjust to new position in the family or to adjust to substitute family.

These goals follow the stages of grief, which we will elaborate on more fully in the next section.

Organisational aspects

A lot of planning goes into running a successful group. It is important to consider, amongst other things, where one will accept referrals from. We allow at least three months before the start of the group to request referrals from appropriate sources (e.g. Health Visitors, Social Services, Child and Family Consultation Service, Hospital Social Work Department). A closing date for referrals must be given and after this families can be contacted and offered a place.

Our referrals are broken down into age appropriate groups:

6–8 years

9–12 years

13–16 years

16 plus

We allocate six places for each group. This, for us, remains an ideal number to work with as it allows, when necessary, individual time for each child, and pair work is also easily arranged. More than six children in any one group can increase control problems, as children, especially the younger ones, often do not have the attention span needed to listen as each child relates his/her feelings, story, news and so on. Seven can be an acceptable number, but eight has the feeling of being overloaded.

Time must be given to considering the content of the programme which may need adapting according to the age-range of the group decided upon. The exercises may vary from group to group, but generally the materials needed are pens, large coloured felt-tipped pens, sheets of drawing and writing paper, paints, glue, old magazines, appropriate reading material (books on bereavement for children can often be obtained through the school lending library service), an empty shoe box (for questions) and tape recorder and music (if using them for guided fantasies and so forth). We have found it useful to provide food and drink (i.e., some orange squash and biscuits). Often the children come to the group straight from school and appreciate some refreshment. It also helps them to relax, and symbolises sharing and caring for each other. These are the basic requirements, the cost of which can be kept to a minimum. However, if budgeting allows we also include a farewell party, which can be a trip to a burger house, a barbecue or a small party.

Our venue is important – easy access, room to run around, and moving from room to room for different tasks, which beats boredom and means that material can be prepared and left out. Outside play areas with swings, slides and so forth also help. Sometimes consideration needs to be given to booking rooms ahead of time to avoid rooms being occupied and necessitating a change of room/s which can be disturbing and can cause confusion. Transport to and from the venue needs careful planning, especially with regard to who is responsible for bringing the child to the group and taking them home. We feel it is not good practice for group workers to undertake this task as it tends to interfere with the running of the group and overloads the workers.

The staffing of the group is, ideally, three workers. This is in order to provide plenty of individual support for the children, allow small groups to operate with one worker for tasks, ensure continuation of the group if one of the workers is absent, and to provide an opportunity for training other staff. Consultation and support for the workers is also important. This should occur at least three times during the run of the group and the time is usually spent discussing group processes, interactions amongst the workers and with the group, and any other related issues.

Time also needs to be set aside for meetings with the family and the referrer. An initial meeting with the family before the group starts is important in order to establish with them the aims and objectives of the group, so parents and carers have some knowledge of the programme. This equips them to deal with any issues the children may bring back from the group. The child referred is also made aware of why they are coming to the group and their consent and co-operation gained. Practical arrangements, such as transport, are also sorted out and the issue of confidentiality explained. We feel the group is a safe place for children to express their feelings and therefore it is important that children know we do not report back on them after each session. At the end of the group, a meeting again with the whole family, is useful in order to feed back generally how the child has progressed in the group, any problems that may have arisen and if any further help is required. Sometimes parents and other family members may need referring on for help in their own right. Parents and carers should always be free to contact group workers or the referrer if any worries or problems arise while the group is in operation.

Meeting with the referrer can be combined with the family meetings, otherwise separate meetings may be useful to guide the referrer to further work with the family or deal with any remaining issues if relevant. A general report is sent in writing to the referrer after the closure of the group.

Documentation

This consists of:

1. Questionnaires for each group member.

2. Evaluation forms.

3. Group and individual reports.

Questionnaires to each member of the group

We felt no relevant questionnaire had been devised especially to meet the needs of the bereaved, so we composed our own questionnaires that allow each group member to rate themselves on six main areas that appear problematic to the bereaved: adolescent depression, school work, isolation, somatisation, anger and anxiety. These areas are scored on a rating scale of 1–10 and are assessed at the beginning and end of the group and at a six month follow-up. Although to date we have had only a small sample and no control groups, our overall findings have been positive, with a significant improvement shown at the six month follow-up.

Evaluation forms

It is useful for both the group members and the group leaders to evaluate each session. The group members can be helped, by means of a proforma, to recall the activities of each session and in retrospect write what they felt about the sessions, their likes/dislikes, what they felt was useful, difficult, interesting or informative. They can also assess for themselves what they feel they have learnt from the overall group experience and comment on the venue, the format and their relationships with other group members. The evaluation helps the members to view their progress through the group and aid, by their comments, adaptations to the programme to make it more relevant and useful to other groups that follow. The group workers need to take seriously the comments the young people make in order to see if the group activities are really meeting the members' needs.

Group and individual reports

It is very useful for the group workers to compile a group report at the end of each session. A record of each session enables the workers:

1. to describe what occurs and the group process

2. to provide data for more detailed evaluation

3. to note significant events as a basis for planning future work.

This conforms with the basic criteria for record-keeping. Writing after sessions also provides a forum for leaders to de-brief and express their feelings. The individual records, kept again after each session, allows for an in-depth look at the way each child operated within the group, any particular factors to be noted, what he/she expressed that session and so on. These notes can form a basis for the report to be given to referrers at the end of the group.

Basic group structure

The programme we have devised consists of 12 weekly sessions of about one and half hours (allowing for transport problems and free time for the group to unwind at the end).

The programme follows the stages of the grieving process and deals with the following general themes:

Sessions	Theme
1	Introductions
2–4	Shock, numbness, disbelief
5–7	Anger, guilt, denial
8–9	Yearning, searching
10	Acceptance, adaptation
11	Evaluation
12	Group 'good-byes'

The needs of a particular group, however, may cause different emphasis to certain parts of the programme and, for example, the normal one session allocated may take two sessions. Flexibility is therefore essential to meet the group's needs, but the order of the sessions remains the same so that the children can progressively experience the stages of grief.

We have adapted various exercises used in other group work approaches to meet the particular themes we are dealing with. However, group workers need to be creative! The content of each session should be as varied as possible to avoid boredom; however, 'over-filling' sessions can result in uncompleted tasks and a sense of frustration. It is helpful to begin and end in a relaxed fashion, with activity sessions in between. Thus a typical session would be:

1. Food and drink.

2. Good news/bad news.

3. Introductory game.

4. Work/activity around theme of the session.

5. Group mural.

6.   Relaxation/free-time.

A continuing theme throughout the programme is that of group sharing and group trust. This begins with the preparation of *food and drink* which everyone takes a turn at and which symbolises sharing. We usually provide something simple like orange squash and chocolate biscuits. If the group takes place during a lunch hour at school, gathering together and eating sandwiches also provides a relaxed way to begin the group. Other groups may wish to begin with ice-breaking games and reserve the food and drink until the middle or end of the group. We, however, in running the groups after school are aware that it may be some time since they have had refreshments.

Good news/bad news/introductory game
To help the joining process, to get to know each other better and to bridge the gap since the last meeting, the group workers and the members relate one good event that has happened to them in the past week (e.g. I played football, I went on a school trip) and one 'bad' event (e.g. I got too much homework, my Mum shouted at me). This, along with ice-breaking games acts as preparation for the more serious work of the group as well as developing interpersonal relationships amongst the group members and with the group workers.

Group mural
Towards the end of the session, we ask the group to produce a *group mural*. This is a large sheet of paper (at least 3 ft. x 3 ft.) on which they draw, paint, or use other materials to create a small picture at the end of each session. This exercise has many purposes:

1.   It helps the children to work together as a group.

2.   It helps to end each session.

3.   It provides a release for otherwise unexpressed feelings.

4.   It can help the group workers to note anything of significance related to a specific child.

5.   The completed mural (at the end of 12 weeks) is a concrete expression of the whole group experience.

Free-time
The group then ends with 5–10 minutes of *free-time* or a *fun-game* which allows them to unwind before going home. Sometimes we introduce a few minutes of *relaxation exercises* which again facilitates a release of emotions before the group ends and helps them to focus on matters unrelated to bereavement, preparing them to face the rest of the day/evening.

Group rules

Beginnings and endings of the group are as important as the work during the session, as these children, often insecure after a bereavement especially if it has been sudden, need to experience 'planned' endings. The structure of the programme helps to reduce stress and give the children a sense of security. *Group rules* are useful for this too. Rules and expectations need to be expressed simply and clearly. Group workers can set ground rules (e.g. it is a safe place to be, confidentiality, no harm to the place or each other). Group members may like to add their own rules (e.g. no bullying or name-calling).

Endings

The final group activity (session 12) is a celebration of the end of the group. Usually the members are reluctant for the group to end. The group workers need to prepare the members for the end of the group by occasionally reminding them of the impending ending (e.g. we are now half-way through the group, we have only two more sessions left). To give the members some control we ask them what they would like to do at the end and how they would like to say good-bye. Ideas have been given for a meal out, a barbecue, a party. We have also taken a group photograph, (along with the completed mural) which is then sent to the members after the group has ended.

Methods, tools and group activities

We employ various types of methods to help the children work through the bereavement process. These include art work, role play, music, sculpting and relaxation.

Art work can be used to encourage the expression of thoughts and feelings both positive and negative, for example:

- a happy memory of the deceased
- their worst nightmare
- what frightens them about death
- design a headstone or write an epitaph
- projections – what will life be like in one and in five years' time.

There are many opportunities to use paint as a medium both for individual work and for the group as a whole. Art helps to express and test out numerous anxieties that they have about life in an attempt to master those concerns (Segal 1984). It helps them to express their fears and fantasies on a non-verbal level. Another non-verbal method of communication is the use of *guided fantasy*. After creating a relaxed atmosphere, soft music can be played to set the scene while the group worker guides the group through a positive experience with the deceased – this can be a meeting with the deceased in a pleasant setting (e.g.

countryside, heaven). Use of music and fantasy can evoke images and free associations that help children resolve repressed feelings and anxieties.

Role play and sculpting can be used to work through a number of issues. In particular they can be used to:

- act out difficult situations at school
- role play a funeral
- sculpting the family before and after the bereavement
- role play other loss situations (e.g. lost in a shop).

Role play, acting and drama helps the children to express their feelings bodily and together seek resolutions to their problems. We also help children to give expression to their angry and negative feelings by acting out specific feelings identified by the children during a brainstorming session. These feelings can be acted out through drama, or symbolised in a drawing (e.g. anger can be drawn as a fire or lion roaring). An extension of this exercise can be to place the symbolised picture onto a body-shaped outline as to where they feel these feelings (e.g. anger can be placed in the stomach or in the mouth). This exercise can help identify the link between illnesses the bereaved child may be experiencing and their internalised feelings.

A visit to a cemetery

Parents'/carers' permission should be obtained for their child to be allowed to go on such a visit. Children also should be told about the outing and be given the choice to go or not. Some children are frightened by visiting graves and would rather not go. For others it is an opportunity to go along with friends in a situation that is not emotionally fraught. The workers treat this as an educational exercise, choosing a cemetery where none of the group members has deceased relatives and providing each child with a work sheet to complete. The children are asked various questions on the sheet (e.g. draw different types of headstone, what is your favourite epitaph, what is the most interesting thing you saw). The children inevitably have a lot of questions to ask as they go round and many of their fears and fantasies are resolved (e.g. belief that they are treading on the dead person and not realising the person is buried several feet underground). For some children it can be a little like systematic desensitisation (e.g. being able to come with the group and stand at the cemetery gate but not go in). We find the children enjoy this session and learn a great deal from it, feeling less frightened and more confident, being able to accept a cemetery as a natural part of their landscape rather than as a frightening phenomena, as it is sometimes presented on videos or films.

Use of a question box

This allows children who are less verbal, or unwilling to voice in the group, a chance to have their questions answered. A question box can be left out each session for group members to write down their questions and put them in the box quite anonymously. At some stage in the group (usually at the session where fears and fantasies are discussed) the box is opened, the questions read out and a debate takes place. Questions are asked such as 'What is heaven like?' 'Can my mummy see me now?' 'Why are people burnt?' Group workers need to find out first from other group members what they feel and think about the questions. The workers can then either inform the group members, that is, provide education, or simply be honest and say we do not know the answer but some people think one thing and some people think another. Respect for children's religious beliefs need to be held and children can accept that there is not one definite answer to a question.

Other group activities can be

- reading appropriate stories (see booklist)
- bring a momento of the deceased and sharing the memories it evokes
- creative writing (stories, poems and so on) linked to themes being explored in a particular session.
- relaxation.

Children need to have as many different forms of expression as possible, because some children find it easier to use some forms of expression rather than others. With a wide variety of creative mediums, group workers can also be assured of meeting most of the children's needs. These exercises can be adapted to meet the age and development level of the child and the needs of the group. It is hoped that through these exercises the child can be helped through their grieving process and enabled to give expression to their internal struggles.

Evaluation

Our evaluation of each group initially comes from our reports and question-naires as outlined earlier. To date we have found no standard method of evaluating the effectiveness of group work with bereaved children as it appears to be a new operational field. However, the reports and questionnaires we use provide a wealth of material for evaluation purposes. We would encourage workers to be as innovative as possible in their approach to evaluation as we have been encouraged by the results we have obtained. The most important information we have gained comes from the comments made by the group members, some of which have been:

- I liked to listen to what the others said, to hear what they think and feel.
- It helped me to feel that I'm not the only one that has the feelings.
- I learnt a lot.
- It made me think.
- (Session 9) made me very upset in the end. But it made me get everything out which I wanted to tell for a long time.
- I've learnt that we all have feelings, even if I might not feel some of them myself.
- (Session 3) was good because we got to know each other's losses.
- It helped me to remember.
- It helped us to understand each other better.
- You know that other people went through what you did.
- It brought back some sad memories. But it did help a lot.
- You felt as if you weren't alone with your feelings.
- It got it all out of your system and it made me feel better knowing that other people had the same feelings as me.
- I think I have learned to cope more with death.
- It has made me a stronger person.
- It has prepared me for when someone else dies.

There were also some significant changes in the group members by the end of the group, for example.

Case A – who had been referred for bereavement counselling because of pains in her legs and difficulties in walking, was, by the end of the group walking quite well and at the six month follow-up was representing the County in cross country running and had entered the Duke of Edinburgh Award Scheme.

Case B – by the end of the group had expressed his anger at never having attended his father's funeral. Talking about the sessions at the bereavement group encouraged the whole family to talk about the death and be more open. They eventually were able to appear on television advising other families on how to cope with a bereavement.

Case C – had a young sister who died. It emerged in the group that he had kept this a secret from his class mates at school for four years, because when he began to tell them they started to laugh and make cruel remarks. In our group he was able to tell the whole story for the first time and felt understood and accepted by the others. This has helped his self-confidence and esteem in his present relationships.

Case D – her mother died and she was described as lonely and isolated at school and rejecting and cruel towards any girl friend her father brought home. During the fantasy journey in particular, and by sharing with another girl who had been through similar experiences to herself, she was able to look to the future more and consider the possibility of having a 'new mother'. At a six month follow up, she had made a happy relationship with Dad's new girl friend and was not so destructive.

We note many positive results from the young people, and their families also report positively about the changes they see and the benefits for the whole family. Unfortunately however, these results are not able to be 'measured' as such.

Conclusion

Having used and refined our methods of group work with successive groups over a number of years, we feel this is a very valid and useful way of working with bereaved children and adolescents. We acknowledge that individual and family work are also viable methods of counselling and this is usually used in conjunction with our group therapy. We nevertheless feel that group work provides specific benefits for the grieving child and adolescent which are unavailable in either of the other.

However, we recognise that more research into the effectiveness of a group work approach needs to be done, especially in relation to teenagers, where the problems of adolescence are difficult to separate from grief reactions. In group work children encourage and support each other in the expression and resolution of their feelings. Identification with others helps them overcome the isolation and stigmatisation a bereavement might bring. We hope that the future will see the development of a group work approach in this field.

References

Heap, K. (1985) *The Practice of Social Work with Groups.* London: Allen and Unwin.

Kitchener, S. and Pennells, M. (1990) 'Bereavement Group for Children'. *Bereavement Care.* 9(3): 30–31.

Pennells, M. and Kitchener, S. (1990) 'Holding back the Nightmares'. *Social Work Today.* 21(25): 14–15.

Preston-Shoot, M. (1987) *Effective Group Work.* London: MacMillan Education.

Segal, R.M. (1984) 'Helping Children Express Grief through Symbolic Communication'. *Social Case Work.:* 590–599.

Stock-Whitaker, D. (1985) *Using Groups to Help People.* London: Routledge and Kegan Paul.

Further reading materials

Brandes, D. and Phillips, H. (1990) *Gamester's Handbook.* Cheltenham: Stanley Thornes.

Heegaard, M.E. (1988) *Facilitator's Guide: For When Someone Very Special Dies.* Minneapolis, USA: Woodland Press.

Jewett, C. (1984) *Helping Children Cope with Separation and Loss.* London: Batsford Academic and Educational.

Training videos

1. That Morning I Went to School.

2. Childhood Grief.

Both videos along with a booklet entitled *Guidelines for Working with Bereaved Children* can be obtained from Sue Smith, Social Work Department, Northampton General Hospital, or Margaret Pennells, Child and Family Consultation Service, Cliftonville, Northampton.

Books for children

Department of Social Work (1989) *Someone Special had Died* London: St. Christopher's Hospice.

Mellonie, B. and Ingpen, R. (1987) *Beginnings and Endings with Lifetimes In Between.* Surrey: Dragons World.

Mystrom, C. (1990) *Emma Says Goodbye.* Oxford: Lion Book.

Simms, A. (1986) *Am I Still a Sister?* Louisiana: Big A and Co.

Varley, S. (1985) *Badger's Parting Gifts.* London: Collins (Lion).

CHAPTER 15

Encopresis

Kedar Nath Dwivedi and Sue Bell

Encopresis refers to the inability to control bowel functions in the absence of a major organic pathology. For clinical purposes it means the passing of a bowel movement in an inappropriate place beyond the age of four years. Paediatricians have tended to distinguish 'Encopresis' from 'Soiling' by calling the involuntary passage of mucous and liquid faeces as 'Soiling' and the passage of stools on inappropriate occasions as 'Encopresis'. Child psychiatrists and others, however, use both terms interchangeably.

There are a number of organic pathologies that can lead to disturbed bowel functions. An anal fissure (small ulcerated cleft in the mucous membrane of the anus) for example, can cause severe pain on defecation leading to the child consciously holding back from passing faeces. Resulting constipation and the loss of tone of the intestinal wall and the sphincter leads to soiling. A defect in the nerve supply to a part of the colon (as in Hirschsprungs disease) can lead to obstruction and results in dilation and hypertrophy of the more proximal segments and disturbed bowel function requiring surgery. Similarly congenital hyperthyroidism and rectal anomalies, spina bifida, intestinal infections and so on, can be responsible for bowel dysfunction.

These organic pathologies are very rare in comparison to encopresis associated with constipation, but without such organic pathologies. Children who have never established bowel control, that is, those who have not been continuously clean for a period of at least six months are considered to suffer from continuous (or primary) encopresis and those who have shown independent bowel control for at least six months before showing instances of encopresis are considered to be of onset (or secondary) type.

Epidemiology

Encopresis is four to five times more common in boys than in girls and the prevalence increases with age. For example, at the age of seven or eight years the prevalence in a study was found to be 2.3 per cent in boys and 0.7 per cent in girls, but lower at the age of ten to twelve years, i.e., 1.3 per cent in boys and 0.3 per cent in girls (Rutter *et al.* 1970). In 50–60 per cent of children the encopresis is secondary and approximately 25 per cent of children with encopresis also have enuresis (Fritz and Armbrust 1982). This may be due to the pressure of the distended bowel on the bladder. The most common time for encopresis has been found to be afternoon and early evening, between 3pm and 7pm (Fielding and Doleys 1988). Encopresis during sleep is very rare and is usually associated with organic pathology such as epilepsy.

The issue of classification and terminology is yet to be resolved as various variables do influence the outcome and choice of treatment. There are, in fact, many schemes of classification in the literature emphasising different variables such as constitutional factors, toilet training, nature of retention, quantity of faecal output, nature of onset and so forth. (Anthony 1957, Coekin and Gairdener 1960, Easson 1960, Davidson *et al.* 1963, Woodmansey 1967, Gavanski 1971, Levine 1975 and Hersov 1985). These attempts are largely based upon theoretical assumptions and clinical impressions. Different conclusions are also due to differing clinical populations of child psychiatrists and paediatricians. One way of classifying the problem would be as follows:

1. Retentive

    (a) Physical in origin (e.g. anal fissure, Hirschsprungs disease).

    (b) Emotional in origin (e.g. phobic, aggressive).

2. Non-retentive

    (a) Continuous (e.g. spina-bifida).

    (b) Onset type (e.g. regressive, aggressive).

Some contributory factors and assessment

Psychosocial and family factors

Bellman (1966) conducted a large epidemiological study on all seven- to eight-year-old school children in Stockholm. She sent questionnaires to their parents and received 8,863 replies. This identified 1.5 per cent of children as encopretic and their parents and teachers were then interviewed for further psychiatric assessment. Nearly half of these children had continuous encopresis while the others were of the onset type. The study revealed various associations such as a family history of encopresis, stressful life events, food refusal, enuresis, anxiety, lack of self assertion, aggressiveness, dependence on mother, defiance, adjustment problems and disturbed family relationships. Many other studies have explored various associations such as with developmental factors (Bemporad *et al.* 1971), psychiatric disturbance (McTaggart and Scott 1959) and family disturbance (Wolters 1978).

Wolters' (1978) study on 46 families with encopresis in the Netherlands revealed that the majority of these mothers married at a younger age than the average Dutch woman and were rather over indulgent while the fathers had little involvement in their families. In a high proportion (67%) of families one or both parents had psychiatric problems requiring professional help and 46 per cent of marriages had sexual problems in comparison to 15 per cent of marriages of parents of dialysis children.

Role of toilet training

A regular cycle of rectal filling and defecation is an important element in establishing bowel control. Continence of faeces cannot be expected without regular use of the toilet. Children may not learn to use the toilet for defecation if the parents are unconcerned about training. Similarly, aggressive or punitive toilet training by parents who may be rather rigid, obsessional and authoritarian can produce neat, meticulous children with constipation and soiling. The toilet training in such a family gets invested with high levels of both tension and importance as the parents find soiling most distressing. Many of these children are immature and show excessive dependence (Hoag *et al.* 1971). Some mothers have a great fear of constipation and use laxatives to excess. For some children soiling may be a mode of expressing their unconsciously felt aggressive feelings towards their parents.

Role of constipation

Chronic constipation is five times more common in children with encopresis than with other children (Fritz and Armbrust 1982). The degree of constipation can be described in four stages (Woodmansey 1967);

1. *Phobic Aversion,* that is, fear associated with defecation which may be due to anal fissures, diarrhoea during infancy or history of enemas, suppositories, laxatives and so on for real or imagined constipation. Fear may also be associated with defecation in certain places or situations, for example, the presence of mother or certain individuals, pot or lavatory flushing. However, when the child is relaxed there is often a respite defecation, usually at the wrong time and place and can easily elicit punishment by the care givers leading to further fear of defecation.

2. *General inhibition* of defecation, until at last the bowel empties accidentally. This is the most common stage of constipation in children with encopresis and again elicits more punishment by care givers.

3. *Retention* and rectal distention because of which more and more amount of tension is required to initiate any defecation reflex. As the rectum does not empty fully, there is faecal displacement, dropping of faecal pellets, or continuous straining.

4. *Impacted* colon due to the hardened solid mass of faeces around which the liquid waste finds its way from time to time, leading to overflow. There is no proper defecation.

Associated psychiatric disturbance

Many children with encopresis have associated psychiatric disturbance in the form of conduct disorder and/or emotional disturbance. However, the psychiatric disturbances are usually the effect of encopresis, associated shame and interpersonal difficulties. Feeling of shame and embarrassment leads to hiding of pants and a reaction of distress, anger or upset if the topic of soiling is mentioned or discussed. This affects the self esteem, leading to poor peer relationships and isolation, educational deficits, emotional disturbance and/or conduct disorder and delinquency. Such disturbances also escalate parental hostility and guilt leading to family disharmony and further stress which makes encopresis worse.

Assessment

Medical examination would be essential to exclude any organic pathology and to assess the degree of constipation. It is also important to elicit a detailed history of the problem, developmental and family background and to determine the type of encopresis and the kinds of treatment that have been tried. Assessment of motivation, isolation, shame, rejection and self esteem etc. in addition to personal profile (e.g. hobbies, exercise and diet) family relationships and any associated psychiatric disturbance is also important for devising adequate treatment.

Some principles of management

There have been several clinical approaches to treat this condition. For example, vigorous catharsis in hospital or at home with the help of enemata, suppositories and oral laxatives has been demonstrated to be successful in children with constipation (Coekin and Gairdner 1960, Davidson *et al.* 1963, Levine and Bakow 1976). However, such 'anal assaults' are likely to intensify the hostile struggle between the child and significant others (Sluckin 1981). There is also a problem of high relapse rate which has been shown to be associated with less vigorous catharsis and lack of compliance (Levine and Bakow 1976). Compliance with treatment may cease if the family members don't find the treatment effective enough. Proper counselling to 'demystify' the treatment process and to prepare emotionally for the treatment can improve the compliance to a great extent (Levine 1982, Wakefield *et al.* 1984).

Positive reinforcement of frequent toilet use and maintaining cleanliness during defined periods of time, with the help of star charts, praise and other rewards have also proved to be effective methods of treatment (Wright and Walker 1977). But, poor compliance is again a problem. Moreover, the child has to stay at home and miss school to implement a very frequent toilet visit, and can be rather emotionally demanding on the parents. A similar regime has been used in hospital in some non-compliant, resistant or severe cases (Neale 1963, Webster and Gore 1980). The child's school may also be persuaded to co-operate and implement the programme at school (Sluckin 1981).

Scapegoating, hostility, enmeshment and other family disturbances greatly influence the treatment process. Family therapy may help to treat such relationship disturbances and minimise their negative influences. However, many families are non-compliant in attending family therapy sessions. Individual or group psychotherapy and play therapy may provide some protection to the child from emotionally negative influences of the school and family and such psychotherapeutic measures can also help in dealing with shame, denial, poor confidence, effects of emotionally traumatic events and other emotional disturbances (McTaggart and Scott 1959).

Though different approaches to treatment have been demonstrated to be successful in certain groups of cases, there has been a growing recognition for the need of combining them as soiling often occurs due to a complex interaction of physical and psychological factors (Wright 1973, Wakefield *et al.* 1984).

Some of the important aspects of the above treatments are summarised below:

Psycho-educational work
Encopresis often evokes strong feelings of shame, revulsion, anger and blame. Parents tend to blame the child for soiling and think that the child does it deliberately and is lazy or hurtful. Exploring these feelings and counteracting wrong beliefs are the most important elements of management. It is very important to explain in detail with the help of diagrams, how inadequate muscular control or reduced sensitivity to the urge to defecate can lead to constipation and encopresis (Levine 1982). The child's carers have to be helped to appreciate how punishment seriously hinders the learning process and therefore rejecting, shaming or spanking can only make the situation worse.

Accurate recording

An on-going record of encopresis and toilet use is essential before starting any specific treatment.

Action plan

The hallmark of treatment is focussed on gains, however small. Depending on the specific situations, a plan of action has to be jointly prepared which includes a variety of tasks. The main purpose is to restore the normal state of emptiness of the rectum. If there is considerable constipation a laxative may have to be used as well and the defecation reflex initiated by the laxative. It can become an opportunity to establish a regular toilet routine. Abdominal massage, hot drinks and other pleasant prompts and cues can be used to establish such a routine. Similarly, regular meals with adequate roughage and exercises should be encouraged. One should check that the child knows how to 'push' and doesn't just sit passively on the toilet. The child should be allowed ample time for defecation to occur, that is, about five minutes. The parents should be prepared for the possibility that it may take several months before the problem is cleared and in fact the situation may get worse in the beginning.

Rewards

Praise, stars, tokens and/or other reinforcers must be mobilised consistently to reinforce even the smallest gains, for example, putting soiled clothes in a Napisan bucket; decrease in the number of prompts required to use the toilet; amount of time stayed on the toilet; number of self initiated toileting; and decrease in frequency of accidents, and so on (Blackwell 1989).

If star charts and reward systems are improperly used they can cause more harm than good. It is therefore essential to define very clearly the behaviour which has to become observable that will be rewarded. Once the system is in operation the reward should only be given for target behaviour. There should be no room for interim bargaining and, once given, the reward should never be taken back from the child. If the system is not working and the threshold needs lowering or if the system has become very successful and has hit the ceiling for some time, then it should be formally renegotiated and new targets set.

Reducing stress

It is important to try to reduce the stress associated with toileting. Children with encopresis are very likely to have been subjected to harsh and punitive attitudes which means that they often feel aversive and distressed towards toileting. If that is the case toileting has to be turned into fun by encouraging the child to bring in toys, books, radio taped story or posters and so forth. If the child is very frightened of the toilet one can desensitise to the toilet by starting at distance from the toilet at which the child is happy and then bringing the child a little closer to it. At each step towards the toilet the child should be praised and rewarded; there is no need to coerce and if the child is too anxious one should not move onto the next step too soon. A procedure like this can be tried up to three times a day until the child is able to sit comfortably on the toilet.

Bowel training

Having attended to the aspects of diet, anxiety, exercise and laxatives, it is important to work out a detailed training programme for establishing a toilet routine. For example, the child should sit down and eat breakfast every morning along with a warm drink. Twenty to forty minutes later he or she should go (or be taken) to the toilet to attempt defecation and could stay for five minutes. Such supervised regular toileting should be continued until the child has established a defecation routine for two weeks. Gradually the responsibilities are handed over to the child, step by step. The aim is to help the child become aware of the sensations and actions associated with appropriate use of the toilet for defecation.

Associated symptoms

Treatment of associated psychiatric disturbance through play therapy, counselling and group therapy to improve self esteem and interpersonal skills is also important. Activities such as swimming can be extremely valuable for raising self esteem. Family therapy can help with disturbed family relationships.

Termination

If there is no evidence of improvement, it is unwise to continue the same treatment plan for more than six months. A break for a while from treatment or a shift in emphasis may be useful. When the treatment is successful it is better to phase out the treatment gradually rather than abruptly, and also to warn the family about relapse so that early evidence of recurring problems (such as larger stools, missed toileting, abdominal pain) can lead to prompt action in a matter of fact way.

Group work with children

A comprehensive treatment programme for encopresis can also be offered in a group setting involving a whole or half a day every week. This could include various structured activities (e.g. yoga exercises, swimming, abdominal massage, lunch, using the toilet, drawing star charts), psycho-educational work and counselling in addition to the use of the group processes for the purpose of treatment. Marital strain, educational deficit, financial constraints, food fads, disciplinary difficulties, scape-goating and over protection are different facets of the problem. Some of the common themes and issues important in such group work are as follows.

Shame

The story of encopresis or soiling is a story of shame, embarrassment and humiliation. Shame is a universal phenomenon and all of us have experienced shame at some point in our lives. The feeling of shame is a very powerful and intense feeling. One wishes the ground beneath would crack open and one could hide, so that no one could see one's face again. The wish to disappear or even die can thus be associated with shame. All feelings have a certain contagious quality. Thus joy, anger, sorrow, shame and so on can spread just by association. It is, therefore, understandable that when a child keeps making a mess in his or her pants, whatever the reason, it is not only he or she who feels ashamed, but also their family, friends, teachers, class mates and others may feel ashamed of the child. Coping with shame is a very difficult task. Even some very successful people are known to have committed suicide in the face of shame associated with the disclosure of their fraud, shoplifting, failing exami-nations, or sexual relationships. Some develop strategies in order to protect the self against further encounters with shame (e.g. denial, internal withdrawal, rage, contempt, striving for perfection, striving for power, transfer of blame, humour). Many mental health problems such as compulsive (e.g. physical abuse, sexual abuse, addictive disorder, eating disorder) schizoid, paranoid, depressive, borderline and narcissistic syndromes are rooted in shame (Kaufman 1987). Thus, using the group processes to work through shame is the most beneficial aspect of group work with this condition.

Isolation

Avoidance of social intercourse or emotionally meaningful relationships can become another means of protecting oneself not only from the real but also from imagined humiliation. Some children with encopresis, therefore, become reluctant to go to school, make friends or enjoy relationships. They tend to lead an insular and isolated life, feeling more and more miserable, tearful, emotion-ally sensitive, and miss out on learning social skills. Some others seek reassur-ance, give up protecting themselves, become dependent on others and soak up others' overprotective, indulgent or hostile feelings.

Thus, knowing the fact that there are many other children who have this problem and exploring each others feelings regarding these matters and finding ways to overcome these in a safe setting of the group and improving social skills can be very therapeutic.

Denial, compensation and blame

Some children defend themselves through disassociation and denial. They switch off, hide their pants, don't even notice the smells or the teasing. Denial is so intense that it may be difficult to offer help. Others, however, fight back in order to compensate for the lost self esteem due to shame. They become aggressive and violent, steal and fabricate and are quick to blame others. It is not just the child who has to struggle with his shame, but also his brothers, sisters, parents and parental figures. The scene is therefore set for the most complex of defensive interactions which can be explored during group work.

Self esteem, social competence, self confidence and self control

Group processes provide opportunities for identification and for mirroring, to notice and cultivate positive aspects of oneself, experiment with social skills and build up self confidence and self control.

Group work with parents

Parents are equally affected by the processes of shame, denial, rejection, blame, hostility, guilt and over-protectiveness. Some think that their child hates them and is trying to get at them by being bone lazy, embarrassing and anti-social. Some parents describe their children as 'Jekyll and Hyde', 'Schizophrenic', 'Possessed by the Devil' and so on. A child's natural response, such as defecating while relaxing (watching TV or playing) and inability to perform while being tense (coerced to sit on the toilet) provide opportunities for the parents to project onto their children feelings and attributes that essentially belonged to themselves or to their partners, in-laws, workmates, parents, siblings and so on.

A group for such parents not only provides a forum for making sense of the physical and emotional problems associated with encopresis in their children but also a source of support to bring about change. It offers a therapeutic opportunity for working through their feelings and perceptions. They learn how to provide positive reinforcements to their children's small successes, as they get in touch with the feelings of the children within themselves.

References

Anthony, E.J. (1957) 'An Experimental Approach to the Psychopathology of Childhood: Encopresis'. *British Journal of Medical Psychology*. 30: 146–175.

Bellman, M. (1966) 'Studies in Encopresis'. *Acta Paediatrica Scandinavia*. Supplement, 170.

Bemporad, J.L., Pfeifer, C.M., Gibbs, L., Cortner, R.H. and Bloom, W. (1971) 'Characteristics of Encopretic Patients and their Families'. *Journal of American Academy of Child Psychiatrists*. 10: 272–292.

Blackwell, C. (1989) *A Guide to Encopresis*. Northumberland Health Authority.

Coekin, M. and Gairdener, D. (1960) 'Faecal Incontinence in Children'. *British Medical Journal.* 5207: 1175–1180.

Davidson, M., Kugler, M.M. and Bauer, C.H. (1963) 'Diagnosis and Management in Children with Severe and Protracted Constipation and Obstipation'. *Journal of Paediatrics.* 62(2): 261–275.

Easson, W.M. (1960) 'Encopresis – Psychogenic Soiling'. *Canadian Medical Association Journal.* 82: 624–628.

Fielding, D.M. and Doleys, D.M. (1988) 'Elimination Problems: Enuresis and Encopresis'. In E.J. Mash and L.G. Terdahl (eds) *Behavioural Assessment of Childhood Disorders* (2nd Edition). New York: Guilford Press.

Fritz, G.K. and Armbrust, J. (1982) 'Enuresis and Encopresis'. *Psychiatric Clinics of North America.* 5(2): 283–296.

Gavanski, M. (1971) 'The Treatment of Non Retentive Secondary Encopresis with Imipramine and Psychotherapy'. *Canadian Medical Association Journal.* 104: 46–48.

Hersov, L. (1985)' Faecal Soiling'. In M. Rutter and L. Hersov (eds) *Child and Adolescent Psychiatry: Modern Approaches.* Oxford: Blackwell Scientific Publishers. Chapter 29: 482–489.

Hoag, J.M., Norriss, N.G., Himeno, E.T. and Jacobs, J. (1971) 'The Encopretic Child and his Family'. *Journal of the American Academy of Child Psychiatrists.* Vol 10: 242–256.

Kaufman, G. (1987) 'Disorders of Self Esteem: Psychotherapy for Shame Based Syndromes'. In P.A. Keller and S.R. Heyman (eds) *Innovations in Clinical Practice: A Source Book.* Sarasota: Professional Resources Exchange.

Levine, M.D. (1975) 'Children with Encopresis: A Descriptive Analysis'. *Pediatrics.* 56(3): 412–416.

Levine, M.D. (1982) 'Encopresis: Its Potentiation, Evaluation and Alleviation'. *Pediatric Clinics of North America.* 29: 315–330.

Levine, M.D. and Bakow, H. (1976) 'Children with Encopresis: A Study of Treatment Outcome'. *Paediatrics.* 58(6): 845–852.

McTaggart, A. and Scott, M. (1959) 'A Review of Twelve Cases of Encopresis'. *Journal of Paediatrics.* 54: 762–768.

Neale, D.H. (1963) 'Behaviour Therapy and Encopresis in Children'. *Behaviour Research and Therapy.* 1: 139–149.

Rutter, M., Tizard, J. and Whitmore, K. (1970) (eds) *Education, Health and Behaviour.* London: Longman.

Sluckin, A. (1981) 'Behavioural Social Work with Encopretic Children, their Families and the School. *Child: Care, Health and Development.* 7: 67–80.

Wakefield, M.A., Woodbridge, C., Steward, J. and Croke, W.M. (1984) 'A Treatment Programme for Faecal Incontinence'. *Developmental Medicine and Child Neurology.* 26: 613–616.

Webster, A. and Gore, E. (1980) 'The Treatment of Intractable Encopresis: a Team Intervention Approach'. *Child: Care, Health and Development.* 6: 351–360.

Wolters, W.H.G. (1978) 'The Influence of Environmental Factors on Encopretic Children'. *Acta Paedopsychiatrica.* 43: 159–172.

Woodmansey, A.C. (1967) 'Emotion and the Motions: an Inquiry into the Causes and Prevention of Functional Disorders of Defecation'. *British Journal of Medical Psychology.* 40: 207–223.

Wright, L. (1973) 'Handling the Encopretic Child'. *Professional Psychology.* 4: 137–144.

Wright, L. and Walker, E. (1977) 'A Simple Behavioural Treatment Programme for Psychogenic Encopresis'. *Behaviour Research and Therapy.* 16: 209–212.

CHAPTER 16

Victims and Perpetrators
of Sexual Abuse

Andy Howard

This chapter will consider the treatment modality of group work in relation to childhood victims and perpetrators of sexual abuse. Reference is made to the predisposing factors which impact both behaviourally and psychologically on these two clinical groups. In addressing the assessment and treatment needs, indication will be given of the methods and approaches which clinicians have consistently found to be most productive.

Victims of sexual abuse

Most of the specific behavioural problems associated with sexually abused children can be understood in terms of inappropriate learned behaviour and maladaptive coping mechanisms which have developed for the purpose of avoiding painful feelings and as an explanation for disturbing events. Berliner (1988) and Finkelhor (1979) stress the importance of dealing with the full range of trauma issues. There is now a substantial body of work which demonstrates that the most effective method of achieving recovery is via the medium of group work. Group work makes a number of contributions to treatment. It enables the reduction of isolation, promotes the development of more appropriate interpersonal and social skills, and provides a safe setting in which children can communicate their distress and regain a sense of power and control over their lives.

The traumagenic dynamics model of child sexual abuse proposed by Finkelhor and Brown (1985) suggests that victims of sexual abuse are damaged in four significant areas. The child is traumatically sexualised by the offender, who exchanges or enforces attention and affection for sexual contact. This is achieved by the offender impressing upon the child misconceptions about sexual behaviour and sexual morality as a means of legitimising his or her actions. The child is rewarded for sexual behaviour inappropriate to their age and stage of development, whilst at the same time being conditioned to equate sexual activity with negative emotions, thoughts and memories.

The child experiences confusion about sexual norms and sexual identity. Sex becomes linked with the giving or receiving of care and affection. Particularly during adolescence and adulthood, the victimised individual can experience negative associations with sexual activity, leading to an avoidance of sexual contact and intimacy. Conversely, sexual abuse may also result in sexual preoccupation and compulsive sexual behaviour. Disturbance in a variety of forms can emerge, including precocious sexual activity or aggressive sexual behaviour. This is particularly evident in dual-status children who have become both victim and abuser.

The child is stigmatised by being blamed, humiliated and denigrated by the abuser. Pressure is brought to bear on the child by the perpetrator and, sometimes, significant others in order to establish secrecy. The child develops a sense of shame and guilt that is often compounded by the actions of other individuals upon disclosure, particularly where shock and blame result. The victim becomes stereotyped as damaged or tainted in some way. A reduction in self-worth reinforces negative comparisons with others, confirming the victim's belief that they are different from their peers. Stigmatisation can manifest itself in criminal behaviour, drug and alcohol abuse, self-harm and attempted suicide.

Sexual abuse, particularly when perpetrated by adults or young people who are in a position of trust, results in a profound experience of betrayal. The vulnerability and dependence of the child is manipulated through the violation of social norms which imply that children can expect to be cared for and protected. Victims may become dependent or introverted and solitary as their ability to judge the reliability of others is undermined. Commonly, feelings associated with grief and loss emerge, manifesting themselves in depression, anger and hostility. It is betrayal that makes children who have been sexually abused vulnerable to further abuse and exploitation. Isolation and anger can become directed into delinquent behaviour. In adulthood an impoverished sense of judgment, allied with vulnerability, may lead to individuals' own children becoming vulnerable to exploitation by potential abusers.

Powerlessness stems from the destructive invasion of the child's body against his or her wishes. The perpetrator uses force or deception in order to involve the child in activities they may feel unable to prevent or protect themselves against. Repeated experiences of fear may be communicated, either directly or indirectly, by children. However, they may be unable to make others believe them. It is powerlessness that contributes to victimisation, through anxiety, fear and reduced efficacy. Children and young people who become abusers subsequent to their own sexual victimisation are acting upon their need to control their environment by identifying themselves with the abuser. It has been suggested that this process may be mediated by gender, making it more likely that boys who have been abused become sexually aggressive. Other behavioural indicators include nightmares, phobias, eating and sleeping disorders, depression and school-based problems.

In assessing the treatment needs of sexually abused children it is possible, by considering their descriptions of experiences and placing these alongside the known dynamics of sexual abuse, to predict the likely impact on the child. By predicting and identifying particular effects the group worker is able to direct the intervention and influence the group agenda with regard to certain issues – aggression, anxiety and so forth.

Group work with pre-pubertal children

When conducting group therapy with pre-pubertal victims of sexual abuse it is useful to involve carers directly in the work being undertaken. This relieves the child of an inappropriate sense of responsibility and accountability for their own protection. It clearly identifies the carer in the role of protector, which is a proper reflection of role. Furthermore, it is the carer, and not the therapist, who will be in a position to ensure their future safety and protection from further abuse. Traditional therapeutic approaches have tended to identify the child as the target of intervention, leaving carers uninformed and left to cope with the resulting behaviour. For the carer, direct involvement in the therapeutic process provides them with valuable insights and information, making them feel truly engaged in the recovery of their child. Empowering carers can lead to more effective use of therapeutic time within the group and allow the work being undertaken the affirmation within the home environment it requires.

The group work programme is based on a multi-dimensional model, including a psychotherapeutic, psychoeducational and skills development component. Psychotherapy addresses the psychological damage which results from sexually abusive experiences. The recognition of both positive and negative feelings towards the perpetrator are expressed by the participants via the therapist working directly with the group process. A psychoeducational approach, concentrating on sex education and self-protection, enhances the child's knowledge base. The exploration and understanding of facts and information is vital and should not be seen as secondary to other therapeutic aspects. It is lack of information and knowledge that is the cause of childhood vulnerability and which makes children easy targets for abusers. Children who have been sexualised and victimised are made more vulnerable as a result of confusion, poor self-worth and faulty learning. Boundary setting on the basis of age, gender and social behaviour confirms the message that children should not be exposed to adult sexual intimacy. The development of skills provides the means for young children to deal with the effects of trauma. Anxiety control through relaxation and visualisation, assertiveness and social skills training can combat behavioural deficits resulting from abusive experiences.

In order to establish meaningful communication with young children a range of media must be offered. They can act as vehicles for the expression of feeling and emotions and the development of understanding of what are often complex concepts. For children up to the age of three years the primary information is best received through the care giver using a variety of non-verbal techniques in order to provide and receive information. When working with children aged between four years and ten years the needs of carers can be met within the group work context which operates parallel to the therapeutic provision for the child. This approach is particularly valuable for foster parents as in many instances seriously abused children will be in the care of the Local Authority. It is important for carers to identify boundaries of confidentiality in order to ensure the protection of individual children and other family members. Sexually abused children can feel as if their lives are exposed to the scrutiny of others, undermining their privacy, and emphasising their victimisation and disempowerment. The perceived risk to other members of the foster family and the negative influence of the acting-out behaviour of the children are significant predisposing factors in placement breakdown. Giving carers the confidence and skills to respond appropriately to difficult behaviour, addressing the fear of contamination, and helping them to provide suitable explanations for their own natural and foster children, contribute to the stabilisation of potentially vulnerable circumstances.

When working with pre-pubertal children it is generally the case that, with increasing age, their reliance on the care giver diminishes, as the impact of peer relations and relative independence comes into effect. It can be useful to provide children aged approximately between four and ten years with a transitional object, such as a valued toy or a piece of art material. During times of stress the child can gain confidence and reassurance from the object in the absence of their carer.

When using art work within the group work context it is interpretations made by the children rather than the workers which provide the most powerful evidence of their experience. The development of stories through literature and writing exercises is a useful means by which the child can gain access to otherwise confused feelings and information. Distressed children commonly develop fears, so toys which reflect their worries and preoccupations can represent, in a less threatening manner, aspects of themselves and others for the group to explore. Monster images allow children to regain a sense of control within the safety of the therapeutic session. A range of glove puppets, indicating strength, wisdom and naivety, for example, can be used by children to set up a fantasy story which reflects their own reality. Using a puppet as a vehicle for communication removes the focus from the child, thus reducing the intensity and psychological pressure. Transformation toys, which demonstrate positive and negative forces, help children to explore the traits of significant individuals in their lives. The perpetrator may appear warm and approachable at times, yet on other occasions behaves abusively and with threat. Transformation is important in that it suggests the possibility of change. Prisms and kaleidoscopes produce altered images, thus helping the child to identify with the concept. Symbols representing emotions, such as anger, sadness, or pleasure, aid confused children in identifying their feelings and, through interactive play, enable the child to express them more directly. In conducting therapeutic group work, play materials and activities can usefully be chosen for their ambiguity, as children need these indirect triggers in order to retrieve painful material.

In group work with children under the age of ten years boundaries of behaviour are clearly reinforced by the worker. It is common in this age group for children to act out with their peers, which means that the group workers must ensure a protective, safe, group environment. On a practical level, staff numbers may be critical in ensuring an appropriate degree of control. Inappropriate, sexualised behaviour within the group is dealt with directly and not ignored. Programmes should include aspects of prevention; however, these need to be more clearly defined and not as oblique as material contained in programmes of prevention designed for children who may not have been abused.

Group work with adolescents

Unlike groups for very young children, groups involving adolescents are usually single gender, due to the greater relevance of sexuality and gender identity in this phase of development. The gender of the groupworkers must also be addressed, particularly given that the majority of perpetrators are male. It has been strongly argued, particularly by feminist therapists working in this field, that a male presence is not indicated. However, providing that the male worker is sensitive to the impact of his behaviour, takes care not to take the lead role, and receives adequate support from a female co-worker, a male can bring an additional dimension to the group process. It can, equally, be argued that a male worker is in a position to represent an alternative model of male behaviour to that which has been experienced by the group participants. A male worker also acts as a focus for the negative feelings participants might feel towards their abuser, thus enhancing the expression of strong and potentially self-destructive feelings.

Careful planning and preparation is required prior to establishing a group including a male worker in relation to the implications this might have on the life of the group, the connection to the aims of the group and the relationship between the group workers. The choice of individual is crucial and must take account of attitude, depth of self-awareness and acknowledgement and understanding of gender stereotypes which prevail in society at large. The most significant difference between groups for adolescent girls and boys is the issue of gender identity. Given that the majority of sexually abused males will have been assaulted by a perpetrator of their own gender, these factors, allied with the homophobic responses within the community, can lead to an increased anxiety and internal conflict about sexual orientation. An additional important issue in offering group work for young males is the recognition of a generalised gender difference in the way communication operates. As the result of their socialisation men tend not to be as open or expressive on a feeling level as women. Therefore the verbalisation and expression of emotion in a male group is likely to be more problematic.

Group work as a treatment modality is particularly useful with adolescent victims of sexual abuse as it reduces the profound sense of isolation endured by many individuals. Acknowledging what has happened with others who have also been abused validates the individual both internally and in the eyes of their peers, helping to normalise their response to the abusive experiences. The group is a forum where empowerment can take place through mutual support, leading to increased self-esteem. The development of communication and social skills occurs simply through the act of taking part and despite the nature of the group work programme. Certain practitioners in the field have suggested that individual therapy can mirror the circumstances in which sexual abuse originally took place in that it can appear secretive, intense and produce a significant power differential between therapist and client. Group work can therefore be seen as less threatening and the participant numbers denote a greater degree of safety.

This does not, of course, mean that group work is indicated in every case. Indeed, a degree of individual work is usually required before a victim is likely to cope with the group work setting. Certain manifestations and pitfalls require constant vigilance on the part of the therapists. Adolescents who have been sexually abused and made to feel special by their abuser can seek to compare experiences in a rivalrous way. Indeed, the competitive ethos evident within a western industrial society is as likely to occur within a therapeutic group as in any other collective situation. Victimised behaviour in some individuals can inevitably lead them to become 'scapegoated' by other group members. From a psychodynamic perspective the group represents family roles, with the groupworkers in the position of parent figures. The need for a group to conform may lead to participants seeking the approval of groupworkers by stating what they think the adults wish to hear rather than the real issues which are concerning them. Conversely, the group may rebel against or attack the group leaders, particularly if they come to represent a coercive authority, causing the leaders themselves to become vulnerable. As the needs of each individual member must be accounted for, progress, and therefore the pacing of a particular group, may become difficult to judge. Participants will inevitably be at different stages in their recovery, which causes the ending phase of the group to be potentially fraught. Victims of sexual abuse feel isolated and alone, which has implications when assessing referrals from the position of gender, race and culture. Placing singleton participants in a group should be avoided, as there needs to be at least a match or pairing that can reduce the potential for 'scapegoating' and alleviate the strong sense of difference felt by most victims. A further contra-indicator when identifying potential participants for a group is the evidence of symptomatic behaviour. If an adolescent is in a phase of actively harming themselves, a group may not be able to contain them adequately. Groups are chiefly about symptom control: therefore the respective agenda and needs may be incompatible.

Sexually abusive adolescents

A sexually abusive adolescent can be defined as a:

> 'young person from puberty up to the age of 18 years who commits any sexual act with a person of any age against their will, or without consent, in an aggressive, exploitative manner'. (Ryan 1986, p.385)

The most recent annual Home Office statistics indicate that of the offenders cautioned or found to be guilty of a sexual offence, 32 per cent were below the age of 21, and 17 per cent were under the age of 16 years (NCH 1992). However, these figures undoubtedly represent a significant underestimate of the true scale of offending, as demonstrated by a British Crime Survey, which suggests that only 10 per cent of sexual crimes are ever reported (Hoghughi and Richardson 1990). The reasons for this are varied and probably not wholly understood, particularly in relation to young people. It is widely recognised from work undertaken with victims of sexual abuse that sexually abusive acts may have been perpetrated against them many times before they disclose. Fear, combined with guilt and shame, may prevent a proportion of children from disclosing at all – a view which would be supported by the significant number of adults who subsequently report childhood abuse through the mental health services. A successful disclosure also relies upon the ability or willingness of the recipient to act upon the information given. Again, the anecdotal material available from victims supports the view that many children are met with disbelief and denial.

Sexual abuse perpetrated by what are predominantly young males has been commonly perceived by the community as an example of normal sexual exploration and experimentation. Within the professional network not only has this attitude led to under-reporting, it has also produced a varied and inconsistent response around the country. In the last 15 years, particularly in the United States, professionals employed within the criminal and welfare services have started to take seriously the significance of adolescent sexual offending. Perhaps the single most important contributory factor in this process has been the findings generated from work undertaken with convicted adult perpetrators which have indicated that most began their offending careers during the adolescent phase. In addition, the histories of both groups demonstrate a high incidence of sexual victimisation in their early years. When this picture is broadened to include other forms of abuse, including emotional and physical, it becomes clear that the vast majority of adult and adolescent offenders have had an experience of being victimised in childhood.

Saunders and Awad (1988) in a review of a sample of studies indicate a range of characteristics which were presented repeatedly. In addition to abuse-related traits, social awkwardness and isolation was a feature, as were academic or behavioural problems in school, psychopathology, including neurotic conduct and personality disorder.

The victimisation of females in our society remains a major unresolved issue, but one that is nevertheless recognised and widely accepted as real. The victimisation of males, by contrast, goes essentially unrecognised despite the fact that males are more likely to become victims of violence than females. In British society males are expected to protect and defend themselves against threat. Consequently, a young male who is unable to cope with a particular circumstance is more likely to internalise a profound sense of guilt, along with feelings of anger and powerlessness. Victims of abuse may produce a learned helplessness or repeated aggression. Victims who do not receive appropriate therapeutic support may experience further victimisation or develop similarly abusive behaviours towards other vulnerable individuals. Sexuality may be an inherent characteristic; however, the expression of that sexuality is determined by the values and boundaries present in society at large.

Assessment

Before considering group work as a modality of treatment it is vital to conduct a comprehensive assessment of each individual. It is important to establish the nature and details of the sexual offence in order to begin to understand the motivation to commit the offence. However, establishing the details of an offence is frequently difficult and the motivation to commit the offence may never become known. Groth and Loredo (1981) propose that eight specific issues should be explored in assessing the adolescent abuser.

1. Difference in age between the offender and victim.
2. Social relationship between the offender and victim.
3. Type of sexual activity.
4. The extent of persuasion, enticement, threat or coercion.
5. The persistence of the sexual activity.
6. Evidence of progression in the nature and frequency of the sexual activity.
7. The nature of fantasies which preceded or accompanied the behaviour.
8. The vulnerability of the victim due to a particular disability or disadvantage.

Obtaining information about the first two items is usually unproblematic, in that reports on the offence will usually be available from the Police and Social Services. Identifying the type of sexual activity is more difficult as many, if not most, adolescent offenders tend to minimise their sexually abusive behaviour either by not describing previous offences, which may remain unknown, or by presenting inconsistent or incomplete accounts of the known offence or offences.

It is important to ask for a sequential description of everything that happened prior to, during and after the offence, including the young person's planning, his impression of the victim's reactions during the offence, the precautions he took in order to avoid discovery, his understanding of how the offence was discovered and his perception of his parents' and other's reactions to the disclosure.

The extent to which persuasion, threats or coercion were used to obtain sexual contact may also be difficult to ascertain. Offenders often tell a plausible story, suggesting that the victim has consented to or provoked sexual activity. Many of these young people are able to persuade relatives, friends and others of their innocence, which can only adequately be challenged when compared with the information contained within the victim's statement.

Determining the persistence of sexual activity and whether there is a progression in the nature and frequency of deviant sexual activity requires questions to be asked of the young person about whether they have engaged in sexually deviant behaviour other than the known offences. Research with adult sexual offenders suggests that several paraphilias can often coexist.

Exploring the nature of fantasies that precede or accompany sexual activity is often a problem with adolescent offenders because they are too embarrassed to talk about them, and therefore co-operation is typically difficult to obtain. Insistence by the young person that they did not experience any sexual feelings or fantasies denotes minimisation and denial.

With regard to the victim, it is important to enquire about the perceptions of the young person in relation to the impact the sexual act had on the victim. Many practitioners suggest that the accounts given by adolescent and adult abusers typically reflect cognitive distortions which underpin their behaviour. Becker and Abel (1985) define these cognitive distortions as involving the belief by the offender that his offence will have a positive outcome for him, and that any negative consequences for both the offender and the victim will be minimal. It can be said that this mode of thinking is the means by which the offender is able to translate fantasy into action.

An unresolved area of controversy in assessing adolescent abusers is the disclosure of information regarding sexual offences otherwise unknown to the justice system. If an assessment is being carried out with a young person who intends to plead innocent to a charge of a sexual nature, addressing the offence during the assessment is not appropriate. Ideally it is best to undertake an assessment after the court has established a finding of guilt and to then carry out the assessment, which then informs plans for intervention prior to sentencing. Such a model is as yet not available within the United Kingdom and sentencing remains a difficult, perhaps idiosyncratic, process.

Treatment

In identifying a long-term plan for the young person consideration needs to be given to their overall functioning. It is likely that an adolescent who has committed a sexual offence will have serious deficits in a number of areas. It is increasingly the case that the treatment plan will include a variety of intervention approaches. Among the community based services, the most frequently described treatment approach includes offender-based group therapy, individual therapy aimed at improving social skills, anger management and the promotion of more appropriate sexual knowledge. The treatment modalities can be combined with family therapy and ongoing supervision by a social worker.

Residential treatment programmes offer focused group therapy, social skills training and individual therapies but may have logistical difficulties in linking these approaches with the family.

Focused group therapy concentrates on the details of the offence, with the aim of enlisting peer group pressure as a means of challenging denial. The aim is to help the adolescent abuser to identify the external and internal events which trigger their sexually abusive behaviour, and to learn to cope with and master these pressures.

At first treatment is directed at confronting denial. The group members must admit their offences openly. Their denial is likely to be well-established and, in part, upheld by cognitive distortions and possibly by inconsistent responses from both family, community and professionals with whom they come into contact.

What sets this approach apart from other forms of group treatment is the degree of confrontation required by the group workers, assisted by peer pressure which is deemed necessary in order to challenge denial appropriately. The success of such a challenging approach can only be assessed in the context of the discomfort and level of unease engendered in a particular individual participant, rather than simply the subjective judgments of the workers involved.

The sexual abuse cycle (Ryan 1987) provides a framework within which the sexual assault process can be defined and examined by considering the individual characteristics of each young abuser. The sexual assault cycle involves the following series of connected stages.

The cycle begins with negative self-image, which can be triggered by a range of emotional situations leading to an inappropriate coping response. Predicting rejection is a reaction to negative feelings, including the development of behaviour which elicits rejection from others, or an active rejection by the adolescent in order to pre-empt a predicted negative response. This position inevitably leads to a deep sense of isolation, withdrawal and self-preoccupation. During the stage of withdrawal, the adolescent abuser may develop fantasies of a deviant sexual nature in order to provide a more potent and positive self-image. For the young abuser, fantasies counter feelings of powerlessness and victimisation, with the aim of recreating their personal negative feelings within the victim. Fantasies lead to the development of cognitive distortions which justify and allow the abusive behaviour to progress. Planning may take place in fantasy or may include an active process of identification and preparation. The final stage is the offence itself and will include activity which reflects earlier aspects of the cycle. It is at the point following a sexually abusive act that the adolescent may experience guilt. However, this may relate more to the risk of being found out than to any real recognition of the victim experience. This short-lived sense of guilt soon lapses and feeds into the abuser's sense of low self-esteem and thus the cycle begins again.

Using the concept of a sexual abuse cycle, the purpose of group work is to help participants become more aware of events which trigger the abusive process and identify different ways of behaving and thinking, in order to enable them to avoid further unacceptable sexual activity. Techniques including brainstorming, role-play and careful analysis of particular situations can help the group refocus aspects of their poor self-esteem into more neutral or positive outcomes. Social skills training, assertiveness and an understanding of sexuality can all contribute to identifying different ways of behaving, thus challenging the expectation that rejection will inevitably take place. The eventual aim of such group work is to prevent the cyclical pattern by helping the adolescent avoid isolation and withdrawal.

In order to understand and gain control of these complex and inter-related responses, a number of methods can be employed. Work between sessions is necessary in order to help the young person consider ways in which daily events contribute to their distorted thinking. Group members might be asked to keep a written record of situations and the feelings that they engender. Sex education and training in the expression of appropriate sexuality can provide both alternative models of behaviour and information which conflicts with distorted beliefs such as the idea that a young child can consent to sexual activity. Group sessions aimed at promoting victim empathy can enable the young person to get in touch with the impact of their behaviour on the victim. Adolescents who are both victim and abuser must learn to separate their own distress as a victim and place blame and responsibility where it belongs, and at the same time accept ownership of their own unacceptable offending behaviour. By confronting cognitive distortion, and challenging the gender-related messages prevalent in society, faulty thinking can be replaced by healthier images and attitudes.

Inappropriate sexual behaviour of younger children

As the connection between sexually abusive behaviour in adolescence and the subsequent development of adulthood perpetration has been made, similarly the incidence of inappropriate sexual activity amongst younger children has now become an area of intervention. Unlike adolescents who may develop sexually abusive behaviour in part due to a history of victimisation or as an inappropriate response to their developing sexuality, clinicians involved with younger children find that a high proportion of them have been sexually abused. Their behaviour can be examined within the context of a sexual abuse cycle. However, the main differences between adolescents and younger children appear to be the manner in which reinforcement takes place. Pre-pubertal children tend to find the exercise of power over their victim the main reinforcing element, whereas the behaviour of adolescent and adult perpetrators is also strongly reinforced by the addictive sexual component, in particular the attainment of orgasm.

The treatment of younger children who abuse can therefore follow a similar programme to that carried out with victims. Two significant areas of difference will be issues arising from the exercise of power and sexual expression. The exercise of power can be usefully addressed in an oblique manner by using examples stemming from incidents of bullying, stealing, rule-breaking and so forth, which in process have a relevance to the sexual component. Much observed behaviour in young children indicates that they have been sexualised and are acting-out their experiences. Therefore, dealing too directly with the sexual abuse within a group context can lead to arousal, which may run counter to the aims of the group and be difficult to control for the groupworkers.

Conclusions

All sexually abused children, irrespective of gender, feel confused and harmed by their experiences. They need encouragement, permission, and an opportunity to talk about the impact of abusive events, and to work through their feelings of isolation and damage. In addition, all such children and their carers require education and empowerment in order to prevent further abuse. Many children will be psychologically disturbed as a result of their abusive experiences and therefore require access to a therapeutic setting where healing can take place. Group work can successfully meet the needs of support, protection and treatment for such childhood victims.

Treatment approaches with adolescent abusers are relatively new in this country, most being based on learning theory and utilising behaviour modification techniques. Unlike groups for abused children where the effect is to promote acceptance and belonging, group work with adolescent perpetrators can be used to challenge poor motivation via peer pressure. Through group work such young people can begin to identify the external and internal psychological events which lead to, or trigger, sexually abusive behaviour. The group provides a forum in which their capacity to cope with and control these pressures can be examined.

References

Becker, J.V. and Abel, G.G. (1985) 'Methodological and Ethical Issues in Evaluating and Treating Adolescent Sexual Offenders'. In E.M. Otey and G.D. Ryan (eds) *Adolescent Sex Offenders: Issues in Research and Treatment.* (Research monograph from the Centre for the Prevention and Control of Rape), Rockville, M.D.: National Institute of Mental Health, 100–129.

Berliner, L. (1988) Interviewing in Child Sexual Abuse. Paper presented at the Glasgow Conference (personal communication).

Finkelhor, D. (1979) *Sexually Victimised Children.* New York: Free Press.

Finkelhor, D. (1986) *A Sourcebook on Child Sexual Abuse.* London: Sage Publications.

Finkelhor, D. and Brown, A. (1985) 'The Traumatic Impact of Child Sexual Abuse: A Conceptualisation'. *American Journal of Orthopsychiatry.* 55(4): 530–541.

Groth, A. and Loredo, C. (1981) 'Juvenile Sexual Offenders: Guidelines for Assessment'. *International Journal of Offender Therapy and Comparative Criminology.* 25: 31–39.

Hoghughi, M. and Richardson, G. (1990) 'The Root of the Problem'. *Community Care.* 838 (1st November) 21–23.

National Children's Home (1992) *The Report of the Committee of Enquiry into Children and Young People who Sexually Abuse Other Children.* London: National Children's Home.

Ryan, G. (1986) 'Adolescent Perpetrators of Sexual Molestation of children'. *Child Abuse and Neglect.* 10, 125–131.

Ryan, G. (1987) 'Juvenile Sex Offenders: Development and Correction'. *Child Abuse and Neglect.* II: 385–395.

Saunders, E.B. and Awad, G. (1988) 'Assessment, Management and Treatment Planning For Male Adolescent Sexual Offenders'. *American Journal of Orthopsychiatry.* 58(4): 571–579.

CHAPTER 17

Group Work with Young Offenders

Julie Harrower

Traditionally, young offenders have been processed through a system which, whilst acknowledging the plethora of contributory factors which might have led to their offending behaviour, including poverty, family background, personality variables, experience of education, and unemployment, has singularly failed to address the goal of reducing the likelihood of further offending by ignoring the very act which set the process in motion, i.e., the offence. Only by understanding offending behaviour in its context, appreciating its irresistibility in some instances, and enabling young people to make informed choices about their behaviour, can any inroads be made into a cycle which at present has horrendous consequences at both an individual and a societal level. Studies in the UK and elsewhere concur that the acquisition of convictions in adolescence is strongly prognostic of future involvement in crime, and other socially maladaptive behaviours in adulthood (Farrington and West 1990; Robins and Ratcliffe 1979; Stattin and Magnusson 1991). It is, therefore, at this point in the cycle that intervention should occur, and group work represents an attractive option for both administrators and practitioners which endeavours to focus on offending behaviour at source. Higher through-put, reduction in labour-intensive techniques, and measurable outcomes all appeal to managers within the criminal justice system but, more important, group work provides for practitioners an opportunity to effectively tackle offending behaviour directly, in a practical and credible way, by facilitating the acquisition of skills which offenders may choose to employ in their efforts to keep out of trouble. Examples of such skills might include learning to control anger, or resisting group pressure; but over and above these specific aims is the desired goal of increased self-knowledge gained within a peer-group setting and rooted in the context of negotiating everyday social interactions. It should be noted from the outset, therefore, that positive evaluation of participation in group work with such aims is very much concerned with broader humanistic objectives than simply the decreased likelihood of reconviction.

Working with young offenders requires a certain amount of bravery on the part of group workers, the sort of bravery which can withstand onslaughts on personal beliefs and values and which reflects a willingness to be completely open and genuine, even when this does not accord with the collective view of the group. Merrit and Walley (1977) describe the ideal group worker as 'creative, non-judgmental, democratic, excited, exciting, sharing, inspiring, strong, sensitive, perceptive, a member of the team, patient, growing, learning, open, alive, honest, exploring, feeling, you!' It does not matter how hip or politically correct your asides, or how up-to-date your trainers are; if you do not appear to be sincere, you will be unable to make connections with your group members. In this sort of group, establishing credibility is rather more important than establishing rapport, and this may best be achieved by laying down the ground-rules from the outset and placing group activity very much within a legal context. Group members are unlikely to have volunteered to participate, but they are present for a reason and they may need to be convinced that their active participation could have unexpected positive consequences.

A tight structure is essential, linked to authoritative control. This should lead to fewer misunderstandings and challenges, but also provides the kind of security which will facilitate self-disclosure. Related to this is the advisability of formulating a contract of expectations at the beginning of the group's life which not only sets out overall decisions concerning meeting time and place and session objectives, but also lays down the rules about confidentiality, so that group members understand that the information which they may disclose within group sessions will go no further. In group work with adolescent sex offenders this condition may need to be revised to take into account unacceptable risk to vulnerable members of the community.

Feindler and Ecton (1986) suggest that group workers of adolescent groups work more effectively as cotherapists than solo, mainly because sharing the task of group workership allows for flexibility, more active involvement, and the possibility of observing the process of change as well as the management of tasks designed to promote change. Moreover, co-workers can serve as models for giving both positive and negative messages in a non-competitive atmosphere.

Group work with young offenders has particular advantages over traditional one-to-one casework. It allows those who are not adept at communicating, either verbally or non-verbally, to participate at their own level of expression and to learn from observing others. An opportunity is also created for 'modelling', whereby group members can learn by demonstration of specific skills or techniques and then by active participation and rehearsal of those skills rather than passively hearing descriptions of appropriate behaviour. The sharing of such experiences in itself can increase the sense of. belonging and motivate change. It also allows group workers to see at first hand what may be inhibiting an individual's social development, rather than just hearing about the problems.

Notwithstanding the advantages of group work for young offenders, there is a problem which will need to be confronted head on, and this is client resistance. In spite of the fact that participation in the group may have been agreed to in order to avoid an even less palatable disposal, most young offenders will not fall into the category of highly motivated clients. They may see no reason to modify their behaviour, feel resentful about the idea of intervention and, as Hollin (1990a) points out, 'their offending, even when accompanied by violence, is something they are good at; it is a skilled behaviour that brings tangible and social rewards − not a problem to be removed' (p.135). It follows, therefore, that group workers are going to have to present some pretty strong and convincing arguments as to why members should engage in a process of change. In addition, they must be prepared to be challenged virtually every step of the way.

The two areas which will be examined here are social skills training, and anger management − both of which rely on cognitive-behavioural techniques developed originally within a clinical psychology setting, but which have the distinct advantage of being tangible and easy to learn by non-psychologists. At the heart of both approaches is an emphasis on assessment using the technique of offence analysis.

Offence analysis

Exploring offence behaviour in an honest and direct way is, of course, essential as a starting point for charting the direction of desired change, but offence analysis rests on a fundamental premise of behaviourist psychology, namely, the principles of operant learning, as exemplified by the work of Skinner (1953 1974). This states quite simply that a person's behaviour is inevitably related to the environmental consequences that behaviour produces. If the consequences are good the behaviour is likely to be repeated, whilst if the consequences are bad the likelihood of repetition is reduced. Behaviour is thus said to operate on the environment to produce changes that may be reinforcing or punishing − hence, behaviour is operant. Operant behaviour does not, however, occur randomly. There are usually cues in the environment which will indicate whether or not particular behaviour is likely to be rewarded or punished. These three elements (cues, behaviour, consequences) combine to produce the A:B:C of behavioural theory, that is, the Antecedent conditions are the signal for Behaviour which produces environmental Consequences. Understanding offence behaviour within the A:B:C framework allows us to 'make sense' of an individual's actions by understanding what function that behaviour has for the individual; in other words, what are the pay-offs and rewards which make it worthwhile to continue along a path which might appear to outsiders to be fraught with difficulties?

McGuire and Priestley (1985), in probably the most widely used manual for working effectively with offenders (and one which has the admirable sub-title of 'Skills and Stratagems for Going Straight'), suggest a straightforward exercise for discovering the essentials of offence behaviour, namely, asking individuals to describe incidents using the '5-WH' device – Who, What, When, Where, Why and How? This can be done on an individual basis but will probably be more productive if done collectively. So, for instance, each question can be broadened in order to force the level of analysis (e.g. 'Who?' can include 'Who suggested the offence?', 'Who was affected by it?' 'Who might have talked you out of it?'). Equally, 'How?' can include 'How could it have been done differently?', 'How could you have reduced the damage done?' and 'How did you feel?' This last set of questions can lead the group into an important area of work, which McGuire and Priestley (1985) call 'Action Replays'. Here group members are encouraged to literally 'do it differently'. They are invited to imagine they are going to direct a video about one of their own offences and may carry this project through. They are then required to write the script, imagining the feelings participants have at various points and, most important, ensuring that this time the outcome is more positive for everyone concerned. This particular exercise is extremely useful because it requires group members to look closely at their offences while at the same time allowing them the opportunity to regain control, and to work collectively. The resulting 'live action' or the video can also be used for 'freeze frame analysis' in relation to other areas, such as the enhancement of social skills.

Such an analysis allows for the construction of A:B:C frameworks. Antecedent events will be revealed as the scene-setters for an incident, for example a particular place, such as a pub or disco; a situation, such as perceived criticism; a time, such as after a few drinks; or the presence, or words of, a particular person or group of people. Behaviour will crucially include more than just observable behaviour (i.e., emotions and feelings; physiological reactions, such as increased heart rate or sweating; and thoughts and intentions). Consequences may include immediate and observed events following an incident, but they will also include the individual's perception and evaluation of events. Moreover, actions do not occur in a vacuum; there is a strong dynamic process of social interaction so one person's behaviour inevitably becomes the antecedents of another's behaviour, while the second person's response serves as both a consequence and a possible precursor to another set of events.

An additional route to information-gathering called FINDS is suggested by Herbert (1987). This includes estimating the Frequency of specific behaviours over a given time span, the Intensity of that behaviour (severity and duration), the Number of behaviours to be targeted, the Duration (how long the behaviour has been in the individual's repertoire), and finally the Sense of the behaviour – the individual's own understanding and explanation of it.

Social skills training

The technique of social skills training (SST) with young offenders became popular during the 1970s, although the seminal work was largely in the clinical field as documented by Argyle (1967) in the UK, and by Liberman *et al.* (1975) in the USA. Argyle (1967) had drawn an analogy between social skills and motor skills, suggesting that both sets of skills could be learned in the same way. In relation to young offenders it was suggested that a deficit in the skills which comprise general social competence might be a contributory factor in their offending pattern. Social skills are usually held to be the almost invisible factors which cement our everyday encounters with one another, the skills which we absorb as children but which subsequently become taken for granted – conversational rules such as knowing how to begin and terminate encounters, how to read the communicational intentions of others, and more basic processes such as listening, looking and smiling at each other appropriately. Patterns of non-verbal communication are seen to be just as important as speech, particularly in relation to cultural, class and gender differences. It is only when someone breaks these 'rules' that our attention is drawn to them and also to our own automatic interactive repertoire – for example, when someone does not use eye contact in a predictable way, or when their tone of voice does not match the verbal content of their speech.

An early study by Piliavin and Briar (1964) into the behaviour of juveniles in their encounters with police officers led them to conclude that demeanour and attitude were crucial predictors of whether or not the young people were likely to be arrested. Fractiousness, failure to display respect, silence and apparent nonchalance were all seen to increase the possibility of arrest. Similarly, Kinzel (1970) found that the social behaviour of offenders imprisoned for crimes of personal violence was different from that of a control group in relation to the 'body-buffer zone' – the degree of personal space people prefer when they are interacting with others. Kinzel found that the violent offenders required a personal space that was on average almost four times larger than the area deemed as comfortable by a group of non-violent offenders. If their defined zone was invaded they reported becoming very anxious, and this tended to happen at distances which others would have regarded as perfectly acceptable.

There is, however, a questionable set of assumptions inherent here, namely that an apparent social skills deficit can be held responsible for offending behaviour and that, consequently, social skills training should effectively reduce recidivism. As Hollin (1990b) points out, it is dangerous to assume that the link is so simple. If social interaction is accepted as being so important, the dynamics of all social encounters must be addressed, not just from the perspective of the offender. In other words, individual change can never be enough to alter completely patterns of behaviour which are so complex and which rely on so many other variables. This does not mean that social skills training is therefore devalued, but that the aims of such training must be both realistic and achievable. An example of the paradoxical nature of this exercise is the work of Spence and Marzillier (1981). They found that six months after SST a group of young offenders had a lower level of convictions than a control group who had not received SST, but when both groups produced self-reports of offending behaviour (undetected offences) the SST group's tally was actually higher. It could be concluded, therefore, that SST had really worked in that these individuals were clearly more able to negotiate successfully encounters with the police and other representatives of the criminal justice system, but if the measure of success was involvement in crime, SST was a spectacular failure. Hollin (1990b) remarks, 'SST is not a cure for crime...(though)... it may be a powerful method of personal change' (p.491).

The major techniques of SST are instruction (clear description of appropriate behaviour); modelling of the social behaviour by another person; practice and rehearsal of those skills via role-play; feedback on performance; and contingent reinforcement for the skill (praise as the required behaviour is shaped). In additional, homework tasks are often set so that the behaviour can be generalised to real-life situations outside group sessions.

McGuire and Priestley (1985) usefully extend the traditional emphasis within SST on micro-skills to broader areas of social ability, including survival skills such as budgeting, shopping, cooking, form-filling, and also the problem-solving skills involved in assessing a situation, weighing up the alternative ways of dealing with it and choosing an appropriate strategy to deal with it. Useful areas in which to examine the skills needed for effective social interaction might include interview situations, talking to the opposite sex, family negotiations, and encounters with authority figures. More specific and relevant situations might include resisting pressure to have more to drink, or refusing an invitation to a potentially violent albeit attractive venue. It is precisely within these areas that the importance of social cognition becomes clear – the way people understand and attempt to make sense of others and their actions. Here perceptions and evaluations are more likely to depend on existing feelings and previous interpretations of encounters than on the current events themselves. So, attitudes to self, self-esteem and self-instruction become additional areas for targeting. Low self-esteem and negative valuing of one's own worth may be a predisposing factor towards offending behaviour, leading to a seeking of status from involvement in illegitimate group activities.

Enhancing self-esteem does not mean creating conceit or self-consciousness, but a valuing of oneself as worthwhile, which should increase self-confidence and lessen anxiety and self-doubt. The 'Who am I?' exercise (Kuhn and McPartland 1954) provides a useful starting point for work in this area. Individuals are simply asked to complete 20 sentences beginning 'I am...' saying something different each time. The resulting sentences can then be divided into positive and negative statements, the balance providing a rough index of self-esteem. Similarly, a self-esteem scale such as that suggested by Rosenberg (1965) can be used where individuals are required to agree or disagree with statements such as:

- At times I think I am no good at all
- I am able to do things as well as most other people
- I wish I could have more respect for myself
- I take a positive attitude toward myself

A numerical score can be obtained which will indicate level of self-esteem. A measure of the possible discrepancy between the way people view themselves and the way they would like to be can be obtained by constructing a list of adjectives, half of which are positive and the other half negative. Individuals are then asked to tick off the adjectives they feel describe themselves, and the adjectives describing the person they would like to be. The resulting positive and negative scores will illustrate the difference between someone's 'actual' and 'ideal' self, but should also generate considerable discussion within the group when comparisons are made.

Simply drawing attention to someone's good points or enabling them to acknowledge that they exist is a step in the direction of increasing self-esteem. When people consider their past experiences there is often a tendency to dwell on the more negative aspects of encounters, and to disregard more positive experiences as being the result of luck rather than the result of worthwhile personal qualities. An effective way of encouraging people to re-evaluate their past is to instruct them to work in pairs and discuss single events which they have felt good about in the past. These events can then be related to the rest of the group. An extension of this idea is the concept of 'positive strokes' based on the work of Berne (1968). Here group members are invited to write something complimentary about another in confidence (a therapeutic version of Consequences) so that at the end of the exercise each individual should end up with a sheet containing some form of praise from all other members of the group. This may be a difficult exercise, particularly in a group which contains wits, but authoritative and good-humoured control should ensure compliance.

Individuals with low self-esteem may maintain their negativity through a process described by Ellis (1962) which involves internal speech attributing blame to themselves for external events. For example, someone whose relationship ends may repeatedly tell themselves that it ended because they are not worth loving, and that all future relationships will end the same way. In this way a self-fulfilling prophecy may be set in motion which ensures that future relationships may well deteriorate, thus confirming the individual's worst fears. Ellis suggests that these self-statements must be challenged and replaced by positive thoughts in a seemingly artificial but effective way. Systematic timetabling of positive thinking about the self and the explicit 'stopping' of negative thoughts are most usefully included in homework assignments.

For the most part, however, SST is designed to help people improve their interactive skills – their competence in dealing with others. Its principal focus is therefore on behaviour, and outcome is usually evaluated in relation to changes in overt behaviour. It is hoped that, in addition, improvements in social skills will be accompanied by changes in self-perception and self-esteem.

Anger control

One of the most critical areas for intervention in relation to young offenders is that of anger and aggression. Problems in these areas can interfere with schooling, family and peer relationships, and may propel adolescents into an escalating spiral in which they may lose control and become enmeshed in a pattern of behaviour from which they may feel unable to escape.

Aggression seems to figure largely in the lives of adolescents and as one of the pioneers of anger control puts it, 'Paradoxically anger is both satisfying and frightening' (Novaco and Welsh 1989, p.129). In his original formulation of the theory of anger control, Novaco (1975) emphasised the role of cognition in the process of emotional arousal which precedes aggression. He suggested that anger often occurs because the individual is already upset about other factors. There is therefore a tendency to displace angry feelings onto inappropriate but available targets. Once sensitivity levels have been aroused people may take things personally when there is no need to do so. Moreover, anger presents itself as a method of taking charge or assuming control when things appear to be getting out of hand. It follows therefore that anger is more likely to occur when people feel unsure and threatened. This may be particularly true for young men who can feel that their masculinity depends on an exaggerated display of outrage which confirms their control of the situation. It is significant that Novaco postulated that anger is often a learned response, in that the individual has a history of responding angrily in previous situations and may have been rewarded for that behaviour.

One of the most important points which Novaco stressed was that anger is common to us all and therefore must serve a useful function, not least in that it alerts us and others to the possibility of that anger turning into aggression. Thus anger *per se* is not seen as a bad thing, but effective control of anger is perceived as a worthwhile goal in order to enable the individual to achieve objectives successfully.

The route by which Novaco suggests anger can be controlled is through the acquisition of strategies of self-control, techniques which will enable the individual to deal with a potentially violent situation without becoming aggressive and without any loss of face. Paradoxically, the use of assertiveness training can ensure that anger is used in a controlled way. The system of stress inoculation is used in a similar way to conventional medicine – individuals are exposed to small doses of provocation in such a way that they can develop the necessary skills to cope with such situations in real life. Tackling these situations within a group of peers not only provides authenticity but can prove an effective reinforcer for the transfer of newly acquired skills.

A typical anger management programme would consist of three stages. First, cognitive preparation focuses on educating group members to recognise their own personal anger patterns. Via an A:B:C analysis of specific situations, as outlined in a previous section, the various cues or 'triggers' can be identified in order to provide information which in future might indicate that anger is likely to occur. The clear links between cognitive, physiological and behavioural components in the anger pattern will be identified in this stage. During the second stage, skill acquisition, the emphasis is on the range of coping skills available in order to deal more effectively with anger-provoking situations. These skills can be usefully divided into two main areas – cognitive and behavioural skills. Cognitive skills include refining attentional abilities in order to identify potential triggers accurately; the use of thought-stopping techniques which will enable individuals to restructure their immediate angry and often irrational thoughts into something more adaptive and positive; and self-instruction strategies which will provide direction in a controlled manner through anger situations. Behavioural skills include relaxation training, assertiveness training, and problem-solving techniques. The final stage of skill application involves putting these newly acquired skills to the test – exposing group members to graduated, stressful anger-provoking situations so that their anger control skills can be applied, initially in role-play but eventually in real-life too.

An excellent outline of a group Anger Control Programme is provided by Feindler and Ecton (1986, pp.70–85) session by session, but some of the techniques suggested can be usefully summarised. Relaxation training is an important area to introduce early on because it will need to be practised both in homework assignments and in future sessions, but it is also a very potent device for illustrating the possibility of gaining control. Using examples of famous athletes who visibly use these techniques and emphasising the notion of training may convince the more cynical members of the group. The most common methods of relaxation are the progressive tensing and relaxation of specific muscle groups, and counting backwards whilst using visualisation or mental imagery of pleasant, calming scenes. Of more immediate use is the technique of breathing deeply in through the nose, slowly exhaling through the mouth and repeating cue words such as 'calm down', 'loosen up', and so on. The rationale for acquiring these skills needs to be explained fully. First, they reduce physiological tension (thereby reducing some of the antecedent cues to aggression); second, they provide a time delay before a choice has to be made of how to respond; and, third, they refocus attention away from external provoking cues to internal control. An additional benefit may be that individuals can become more in tune with their own bodily states to such an extent that they can learn both to observe, and ultimately influence their own levels of tension.

Assertiveness training is included in the programme to provide alternative responses to aggression, but initially the distinction between passivity, assertion and aggression may need to be demonstrated. The use of assertion techniques should allow individuals to de-escalate conflict situations while maintaining personal rights and a level of self-control. Acquisition of assertion skills will involve practice and role-play of specific techniques such as the 'broken record' (simply repeating a request calmly without escalation but with perseverance); 'emphatic assertion' (recognising the other's feelings but repeating the request nonetheless); and, 'fogging' (confusing the provoker by agreeing with their insult).

The cognitive component of the programme includes positive self-instruction, and thought-stopping techniques. It may be worth reminding group members that talking to oneself is quite normal, but that occasionally what we tell ourselves may be wrong and result in negative consequences. For instance, convincing ourselves that someone is looking at us strangely and that they therefore deserve a response if they continue may result in an explosion which was probably warranted not by events alone but the interpretation of those events. Thought-stopping is precisely what it sounds like: saying 'stop' or 'no' to unwanted thoughts, interrupting a sequence of events and then replacing the unwanted thoughts with the possibility of alternative and more positive responses. Initially, rehearsal may be needed with group members describing events out loud, and others shouting out when interruption is required. Eventually, individuals should be able to recognise when unhelpful sequences are beginning and interrupt themselves, with statements such as 'Calm down, there's a way to avoid this, and it will lead to a rewarding result'. Positive self-instruction takes the form of replacing negative self-statements with positive ones such as 'I can handle this without losing my temper' or 'I'm just going to think through the alternatives and work out the best approach', and, most important, 'I'm in control of this situation and the outcome.' Learning these self-statements is the first step, followed by repeated rehearsal through role-play. Effective transfer of these cognitive skills to real-life situations requires self-monitoring which can then serve as reinforcement. Thus, if conflict situations are resolved, self-statements along the lines of 'I did a great job controlling myself there' or 'I handled that pretty well without getting angry' will be appropriate. Alternatively, if conflict is not resolved appropriately the self-statement should be 'I tried my best, but I'm not going to continue to be upset'. This sort of evaluation serves a feedback function but also increases the probability of subsequent performance of anger control skills.

Conclusion
Only a limited range of cognitive-behavioural techniques have been reviewed here, and since offending behaviour itself is a multi-faceted phenomenon any attempt to change it must include a vast array of techniques from which to

choose the most appropriate approach. Group work would, however, seem to have distinct advantages over the more traditional approaches to problematic behaviour in that it allows opportunities for exploration and practice of alternative modes of behaving within a safe and supportive environment. Moreover, the sharing of experiences and misconceptions can increase commitment and motivate long-term personal change, which allows broader issues to be addressed, rather than chasing the often illusory goal of simply reducing recidivism.

References

Argyle, M. (1967) *The Psychology of Interpersonal Behaviour.* Harmondsworth: Penguin Books.

Berne, E. (1968) *Games People Play.* Harmondsworth: Penguin Books.

Ellis, A. (1962) *Reason and Emotion in Psychotherapy.* New York: Lyle Stuart.

Farrington, D.P. and West, D.J. (1990) 'The Cambridge Study in Delinquent Development: A Longterm Follow-Up of 411 Males'. In H.J. Kerber and G. Kaiser (eds) *Criminality: Personality, Behaviour and Life History.* Berlin: Springer-Verlag.

Feindler, E.L. and Ecton, R.B. (1986) *Adolescent Anger Control.* Elmsford, NY: Pergamon Press.

Herbert, M. (1987) *Behavioural Treatment of Children with Problems.* London: Academic Press.

Hollin, C. (1990a) *Cognitive–Behavioural Interventions with Young Offenders.* Elmsford, NY: Pergamon Press.

Hollin, C. (1990b) 'Social Skills Training with Delinquents: A Look at the Evidence and Some Recommendations for Practice'. *British Journal of Social Work.* 20: 483–93.

Kinzel, A.F. (1970) 'Body Buffer Zones in Violent Prisoners'. *American Journal of Psychiatry.* 127: 99–104.

Kuhn, M.H. and McPartland, T.S. (1954) 'An Empirical Investigation of Self-Attitudes'. *American Sociological Review.* 19: 68–76.

Liberman, K.T., King, L.W., De Risi, W.J. and McCann, M. (1975) *Personal Effectiveness.* Champaign, IL: Research Press.

McGuire, J. and Priestley, P. (1985) *Offending Behaviour.* London: Batsford.

Merrit, R.E. and Walley, D.D. (1977) *The Group Leader's Handbook: Resources, Techniques and Survival Skills.* Champaign, IL: Research Press.

Novaco, R. (1975) *Anger Control: The Development and Evaluation of an Experimental Treatment.* Lexington, Mass.: D.C. Health.

Novaco, R. and Welsh, R.E. (1989) 'Anger Disturbance: Cognitive Mediation and Clinical Prescriptions'. In K. Howells and C. Hollin (eds) *Clinical Approaches to Violence.* Chichester: Wiley and Sons.

Piliavin, I. and Briar, S. (1964) 'Police Encounters with Juveniles'. *American Journal of Sociology.* 70: 206–14.

Robins, L.N. and Ratcliff, K.S. (1979) 'Risk Factors in the Continuation of Childhood Anti-Social Behaviour into Adulthood'. *International Journal of Mental Health.* 7: 96–116.

Rosenberg, M. (1965) *Society and the Adolescent Self-Image.* Princeton: Princeton University Press.

Skinner, B.F. (1953) *Science and Human Behaviour.* New York: Macmillan.

Skinner, B.F. (1974) *About Behaviourism.* London: Cape.

Spence, S. and Marzillier, J.S. (1981) 'Social Skills Training with Adolescent Male Offenders'. *Behavioural Research and Therapy.* 19: 349–68.

Stattin, H. and Magnusson, D. (1991) 'Stability and Change in Criminal Behaviour up to Age 30'. *British Journal of Criminology.* 31(4): 327–46.

CHAPTER 18

Race, Identity and Culture

Barbara Coward and Pratima Dattani

'It had occurred to Pecola some time ago that if her eyes, those eyes that held the pictures, and knew the sights – if those eyes of hers were different, that is to say, beautiful, she herself would be different...

Each night, without fail, she prayed for blue eyes. Fervently, for a year she had prayed. Although somewhat discouraged she was not without hope...

Thrown, in this way into the blinding conviction that only a miracle could relieve her, she would never know her own beauty'. (Morrison 1970 p.34–35)

This chapter will consider the reason for the need for specific group work with Black children and young people. The experience of Black children and young people growing up in this society, the philosophy of the Roots Identity Group, the importance of good planning and preparation and good practice models in work with Black children and young people will also be addressed. The term 'Black' throughout our work and in the context of this chapter is used to define people who suffer the effects of racism because of their 'non-white' skin colour. While accepting that there are major differences in culture, language and religion between African Caribbean people and Asian people, both these groups are subject to discrimination and prejudice because of their skin colour. It is this experience, we believe, that unites 'Black' people in this society. Within the context of the groups the differences were recognised and celebrated, enabling Asian and African-Caribbean children and young people to have confidence in their sense of their own identities. Racism within the context of the groups was defined as:

'A belief that Black people are inferior to White people in relation to their culture, religion, intellect, beliefs, lifestyles. An ideology developed by White people backed by pseudo scientists, historians, literary persons, religious and missionary bodies, academics, politicians and media supporting the belief that physical criteria determines intellectual and other abilities'. (MacDonald 1991 p.vi)

Evidence from studies clearly demonstrates that by the age of three children distinguish skin colours and attach values to them (see Milner 1983 and Kunjufu 1984). Unless they are given accurate information, young children learn that light skin colours are valued positively and are more acceptable than dark skin colours which are associated with what is inferior and fearful. It is imperative that in this society, both Black and White children are supported in the acquisition of positive self-images and a 'balanced' view of themselves, their history and heritage and the injustices within this society. For many White children reinforcement of a positive identity is acquired through the family, the media, literature, the law, the arts, education and science. For many Black children, however, some of these same systems, from a very early age, consistently destroy the positive historical contributions of Black people to this society, including their contributions to science, the arts, business, literature, the media, and so forth. It is not surprising, therefore, that images portrayed through these systems provide a distorted reality of Black and White. 'Blackness' is often portrayed as dirty, bad, dangerous, violent and frightening while 'Whiteness' is portrayed as good, clean, pure, and so on.

It is important to acknowledge that *all* children, Black and White, can be damaged through this process. Black children, unless positively and deliberately, assisted, may internalise racist messages, while White children, by being exposed to only a limited Eurocentric environment and view of the world, are denied opportunities to develop positive attitudes towards other people and ways of life (Dwivedi 1993). White children should be enabled to be proud of themselves but should not grow up believing themselves to be superior to Black people. Within the education system the issue of identity, race and culture has expressed itself in many schools through 'multi-culturalism'. Here the emphasis has been predominantly on the tolerance of cultural difference. So, for example, in schools, religious festivals may be celebrated, Black pictures may be visible and there may also be books featuring Black people available to children. The education system, however, has not addressed itself to the extent of looking at the effects of racism on Black children and young people. 'Multi-culturalism' has not eradicated the low expectations teachers have of Black children and young people or justified why there are still many debates in respect of the under achievement of Black children and young people within the education system.

While there is now some move towards developing anti-racist curricula and practices within the education system and, similarly, within the social work profession, progress is slow and political fights are having to be fought at all levels by Black people – Black educationalists, Black social workers, Black parents, children and young people.

It is our view that many Black children and young people 'start out' holding positive images of themselves and of being Black. This is often gained through their own family life styles, the cultural environment in which they were born and their access to Black adults as role models. However, as has already been highlighted, experiences of racism begin from a very early age and is likely to continue to gain momentum as the child progresses in age.

It is within this background and context that, we believe, Black children should be empowered to take control of their own lives. They should be given the opportunity to sustain self-worth, positive racial and cultural identities and the confidence to live rich and fulfilled lives. The basic philosophy of our work with the Roots Identity Group started from this premise. During the preparation for the groups, Cross's (1971) five stage model of Black person's journey towards securing a confident Black identity was, we felt, a very relevant starting point. Cross's (1971) work, supported by empirical research, describes the process of change through following stages that many Black people undergo (Maximé 1986).

Life stages

The pre-encounter stage

The person's world view, at this level, is White-orientated (Eurocentric). He or she will even deny that racism exists.

The encounter stage

The person now experiences or observes a situation that brings him or her face-to-face with racism. The experience is so shattering that it forces the individual to reinterpret his or her world.

Immersion-emersion stage

'This stage encompasses the most sensational aspects of Black identity development' (Cross 1971 quoted in Maximé 1986 p.108). The person struggles to remove all semblance of the old identity while intensifying 'Blackness'. Unfortunately, because the identity process is not positively founded, typical behaviours include, sometimes, the disparagement of White people while deifying Black people.

Internalisation stage

The individual has now managed to separate the old identified self and the new self, thus moving towards a positive Black identity.

Internalisation – commitment stage

Here the individual advances on the previous stage by involving him or herself in Black groups or community issues.

It is our personal view that in order to feel good and proud of being Black, individuals have had to undergo years of struggle involving, as Cross (1971) describes very painful experiences. Moreover, survival for many Black people has developed from inspiration gained through conscious attempts to unearth the richness and achievements of Black people and Black cultures. In an attempt at re-educating Black children and young people, the group work we undertook was to provide *positive* and *honest* facts about Black people and their contribution to this society and the world.

Thoburn's (1988) model describing the promotion of positive and healthy development of a child's identity is given below. We have specifically incorporated within this model how Black children and young people could be helped to acquire a positive and healthy racial identity. It was these categories which helped to define the areas of work in the sessions.

Self-esteem

According to Thoburn (1988) self-esteem is a product of a sense of permanence and identity. *Permanence* includes security, belonging, family life, being loved and loving. *Self-esteem* creates the capacity to grow and make new and satisfying relationships as an adult.

Identity

Promoting the positive and healthy development of a Black child's *Identity* includes the following:

KNOWING ABOUT BIRTH FAMILY

- Knowing our origin, racial and historical heritage.
- Appreciating and acknowledging our strengths, and that of Black people.

KNOWING ABOUT PRESENT AND PAST RELATIONSHIPS

- Documenting life and family events through recording (e.g. photographs, stories from the past, mementos).
- Capturing and storing richness of Black lifestyles and experiences.

FITTING THE PRESENT WITH THE PAST

- Acknowledging the historical effects of racism
- Learning from strengths of Black family life and contributions of Black people.

- Asserting the right to be treated with respect and dignity as an individual and a human being.

CONTACTS AND INVOLVEMENT WITH OTHER BLACK PEOPLE

- Access to Black role models (e.g. Black teachers, schools, substitute carers, social workers).
- Involvement in Black community and youth organisations.

BEING VALUED AS THE PERSON YOU ARE

- Feeling positive about being Black.
- Sharing and caring for and with other Black people.
- The capacity to have a positive racial identity and the confidence to live a rich and fulfilled life.

Roots identity groups

Group work specifically aimed at Black children and young people with the purpose of looking at their identity, race, language, culture and religion, now a specific requirement of the Children Act 1989 (MacDonald 1991), was on our part conscious, deliberate and a positive act of re-dressing negative images built up under the influence of the wider society. The Roots Identity group work we felt would, for some Black children, be the beginning of a process in the development of a positive Black identity. That is, it would instil a deeper sense of confidence and pride and provide some of the skills and tools for Black children and young people to live and survive in a racist society.

There were obvious limitations on how much could be achieved given the short term nature of the project. In 12 sessions, on a fortnightly basis, we hoped to structure the work to enable young people to share and learn from each other, to convey that learning about oneself can be interesting and fun and enable Black children and young people to acknowledge that the 'problem' was not of their making but that of history and the wider society.

Facilitators were asked to incorporate within sessions specific work on race and racial heritage, Black history, religion and culture, languages, food (cooking and sharing), visits to Black restaurants, museums, concerts and plays. It was felt essential also to have specific sessions on relationships, sexuality and marriage, as appropriate to the ages in the groups. The overriding emphasis of all sessions, therefore, was developing life and coping skills as Black people within this society. In addition, the facilitators, together with the participants, were asked to consider the plans for the future (i.e., need for self support groups, further ongoing identity work, suggestions for Black children and young people in care, and so on). A residential weekend was also planned at the end of the 12 sessions in order to consolidate some of the work, for the children to enjoy being with each other over a longer period of time and for all the facilitators and co-ordinators to evaluate and monitor with the participants all previous group sessions.

From the evidence of need (see below) it was apparent that we required two groups, one for the age group 7–11 years and one for the age group 12–16 years. We recognised early on that the age span was wide for both groups. However, the need was so great and limited resources meant that we could not justify refusing individuals from attending.

The needs of Black children and young people

In a period of 12–15 months, our attendance at Child Protection Case Conference and Statutory Child Care Reviews where Black children and young people were involved revealed a pattern where specific work was being requested, or was recommended by ourselves, on developing positive self images for Black children and young people.

Almost without exception, we were required to offer advice, support, suggestions of dealing with and resolving the effects of racism on Black children and young people.

There were many incidents of Black children and young people being subjected to racial abuse, harassment and intimidation in neighbourhoods. There were some Black children who identified themselves as anything else but Black (i.e., Italian, Spanish, and so on). Some Black children and young people were known to be in fear of Black people or became extremely distressed when anything about Black people was mentioned or at any suggestion that the child had Black parentage. Some social workers related examples where there were tears and distress amongst Black children and young people when they were asked to define their ethnic origin through formal procedures. Moreover, in some instances the child or young person was encountering racism within his or her own family (i.e., where there were White carers, parents, grandparents, uncles or aunts). Most of these experiences, attitudes and behaviours were in addition to behavioural difficulties and other concerns within the home or school.

Many White workers expressed real difficulties in tackling this kind of work. Consequently, many children who had required identity work for many years had been deprived of this input. In some cases the need for identity work had been identified some ten years earlier but no work was offered to children or their carers.

Sadly, some young people between 15 and 18 years, with the most severe identity problems, could not be helped by this group, as it was considered that more intensive work was required to undo the damage that had already been done. Moreover, approximately 50 per cent of the original target group with quite severe identity problems refused identity work when it was eventually offered.

Alongside these groups we recognised the need for working with and helping carers to appreciate the positive benefits that Black children and young people could gain from attending these groups. A carer's group was set up to provide the opportunity for carers to acquire a greater insight, understanding of the need for and benefits of racial identity work and to address the effects of negative self images on children's physical and psychological development. It also provided a forum where the carers could learn practical skills of building and reinforcing a positive racial identity and we hope, reduce their anxieties about discussing these issues.

Although many carers and parents expressed their verbal support, only a small proportion of the carers (3+) actually participated throughout the six sessions planned for them. While for some this was because of practical arrangements, we believe others found the idea of specific work on 'race issues' threatening. In the end, in order to utilise the resource of this specific group, some Black and White substitute carers were given access to this group. The children and young people's groups, however, remained closed groups, once the selection of individuals was made.

Preparation and planning

Resources of Local Authority Social Services Departments are at the best of times limited and often priorities of work and racist attitudes do not allow for specific programmes of work for Black children and young people. It was in this context that our resources had to be defined. Furthermore, this project was seen essentially as a pilot in order to encourage the department of the need for the work to be given priority and to secure long term mainstream funding. A budget was agreed with senior managers based on payments for four facilitators, transport costs, cost for activities and a residential weekend.

Facilitators were selected for the groups after a two day training programme organised for over 12 workers. Out of this group two female Asian facilitators and two African-Caribbean facilitators were selected. Facilitators had to demonstrate a commitment and enthusiasm for identity work with Black children and young people. They needed to have an experience of and a clear idea of how racism affects Black children and young people. In addition, the facilitators needed to have experience of direct work with Black children and young people and their families.

Our contract with them also required them to have the ability to offer adequate time and consistency over the duration of the groups and be available for training, supervision and planning sessions. While we would have liked to have had Black male facilitators, we were unable to identify any from these groups.

All facilitators would be paid for their work and, although one facilitator worked for the department, this work was considered to be over and above her duties as a specialist social worker. This arrangement was to ensure that we received the full commitment of the facilitators and was an attempt to demonstrate that Black workers should be recognised for their specific skills and experiences.

For the carers group, two family placement workers (plus facilitators of the carers group) also attended the two training sessions. The Family Placement Unit (Fostering Section) saw this work as part of their remit and selected two Black (one Asian and one African-Caribbean) facilitators and two White facilitators. The carers' sessions were co-facilitated by a Black Clinical Psychologist, who had also facilitated the training sessions for the children's group facilitators.

The first two-day training course covered specific work on how identity and self-images are built up and how Black people can build positive identities in spite of negative influences from society. There was considerable focus on our own experiences of racism in childhood and adulthood and these experiences were used as solid examples to learn from. Experiential exercises on discovering and developing survival skills were used to enable facilitators to pass these on to the Black children and young people they would be working with. Some group work theories were also addressed.

The pooling of the personal and other resources that can be used with Black children and young people was an important feature of the training. Overall, the training was intended to enable us to realise our strengths and weaknesses, the abilities to pass on positive aspects of being Black, and to ensure that we as individuals do not do further damage to already vulnerable Black children and young people.

One follow-up training day was held prior to the actual start of the sessions to consider the referrals; look at specific exercises which could be used; the resources at our disposal; videos; books; poster; and so on. This session was also used to consider the type and methods of monitoring outcomes. Overall this day was a team-building exercise between the facilitators and organisers.

In order to gain maximum co-operation and support from social workers and to allay any concerns and fears that they may have had, detailed briefing sessions were held. This opportunity was used to discuss the purpose and philosophy of the groups, details of practical arrangements, their role in supporting the child/young person and the carers, and to introduce them to the facilitators. A second formal session with social workers was held half-way through the planned 12 sessions to give feedback on areas of concerns or development in respect of the children referred.

Publicity of the groups within the department was important in highlighting the need and encouraging referrals. A colourful leaflet with good, clear information about the aims and objectives of the groups was produced and distributed well in advance of the start date. In addition, social workers were individually pursued and encouraged to make referrals of the known Black child and young person we had had contact with.

The planning, co-ordination and supervision was undertaken by ourselves and on the whole involved the administration of finance, assistance with practical arrangements (e.g. transport, ordering food, booking rooms, liaison with social workers and carers).

Supervision involved group supervision sessions once a fortnight and involved discussions about the importance and parameters of confidentiality, individual child/young person's experiences, support and reassurances for facilitators about their input and sessions (i.e. the content and planning of these at a pace the young people were dictating). In addition, the facilitators were offered opportunities for informal discussions. These sessions proved valuable in generating enthusiasm, team-building and increasing our commitment to the furtherance of these groups. It also highlighted yet again the most painful experiences that Black young people encounter, confirming for us the need for these groups and making us realise the enormity of the task we were undertaking.

Experiences within the groups

Within many Social Services Departments, there are often very few positive images of Black people visible. For the Roots Group it was felt important that money and time be spent on locating positive images of Black people that the children could relate to. Consequently, for every group session, the rooms which were being used were carefully prepared with many positive images of Black people depicting famous past and present contributors, different types of religions, art, different Black countries and lifestyles and cultures of Black people. In addition, participants had access to books, magazines, articles and tapes throughout the sessions and were able to take some materials home. The facilitators themselves were also used as positive role models, their backgrounds including lecturer, manager of a Women's Training Agency, manager of a Counselling Agency and a specialist social worker – undertaking therapeutic work with children. It was our view, reinforced by feedback from our contact with and experiences of the children, that some had had very few opportunities in their lives to come across Black adults who were in responsible positions. While the importance of Black role models has not been scientifically evaluated, we feel that the participants appreciated learning positives of being Black from Black people who came from a variety of backgrounds. From our contact with the group we also observed that there was considerable warmth and affection shown to the facilitators by the participants.

For every session facilitators had to demonstrate their respect for each other and the participants, and to encourage this within the group as a whole. Clear ground rules were established by the facilitators and participants at the sessions. It was found that many children and young people were at various levels of awareness of being Black and of their experiences of racism. Each individual was, therefore, encouraged to discuss and take information at their own pace and level of understanding and some were offered individual work outside the session to build on what they had learnt.

The following are extracts from some of the facilitators' recordings:

> 'This session was the beginning of our attempts to instil positive images of being Black whilst simultaneously demonstrating that neither Black or white was superior. We felt this was necessary because by the fourth session some of the children had developed a greater self image of being Black and were beginning to see being White in a negative way.'

> 'This session was largely discussion based. Children were given different pot paints and brushes, they were asked to mix different colours and see what colours they could make. They came up with a range of colours and concluded that the colour Black or White could not be made. Before we read the poem "Who's is Coloured", we asked them if they were coloured. They all agreed, so they were shocked when we said that it is our view that we weren't coloured. After the poem they too agreed that they were not "coloured". The purpose of using colour as the theme of discussion was to give the children the opportunity to look at their skin colour and assess what colour they were'.

> 'This session was the beginning of our attempts to highlight positive images. We divided the group into two teams who then competed with each other in labelling a world map. This got the children's interest and generated a good team spirit.

> This highlighted names of countries that would be used as a basis of discussion in later sessions. Also to show the variety and richness of other countries resources, etc'.

> 'The purpose of this session was to look at some of the experiences they had in being Black and to encourage the children to discuss these.

> We looked at the colour Black and on a flipchart paper wrote down names that children get called because they were of a different colour. They came up with a list of negatives and told us how they felt because they were 'nearly black' or Black. We looked at how assertively to rise up to negative name calling. We came to the conclusion that we as a group were Black. We used their experiences of negative put downs through role play and looked at how we could handle the situation differently. All of the group supported and gave positive ideas'.

> 'This was a very positive session. A number of strategies were devised on how to deal with name calling. For children whose preferred strategies were aggressive means, we took every opportunity to reinforce more positive methods.

The video *Eye of the Storm* was shown. This video focused on an experiment by an American teacher highlighting the experience of racism and discrimination through the use of labelling the group as brown eyes and blue eyes, creating an "In group" and an "Out group". Children discussed this and related experiences of theirs as being an "Out group". Hurt and aggression were discussed'.

'We had written a series of stories from our own experiences. We incorporated prejudice, discrimination and racism. The children took it in turns to read the stories. At the end of each story they had to decide if there was racism, discrimination or prejudice involved. Some of the stories were role played. There was no racial division between the Asian and African-Caribbean children, all worked and played well together. The only division that clearly emerged was between the boys and girls. The dynamics were good in the group. The older children helping the younger. It was a supportive and caring group'.

'With the aim of introducing the subject of colour classification, the young people were divided in groups of four and were given a number of pictures of people from different racial backgrounds. Then they had to discuss amongst themselves which of the two boxes (the white box or black box) they would put each of the pictures they looked at. After much discussions amongst themselves they, put all the people who were non White in the black box − i.e. Asian, Chinese, African, African-Caribbean, etc. This exercise was to set the scene for future discussions on Black and White people'.

'In this session we looked at Black Heroes in History − Martin Luther King, Mary Seacole, Gandhi, Amerita Sher-Gill, etc. This session highlighted that racism exists and does exist even within the schools. It showed that Black people can rise up and achieve, despite many barriers'.

Food

Out of all the activities within all the sessions, those connected with food had the most noticeable effects, reflecting its importance. Both African-Caribbean and Asian food was provided at each session. This allowed many of the children and young people to try different foods for the first time. While the nourishment aspect and the sharing of food with others was important, it also generated much discussion among group members. This led to considerable respect for, and valuing more, different eating habits and cooking methods, and the acceptance of the difference and richness in each other's food.

For us as organisers and facilitators, one little initial measure of 'success' was that most children and young people even took food home to share and discuss with their families.

In addition to some of the sessions highlighted above there were two other major sessions which played a central role in the groups activities. A cultural evening, planned with the involvement of the children and young people, focused on celebrating music and dance within the Asian cultures. For this event both the senior and junior groups came together for the first time. Carers, parents and the children's respective social workers were invited to this session. As a learning tool this session emphasised and reinforced some of the positive features readily at hand in the Black communities, of which the children and young people could be proud.

During the course of the 12 planned sessions, there was much frustration felt by the children and young people and facilitators, because they felt that the 2 hour sessions did not give them sufficient time to undertake more detailed work. Consequently, a weekend residential to the countryside in Northamptonshire (away from distractions!) was built into the programme. As well as catching up on previous unfinished work, the children had the opportunity to participate in a full range of activities, such as art work, learning to cook African-Caribbean and Asian meals, health and beauty sessions, and so on. In addition, the children had the opportunity to participate in an African-Caribbean cultural evening where African-Caribbean and other popular songs were much in evidence.

Important features of this weekend not only entailed giving the children opportunities to acquire practical life skills, but there were also opportunities to meet other role models who volunteered their help and support to enable the weekend to go as smoothly as possible. One such volunteer gave the children and young people a very positive talk on how she coped with racism and discrimination, essential practical coping skills for Black children in this society.

This weekend proved to be a great success, with much caring and respect for each other and it proved of great importance with respect to both the African-Caribbean and Asian cultures. The following is an extract from the facilitators' recording of this event.

> 'The weekend away gave us the opportunity to catch up on unfinished work. We managed to do this productively and the children worked really well.
>
> The different environment and the open free areas for play enhanced the children's openness to discuss more freely things perhaps they did not want to before.
>
> In addition to the more formal teaching sessions we were able to include sessions such as practical cooking skills, the designing of a 'Roots' logo for T-shirts, traditional Asian and African-Caribbean games etc. Some of the children found the journey far too long but, once they arrived everything went well. That is not to say that they were all on their best behaviour at all times. The task of trying to get

a number of excited children to sleep, for example was not an easy one. But all in all it was an extremely productive and enjoyable event'.

Evaluation

In group work focusing on identity issues, it is important to acknowledge and convey to participants that such a short term input is only a starting point in what could be a long journey in unearthing, building and creating a positive racial identity. It is also essential that Black children and young people are given a realistic picture, and that they are informed that the process can be painful, and will often involve insecurity and resentment from White family members, friends and associates. Moreover, a positive Black person can seem threatening to many Black people, who may have adopted coping strategies such as avoidance, denial of racism and racist practices or collusion with racist attitudes, behaviour and practices.

However, the need to prepare Black children and young people for the realities of this society, could mean that the message that is conveyed is only one of the struggles and pain. It is essential, however, that Black children and young people also realise and appreciate that learning about oneself, one's history and heritage can be fun, interesting and can lead to years of exploration and exciting new discoveries.

The following is an extract of the children and young people's comments. These comments were gathered through the evaluation:

> 'I thought it would be boring, but it has really been good'.
>
> 'I thought we'd have to do reading and writing, like going to school, but is has been excellent doing all these different things'.
>
> 'I thought that there would be loads of personal questions about my mum and dad, but there haven't been, and it has been really nice'.

During the evaluation of the identity groups, it was the view of both the co-ordinator and the facilitators that it was not necessarily essential to use any recognised psychological tools to ascertain the views of the participants, but what was more important was to use measures which the children and young people themselves felt comfortable with. The evaluation sessions were therefore conducted in a very relaxed style and were facilitated by a co-ordinator, whose background was research, and who also knew the children. The following are the main areas which were covered:

> Why did they think the groups were set up? What had they expected the groups to be like and how did that compare to reality? (Some of the children and young people's comments have been highlighted above). What had they most/least enjoyed about the groups? What did they feel they had gained/learnt from the groups? What did they want to happen about the groups in the future?

Many of the views expressed were common to both the senior and junior group. The following are a few typical responses:

> *Why did you think that the groups had been set up?* In general (articulated to a greater or lesser degree) the young people replied that the Identity groups were set up because there are a lot of Black children 'in care' who needed to learn more about being Black and being proud of being Black.

> However, a comment was also made by one young person that they had just been told they had to come, without really having the reason for the group or their participation in the group explained to them. This highlights how important it is that preparatory work and support is given to each individual child or young person prior to their inclusion in groups such as this.

> *What did you most/least enjoy about the Identity groups?* 'I enjoyed everything – talking, videos, role plays. I enjoyed the activities. I liked working with the others in the group and with the facilitators'. I enjoyed talking about Black people. I enjoyed the dancing.

> …and everybody in the group commented on how much they had enjoyed the food.

Members of both groups were unwilling to say anything negative about the identity sessions in terms of stating what they had 'least enjoyed'. This may be because they did not want to upset anyone or did not know what the consequences of saying what they least enjoyed would be. On the other hand, it may simply be that, as they themselves said, 'there isn't anything that we didn't enjoy'. Although to be strictly truthful, one person said that they thought one of the facilitators was 'bossy'; however, all the other members of the group defended this facilitator and said that they thought she was 'kind, helpful and fun'. The facilitator was not present in this evaluation session, so her presence could not have been said to influence these comments. Another young person said that they least enjoyed having to 'clear up' after the sessions were over.

> *What, if anything, do you feel that you gained/learnt from being part of the identity groups?*

> 'We learnt more about ourselves and about being Black'.

> 'I learnt to be more confident about myself'.

> 'I learnt about the experiences of older Black people'.

> 'I learnt about Black heroes'.

> 'We learnt not to quarrel with each other'.

> 'We learnt about hair care and personal care'.

> 'We learnt about fashion and music'.

'We made new friends'.

'I learnt how to say things assertively'.

'I learnt about the different backgrounds of Asian and African-Caribbean people'.

'We learnt about African-Caribbean and Asian cuisine'.

'We learnt to swap ideas'.

'I learnt to be positive and proud of who I am'.

'I learnt that some White people are racist and that some white people are not'.

'Some White people think they are superior – I learnt that is cobblers'.

In addition to the evaluation exercise with the children, social workers and carers were also requested to make written responses regarding their views on the impact of the identity group on the children and young people they had referred.

Although the evaluation exercise cannot make claims to be scientifically sound, nor can it show what the long term effects on being part of the identity groups will be on the children and young people, it does, however give an insight into what had started to be achieved in the identity groups. Of equal importance is that it highlighted what could have been achieved in the past, if this service had been provided and, most important what could still be achieved if groups are provided on a long term basis.

Ending

Identity work of this nature requires careful thought and preparation as to how the groups should formally be ended, especially in view of the fact that the goal or target for each individual will be different and is essentially a long term one. It was therefore felt that the ending of the group should be creative, lively, colourful in the hope that it would have a lasting impact on the children and young people.

A presentation evening was decided upon which incorporated all the above elements. Here the children and young people, facilitators and co-ordinators celebrated their achievements thus far. Parents and carers, social workers and 'community supporters' were also invited.

Both the children and facilitators were presented with certificates, signed by the Director and presented by an assistant director. In addition, there were songs from Black artists, speeches from the facilitators and co-ordinators, songs from group members and music and food for all to enjoy.

Although the children and young people wished for the groups to continue in the future, and in particular for their individual groups to continue as a support group, as yet meaningful resources by the Social Services Department have not been identified.

Conclusion

It is our view that all Black children and young people should be supported to acquire positive self images and be given opportunities to gain a 'balanced' view of themselves, their history and heritage. In our experience, many Black people, especially children, do not have structured, formal or easy reference points to discuss their experiences of being Black in a predominantly White society. We feel that it is in all our interests that Black children and young people – as part of this society's future – need to be 'enabled' to develop a sense of security and confidence and to be encouraged to be clear and positive about being Black. The following poem written by V.J. Moncrieffe (1990) highlights the concerns and importance of acquiring a positive Black identity.

> A Tree without Roots will wither and die,
> A House without solid foundations is bound to crumble,
> A child can have abundance of love but still flounder,
> If there is no self concept, no sense of culture or heritage.

It is our belief that the groupwork we undertook with Black children and young people within the context of a social services department are easily transferable to the work of other statutory agencies, such as schools, youth clubs, voluntary organisations and also Black and White community centres.

The following model illustrates the areas that need to be addressed in delivering good quality services to Black and White children and young people:

Philosophy/ideology
Should include:

1. The need for all children to have, a history, security, belonging, family life – being loved/loving and permanency.

2. For all legislation to incorporate detailed provisions catering for specific needs of Black children and young people.

3. For policy and practices of voluntary and statutory agencies to take account of the realities of this society and hence the specific needs of Black children and young people.

Planning
Should include clear strategies which incorporates the following:

1. Conveying through images and other communications that Black children and young people are valued in this society. Ensuring that

Black children and young people have access to positive role models at all levels.

2. Making available good quality information, books, videos, etc.

3. Enabling Black and White children and young people to acquire knowledge of racial/cultural heritage, race and racism.

4. Making arrangements for Black Awareness and anti oppressive training for all service providers and carers.

Resources

Should take account of:

1. Human Resources – workers to have experience and proven commitment/track record of anti-racist and anti-oppressive practices in their direct work with Black and White children and young people.

2. Commitment – Policy makers and senior managers to demonstrate consistently their commitment to the needs of Black children and young people.

3. Financial – Recognising that appropriate work: with Black children/families at an early stage could be cost-effective in terms of preventing serious mental health problems, which would require greater financial outlays.

Implementation

Should include:

1. Appropriately skilled and qualified Black and White staff.

2. Consultation, involvement and participation of skilled Black people, parents/carers and Black children and young people in the planning and implementation of services.

Monitoring/evaluation

Should incorporate:

1. A complaints procedure, which should have a clear Black Perspective and appropriate investigating systems involving skilled and independent Black people.

2. Regular and consistent monitoring systems which should identify gaps in services and specific target and timescales for change.

Acknowledgements

We would like to thank: Heather Paul, Caroline Comrie, Dollar Abbott, Indrajit Bhogal, Cheron Byfield, Marcia Parchment, Jagtar Bal and Coventry Social Services, for their valuable contribution to this work.

References

Cross, W.E. (1971) 'The Negro-to-Black Conversion Experience: Towards a Psychology of Black Liberation'. *Black World.* 2 (July) 13–27.

Dwivedi, K.N. (1993) 'Ethnic Minority Children'. In V.P. Varma (ed) *Coping with Unhappy Children.* London: Cassell.

Kunjufu, J. (1984) *Developing Positive Self Images and Discipline in Black Children.* Chicago, Illinois: African–American Images.

MacDonald, S. (1991) *All Under the Act? – A Practical Guide to the Children Act 1989 for Social Workers.* London: The Racial Equality Unit (REU).

Maximé, J.E. (1986) 'Some Psychological Models of Black Self Concept'. In S. Ahmed, J. Cheetham and J. Small (eds) *Social Work with Black Children and Their Families.* London: B.T. Batsford. pp.100–116.

Milner, D. (1983) *Children and Race: Ten Years On.* East Grindstead: Ward Lock Educational.

Moncrieffe, V.J. (1990) Unpublished book of poems (personal communication).

Morrison, T. (1970) *The Bluest Eyes.* London: Pan Books.

Thoburn, J. (1988) *Child Placement: Principles and Practice.* Aldershot: Wildwood House.

Part 5

Contexts and Settings

CHAPTER 19

Group Work in Schools

Carol Coppock and Kedar Nath Dwivedi

The need for groups

As highlighted in the chapter on Group Work in Child Mental Health Services in this volume, up to 20 per cent of children experience emotional and behavioural difficulties requiring help and support. These problems are of a moderate to severe nature in nearly 7–10 per cent of the children and the prevalence of these difficulties tends to increase in proportion to the age of the child or adolescent. Those living in urban areas have a higher prevalence than those living in rural areas. These problems may manifest themselves in aggressiveness, delinquency, drug abuse, sexual acting out, eating disorders, or school refusal, which are stressful, not only to the pupils who are suffering from these disorders, but also to other pupils and their teachers.

The Committee of Enquiry into Discipline in Schools (Department of Education and Science and the Welsh Office 1989) found the teachers in their survey were also very concerned about the cumulative effects of disruption to their lessons caused by relatively trivial but persistent misbehaviour. At least 80 per cent of teachers had encountered behaviours showing 'lack of concern for others', 'unruliness while waiting', 'running in the corridors', general rowdiness, horseplay or mucking about' and 'persistently infringing school rules'. Such behaviours were encountered at rates from daily to at least once a week. The committee emphasised the importance of finding ways of creating an atmosphere in school in which pupils do not even think of being aggressive, at least towards their teachers.

Disturbance in children also reflects the extent of social and family breakdown, physical, sexual and emotional abuse, and neglect. Children react differently to emotional pain; some refuse to grow up, while others grow up only to repeat the cycle of abuse and violence to others. The need has grown to address a large number of these psychological and mental health issues in

the school setting. There are already a variety of psycho-educational programmes dealing with such topics as solvent abuse, teenage pregnancy, sexual
abuse and AIDS, which can be used in schools. A major problem in attempting
to tackle any one of these separately is that the very pupils who need most to
work through these issues are the ones who become most defensive when
approached in a formal way.

One of the central issues when addressing most of these problems is the
ability to get in touch with one's own and others' feelings and to manage these
feelings more effectively. Feelings of anger, anxiety, jealousy, fear, suspicion,
and craving for attention are almost universal, but their crippling intensity in
some individuals make such individuals vulnerable to a variety of problems.
One way of meeting some of these needs is to set up an on-going group of
vulnerable pupils to explore and learn about interpersonal relationships and
group processes. Such an experiential group in a caring, trusting, non-judgemental, non-demanding and co-operative learning atmosphere can facilitate the
process of getting in touch with deeper feelings, sharing these feelings,
concerns and conflicts, and learning from each other's experiences. A group of
this kind could become the hub of health education and psychosocial skills
training and could facilitate children's psychological growth, enriching them
with self-awareness, self-esteem, self-confidence and self-control. Jones (1971),
describing group work with adolescent girls in a comprehensive school,
commented: 'What girls are most interested in discussing are problems which
come within their own range of experience. The main part of the discussion
concerns the normal problems of adolescence: worries about menstruation and
moodiness, conflicts with parents about going out and having boyfriends,
anxieties over appearance or about the way to behave in a new situation,
problems of having nowhere to go in the evenings and no friends in their
neighbourhood' (p.47).

Advantages and disadvantages of a school setting for group work

The more familiar interpretation by teachers of the words 'group work' is as a
method of co-operative learning. Children in schools spend a great deal of
their time in groups. One could be forgiven for assuming that schools make use
of group work methods and group processes. Unfortunately, this is not the case
generally. Bennett et al. (1984) discovered that what generally passed for group
work was in fact collections of children sitting closely together, but engaged
on individual tasks. Slavin (1985) highlighted the situation as follows:

> 'why have we humans been so successful as a species? We are not strong
> like tigers, big like elephants, protectively coloured like lizards, or swift
> like gazelles. We are intelligent, but an intelligent human alone in the
> forest would not survive for long. What has really made us such
> successful animals is our ability to apply our intelligence to

co-operating with others to accomplish group goals. From the primitive hunting group to the corporate boardroom, it is those of us who can solve problems while working with others who succeed...

'Because schools socialise children to assume adult roles, and because co-operation is so much a part of adult life, one might expect that co-operative activity would be emphasised. However, this is far from true. Among the prominent institutions of our society, the school is least characterised by co-operative activity...' (p.5)

There is, therefore, great potential in the school setting for groups whose purpose is the promotion of mental health and the helping of children with emotional and behavioural problems. There are several advantages to setting up groups in school. One is that the pupils involved are familiar with the environment they are working in; this can relieve the stress for some pupils suspicious of new situations and meeting new people. The pupils in the group may already know each other, at least by sight, and will quickly be able to build up a rapport with the others in the group. Issues relating to the school situation can be dealt with directly and with the particular pupils involved, for example bullying, name calling, isolation of a particular pupil. Any positive effects that the group might have will directly reflect in the school setting. It may be that the school is able to organise group work so that it is part of the curriculum, thus taking away the overtness and specialness of the work and enabling the activities to be related more directly to the pupil's needs within school. Many pupils may not be very cooperative, or may feel stigmatised if they are asked to attend groups elsewhere (e.g. in Child Psychiatric Services). Limited resources in such services cannot meet all the demands, either.

Group work can help pupils to form better relationships with their peers and with their teachers, which can directly affect behaviour in the classroom. Any school which is contemplating setting up groups should be aware of the differences between the role of a group worker and that of a teacher, which can lead to a conflict of interest. Pupils and teachers may not be able to reconcile their different roles in and out of the group. The question of confidentiality needs to be carefully thought out. Group work is an area which requires a great deal of commitment from staff and a change in teaching style during the sessions, which may not be a comfortable role for all staff and therefore not a role that every member of staff will want to take on.

Practical considerations

If a school decides to establish groups, there are a variety of practical considerations which need to be thought through prior to the commencement of the group work. First there are the constraints of the timetable which face any new course which is being established in the existing curriculum pattern adopted by the school. Groups can, of course, be run at lunch time or after school but this will change the emphasis of the group and may preclude those less-motivated pupils who, none the less, are very needy. If group work is to establish itself as an important part of a pupil's school experience then it needs to take its place within the curriculum alongside other cross-curricular themes. It may be that group work could be incorporated into a Personal and Social Education Programme or it may be that there is a Low Achievers Project where many of the most needy pupils are catered for, because of their learning and/or emotional and behavioural difficulties.

Another important consideration is the room in which group work is to run. It needs to be a comfortable, well appointed room, with easy chairs and space to move around if necessary. It should not be overlooked or overheard in any way. The provision of a flipchart and pin boarding can be useful. It is also pleasant to be able to have refreshments available if required. The idea is to create a warm and caring atmosphere in which the pupils can relax.

The staff involved in running groups play a key role. They need to be able to listen to young people and create the right sort of atmosphere for talk. They need to be conversant in techniques for encouraging groups to talk and in how to manage groups in a variety of situations. Of course much of this comes with experience, a comprehensive training programme and backup. It is vital that staff running the group are aware of their Local Authority Guidelines and Procedures on Child Abuse and they will need to agree upon a definition of confidentiality as it applies within the school. Teachers will need to have thought out the implications of their new role as group worker and how this will differ from that of a class teacher.

The number of pupils in a group needs to be considered. As the ideal number is agreed to be between six and eight pupils, this may have implications for general staffing levels. Other staff taking larger groups to accommodate group work will need to be convinced of its value. What will the group be called? How can it gain credibility? Pupils may see it as a talking lesson and therefore of no value compared with a lesson where they are expected to do lots of writing. Finally, there will need to be a way of evaluating the work done; in the present climate of cost effectiveness it is not enough to say 'I think it is helping' – there needs to be a formal evaluation process so that all involved can assess the effectiveness of group work.

What sort of group?

The criteria by which a group is formed are wide and varied. A single sexed group which deals specifically with issues related to gender can serve a useful purpose. Often these groups are more frank about sexual feelings than when they are discussed in a mixed group. Mixed groups can provide an opportunity for boys and girls to share their feelings on different issues. Sometimes it is useful to convene a group of pupils of around the same age, and there can be times where a broad spread across the age range is more suitable. When dealing with issues such as bullying it may be useful to have a group of perpetrators and a group of victims or a mixture of both.

A group can be run for a set number of weeks with an identified group of pupils which stays the same through all the sessions. This is known as a closed group. Conversely, an open group is where the timing of the sessions is constant but a small number of individual pupils join or leave the group on a rolling programme. Groups can be run on or off the school premises, perhaps at a youth club or at a Child and Family Guidance Clinic. Groups, as mentioned previously, can be run in school time or as an extra-curricular activity, either at lunch time or after school. Groups can be staffed in a number of ways: by full time members of staff, adults other than teachers, Child and Family Guidance staff, Education Welfare Officers, staff from the Special Educational Needs Support Service or by a combination of these professionals. Pupils can be selected for groups because they have a common difficulty (e.g. bereavement or are victims of bullying or have poor social skills) or they can be selected on a more random basis.

What next?

Once a school has decided to adopt group work it is important that the preparation and ground work are completed before the groups commence. As discussed in the previous section, a decision needs to be taken as to who is going to run the group. Once this has been agreed upon, training can begin. This should aim to familiarise staff with the philosophy of group work. Training could be in the form of a seminar with one group member reading a relevant paper or article, summarising this and presenting it to the rest of the staff group for discussion. It might include some experiential learning with one member leading some group work. It can be useful for one or more members to observe and participate in groups which are already running, possibly in other establishments. There may also be courses available locally which potential group workers could attend.

It is vital that all staff in the school are kept informed of what is being planned so that they too are well prepared prior to the commencement of the groups.

Once the participating adults have completed their training, thought needs to be given to the pupils who are going to be involved in the group sessions. How are they to be selected? Will this be done by establishing a referral system? Who will then prioritise the need of the individuals concerned? Will one person (such as the Special Needs Co-ordinator), the pastoral staff, or those running the group do the selecting? Maybe there will be a formal referral system with a proforma to be completed, which would then be discussed by the group leaders. Will any account be taken of the age, sex or needs of the pupils? For example, will it be a girl's group of 14–15-year-olds, or a mixed group of students aged 13–16 who have been the victims of bullying?

It is important that the pupils who are selected for group work are approached in a way which will not make them antagonistic towards the idea of participating in such a group. They will need to be prepared before joining a group as to what is expected. Parents will also need to be consulted and informed. Some schools might wish to establish group work as part of a low achievers course and/or as part of their PSE programme, thus making group work much less overt and possibly more acceptable to both parents and pupils.

The location for group work needs careful thought. A room can destroy or support the work going on in the group. It needs to be a comfortable room where pupils can relax – not too big, but not cramped. There needs to be space to move around but not to get lost. Comfortable chairs which can be drawn into a circle and, ideally, some tables should be available. Facilities for making refreshments would be useful. The room should not be overlooked by others in the school. There are advantages to running the groups on the school site. Time is not wasted in travelling. There is more flexibility on the timetable and staffing and the pupils can feel that group work is not a separate issue from school. There are, however, times when a group would be better run off-site, such as a group for pupils who are long term truants from school.

Once the groups are running, a time needs to be allocated for the staff involved to meet on a regular basis to plan and discuss how the groups are developing and to reflect upon the issues raised by the groups and what their response should be. Expert on-going supervision will be necessary. Groupworkers may have to face a variety of issues which will need to be talked through with colleagues. It is useful if group workers keep a diary recording the key points raised in any group session. Groupworkers will also need time to liaise with pastoral staff and to plan activities.

Group sessions

The primary aim of group work is to create the right atmosphere for pupils to get in touch with their feelings and to appreciate the feelings of others. How is this done? The practicalities and domestic arrangements have already been discussed. The day arrives, there are eight pupils in a room with the group worker(s), what is going to happen? Clearly, it will take time to gain the trust of these young people. They may feel uncomfortable and shy, they may behave inappropriately, monopolise conversations, put others down. Mutual trust may be built in a number of ways, for example by routines and activities which provide a framework for the group to work within.

Routines

These are a sequence of activities which occur at the commencement of each session or block of sessions. If it is a closed group with a definite start and end date with the same pupils then it is pleasant to start the first session with introductions. Each group member introduces themselves and tells the group one thing about themselves. The serving of refreshments at the session can be a way of breaking the ice, as pupils busy themselves with the preparations: boiling kettle, asking who takes sugar, and so on. Similarly, it can round off a series of sessions if there is a goodbye session where pupils are invited to comment on how they have enjoyed, or not, as the case may be, the group sessions. An evaluation sheet can be a useful way of recording their thoughts and opinions on the sessions.

In an open group, where members are joining and leaving the group on a roll-on roll-off programme, the technique of introducing a new member can still be employed, perhaps by encouraging an existing member of the group to introduce the new member.

Beginning the session with a sharing of news can be a good way to get the group 'warmed up' before moving on to the main objective of the session. This could take the form of each group member reflecting on their week or the previous evening's events, or identifying one good and one bad thing that has happened to them in the week. An activity which requires the group to move around and work as a team could be used as 'energisers' to encourage the group to participate and work together.

Establishing the ground rules of the group is very important. It is quite useful if group members remind themselves of the rules at the commencement of each session. These could also be displayed on the wall of the room. The sort of rules which might be established are:

- Do not talk when another person is speaking
- Do not interrupt when another person is speaking
- What ever is said within the group situation is confidential to the group and should not be talked about with anyone outside the group without the group's permission.

It is best if each group can devise their own set of rules to which they agree to adhere.

Confidentiality

In a school setting the group members are in contact with each other throughout the school day either in classes or in other activities. This can be helpful because the members can provide support to each other between sessions. However, this can also provide opportunities for violations of confidentiality or the escalation of hostilities and conflicts that may have appeared in the group session (Berkovitz 1989). It would be important to emphasise in the group and to create a school culture whereby such violations of confidentiality are actively discouraged and the conflicts belonging to the group are brought back to the group for resolution.

It is also important to stress the point made earlier in this chapter that the groupworkers too need to have considered their own position on confidentiality. Although they may agree to keep the confidence of the group, it should be made clear to the group that in certain circumstances this is over-ruled by the guidelines laid down by the local authority on such issues as child abuse disclosures. Clearly, if a pupil talks openly about being involved in breaking the law or in experimenting with drugs it can compromise the groupworker's position. Many schools and local authorities publish guidelines on giving confidential advice to students; group leaders need to be aware of these. This is one reason why it is useful to have two groupworkers. They can evaluate the sessions and offer mutual support in and after the sessions.

Activities

To encourage pupils to express their feelings openly within the group situation can be a very difficult task. It is useful to be prepared to begin the session with an activity which brings the group together and can offer a common theme for discussion. These activities should not be seen as the *raison d'etre* for the session, but rather a process by which a group can be helped to get in touch with their feelings and express them.

Cards can be a very useful tool. The group worker prepares a set of cards based on a theme, each group member takes a card in turn, thinks about their response and shares this with the rest of the group. Others are then invited to make their comments. An example of these cards would be on the topic of 'getting on with parents' and one card might say, 'You want to go to a party which finishes very late, your parents want you to be home by 10.30pm. What would you do? How do you feel?'. Another use of cards would be to present various adjectives which describe feelings, such as 'aggressive, 'angry', 'sorry'. Each member of the group takes a card and then describes a situation when they have felt like this. These cards could be used to help pupils to describe how they are feeling at that moment.

Cards can be used successfully in a programme aimed at building the pupil's self-esteem. Statements such as 'the person with the nicest smile', 'the person I would trust with a secret', 'the person who would lend me their last £5', 'the person who works hard', are prepared prior to the session. These cards are dealt out, one to each group member and on a given signal they are given to the person to whom it is most appropriate. It is important in this activity that the group worker ensures that no one is left without a card. At the end of the activity the group discuss how it felt to receive a positive comment about themselves.

Other activities which could be employed are mentioned briefly here but are developed in other chapters of the book. These are physical games, such as trust games, or games where there is physical contact in a safe situation. Art work can be a way of encouraging pupils to communicate their feelings in a non-verbal way, as can mime and other techniques of drama such as the use of role play which can give pupils the opportunity to experience or to act out particular situations. Skills such as assertiveness and active listening can be introduced and explored within the group.

Theme orientated structured short term groups

As has been mentioned already, closed groups can be run in schools on a short term basis, on psycho-educational lines in a rather structured manner for specific themes such as bereavement, social skills, anger management and bullying.

Various aspects of group work with bereaved children have already been discussed in the chapter on bereaved children and adolescents. In any school there may be a number of children who have experienced loss or bereavement and may be 'stuck' in one of the stages of grief such as shock, disbelief, denial, anger, guilt or depression. Many children who appear to be withdrawn, violent, disruptive, delinquent or involved in substance abuse may in fact be trying to cope with the unbearable pain of loss or bereavement, even though it occurred a long time ago. The school may decide to use competent staff to help these children by employing group work techniques in the school setting. For example, at Sponne School in Towcester, Northamptonshire, the school nurse and a teacher ran a closed group for eight children for eight weeks. Each session was held at lunch time when a packed lunch was provided and eaten by the children during the group sessions. Teachers suggested which children would benefit from the group, and time was allowed for the groupworkers to discuss individual children with their teachers and also for group members to have time with the group workers on an individual basis. The sessions included various structured exercises and games as well as group discussions to help the group members to get in touch with their feelings and make sense of these (Jones et al. 1992).

A major concern in most schools is the occurrence of disruptive and violent behaviours. One reason for this type of behaviour is the lack of socially appropriate interpersonal skills in many such pupils. For such children and adolescents, Social Skills Training in a group setting may prove to be effective. Van Hasselt et al. (1979) cited over twenty studies which highlighted the relationship between childhood social functioning to adulthood psychological disturbance. Through a social skills training programme children can be helped to acquire a repertoire of behaviours for coping with day-to-day situations and difficulties such as asking for help, dealing with bullies and handling criticism appropriately. A variety of methods such as group discussion, modelling re-hearsal, roleplay, homework and feedback diaries can be combined to produce the maximum effect.

Verduyn, Lord and Forrest (1990) reported the outcome of such school based social skills programmes in an Oxfordshire Middle School. They noted that all children from 10 to 13 years (following the obtaining of parental consent) were screened to identify those who were observed to have behavioural problems and/or experienced difficulties in social interactions. The screening was done by asking teachers to complete the Rutter's Scale (Rutter 1967) and by asking all children to complete a standardised sociometric questionnaire (MacMillan *et al.* 1980) requiring each child to nominate the three children in his class with whom he would most like and the three with whom he would least like to play, sit and work. A social behaviour checklist was completed on each child before and after the program by both teachers and parents. The children completed a Social Situation Checklist (Spence 1980), a Self-Esteem Inventory (Cooper-Smith 1967) and a weekly diary of the activities. From this screening process 34 pupils were identified for the social skills program and control on a random basis. Seventeen of the children were sub-divided into four groups for eight training sessions of one hour, twice a week and four booster sessions. Although there was no 'placebo' treatment for the control group, the results of the study demonstrated significant and specific changes in the children's social behaviours. The improvements were present even at the follow up session six months later.

It is also important to aim for cognitive changes when helping children with emotional and behavioural difficulties (Spence 1983, Kendall 1984). For example, the occurrence of delinquent or aggressive behaviours may represent performance deficits associated with interfering emotional arousal. Arousal of anger often serves as a cognitive mediator of aggressive behaviour. In the chapter on young offenders in this volume, the principles of group work for anger management are also outlined. Feindler, Ecton, Kingsley and Dubey (1986) have shown the effectiveness of group anger control training with adolescent boys who were patients in a psychiatric hospital. Feindler and Ecton (1986) describe in detail the techniques of anger control training for adolescents in any setting. Lochman, Nelson and Sims (1981) reported on an anger control treatment programme with aggressive elementary school children. Group sessions were run on a twice weekly basis for 40 minutes each. The children were taught how to stop initial aggressive response, how to relabel cognitively the so-called threatening stimuli and how to solve problems by generating alternative options. They were helped to become more aware of their physiological changes so that they could use these changes (anger arousal) as signals for getting into problem solving mode. Their unhelpful thoughts such as 'I want to get back at my teacher and my mum for making me miss my favourite TV programme', were altered to the more helpful, 'If I stick to the homework rules I can watch my favourite TV programme'. The effectiveness of the treatment programme was evaluated by the use of Walker Problem Behaviour Identification Checklist (Walker 1976) before and after the training. The program was more effective in helping children with problems of acting out rather than children with the problems of distractibility or immaturity.

Feindler, Marriott and Iwata (1984) reported on a study of the effectiveness of group anger control teaching for junior high school delinquents. On the basis of high rates of classroom and community disruption 36 multi-suspended adolescents were chosen from an in-school sample of 100 students. They were randomly assigned to one of the three treatment groups or to a non-contact control group. Training included practising relaxation, thinking ahead, assertion without aggression and appropriate self evaluation and self instructions, for example 'I am going to ignore this boy and keep cool', 'He is just jealous because I did so well in my test', and so on. It was found that there were significant changes in the self control rating scales (Kendall and Wilcox 1979) of the children in the groups.

Evaluation

It is important that any new work done in a school setting is evaluated for its effectiveness. It can be difficult to evaluate something as intangible as the benefits of group work. Evaluation needs to take place at various levels, involving the whole staff, the group leaders and the pupils. A variety of techniques can be employed. An evaluation sheet may be used to encourage the pupils to evaluate what went on in the group sessions. This could be used by staff as well. A questionnaire to be completed by the staff might give a valuable insight into staff perception of the role of group work. Individual pupils or groups of pupils could be invited to 'give evidence' on what they think of group work. Groupworkers can evaluate each session in their log book, perhaps using previously agreed headings. Because it is so difficult to quantify the benefits of group work there necessarily has to be an element of trust and belief that group work can help young people in the long term.

Staff and pupils must be realistic in their expectations of a group. Nothing will change immediately. Helping young people to get in touch with their feelings and learn to express these feelings will take time, but the outcomes can be very rewarding and offer a new perspective on their situations.

An example of group work in an upper school

(The names of pupils mentioned in this section have been changed, but the experiences described arose from group work sessions which were run at Weston Favell Upper School, Northampton.)

In 1988 a group of staff came together to discuss the possibility of helping young people in school who were experiencing emotional or behavioural difficulties. It was agreed that there needed to be a mechanism for dealing with such topics as drug abuse, sexuality and family matters in a directive way with these pupils. It was agreed to look at tackling these issues through a group work approach.

A training programme consisting of a number of sessions to gain insight into the procedures and connotations of group therapy involving the adolescent were organised. This enabled the staff involved to acquire enough knowledge and expertise to be able to conduct group therapy sessions within the school. In addition, one member of the group was able to observe experienced staff working with groups attending the Ken Stewart Family Centre (Child and Family Consultation Service) for a period of six months.

Following these training sessions a group of ninth year (13–14 years) pupils displaying behavioural difficulties were identified to take part in a pilot scheme. It was a mixed group of eight pupils working with two group workers. The group met at the same time and in the same place within the last session of a morning or afternoon. Each pupil was seen individually, to 'sell' the idea and a carefully worded letter was sent home allowing parents the opportunity for discussion. Regular meetings were held with a member of the Child and Family Consultation Service to discuss 'progress' and issues arising.

The pilot scheme proved to be worthwhile in highlighting the difficulties in running such a group:

1. Withdrawing pupils from a lesson meant that the pupil could use this as a weapon when they wanted to withdraw from the group activities.

2. The pupils were withdrawn from various areas of the curriculum, which meant that there was little sense of group purpose.

Despite these difficulties it was still felt to be a valid approach to the presenting problems.

Most pupils who took part in the pilot scheme opted for the BTec Foundation studies programme in their 10th year, aimed mainly at low achieving pupils or those with learning difficulties. It was therefore possible to embed group work into their curriculum by running groups during core time which was part of their course. In this way many of the organisational problems encountered in the pilot scheme were eradicated and pupils did not perceive group work as anything special, but rather as part of their total curriculum. Small numbers of pupils were withdrawn from core lessons for a period of ten weeks (1 x 45 minute sessions). Each session was loosely based around a theme, but the activity was secondary to the problems the group came with or brought forward during the time. For example, the session might start with cards outlining situations occurring at school and at home but issues arising from the group might over-ride these. The areas covered by the group were very wide ranging; home issues often arose and the adults working with the group were surprised at the honesty and the depth of the information and feelings being brought forward and shared with the group.

Later on in the course single sexed groups were established. There were very different patterns of behaviour in these groups from those in mixed groups. All male groups seemed to be able to lay aside the fact that the group workers were teachers and women when the topic of sex arose, as it most frequently did! Most of the discussion was of an indirectly challenging nature, but the boys were able to express their feelings of uncertainty and inadequacy in the safe environment of the group. It was noted that in all the groups the pupils became better at listening and making sense of each other's feelings. The feedback at the end of the sessions from the pupils was that they knew each other better and identified a need for 'time to talk' which they didn't feel was available to them at any other time; some pupils requested that the group continued. It was felt by the group workers that the pupils were more aware and sensitive to others in the group. Behavioural problems were not eradicated from these sessions; however, there was the opportunity to work through the group, use peer pressure and encourage individuals to look at themselves. There was some evidence to suggest that the group work led to better pupil relationships within the BTec Foundation Programme generally.

The staff involved in the group work sessions felt that, although perfection was not achieved, time and opportunity had been created for the pupils to talk to each other in a non threatening, safe forum about issues which are important within their lives. By embedding the sessions into the curriculum it was possible to recreate the groups at any time it was felt necessary. Groupworkers commented that it was quite noticeable that pupils involved with group work were rarely absent for their sessions; sometimes they made an appearance in school especially for the sessions!

It is hoped that other teachers will want to become involved in setting up groups in their schools. A support group has been formed which meets twice a term which offers guidance to teachers who are considering starting a group in their school, help and advice for those already running groups and for others the opportunity for further training.

Case examples

John

John is fourteen; he says he is very unhappy at home. The relationship with himself, his mother and her partner are very strained. He has run away from home on several occasions. He does not like school and has rejected any structure which might offer him support within the school system. He frequently truants and is becoming increasingly isolated from his peer group. On the first two occasions that the group met, John had to be escorted into the room by a member of staff. He made it quite clear that he did not want to be part of the group activities. Gradually he relaxed and eventually proved himself to be the most perceptive member of the group and declared it to be his 'best' lesson. He has begun to transfer his increased assertiveness into other situations in which he finds himself and his self-esteem has improved. Instead of leaving the school site when he finds himself in an unhappy situation he now approaches his form tutor or finds a quiet place to work, such as the library. His negotiating skills with adults are much improved.

Stephen

Stephen is a fifteen-year-old who was being bullied by many of the pupils in his groups and around the school. He was able to gain status within the group by sharing his skill with words. His self-esteem rose and he reported that he is more able now to cope with the bullying because he is better at words than the bullies.

Tracy

Tracy is fifteen and is exploring the feelings about her relationship with her parents and her boyfriend. She was able to appreciate her parents' point of view about her sexual activity. Instead of continuing with the shouting matches she was having with her mother, she decided to write down how she was feeling in a letter to her mother. The group had helped her to reach that decision.

It was noted that relationships could often be 'mended' in groups. For example, two girls who had been at loggerheads for some time and brought their silences to the group were eventually reconciled when one of the group members decided to leave the room until the two had 'made it up'.

Conclusion

Group work is a technique for helping young people to recognise and accept their feelings and to respect the feelings of others. It can be employed in a variety of context and for a variety of purposes. The techniques of group work can be used across the curriculum and many Personal and Social Education Programmes rely heavily on the ideas outlined. What these programmes may not offer the pupils is a non-critical and supportive environment where there is the opportunity for growth, development, and a change of attitude. Group work in the school setting offers the opportunity for the work to be carried out in an environment which is often more acceptable to both parents and pupils alike.

Acknowledgements

The authors of this chapter would like to thank Judy Jennings and Susan Wright from Northampton SENSS EBD and Margaret Richards and Lorna Jones from Weston Favell Upper School

References

Bennett, N., Desforges, C., Cockburn, A. and Wilkinson, B. (1984) *The Quality of Pupil Learning Experiences*. London: Lawrence Erlbaum.

Berkovitz, I.H. (1989) 'Application of Group Therapy in Secondary Schools'. In F.J.C. Azima and L.H. Richmond (eds) *Adolescent Group Psychotherapy*. Madison: International Universities Press. Ch. 7: 99–123.

Cooper-Smith, S. (1967) *The Antecedents of Self Esteem*. San Francisco: Freeman.

Department of Education and Science and Welsh Office (1989) *Discipline in Schools: Report of the Committee of Enquiry Chaired by Lord Elton*. London: Her Majesty's Stationery Office.

Feindler, E.L. and Ecton, R.B. (1986) *Adolescent Anger Control: Cognitive Behavioural Techniques*. Oxford: Pergamon Press.

Feindler, E.L., Ecton, R.B., Kingsley, D. and Dubey, D.R. (1986) 'Group Anger and Control Training for Institutionalised Psychiatric Male Adolescents'. *Behaviour Therapy* 17: 109–123.

Feindler, E.L., Marriott, S.A. and Iwata, M. (1984) 'Group Anger Control Training for Junior High School Delinquents'. *Cognitive Therapy and Research* 8(3): 299–311.

Jones, A. (1971) Groupwork in a Comprehensive School. *Groups: Annual Review of the Residential Child Care Association*. 18:40–47.

Jones, A., Allen, M., Bell, J. and Shaw, M. (1992) Thursday Group at Sponne School Towcester, Northants. (Personal Communication).

Kendall, P.C. (1984) 'Cognitive Behavioural Self Control Therapy for Children'. *Journal of Child Psychology and Psychiatry* 25: 173–179.

Kendell, P.C. and Wilcox, L. (1979) 'Self Control in Children: Development of a Rating Scale'. *Journal of Consulting and Clinical Psychology* 47: 1020–1029.

Lochmann, J.E., Nelson, W.M. and Sims, J.P. (1981) *Journal of Clinical Child Psychology:* 146–148.

MacMillan, A.S., Kolvin, I., Garside, R.F., Nicol, A.R. and Leitch, I.M. (1980) 'A Multiple Criterion Screen for Identifying Secondary School Children with Psychiatric Disorders'. *Psychological Medicine* 10: 265–276.

Rutter, M. (1967) 'A Children's Behaviour Questionnaire for Completion by teachers: Preliminary findings'. *Journal of Child Psychology and Psychiatry* 8: 1–11.

Slavin, R.E. (1985) 'An Introduction to Cooperative Learning Research'. In R. Slavin, S. Sharon, S. Kagan, R. Hentz-Lazarowitz, C. Webb and R. Schmuck (eds) *Learning to Cooperate, Cooperating to Learn*. London: Plenum (pp.5–15).

Spence, S.H. (1980) *Social Skills Training Children and Adolescents. A Councellor's Manual*. Windsor: NFER.

Spence, S.H. (1983)' Teaching Social Skills to Children'. *Journal of Child Psychology and Psychiatry* 24: 621–627.

Vann Hasselt, V.B., Hersen, M.M., Whitehill, M.B. and Bellak, A.S. (1979) 'Social Skill Assessment and Training for Children: An Evaluative Review'. *Behaviour Research and Therapy* 17: 4113–4139.

Verduyn, C.M., Lord, W. and Forrest, A.C. (1990) 'Social Skills Training in Schools: An Evaluation Study'. *Journal of Adolescence* 113: 3–16.

Walker, H.M. (1976) *Manual for Walker Problem Behaviour Identification Checklist.* Los Angeles: Western Psychological Services.

CHAPTER 20

Group Work in Residential Child Care

Bernie Evans and Paul Cook

Residential establishments exist to cater for the needs of society or of an individual that they cannot meet themselves. A residential establishment can facilitate a process that cannot be achieved outside the establishment, or cannot be maintained by any other means. This can cover a wide area of needs, including learning, treatment and many forms of care.

A residential establishment may be regarded as one group within an aggregate of groups. A group is defined 'as a collection of people who spend some time together, see themselves as members of a group and are identified as such by others outside the group' (Preston-Shoot 1987 p.7). Where mutual respect exists it is possible to attain a high standard of care in a residential setting. It is essential, if success is to be achieved, that a good quality of communication is practised and an awareness of group processes and interaction are understood.

A group work process is in action in residential settings informally by virtue of the very fact that people are living together in an environment such that group situations cannot be avoided, i.e., having to share communal facilities such as bathrooms, or a TV Lounge. Thus groups can occur formally and informally and both can be equally effective.

Knopka (1963) states 'social group work is a method of social work which helps individuals to enhance their social functioning through purposeful group experience, and to cope more effectively with their personal group or community problems' (p.5). This is put into effect on a daily basis in residential establishments in an informal way. Clients can learn to function better and enhance their social skills from participating in something as simple as sitting down and having a meal with a group of people, to taking part in a group discussion.

Research findings from social psychology (Sherif and Sherif 1969) clearly indicate that under certain conditions individual's behaviour and attitudes are influenced by groups. A child who has been displaying inappropriate or unacceptable behaviour in the community may, once admitted into a residential establishment, be influenced by the environment and by her or his peers and, if entering a stable unit, change their behaviour to conform with that of their peers. Most of this occurrs as informal group work.

There is another side of residential care that needs to be discussed. There is a trap to group living in a residential environment that denies young people their freedom. Living under a regime can induce institutionalisation and not encourage individuals to develop their own personality to the full. For some the lack or loss of opportunity to do what most people do for themselves can hinder their social skills. For example, frequently young people in residential care do not have the opportunity to see how food is purchased and then prepared, something which many of us take for granted and which is a normal part of our socialisation pattern. This can not only deprive them of important emotional experiences but also of the ability to acquire the basic social skills necessary if they are to gain confidence and ability in their own lives, and exercise choice wisely. One approach to combat this is to increase the level of participation of residents in the daily running and routines of the unit. Another approach is to prepare the young person for the independent life they are about to encounter. If a residential unit has the space to offer independence training it could, for example, encourage a young person to prepare their own dinner, or spend some time alone in their room, trying to simulate the situation they may encounter after leaving a care situation.

There are some people who find the intensity and the intimacy of one-to-one relationships when understanding counselling or treatment programmes difficult, and are much more comfortable with a group of peers. This can be true for many adolescents who can feel threatened by individual sessions with adults, especially those in authority. The right balance needs to be met if the work is to be successful. Yet it is a very difficult task to balance the role of the carer and controller with counsellor. A period of settling in must elapse and the young person be sufficiently confident in their environment, displaying trust towards their carer and their peers before the opportunity rises for work with the young person on the difficulties and life problems that have often precipitated admission to the residential unit. The growth of these problems are too numerous to mention, but they clearly differ from one residential unit to another and, more important, from one resident to another. For example, young people in care often suffer from many different forms of deprivation, emotional, social and educational. It is one of the tasks of the residential unit to erase some of these effects through appropriate channels.

We once worked with a 17-year-old young man who expressed an interest in mechanical farming and wanted to go to college to obtain a qualification in this area. However, he had not attended his school on a regular basis due to many personal difficulties within his family. As a result of sporadic attendance, he had no formal examination qualifications and his general ability was below average. This, however, did not deter us from encouraging him to return to college to obtain the necessary GCSE to enable him to continue further. This actually appears a quite simple and logical task, but the young man was very anxious about returning and being in a group with others. As a way of helping him prepare, he was enrolled in the local Judo group, an activity which he enjoyed, yet ensured that at the same time he was part of a group process.

When working in a residential setting, the knowledge and ability to display skills in group work are needed in many areas. It is essential for harmonious living to be achieved that the resources of residential group living are managed appropriately; for example coping with the daily tensions that arise, integration of new arrivals, the preparation of young people who are about to leave care, and the facilitation of personal growth, problem solving and social functioning.

Given that residential care is the first point of contact with work for the majority of workers, one of the difficulties of putting these theories into practice is that most residential workers have had little or no training in the way of conceptual models to guide them. As a result of this it is the responsibility of the few specialist workers to create a clear conceptual and practised approach for all workers to implement. Criteria are needed for guiding the workers when organising a planned group occasion and are equally important when doing informal group work, for example at meal times, or when just sitting in a group chatting. A starting point with group work is for the carer to examine their own values and attitudes and to be aware enough not to impose their values on the clients.

Residential workers undoubtedly face difficulties when attempting formal group work with their clients. As we have said, many residential workers have had no formal training, often coming from a work background that bears limited resemblance to their present employment. The result of this situation is that young people who are deprived or disturbed are cared for and treated by individuals who, despite showing motivation and commitment, have little theoretical base to work from when implementing treatment programmes, or trying to understand that attitudes and behaviours of the young people in our care.

Within the residential setting certain problems have been experienced which, if not addressed, can lead to the failure of the group work process. Issues within staff groups have caused difficulties; these revolved around staff members' behaviour, for example feeling that staff undertaking the group work have an easier task than those working with the rest of the group. On occasion staff who may have attempted similar work which has not been successful may have a cynical attitude to those undertaking group work. This requires challenge by the staff team as it provides an unhelpful attitude and undermines the commitment and enthusiasm of both workers and young people.

As will be familiar to those who work in residential settings, rota changes, due to illness, or particular crises in the unit, new admissions, children who go missing, or who may have unexpectedly left (e.g. Custodial Sentence at Court) can cause problems for the continuity of the group. Peer dynamics, young people who following a disagreement may also affect the way the group was set up initially. It is very important that the group workers are supported by their colleagues and encouraged in the work they are attempting to achieve, or the group may lose its continuity, and the clients' interest could diminish. Other staff members can sometimes unintentionally sabotage a group. For example, if a young person is protesting that they do not wish to attend, and it is for no apparent reason, other than, say, a film is on the television, staff may not sell the group in a positive way and encourage the person to attend, thus almost colluding with the young person and minimising the purpose of the group. Also, if in their past experience they have seen or taken part in a group that has been unsuccessful they may be sceptical about the usefulness of the new group, only offering negative advice and support to their colleagues.

As has been noted previously, workers and group members may experience difficulties over roles. For example, 'confidentiality' within the group may manifest itself often in the way young people find it difficult to accept the differing roles of staff from groupworker to staff member within the unit. Young people often feel that what they have said in the group setting is affecting the way they are treated outside the group. A young person who has told a member of staff about 'drug taking' may then feel that a staff member speaking to them about another matter is really being critical of what has been said in the group. Equally, keyworkers of the young people within the group will require lines of communication so as to ensure they do not feel their work is being undermined. Working in partnership, with common and clear goals understood by all is very important. The role of supervision cannot be overstated to aid good practice during this process.

Group work is a more visible method of working than individual work and therefore tends to attract proportionately more attention within a Unit. This can result in a higher expectation of 'success' than less visible individual work. In residential work, social workers spend many of their working hours with colleagues and clients in the company of a 'shared' group situation. This high visibility to peers and clients can highlight human failings and group failings which will be hard to conceal. It is important, therefore, that these are acknowledged and shared, not minimised, so workers and clients feel supported and valued. Group work involves sharing both by the clients and social workers, and much effort and careful thought needs to go into planning when setting up a formal group in a residential setting.

From our experiences of group work in a residential establishment catering for adolescents of a mixed gender who were extremely disturbed or disruptive in their behaviour, we found that their behaviour in the group appeared to be very different from the way they interacted normally. This is what the workers set out to achieve; they wanted to create a relaxed environment. They chose the four young people very carefully, making sure all those chosen were reasonably equal in status. (For example, if you ran a group of mainly boys who were car thief's and put an adolescent sex offender in the group, the others would minimise their own behaviour in comparison with the sexual offender; he may also be subjected to much ridicule and scapegoating which would not only be inappropriate but damaging to his treatment.) They also let the group set their own rules regarding smoking, acceptable language and so on. This made the young people own their group. It was in this environment that the workers noticed a change in the young people, finding that they would communicate more freely. Some who were very introvert in the large group found it easier to communicate and benefited greatly from being listened to. Another area in which we noted a change in behaviour was with the young people who normally acted in a 'Bravado Way', who allowed their barriers to drop, obviously feeling safe and secure enough to do so. Equally, groups who play together, stay together. It was therefore important that, within the group sessions, the group 'celebrated the activity and achievement and took time out to enjoy each other'(Benson 1987 p.190). This they did by enjoying refreshments made by one of the group members.

The group workers also appreciated the need for further training in comprehending group processes and interactions. Now residential workers can receive training from courses specialising in group work to supplement their own self learning. Group work requires a very high level of commitment, and this needs to be appreciated fully by group workers in a residential setting. Should the worker run single sex, mixed sex groups and groups for minority ethnic children? It is possible to run all types of group successfully. However, it is very important, if attempting to run mixed groups, that one has the correct balance, as it could be very detrimental to the gender or group in the minority. It also has to be balanced with young people at a similar level of maturation. Initially, a mixed gender group may have a higher anxiety level than a single sex group, which may result in the worker having to intervene excessively to bring down the level of anxiety. Nervous sexual banter, boisterous interchange and possible sub-grouping may occur and impede the development of the group. Unless this is addressed it can lead to a high non- attendance record and lack of interest in the group by certain members. If the initial anxiety can be overcome, a mixed group provides a good arena for examining and rehearsing male/female relationships and examining and challenging sexist and gender stereotyping.

The effective group worker requires certain qualities to be able to form therapeutic relationships with the group, and the ability to relate equally to all members without a particular focus on individuals. Workers need to demonstrate an empathy and genuine warmth, to create a safe, trusting environment. Many young people have often previously participated in groups that have been unsuccessful. Therefore, workers require skills and understanding to facilitate self disclosure and openness to interpret and analyse group dynamics and challenge and stimulate and openness to interpret and analyse group dynamics and challenge and stimulate when required. Communication, both verbal and non-verbal and the ability to actively listen are key skills. Many young people often feel that their views and opinions are not listened to by workers in units, therefore workers should actively listen and acknowledge contributions. With this in mind, young people need to be actively involved in the setting of group rules and norms and set limits on their own behaviour. Groupworkers should be able to demonstrate the ability to challenge, keep time, boundaries and, most important, resist manipulation.

One example of how we have involved young people in a group was through a Motor Cross Club. The rational of the club is to achieve different skills, build confidence and personality. Team work is also a very important aspect, as is learning to consider others and building relationships. When someone joins the group their knowledge of the workings of the bike, or the skills and techniques required to ride are limited. Here a young person who has been in the group, who has the necessary experience, acquires the skills to pass this knowledge on. It is also an opportunity for re-channelling the energy of delinquent excitement.

A boy was admitted to the unit for stealing motor cars and bikes. He was unable to appreciate that his actions were highly dangerous not only to himself but also to others; individuals he stole from and others he injured were deeply affected and hurt, and therefore his behaviour was not acceptable. Through the group process of the Motor Cross Club, he was able to identify alternative strategies for his behaviour. He also learnt that many other skills were necessary requirements, such as preparing the track to ride on, the maintenance of the bikes, the learning process of how to ride safely, the need to be patient and committed, because on joining the group it would be at least eight weeks before riding. At the end of his stay he was able to learn a variety of psychological and interpersonal skills and also see the affect his behaviour had on others. This was possible as the group had offered support, he had felt significant and worthwhile and, through a sharing of feelings, had received feedback on his help to others, being liked and valued for himself.

Many group situations are enhanced when co-working with a colleague within a residential setting, which has the potential to be highly stressful. Co-working offers mutual support for workers; it also increases the range of skills and experience that can be brought to the group. Sharing tasks and functions, whilst ensuring continuity, particularly if one worker is absent, are key advantages. Working together also provides opportunities to have two perspectives on observations, interpretations and feeding back interventions. Two workers provide opportunities to work in sub groups if required. To be effective as a partnership, workers should ensure that they are familiar with each other's style and way of working, follow similar approaches that complement each other and be committed to working together.

Generally, smaller groups (6–8 residents plus workers) are more effective: 'Large enough for stimulation, small enough for participation and recognition' (Brown 1986 p.55) Residential Units that are now providing the most effective care for young people do so in smaller group living situations (maximum ten young people) with at least an equal number of social work staff (plus night supervision). Smaller groups enable relationships, trust and cohesion to develop more quickly and provide opportunities for more participation, face-to-face communication and individual recognition.

The membership of any group is a critical factor in determining how effectively it can operate. The opportunities of selection may be limited by self selection, referral of the presence of a resident population. Providing a commonality of need and purpose are present, groups have a positive chance of being successful. In terms of selection the worker has to consider not only the individual's past history but also their potential in terms of how they are likely to relate and interact with other possible members. In some settings it may be possible to have a pre-selection interview or meeting when both have the opportunity to view each other. Whenever possible, young people should be self motivated to join the group; however, workers should encourage, help and support those whose participation would be beneficial. Anxieties and fears of group interaction may require clarification, preparation,support and encouragement.

Workers will need to demonstrate the ability to work in an anti-discriminatory way. Dominelli (1988) suggests that workers need to be able to work with anyone, across racial divides and sexes, and have an empathy based on knowledge of differences between black and white people and their significance rather than the pretence that all people are the same. The range of problems, needs and abilities of young people need to be fully considered. Some young people's diversity of problems may dominate a group to the detriment of other members. Some young people may also require particular support regarding areas of confidentiality that may then create personal problems with the larger group. Groups will need to have a particular focus on the racial, religious, linguistic, cultural and gender needs of the young people they work with. Workers may need to build into the group help for members in respecting the individual needs of members of the group, as well as having a clear understanding of their own attitudes and values and how they may effect their methods of working. On setting the age limit for the group, workers should also consider the actual level of functioning of group members. For example, many older young people function chronologically younger than their years and may benefit from opportunities for working in a different group setting.

Workers have to be clear as to the óverall purpose of the group, and not be over ambitious in their objectives, particularly in the initial attempts at group work. Groups may wish to focus on a particular issue, for example on building the self esteem of its members, developing social skills, providing education on sexual behaviour, drugs and alcohol abuse, social treatment and discussion. Other groups may wish to focus more on feelings and abuse young people may have been subjected to.

Once planned, it is important that timings are strictly adhered to, to give a structure to the group sessions and enhance members' sense of security. Workers should ensure that they review their own experience to undertake group work and be aware of their feelings and expectations. An experienced supervisor should be identified and available for regular consultation. Workers should also actively engage the support and approval of their management which will be invaluable in supporting them when residential units are under pressure for staff resources. Workers should be clear what records they are to keep and the access to other professionals and young people should be clear from the outset. Many groups can be a very productive and rewarding experience. However, for a variety of reasons a group can also be frustrating and negative within a residential setting.

Problems can be expressed in a variety of ways however, within open residential settings, certain problems can dominate. Often retaining regular attendance can be a major issue: young people may be missing from the unit at key times, be late, attempt to finish early or threaten to leave. Conflicts due to young people monopolising the group may lead to absence or hostility, or behaviour such as ridicule. Impatience causes difficulties and if not handled confidently by workers lead to 'scapegoating' of certain members. This involves focusing negative and unacceptable feeling onto a vulnerable member, often blaming then rejecting them from the group. In this situation it is easy for the worker to take sides with the young person who is being subjected to 'scapegoating' but it is important that the group is made aware of what is happening and asked to comment on it. Within social work, handling conflict can provoke concern, apprehension and even fear. As within all social work settings, handling conflict becomes part of every day life and practice, and can be particularly daunting within a residential setting. Having the courage to confront issues and be supported is of prime importance.

Workers within the group will need to be aware of avoidance by members of certain tasks or issues. This may take the form of distracting the group, challenging the value of the group and avoiding pressing issues, which may lead to misunderstanding, not listening, a lack of trust and withdrawal. It is important that workers allow the group to take responsibility and not rely just on workers for decisions, whilst retaining some structure, by thanking contributors and by body language or a more directing approach, saying they wish to hear from other members. It is important that this is done with care; it better to engage a silent member by saying 'I think you said something interesting about last week, Linda', than 'You haven't said anything about today, Linda'.

Workers may also need to understand the various meanings of silence, which is a very powerful form of expression indicating a wide range of feelings, from resistance, disinterest, to positive feelings or reflections of calmness of thought. This requires a diagnostic understanding and group work skill. Equally, 'latent' communication can present a problem. This is where the group is observed to be preoccupied with an unrelated topic,but is in fact concerned with an issue that as a group it cannot, for some reason, talk about openly (Heap 1985). The group's ability to cope constructively with problems can provide useful feedback on progress. Total resolutions may not always be possible and members may have to tolerate or cope with the presence of unresolved issues. Problems with the group are best solved through communication, discussion of issues, negotiations, compromise or even voting. The open sharing of experiences which allows for emotional release in a safe environment can allow for questioning and feedback whilst providing reassurance for group members. Support from within and outside groups, positive encouragement, 'a pat on the back' are most welcome for workers and group members in providing encouragement. Specific techniques such as sculpting, role reversal, role play, psychodrama can also be used to develop awareness and insight, promoting positive reinforcement and the teaching of new skills, such as problem solving.

The process and progress of a group needs to be carefully monitored and evaluated. This feedback helps the group to teach and reach its full potential. Various observations of group members, written records, feedback from supervisors and colleagues are all sources of information towards evaluation.

References

Benson, J.F. (1987) *Working More Creatively With Groups.* London: Tavistock Publications Ltd.

Brown, A. (1986) *Groupwork.* London: Heinmann Educational Books.

Dominelli, L. (1988) *Anti-Racist Social Work.* Basingstoke and London: MacMillan Press Ltd.

Heap, K. (1985) *The Practice of Social Work with Groups: Systematic Approach.* London: Geoage Allan and Urwin.

Knopa, L. (1963) *Groupwork in Social Work.* London: Heinemann Educational Books.

Preston-Shoot, M. (1987) *Effective Groupwork.* London: MacMillian Press Ltd.

Sherif, M. and Sherif, C.W. (1969) *Social Psychology.* New York: Harper and Row'.

CHAPTER 21

Group Work in Child Mental Health Services

Kedar Nath Dwivedi

A number of mental health services for children and adolescents have been using group work as an important component of treatment, often in conjunction with other treatment modalities such as Family Therapy and Individual Psychotherapy or Counselling. Group work is particularly suitable for the treatment of children and adolescents and is also a greater value for money in the light of the limited resources in most Child Mental Health Services. The Child Mental Health Services do also provide training, consultation, supervision, liaison and support to other agencies working with children and adolescents (where group work is a frequent way of working) and thus play a valuable role in preventive, promotive and rehabilitative aspects of mental health as well.

In this chapter there is an attempt to briefly examine the impact, extent, types and causes of the mental health problems in children, the nature of child mental health services and aspects of group work within such services.

The impact of child mental health problems

'In years gone by, many people tended to regard children's psychiatric disorder as not worthy of serious attention. The assumption had been that most disorders are no more than an exaggeration of normal growing-up pains. I think it is fair to recognise that the term 'Child Guidance Clinic' has rather tended to reinforce that prejudice, in that it seems to imply that all that is needed is a bit of sound advice and support'. (Rutter 1991 p.1)

Unfortunately, psychiatric disorders in children not only cause considerable immediate distress and suffering in the child but also have a tendency to persist and can be a precursor of adult mental disorders.

In the Isle of Wight study (Rutter *et al.* 1970), for example, the psychiatric disorders in ten-year-old children had usually been present for several years already. Richman *et al.* (1982) found that in 60 per cent of the three-year-old children with psychiatric problems, the problems were still present at the age of eight years. Similarly, in the Isle of Wight study (Rutter 1979) over half of children who had psychiatric problems at the age of ten years continued to have these problems five years later.

The long term risks are particularly important in conduct disorders. Nearly 50 per cent of children with conduct disorder may grow out of it but the remaining tend to have problems even during adulthood (Robins 1966). In fact in one study nearly two thirds continued to have pervasive psychological problems in adult life (e.g. high rates of marital breakdown, their children being taken into care, unemployment, poor social relationships and recurrent depression) (Rutter 1991). Thus the link is not only with the psychopathic personality disorder but also with depressive illness. Childhood violence or aggression, in a study by Zeitlin (1966), was followed by personality disorder or psychosis in a considerable proportion of cases.

Similarly, childhood depression increases the risk of affective disorders in adult life (Harrington *et al.* 1990). A long term follow-up study of school children with school refusal revealed that 12 per cent had marked agoraphobia in adult life (Berg and Jackson 1985). Nearly 72 per cent of children with obsessional symptoms were found to have the same symptoms as adults in a study by Zeitlin (1966). Childhood phobias also showed considerable continuity. Drug addiction and alcoholism in adults are associated with the use or abuse of dependence-producing substances in childhood (Kandel 1978). Hyperactive children, in contrast to their siblings, tend to grow up with an increased risk of accidents, geographical moves and lower educational status (Weiss *et al.* 1985). Adulthood disorders and variations of sexual orientation (transsexuality, transvestism and homosexuality) usually have their origin in childhood (Green 1975).

All children react differently to the emotional pain they experience; each child is a unique individual. Many children are overwhelmed by family conflicts, divorce or death of their loved ones, lack of loving concern, neglect and physical, emotional or sexual abuse. There are some who find it so unbearable that the only alternative they have is to cut themselves off from the world or refuse to grow up. Some blame themselves for what has happened, while others grow up only to repeat the neglectful or violent behaviours shown to them. There is an urgent need to recognise these frightened and damaged children and help them to make sense of and deal with their conflicting feelings. Such a help not only alleviates the intense suffering of the moment but also prevents a great deal of psychiatric disturbance in the future, especially personality disorders that lead to violence, alcohol, drug and sex abuse, accidents, family breakdowns, poverty, crime and so on, draining the meagre resources of welfare and health agencies. If there are no resources to help these children, they and their future children face a very bleak future (Miller, undated). Early intervention would not only improve adjustment during childhood and adolescence but would also reduce the incidence of psychological distress in adulthood (Lewis 1965).

The extent of child mental health problems

An estimate by the Department of Education and Science (1978) pointed out that 20 per cent of children had need of help and guidance at some time during their development from birth to years of age. Surveys of general populations have shown that the prevalence of persistent and socially handicapping mental health problems amongst children aged 3–15 years in developed countries is about 5–15 per cent (World Health Organisation 1977). Thus, in a population of a health district of 250,000, one may expect to find between 5000 and 15,000 children with considerable mental health problems. Many health districts have a much larger general population.

The Royal College of General Practitioners Working Party on Prevention of Psychiatric Disorders in General Practice pointed out that psychosocial factors are very relevant in about half of a GP's consultation with children (Bailey *et al.* 1978)

In general, child mental health problems are more common in boys than girls, more frequent in adolescence than in earlier childhood and more common in children living in inner city areas than those living in small towns and rural areas. Children with adverse psychological circumstances, educational difficulties and physical ill health, particularly neurological problems, are much more vulnerable to psychiatric disorders. Help should, therefore, also be made available in Social Services, Education and Child Health settings, in addition to a specific Child Mental Health Service.

Evidence also indicates that many forms of child psychiatric disorders, such as juvenile delinquency, suicide, eating disorders, alcohol and drug abuse, are becoming much more frequent (Rutter 1979, 1991). There has been a substantial increase in the rate of divorce, unemployment, abuse and in the impact of mass media but a decrease in the role of religion and moral values. During the last decade the rate of homelessness doubled in this country (Oldman 1990). These factors are bound to contribute to the increase in childhood psychiatric disorders.

The nature of child mental health problems

The concept of 'disease' is not particularly helpful when considering psychiatric disorders of childhood, because only a very small proportion of such disorders constitute conditions qualitatively different from normal development, (autism, childhood psychosis). Most disorders are, therefore, quantitatively rather than qualitatively different from the norm. However, this is not just an issue of statistical abnormality but also one of suffering, and impairment of personal development as a consequence. Very high intelligence, for example, may not be regarded as a psychiatric disorder if it is not handicapping, although this may be statistically abnormal. Thus, mental health problems in children and adolescents are 'abnormalities of emotions, behaviour or social relationships sufficiently marked or prolonged to cause suffering or risk to optimal development in the child or distress or disturbance in the family or community' (Kurtz 1992 p.6).

There are many ways of classifying these problems. For example, The American Psychiatric Association (1987) in its Diagnostic and Statistical Manual of Mental Disorders (3rd Revised Edition) classified various developmental disorders, disruptive behaviour disorders, anxiety disorders, eating disorders, gender identity disorders, tic disorders, elimination disorders and other disorders. The multi-axial classification in child psychiatry (Rutter, Shaffer and Sturge 1975 and Rutter, Shaffer and Shepherd 1975) is based upon The International Classification of Diseases (World Health Organisation 1978) and includes not only the psychiatric syndromes (axis 1) but also specific delays in development (axis 2), intellectual level (axis 3), medical conditions (axis 4) and abnormal psychosocial situations (axis 5). Steinhausen and Erdin (1991) have compared the diagnoses of Child and Adolescent Psychiatry Disorders in ICD-9 (World Health Organisations 1978) and ICD-10 (World Health Organisation 1987 and Rutter 1989).

The National Casemix Office (1991) has also produced a classification system that includes various psychiatric disorders of children mainly for the purposes of business planning and management. Some of the common disorders mentioned already are briefly outlined below.

Conduct Disorders

These refer to children who show a persistent pattern of antisocial behaviour with significant impairment in everyday functioning and who may be unmanageable by parents or teachers. These behaviours may include lying, cheating, stealing, hitting, oppositional and defiant behaviours, poor peer relationships and destructiveness. Nearly 4–10 per cent of children may be suffering from this problem, which is significantly more common in boys than girls (Rutter, Cox *et al.* 1975).

Emotional Disorders

These involve considerable emotional distress or suffering for the child, such as feelings of inferiority, self consciousness, social withdrawal, shyness, anxiety, crying, hypersensitivity, depression, chronic sadness. The symptomatology may be similar to adulthood 'neurosis' (e.g. anxiety states, depressive disorders, obsessive compulsive conditions, phobias, conversion hysteria, hypochondriasis). However, these disorders in children are usually undifferentiated and are difficult to categorise clearly and are therefore known as Emotional Disorders. These occur with the same frequency in both boys and girls. Nearly 2.5 per cent of preadolescent children living in small town communities suffer from these disorders and the prevalence increases in adolescence and in children living in city areas (Rutter 1973, Rutter *et al.* 1976).

Developmental Disorders

Disproportionate delays in the development of certain functions or skills arise due to an interaction between various environmental and constitutional factors. These are more common in boys than girls. Developmental disorders of speech and language occur in some 1–5 per cent of children; regular bedwetting is present in about 3 per cent of 10-year-old children; and reading retardation in children of normal intelligence is found to be present in about 3–10 per cent of children (WHO 1977). There is also a developmental component in the development of stammering and tics.

Hyperactivity

Nearly 2 per cent of children show nonsituational or pervasive hyperactive behaviour with distractibility, reduced impulse control and poor attention span. Often there are associated educational problems and conduct disorder.

Psychoses

Autism and disintegrative psychoses are known as 'psychoses specific to childhood' as they specifically start in childhood. Autism begins in infancy and consists of an inability to develop relationships with people, a delay in speech acquisition, the non-communicative use of speech after it develops, pronominal reversal, delayed echolalia, repetitive and stereotyped play activities, an obsessive insistence on the maintenance of sameness, a lack of imagination, a good rote memory, and a normal physical appearance (Kanner 1943). Nearly three-quarters of these children also have learning disabilities. Nearly 2 per 10,000 children may suffer from autism (Lotter 1966); however, milder forms of Autistic Spectrum Disorder or Autistic Psychopathy (Asperger Syndrome) may be more common, characterised by gross social impairments, obsessive preoccupations or circumscribed interest patterns.

Disintegrative psychosis occurs after nearly 3–4 years of normal development and may be due to an organic illness of the brain (e.g. measles or encephalitis). This leads to a profound regression and behavioural disintegration (Rutter 1977). Toxic confusional states and drug induced psychoses can also occur in childhood. Very occasionally, manic disorder can also begin in adolescence. Schizophrenia as seen in adults can occasionally begin in later childhood or adolescence but has the same features (e.g. thought disorder, hallucinations, delusions and disturbances of mood, perplexity and blunting of affect). At present, however, it is not possible to diagnose children who may later develop schizophrenia.

Others

Other problems can include disorders of sleep, eating and defecation. Nearly 15 per cent of 3–4-year-olds and 10 per cent of eight-year-olds have problems of settling, and 10–20 per cent of pre-school children have problems due to nocturnal waking (Richman *et al.* 1982). Parasomniac problems include persistent nightmares, night terrors, sleepwalking and sleeptalking. Problems of insomnia and hypersomnia can also be found in adolescents (Hill 1989). Failure to thrive in young children, and obesity and anorexia in older children and adolescents, may be associated with family relationships, as is refusal to attend school. Encopresis is usually associated with poor toilet routine and constipation and may be present in 2.5 per cent of boys and 1 per cent of girls at the age of seven years.

The contributory factors

Psychiatric disorders in children are invariably of multifactorial origin and are produced by the interplay between the child's constitution, child's past experiences and the child's living context (family, school, peer group, and so on). It is, therefore, very important to keep the Interactional model in mind whilst managing such problems, that is the interaction of three Ps: the Precipitating factors impinging upon the Predisposing elements and Perpetuated by situational factors.

Biological factors

Although very few mental disorders in childhood are inherited as such, genetic factors do influence children's temperament and personality. Maturation, physical appearance, gender, brain dysfunction or damage and physical disease or disability also influence the vulnerability to psychiatric disorders in children.

From infancy onwards children vary greatly in their *temperamental* attributes. These differences result from an interaction between genetic and other biological factors and the child's life experiences. However, such temperamental differences are of great significance in the child's development, personality and susceptibility to problems. These influence the way other people behave towards the child and the range of situations the child is exposed to. The temperamental differences also influence the child's perception of the environment, competence and vulnerability to a variety of stresses. For example, in one study a quarter of infants were found to be non-cuddlers (Schaffer and Emerson 1964). Infants with adverse temperament, like those with poor routines, low adaptability and intensely negative mood swings, are more vulnerable to later problems.

Developmental delays, brain dysfunctions or damage and physical ill health or handicap can also impinge upon psychiatric disorders. Nearly half of the children with delayed speech *development* have behaviour problems. Nearly 70 per cent of children with enuresis have a positive history of enuresis in first degree relatives and the concordance rate in monozygotic twins is roughly double (68%) than that in dizygotic twins (36%) (Bakwin 1961). Between 15 and 40 per cent of children with enuresis were found to have behaviour problems in a study by Rutter *et al.* (1973).

Prevalence of psychiatric disorders may double in children with *physical disorders* not affecting the brain (11.5% vs. 6.8%) and five-fold in children with brain disorders. Chronic physical or mental handicap may also be associated with lack of sensory stimulation, emotional deprivation, lowered self esteem, restriction on physical activities, stigmatisation and problems associated with recurrent hospitalisation and side effects of drugs, and so on.

Cognitive factors

Cognitive impairment may also be due to a combination of psycho-social deprivation and biological factors, such as brain damage or learning disability. The risk of poor mental health may stem directly from the underlying factors or maybe the result of school failure. Educational deficits are, therefore, often associated with psychiatric disorders in children. In the Isle of Wight studies (Rutter *et al.* 1970) nearly a quarter of children with specific reading disability had conduct disorder and a third of conduct disordered children had reading disability, compared with only 4 per cent in the general population.

Patterns of upbringing

Lack of concern and brutal, restrictive, punitive, repressive and inconsistent child care increase the risk of mental health problems. Similarly, children who are unwanted or who experience rejection, hostility, serious family discord or multiple changes of parent figures become vulnerable to mental problems. Lack of play opportunities, of conversational interchange and of positive interaction with family members and others, and experience of parental deviance such as criminality, or mental disorder in parents, also affect the mental health of children. The nature of staff–child interaction at school and peer group influences have important impact on children's psycho-social development. Recent findings (Dunn and Plomin 1990) suggest that children are also affected by the fact that in comparison to their siblings they are less loved.

Socio-economic factors

Although increasing affluence may not decrease the mental health problems in children, poverty may often underlay a whole cluster of psycho-social factors that impinge on children's mental health (e.g. family breakdown, overcrowding, educational disadvantage, delinquency, loose family ties). Thus, Kurtz (1992) lists the following circumstances that increase the risk of child mental health problems.

1. Families suffering from socio-economic disadvantages or family discord (Earls and Jung 1987), which may be due to unemployment, divorce, living alone or homelessness (Graham 1986).

2. Parents suffering from psychiatric illness, notably maternal depression (Richman 1977).

3. Child abuse. At 31st March 1991, 4.2 per thousand children under 18 were on local authority child protection registers in England (Kurtz 1992).

4. Some physical illnesses, especially chronic conditions (such as diabetes and cystic fibrosis). Severe conditions and conditions with sensory deficit or brain damage.

5. Learning difficulties, especially with regard to reading.

6. Learning disability. Nearly 40 per cent of severe learning disabilities children (IQ below 50) can have severe psychiatric disturbance (Graham 1986).

7. Young offenders. A third of young men aged between 16 and 18 years who have been sentenced, have been found to have a primary psychiatric disorder (Gunn *et al.* 1991).

The nature of child mental health services

'...successful development of any academic or professional discipline depends ultimately on its intellectual or technical capital, which by nature must be derived from as wide a range of other disciplines as possible. The metaphor that may be helpful here is that of a plant thriving because it has a deep and wide network of roots spreading in all directions, seeking nourishment wherever possible'. (Guze 1983 p.1–2)

The child mental health services have been multi-disciplinary from their beginning in 1920s and 1930s as 'the product of a confluence of expertise from paediatrics, asylum medicine, the training and custodial care of the mentally retarded, psychoanalysis, psychology, psychiatric social work, remedial education and criminology'. (Parry-Jones 1992). This has also meant a wide variation in assessment and treatment styles and the recent introduction of general management principles with an emphasis on budgeting, control and management of resources and development of a line management culture has tended to pull apart such multi-agency and multi-disciplinary services.

For example, educational psychologists have withdrawn their services from most clinics and run an independent educational psychology service, and almost all of their energy is consumed in assessing the children under the 1981 Education Act. Many clinics have either lost the support of their social workers or the nature of their support has been substantially reduced and altered. It is rare to find clinics with such therapy staff as an art therapist, drama therapist, child psychotherapist, or occupational therapist. To create posts of family therapists and/or group therapists is still more difficult.

The manpower of child psychiatrists is also very inadequate in most clinics. The Royal College of Psychiatrists (1991) recommended at least three consultant child and adolescent psychiatrists per 200,000 general population, but most clinics are far behind even this minimum norm. For example, in our own clinic, there are only two consultants for a population of 314,000.

> 'In some parts of the country, there is evidence of prolonged lack of funding, resulting in marked shortfall of manpower by any standards and in poor working conditions, rendering child and adolescent psychiatry a truly 'Cinderella' service. Under such circumstances, opportunities for involvement in less urgent clinical activities, such as preventative or health promotion programmes are likely to be absent or minimal'. (Parry-Jones 1992 p.5)

'The Health of the Nation' (Secretary of State for Health 1991) has a target for reducing the suicide rate. Four hundred young people out of every 100,000 aged between 15 and 19, attempt suicide each year and three succeed. At least a quarter of these young people have serious psychiatric disorders. Nearly 10 per cent of boys and 3 per cent of girls who attempt suicide go on to kill themselves (Kurtz 1992, Taylor and Stansfeld 1984, Otto 1972). 'How are hard pressed child and adolescent psychiatrists to meet the demand for reducing the suicide rates in young people in addition to other increased demands on their time and dwindling resources?'. (Black 1992 p.971) Lack of hard data to demonstrate the concrete effect of resources on such services and interventions, and the more recent introduction of the spirit of market forces have meant a further increase in vulnerability of the services to heavy cost containment pressures.

On the other hand, there has been an ever widening compass of clinical demands on child mental health services. For example, the referrals to our clinic in Northampton tripled within a decade. The increase in referrals to the child mental health services reflect the increase in family breakdowns and reconstitutions, unemployment, drug abuse and also the decline in residential resources for children in social services and education departments. The recent explosion in sexual abuse problems have also made considerable clinical demands on these services, which consume enormous time in arranging assessment, treatment, evidence for the courts and which can be emotionally very draining.

The child guidance movement that started first in America in the 1920s and then spread to other countries, including the UK, was initially driven by the psycho-analytical ideas that psycho-pathology in adults had its origin in arrested psycho-sexual development during childhood, and if this could be treated or prevented in childhood, children would grow up as adults free from mental illness (Robins and Jegede 1980). The services consisted of a comprehensive assessment by a multi-disciplinary team (i.e., child psychiatrist, educational psychologist and psychiatric social worker) and the formulation of a program of psychotherapy for the child and family. Unfortunately, only a few children returned for such a treatment (Bahn et al. 1962). Most children felt restless and reluctant in the face of a long confessional conversation with a psychotherapist. The parents of acting-out children typically had behaviour problems of their own and were very poor at keeping appointments or following suggestions about handling the child at home. The effect of this technique on adult mental disorders did not prove to be very beneficial either (McCord 1978).

This disillusionment with the traditional child guidance technique has led to the development of various alternative approaches, such as behaviour therapy, chemotherapy, family therapy, group therapy, milieu therapy (e.g. classroom management) and training teachers and parents in their effectiveness and so on. However, many of these approaches also have their own limitations. The child psychiatrists are now very reluctant to use psychotropic medication for children because of the side effects. In fact, the stimulant medication (Ritalin) prescribed for hyperactive children has been generally withdrawn from the market. Both behaviour therapy and family therapy require greater parental co-operation, commitment and effort than may be forthcoming in many families. Also, many children find it difficult to share their feelings in an individual therapy setting or family therapy setting. However, it is easier to do so in a group setting with others of a similar age (Corder et al. 1981, Ginott 1961). Such a group setting is much more conducive for sharing of feelings because, if one member is able to do so, others are helped by the processes of identification, modelling and projection.

The role of group work

In terms of manpower and time the group therapy approach is much more economical than any other approach. However, group therapy may have to be supplemented with family therapy and, at times, individual therapy as well. In group settings some children resist focusing on the relevant issues on their lives outside. Thus, linking the group therapy with family therapy and individual therapy helps to recycle relevant materials.

It is much better if the group work service acts as a tertiary service. All the referrals, therefore, should be received and assessed by the child mental health service, acting as a secondary specialist service. If group therapy is deemed appropriate (in addition to or instead of any family work, individual work and liaison), the child could then be referred to the particular group with regular feedback and 'recycling' of therapeutic effects maintained. This allows the systemic perspective to remain alive and effective.

As none of the child mental health services, to our knowledge, has an establishment for 'Group Therapist' post, the interested professional within the service with some experience and training will have to take on this responsibility with the support of the rest of the team. There are several introductory and advanced courses in group work, usually in association with the Institute of Group Analysis and/or European Group Analytic Training Institutions Network (EGATIN), but the main emphasis in most courses is on group work with adults, except in the 'Introductory Course on Group Work with Children and Adolescents' at Northampton.

Some of the organisational details that are applicable to setting up groups in different settings and the use of different therapeutic styles are already outlined elsewhere in this volume. Here it may suffice to mention that the clinic setting has its own limitations because of a very wide range of ages and clinical conditions.

One may choose to set up a group on a particular theme, if there is a sufficient number of suitable children from a particular age band in the clinic. Conditions such as sexual abuse, bereavement, school refusal, conduct disorder, anger management, social skills, encopresis, asthma, or chronic illnesses, are some of the examples. Such a group can be a time-bound closed group using a structured approach with considerable emphasis on the psycho-educational aspect of treatment. Each session may need to be planned beforehand with a clear beginning and ending. One may have a system of receiving referrals of children of any age suitable for a group and run a closed, time-bound structured group for a particular age band while accumulating enough referrals for another age band group.

Heavy structuring of the therapeutic input has an economic advantage; can quickly access certain emotional materials and can produce lasting changes through the rituals of the exercises. However, the scope for flexibility, spontaneity, due regard to uniqueness of each individual's circumstances and the connectedness with a variety of other issues may not be adequate. It is also possible for a child who has completed a structured psycho-educational group on a particular theme, then to join a group that is not so structured or constrained in terms of time or themes. This may help consolidate therapeutic changes at much deeper and wider levels.

If it is possible to create and organise staffing in a systematic manner on a long term basis, the service may be able to run concurrent groups for different age bands. These may be open, slow open or closed, structured or unstructured and homogeneous or heterogeneous groups, with a structure for processing referrals, discharges, feedback, liaison, consultation and supervision, as we have managed to arrange in our service at the Ken Stewart Family Centre. However, turnover of staff and limited availability of skilled staff and training opportunities can be problematic.

It is very important that the staff running such groups are adequately skilled and supported. The group situations through the processes of projective identification can easily unleash destructive forces in staff. A great deal of skill and effort is needed to hold things together (Lucas 1988), to maintain boundaries (Behr 1988) and to balance permissive creativity with limit setting. The staff also need to be protected from other intrusive commitments and should be offered opportunities for regular reflection and ongoing training. As many families may not be able to provide transport for these children on a regular basis, the service should also be able to offer such a facility (Farrell 1984).

For many children with feelings of neglect, hurt, rejection, abandonment, loss or alienation, the group can assume the significance of a transitional object. Even a video system can become an object of transference (Mallery and Navas 1982). Certain behaviours can induce, trigger and arouse feelings and behaviours in others and recreate the day-to-day problems in life outside the group. The setting of the group, therefore, becomes more conducive to getting in touch with each other's feelings. If one member is able to share some of these feelings, others are also helped by linking and emotional feedback. It also provides opportunities to experiment with alternative view points, feelings, behaviours and changes in a safe setting. The sense of competition, group pressure, modelling and reinforcement also help to initiate and accomplish change (Slavson and Schiffer 1975).

Groupwork in psychiatric in patient services for children and adolescents

Kahn *et al.* (1992) describe a group as a 'milieu biopsy' in an inpatient setting because of the correspondence between the characteristics of the treatment environment and dynamics within therapeutic groups on the ward. Thus, staff can use insight gained through groups in the management of their wards and create an atmosphere or climate that is more therapeutic.

Straight and Weekman (1958) spell out three important ingredients of residential psychiatric treatment of severe conduct disorder and delinquency: (1) withdrawals from groups as necessary for control, (2) use of tangible incentives for remaining in the group (i.e., extra activities such as parties) and (3) individuation of limits. Appropriate limit setting helps with impulse control and reality testing, as permissiveness perpetuates their acting out of omnipotent fantasies in the group situation.

Rinsley (1972) points out 'Even severely ill adolescents are capable of full engagement in an expressive analytical process provided that the therapist, together with the wider aspects of residential milieu, supplies consistent controls and sets predictable limits for acting out' (p.233).

In group work using play therapy with early latency age children with problems of severely impulsive behaviour in a psychiatric residential treatment setting, Abramson et al. (1979) found the separation issues sparked by new admissions and discharges constituted one of the most recurrent themes.

Rosenberg and Cherbuliez (1979) described group work in an impatient unit for 5–12-year-old children who were admitted in relation to autistic behaviour, fire raising, suicidal behaviour, and so on. The group provided a corrective emotional experience in terms of verbal and social skills, enhancement of self esteem, cohesive peer grouping, enjoyment from play and trusting of others. The authors report that directiveness, structuring and active restraints were more effective than their earlier reliance on a non-directive psychoanalytic interpretative stance.

Williams et al. (1978) emphasise the role of confrontation, clarification of feelings, modelling and limit setting in group work with children in an inpatient unit. This helps to facilitate each child's social development 'particularly with respect to impulse control, co-operation and observing ego capacity' (p.32).

Evans (1965 1966) highlights the intense and rapid swings of feelings that adolescents in a psychiatric inpatient setting demonstrate toward the group worker. In the light of the above, external controls are needed to provide them with some stable framework and security while they sort out their thoughts and feelings. He describes the liveliness of an important adolescent group where the group worker is constantly struggling to keep the group intact (Evans 1988). Members refusing to come to the group exhibiting various manic, withdrawn and other acting out behaviours stretch the capacity of the group worker to the limit and often beyond. 'Here we have an impulse-ridden youngster with a low tolerance of anxiety who is immature, highly oppositional and normally wanting to rush out of the room, unable to discuss a serious topic and stating she would not prosecute her step father for incest because she was to blame' (p.112).

In situations like these the research literature, according to Evans' (1988) review, is also of not much help. However, there is an 'over-riding need to find a language to communicate directly with the adolescent, the right words to help an immature, disturbed adolescent feel understood, cared-for and worth-while, not patronised or "psychologised'" (Sevitt 1988 p.116). For example, within minutes of the group worker articulating the confusion and dilemma of the above mentioned girl, her manic behaviour subsided in the group session.

References

Abramson, R.M., Hoffman, L. and Johns, C.A. (1979) 'Play Group Psychotherapy for Early Latency Age Children on an Inpatient Psychiatric Unit'. *International Journal of Group Psychotherapy.* 29: 383–392.

American Psychiatry Association (1987) *Diagnostic and Statistical Manual of Mental Disorders (Third Edition Revised).* Washington D.C.: American Psychiatric Association.

Bahn, A.K. (1962) 'Diagnostic Characteristics Related to Services in Psychiatric Clinics for Children'. *Milbank Memorial Fund Quarterly.* 40: 289.

Bailey, V., Graham, P. and Boniface, D. (1978) 'How Much Child Psychology does a General Practitioner do?' *Journal of the Royal College of General Practitioners.* 28: 621–626.

Bakwin, H. (1961) 'Enuresis in Children'. *Journal of Paediatrics.* 58: 806–819.

Behr, H. (1988) 'Group Analysis with Early Adolescents: Some Clinical Issues. *Group Analysis.* 21: 119–133.

Berg, I. and Jackson, A. (1985) 'Teenage School Refusers Grown Up: A Follow Up Study Of 168 Subjects, Ten Years after Inpatient Treatment'. *British Journal of Psychiatry.* 147: 366–370.

Black, D. (1992) 'Mental Health Services for Children'. *British Medical Journal.* 305: 971–2.

Corder, B.F., Whiteside, L. and Haizlip, T.M. (1981) 'A Study of Curative Factors in Group Psychotherapy with Adolescents'. *International Journal of Group Psychotherapy.* 31 (3): 345–354.

Department of Education and Science (1978) *Special Educational Needs.* Report of the Committee of Enquiry into the Education of Handicapped Children and Young People. London: HMSO.

Dunn, J. and Plomin, R. (1990) (eds) *Separate Lives: Why Siblings are So Different.* New York: Basic Books.

Earls, F. and Jung, K.G. (1987) 'Temperament and Home Environment Characteristics as Causal Factors in the Early Development of Childhood Psychopathology'. *Journal of the American Academy of Child and Adolescent Psychiatrists.* 26: 491–498.

Evans, J. (1965) 'Inpatient Analytic Group Therapy of Neurotic and Delinquent Adolescents: Some Specific Problems Associated with these Groups'. *Psychotherapy and Psychosomatics.* 13: 265–270.

Evans, J. (1966) Analytic Group Therapy with Delinquents'. *Adolescence.* 1: 180–196.

Evans, J. (1988) 'Research Findings and Clinical Practice with Adolescents'. *Group Analysis.* 21 (2): 103–115.

Farrel, M. (1984) 'Group Work with Children: The Significance of Setting and Context'. *Group Analysis.* 17 (2): 145–155.

Ginott, H. (1961) *Group Psychotherapy with Children.* New York: McGraw-Hill.

Graham, P.J. (1986) 'Behavioural and Intellectual Development in Childhood Epidemiology'. *British Medical Bulletin.* 42 (2): 155–162.

Green, R. (1975) 'The Significance of Feminine Behaviour in Boys'. *Journal of Child Psychology and Psychiatry.* 16: 341.

Gunn, J., Maden, A. and Swinton, M. (1991) 'Treatment Needs of Prisoners with Psychiatric Disorders'. *British Medical Journal.* 303: 338–341.

Guze, S.B. (1983) 'Child Psychiatry: Taking Stock'. *Comprehensive Psychiatry.* 24 (1): 1–5.

Harrington, R., Fudge, H., Rutter, M., Pickles, A. and Hill, J. (1990) 'Adult Outcome of Childhood and Adolescent Depression'. I. Psychiatric Status. *Archives of General Psychiatry.* 47: 465–473.

Hill, P. (1989) 'Sleep Disorders in Childhood and Adolescence'. In J.A. Horne and M.L. Page (eds) *Current Approaches: Sleep Disorders.* Southampton: Duphar pp.20–39.

Kahn, E.M., Sturke, I.T. and Schaffer, J. (1992) 'Inpatient Group Processes: Parallel Unit Dynamics'. *International Journal of Group Psychotherapy.* 42 (3): 407–418.

Kandel, D.B. (1978) (ed) *Longitudinal Research in Drug Use: Empirical Findings and Metholodogical Issues.* Washington: Hemisphere.

Kanner, L. (1943) 'Autistic Disturbances of Affective Contact'. *Nervous Child.* 2: 217–250.

Kurtz, Z. (1992) (ed) *With Health in Mind: Mental Health Care for Children and Young People.* London: Action for Sick Children.

Lewis, W.W. (1965) 'Continuity and Intervention in Emotional Disturbances: A Review'. *Exceptional Children.* 31: 465–475.

Lotter, V. (1966) 'Epidemiology of Autistic Conditions in Young Children. I. Prevalence'. *Social Psychiatry.* 1: 124–137.

Lucas, T. (1988) 'Holding and Holding-On: Using Winnicott's Ideas in Group Psychotherapy with Twelve to Thirteen year olds'. *Group Analysis.* 21 (2): 135–151.

Mallery, B. and Navas, M. (1982) 'Engagement of Pre-Adolescent Boys in Group Therapy: Videotape as a Tool'. *International Journal of Group Psychotherapy.* 32 (4): 355–366.

McCord, J. (1978) 'A Thirty Year Follow Up of Treatment Effects'. *American Psychology.* 33: 284.

Miller, J. (undated) *Breaking the Cycle of Misery.* London: Child Psychotherapy Trust.

National Casemix Office (1991) *Health Care Resource Group: Definitions Manual: Section P: Diseases of Childhood.* Lymington: National Casemix Office.

Oldman, J. (1990) *Who Says There's No Housing Problem? Facts and Figures on Housing and Homelessness.* London, Shelter, National Campaign for the Homeless.

Otto, U. (1972) 'Suicidal Acts by Children and Adolescents: A Follow up Study'. *Acta Psychiatrica Scandinavica.* 233 (suppl): 5–23.

Parry-Jones, W. (1992) 'Management in the National Health Service in Relation to Children and their Provision of Child Psychiatric Services'. *ACPP Newsletter.* 14 (1): 3–10.

Richman, N. (1977) 'Behaviour Problems in Preschool Children: Family and Social Factors'. *British Journal of Psychiatry.* 131: 523–527.

Richman, N., Steveson, J. and Graham, P. (1982) *Preschool to School: A Behavioural Study.* London: Academic Press.

Rinsley, D. (1972) 'Group Therapy Within the Wider Residential Context'. In I.H. Bekovitz (ed) *Adolescents Grow in Groups: Experiences in Adolescent Group Psychotherapy.* New York: Brunner/Mazel. 233–242.

Robins, L. (1966) *Deviant Children Grown Up.* Baltimore: Williams and Wilkins.

Robins, L.N. and Jegede, R.O. (1980) 'Mental Health'. In F. Falkner (ed) *Prevention in Childhood of Health Problems in Adult Life.* Geneva: W.H.O. 121–134.

Rosenberg, J. and Cherbuliez, T. (1979) 'Inpatient Group Therapy for Older Children and Preadolescents'. *International Journal of Group Psychotherapy.* 28: 393–406.

Royal College of Psychiatrists (1991) 'Consultant Norms in Child Psychiatry'. *Psychiatric Bulletin.* 15: 238–239.

Rutter, M. (1973) 'Why are London Children so Disturbed?' *Proceedings of Royal Society of Medicine.* 66: 1221–1225.

Rutter, M. (1977) 'Infantile Autism and Other Child Psychoses'. In M. Rutter and L. Hersov (eds) *Child Psychiatry: Modern Approaches.* Oxford: Blackwell pp.717–747.

Rutter, M. (1979) 'Protective Factors in Children's Responses to Stress and Disadvantage'. In M.W. Kent and J.E. Rolf (eds) *Primary Prevention for Psychopathology Vol. 3: Social Competence in Children* (pp.49–74). Hanover, N.H.: University Press of New England.

Rutter, M. (1989) 'Annotation: Child Psychiatric Disorder in ICD-10'. *Journal of Child Psychology and Psychiatry.* 30: 499–513.

Rutter, M. (1991) 'Services for Children with Emotional Disorders: Needs Accomplishments and Future Developments'. *Young Minds Newsletter.* No. 9: 1–5.

Rutter, M., Cox, A., Tupling, C., Berger, M. and Yule, W. (1975) 'Attainment and Adjustment in Two Geographical Areas. I. The Prevalence of Psychiatric Disorder'. *British Journal of Psychiatry.* 126: 493–509.

Rutter, M., Graham, P., Chadwick, O. and Yule, W. (1976) 'Adolescent Turmoil: Fact or Fiction'. *Journal of Child Psychology and Psychiatry.* 17: 35–56.

Rutter, M., Shaffer, D. and Shepherd, M. (1975) *A Multi-Axial Classification of Child Psychiatric Disorders.* Geneva: World Health Organisation.

Rutter, M., Shaffer, D. and Sturge, C. (1975) *A Guide to a Multi-Axial Classification Scheme for Psychiatric Disorders in Childhood and Adolescence.* London: Institute of Psychiatry.

Rutter, M., Tizard, J. and Whitmore, K. (1970) (eds) *Education Health and Behaviour.* London: Longman.

Rutter, M., Yule, W. and Graham, P. (1973) 'Enuresis and Behavioural Deviance: Some Epidemiological Considerations'. In I. Kolvin, R. MacKeith and S.R. Meadow (eds) *Bladder Control and Enuresis. Clinics in Developmental Medicine:* 48, 49. London: SIMP/Heinemann.

Schaffer, H.R. and Emerson, P.E. (1964) 'Patterns of Response to Physical Contact in Early Human Development'. *Journal of Child Psychology and Psychiatry.* 5: 1–13.

Secretary of State for Health (1991) *The Health of a Nation.* London: HMSO.

Sevitt, M. (1988) 'Discussion on Paper by John Evans'. *Group Analysis.* 21 (2): 115–117.

Slavson, S.R. and Schiffer, M. (1975) *Group Psychotherapies for Children.* New York: International Universities Press.

Steinhausen, H.C. and Erdin, A. (1991) 'A Comparison of ICD-9 and ICD-10 Diagnoses of Child and Adolescent Psychiatric Disorders'. *Journal of Child Psychology and Psychiatry.* 32 (6): 909–920.

Straight, B. and Weekman, D. (1958) 'Central Problems in Group Therapy with Aggressive Boys in a Mental Hospital'. *American Journal of Psychiatry.* 114(11): 998–1001.

Taylor, E.A. and Stansfeld, S.A. (1984) 'Children who Poison Themselves. I. Clinical Comparison with Psychiatric Controls'. *British Journal of Psychiatry.* 145: 127–35.

Weiss, G., Hechman, L., Milroy, T. and Perlman, T. (1985) 'Psychiatric States of Hyperactives as Adults: A Controlled Prospective 15 Year Follow Up of 63 Hyperactive Children'. *Journal of American Academy of Child Psychiatry.* 24: 211–220.

Williams, J., Lewis, C., Copeland, F., Tucker, L. and Fregan, L. (1978) 'A Model for Short Term Group Therapy on a Children's Inpatient Unit'. *Clinical Social Work Journal.* 6: 21–32.

World Health Organisation (1977) 'Child Mental Health and Psychosocial Development. Report of a WHO Export Committee'. *WHO Technical Report Series.* 613 Geneva: WHO.

World Health Organisation (1978) *Mental Disorders: Glossary and Guide to their Classification in accordance with the Ninth Revision of the International Classification of Diseases.* Geneva: WHO.

World Health Organisation (1987) *ICD-10: 1987 Draft of Chapter V, Mental and Behavioural Disorders.* Geneva: World Health Organisation.

Zeitlin, H. (1966) 'The Natural History of Psychiatric Disorder in Children'. *Maudsley Monograph No. 29.* Oxford: Oxford University Press.

CHAPTER 22

Group Work in the Youth Service

Janet Adams

Introduction

The work of the youth service focuses on young people who are going through the transitionary stages of adolescence and it takes place in both one-to-one and group settings. This chapter will focus on the role of the youth worker in the group setting through examining: what a group is, formal and informal groups, interventions, group norms, functional and behavioural roles, pecking orders and hierarchies, decision making and the stages of group life. An outline of the broad aims of the youth service, the settings in which it operates and its underpinning values are a necessary part of this introduction in order to put the job of the youth worker into context.

The youth service – aims and settings

The youth service works with young people during the period of adolescence and aims to help them develop into adults who have a feeling of self worth, are able to make informed choices, are empowered and in charge of their lives. Adolescence is a time of physical and emotional change when the young adult is beginning to discover who and what they are. It can be a time of peaks and troughs of emotion which often result in dramatic mood swings and erratic behaviour. The youth service recognises this period in young people's lives as significant and uses 'social' or 'informal' education to address the needs and issues that surround adolescence. Youth work uses informal settings for educational purposes and aims to increase social skills, encourage awareness of self and others, and provide non-directive support.

The work takes place in a variety of settings including Youth Clubs, Community Centres, Counselling and Information Agencies, Drop-In Projects, Arts Centres, pubs and the streets. Whilst youth work happens in a variety of settings, the same underpinning values apply: starting where young people are and a belief in the right of self-determination.

Youth work and groups

Youth workers need to be a part of the lives of the young people with whom they work, whilst at the same time recognising and owning their position as adults. In this sense, youth workers are not a part of and cannot be a part of the groups with which they work; their role and function are different. They are 'outside' the group by virtue of the fact that they are not young people and yet they need to be an integral part of the group in order to do their work. This is an inherent tension which can only be addressed by ensuring that the interventions made by the worker are welcomed and wanted by the group or groups with whom they are working. Leighton (1972) concurs with this view and goes on to stress the need for such co-operation if the outcomes of the work are to have real value.

> 'If the agency and the worker are seen as offering external, (that is external to the group), expertise such expertise can only be really effective if the group itself is desirous of change, that is change in the way it handles responsibility, planning, action and is helped to face up to the consequences of such responsibility. Real growth in social educational terms will only come when each member of the group feels a part of such decision-making and shared responsibility and realizes that there is a problem inherent in the resolving of individual self-determination and group self-determination'. (p.200)

Recognising one's own needs (individual self-determination), and the corporate needs of others (group self-determination), can be described as part of the natural process of adolescence. Most teenagers who make use of youth service provision are young people going through that natural process which includes behaviours and settings that range from drug-taking in car parks, petty theft and truancy from school, to doing 'A' level homework in the club coffee bar, involvement in local youth councils and participation in the Duke of Edinburgh Award Scheme. In each and all of these settings the youth worker attempts to build meaningful relationships that will achieve the aims of the service. These relationships need to be based on trust, mutual respect and warmth; the worker needs to meet with young people on their own ground, and as far as possible, on their own terms. This 'ground' is usually a group of some sort.

What is a group?

A group may be described as three or more people who have come together to achieve a specific task (any task, ranging from a structured fund raising activity to an unstructured social gathering), the completion of which will involve interaction with one another. Hence a bus queue is not a group, neither is a crowd of spectators. Although dated, the following definition, (Cartwright and Zander 1968), of a group still holds:

> 'A group is a collection of individuals who have relations to one another that make them interdependent to some significant degree. As so defined, the term group refers to a class of social entities having in common the property of interdependence among their constituent members. But it is not true that any arbitrary collection of people, such as all students whose last names begin with a given letter, constitute a group. For a set of people to qualify as a group, they must be related to one another in some definite way'. (p.46)

Groups are usual, everyday settings in which both young people and adults find themselves. These can be described with general headings such as: family group, social group, task group, interest group.

Young people will have choice about some of the groups to which they belong and limited or no choice about others. They will, for example have no choice about the school class they are in but will be able to choose which people, within that class form their friendship group. The class itself can be described as a 'formal group' and the friendship group an 'informal group'. The youth service offers young people a number of formal group settings, such as those listed earlier, and within these formal organisations informal group settings are encouraged as forums for the development of social and personal skills.

Formal and informal groups

A formal group can be described as a society, club, organisation, political party and so on. Formal groups have 'public' rules, conditions for membership and expectations that are clear, overt, precise and explain the requirements for the title of 'membership' to those who may wish to seek it. In this sense, formal groups require formal membership.

Informal (or 'social') groups also have conditions for membership, expectations and rules (termed 'norms' in an informal setting), but these are only known in detail to the existing membership and may change more frequently than in formal groups, as the group grows and develops. Names such as gang, posse, crowd, set, are used to describe informal groups. The adherence to 'norms' within an informal group are no less stringent than the adherence to 'rules' within a formal group.

Youth workers need to be able to form relationships with young people in both of these settings – formal and informal. Batten (1967), when describing the non-directive approach to group work, recognises both the formal and informal group as valuable forums for enabling young people to think for themselves.

> 'A worker can provide stimulus and help in any of a wide variety of formal and informal situations. In a youth club, for instance, the

> "worker" will be the youth leader or one of his helpers, and the "group" either a formal group such as a members' committee, or an interest group, or an ad hoc informal group which consists of only a few members talking things over in the coffee bar. Whoever the worker may be and whatever the group, in so far as he aims to help the group to do their own thinking for themselves, he will attempt to stimulate and structure the thinking process by asking questions'. (p.45)

The formal setting may be 'owned' by the worker in the sense that they are the organiser of the task/activity group, or the leader of the club and therefore will have a defined 'role' and 'right' to be involved. The worker needs no reason or justification for introduction to such a group.

The informal setting is 'owned' by its members and does not offer such easy access to the worker as the formal setting. Relationships are the basis upon which informal groups meet: the task or function of an informal group may simply be a party or an outing. In order to understand the pattern of relationships within an informal group the worker must observe and interpret the behaviour of group members in accordance with the norms of the group. Button (1982), links recognition of the group norms to levels of control within a group.

> 'The way that the group behave together, including even their relationships with one another, will be strongly influenced by the prevailing norms of the group. It is vital for the worker to discern the patterns of normative control as rapidly as possible. The experienced worker will begin to sense the controls from the moment they make contact with the group, although the more subtle forms of control may be quite difficult to discern'. (p.26)

While Button talks about experienced workers being able to 'sense' controls, it could be argued that the use of the word 'sense' implies an inborn gifted ability, rather than a learnable skill. Controls may be operating covertly, but there will be evidence through individual behaviour to indicate where the control is coming from and on what basis. When observing and/or working with a group it is important for youth workers to believe that this evidence is seeable, hearable and learnable, if they are to be effective.

Work with young people in both formal and informal groups within the youth service will rely on self selecting and voluntary membership. The group's reason for existing will differ from group to group and most groups will have an undetermined life span. A small percentage of youth service clientele are referred by the Health Service and Social Services.

Interventions

Interventions are not necessarily made because the worker views the group as having or being a 'problems' (although that may be the case), but because that is the forum in which young people are choosing to meet and, by appropriate intervention, the youth worker can facilitate growth and development. Groups are made up of individuals who are defined a 'group' because of a common task. The aim of the group is to achieve the chosen task, such as build a carnival float, organise a party, canoe a river or just have fun together. Facilitating achieving the task is not the only area on which the worker needs to focus – equally important is the individual in the group and the group itself.

All three aspects need maintaining by the worker, rather like juggling three balls in the air. If too much attention is paid to one, another may fall.

The maintenance of the TASK centres around:

1. Identification

2. Realism

3. Commitment

Maintenance of the GROUP is about:

1. Identity

2. Roles

3. Atmosphere

Maintaining the INDIVIDUAL relates to:

1. Participation

2. Relationships

3. Behaviour

Take, for example, a group of young people who have come together to build a carnival float. The task is clear, the theme is agreed and individuals agree to take on specific jobs. If the worker becomes too involved with achieving the task they may overlook, or not take seriously, possible dissatisfaction of the individual or individuals. Likewise, if the worker is focusing too strongly on individual dissatisfactions this may prevent or delay the task from being achieved. It may be that the worker decides it is better, in certain circumstances, to change or abandon the chosen task in favour of the group, or that, for the sake of the task, it is deemed better for an individual no longer to have group membership. There is no 'correct' formula; each youth worker weighs up the situation and responds to it according to their knowledge of the group and the current circumstances.

To take these decisions and to make effective interventions the youth worker needs to know how the group functions, and in particular to have an under-standing of group norms and behavioural roles. This information has to be gathered gradually over a period of time as part and parcel of getting to know members of the group.

Norms

When an informal or social group meet together regularly, certain behaviours are recognised as acceptable or unacceptable. These are not overtly decided; if they were they would be described as rules or regulations, not norms. At the point at which a norm is overtly agreed, for example 'no smoking in one part of a room', it ceases to be a norm and becomes a rule. It could be argued that most rules and regulations are, in fact, codified norms. Norms arise as a result of the interactions and subsequent feelings of group members.

Examples of this can be seen in school staff rooms where everyone 'knows' that a particular chair is occupied by a certain person or, when someone makes coffee the 'norm' is to offer to make a drink for whoever else is in the room. Homans (1968), talks of a norm as being the thoughts present within the minds of group members and makes reference to some norms being more easily interpreted than others.

> 'A norm, then, is an idea in the minds of the members of a group, an idea that specifies what the members should do, ought to do, are expected to do, under given circumstances. Just what group, what circumstances, and what action are meant can be much more easily determined for some norms than for others'. (p.123)

Groups don't sit themselves down and consciously decide what norms they will adhere to; norms develop and change as part of the life of the group.

An individual group member will know when they or others are adhering to or breaking a norm, even if they are unable to identify where the norm has come from or why it is an expected mode of group behaviour. Homans (1968), makes reference to this in relation to a group's 'memory'.

> 'Norms often arise from the diffuse interaction of the members, who associate together for a while, and then, as if overnight, the group norms crystallize and take shape. One day they were followed, though not consciously held; the next day the group is aware of them. The origin of the norms, if it was ever known, is apt to be forgotten. The group has no memory of a time when the norms were not held, be that memory short or long'. (p.417)

Whether the group remembers where their norms came from or not, the importance of familiarity with and understanding of group norms is crucial information for the youth worker in order that they may decide which and whether to challenge the norms they see in operation. If the norms of a group of young people includes stubbing cigarettes out on the floor or using sexist or racist language, the worker may consider that these are behavioural norms that need challenging. This, in turn, may prove difficult for a worker if the displayed behaviours within the group conflict with that worker's own values. This could be called a conflict between behavioural and functional role, the worker may experience some conflict of role between themself as 'themselves', (behavioural role), and themself in the role of 'youth worker', (functional role).

Roles

Roles fall into two groups, behavioural and functional. Behavioural roles are determined by the nature of interactions between people (e.g. challenger, pourer of oil). Functional roles are predetermined and stem from the position a person holds (e.g. job title, parent). The latter are clear, easy to recognise and there is usually a shared perception of the role and its validity. However, behavioural roles are less clear, less easy to recognise and there may not be a shared perception by other people of that role.

Behavioural roles describe the behaviour of individuals within groups by generalising about 'types' of behaviour and giving those 'types' names. 'Clown', 'pourer of oil' and 'stirrer' are each part of common language. For example, Argyle (1983) uses the following descriptions and names for behavioural roles:

> 'Each kind of group has a characteristic set of roles which are available, though the roles of task and socio-emotional leader may occur in every kind of group. A role of "leader of the opposition" is often found in juries, work-groups and T-groups. These roles appear for various reasons – because there are jobs to be done in groups, (task leader), because groups have certain common structures, (leader of the opposition), because members with different personalities want to behave differently, (socio-emotional leader), and because members want to present themselves as unique individuals, (joker, scapegoat)'. (p.171)

Klein (1970) relates behavioural roles firmly to task groups and the functions necessary to carry out the task.

> 'In all task-related groups the following useful functions have to be performed: giving information, asking for contributions from other members, making proposals, and maintaining morale. The roles corresponding to these functions are respectively: the expert, the facilitator, the co-ordinator, and the morale-builder'. (p.141)

Behavioural roles are not fixed and fluctuate for most people, depending on the setting they find themselves in – being the 'expert' with the crowd in the bar does not necessarily equate with being the expert when at home with the family. Behavioural roles can be consciously assumed by individuals, (such as joker or leader) but, if the individual is not perceived or valued in that role by other members of the group, conflict and/or confusion can result. Similarly, a group can ascribe a behavioural role to a group member by treating them in a particular way, such as blaming them for all ills (scapegoat), or by always seeking and valuing their opinion (leader). When an individual finds that they are always expected to behave in a certain way by other group members and are not 'allowed' or taken seriously when behaving in another way, this can be called being 'role bound'. For example, a person who adopts a flippant joker role regularly at group gatherings, and is known as the person who always 'cracks the joke', will find it extremely difficult to contribute a suggestion that will be taken seriously by other group members. Button (1982) suggests that being role bound may be as a result of repeated patterns of behaviour in an individuals life, affecting the individual in other settings, not just within a single group.

> 'Quite often the stereotype role we see in the group is symptomatic of the way that the youngster concerned conducts himself in almost every department of life: he finds it difficult to present himself in any other way. This is a behavioural style he has developed in order to attract his share of attention even if that attention is hostile or painful. There is usually also the complicating factor that those around him are similarly fixed in their expectancy of him, which is likely to make more difficult for him to change should he wish to do so'. (p.59)

The youth worker needs to identify the behavioural roles within the group with whom they are working in order to identify (a) where the power lies, (b) where/if there is conflict, and (c) what intervention to make, for what purpose, with whom and when.

Hierarchies and pecking orders

Hierarchies and pecking orders relate to functional and behavioural roles and to formal and informal groups respectively; i.e., within an informal group one could talk of the types of behavioural role adopted and the subsequent effect on the pecking order; or, within a formal group the different functional roles and how they fitted within the hierarchy.

For youth workers to make effective interventions with young people, it is helpful to have a 'framework' that can be put around the reality of individual's behaviour in groups. For example, within a regular informal gathering of young people in the coffee bar, the individual who finds themselves the role-bound 'joker' may experience surprise and possible role conflict when they find they have been nominated as the organiser of members committee meetings. Whilst this may sound insignificant, the change from a safe and known behavioural role within an informal group, to a functional role within a formal setting may be a very significant opportunity for that young person to 'try out' new behaviours or break a mould that others expect them to fit. The youth worker may or may not be instrumental in the nomination; the important thing is that the opportunity to make an intervention, either before or after the event, is recognised.

Status and power is easy to recognise within formal settings; the powers and responsibilities of the committee chair are known, likewise those of the team captain or the gang leader. The relationship of the secretary or the coach to the chair or team captain is known and open and forms the hierarchy of that group. Within an informal setting status and power is acquired in a number of different ways (e.g. physical strength, charisma, knowledge or skill, time served or age, functional role, ownership of needed resources, gender, class, race and by association); this forms the pecking order within the group. Within some informal groups, individuals may rise within the pecking order because they have the required resources (e.g. it's my ball, you can't play), or by association with another person of recognised status, (e.g. you must let me in, my brother is a friend of the owner). In street gangs physical strength plays a large part in deciding who is 'top dog', whilst in other groups or other settings, knowledge and/or skill (knowing the ropes), will elevate an individual in the eyes of their peers.

The youth worker needs to be able to 'read' the interactions of group members and make sense of what is happening within the group so that they can assess for themselves what is assisting or hindering any one individual to gain a place in the pecking order that they as a group member feel comfortable with. Discussion and debate will flow freely and constructively in a group where individuals have chosen and therefore feel comfortable in their place within the pecking order. This freeflow exchange of ideas and thoughts is necessary for formal and informal groups if they are to make effective decisions.

Decision making

Within a formal group where there are clear functional roles and a hierarchy that is public, decision making will have a set structure. This structure could take one of a number of forms: open voting with or without a percentage requirement; the chair/leader/captain makes the decision; secret ballot; short straw; the individual deemed to have the most skill/knowledge; continual discussion/debate until a unanimous decision is reached, and so on. It really doesn't matter what the structure is, the important thing is that there will be a structure within a formal group setting where roles are functional and a hierarchy exists.

However, within an informal group where roles are behavioural and pecking orders exist, decision making is a more complex process to identify. When an informal group is faced with a decision that is of no great importance to them and no real urgency is felt, they are quite likely not to make a decision at all, or for individuals to offer suggestions casually that never really get taken up; this can be described as 'apathy'. Sometimes two people who agree with each other can push their chosen decision forward for a whole group; this dynamic can be described as a 'pairing'. Three or more individuals within a group may band together to do the same thing, forming what is termed a 'minority clique'. The group may decide to opt for a 'formal vote' based on the majority ruling or, if they are prepared to discuss for longer, could reach a 'compromise', where individuals are prepared to both 'give' and 'give up' in order to reach agreement. Forceful people within an informal group may use persuasion, either physical or verbal, in order to achieve their own ends; this is called a 'forced consensus'. A 'false consensus' is one where agreement is officially recognised but not in reality felt by the group. A 'true consensus' is one where each member has in one way or another been 'heard' by the others and mutual agreement is reached.

This, then, produces a priority order list that can be applied to the way in which groups make decisions:

- apathy
- pairing
- minority clique
- formal vote
- compromise
- forced consensus
- false consensus
- true consensus

The role of the youth worker is significant in helping informal groups to work towards achieving a true consensus where appropriate decisions that include the views of all members are made. The relationship that the worker has with the members of the group is crucial to the extent of the influence they will be able to wield. This influence needs to be balanced with a belief and adherence to the right of young people to self-determine their actions, both as individuals and as members of groups. It is a difficult and sensitive balance to achieve and only by being able to interpret behaviours within groups, against a theoretical framework, can the worker hope to make sense of the interactions that make up the dynamics of a group.

The stages of group life

All groups, whether formal or informal, will go through a number of different stages. Tuckman (1965), Llewelyn and Fielding (1982) describe these stages as forming, storming, norming, performing and mourning.

> *Forming* is the initial coming together of a group, any group, where the criteria for membership and the purpose of the group is known. This could be a committee meeting in the case of a formal group, or an eighteenth birthday party in the case of an informal group.

> *Storming* is when the group begins to sort out its behavioural roles and individuals within the group begin to find out where their place in the pecking order is. People make bids for power and relationships begin to form. The word 'storming' indicates a negative or argumentative

atmosphere; this is not necessarily so, the storming process is just as likely to be co-operative and smooth as it is to be 'stormy'.

Norming is a time when the group has formed an idea of who is who and is accepting of the reality of the situation. Functional roles are decided upon and rituals and procedures are agreed. Decisions are made with regard to how, when and by whom things will be done.

Performing is the time when the group begin to achieve the set task, i.e., the meeting makes decisions or the party really starts to swing. There is co-operation and combined effort amongst all group members.

Mourning occurs, or may occur, when the group's original reason for being a group has ended and the life of the group is 'officially' finished. In this situation a group may decide to find an alternative forum in which to meet, or another task to achieve so that they can continue being a group, or they may acknowledge the inevitable and find some way of saying goodbye. Reunions and final parties are a feature of the mourning phase.

The stages of group life are not necessarily easy to recognise. A group may move to the norming stage within minutes of forming, seemingly missing out the storming stage altogether. If a group moves too quickly into performing without clearly agreeing roles and responsibilities (storming and norming), they may fail to perform successfully. This will inevitably revert the group to the storming stage when a process of 'how come it went wrong', and 'whose fault was it' will begin. Most groups will revisit the first three stages regularly for a number of reasons: each time the task changes; when a member leaves; when a new member joins; when external influences affect the group.

It is essential for youth workers to be able to recognise these stages and make interventions that will enable the group to move towards the performing stage. Some groups never get to achieve the task, (i.e., they never reach the performing stage) and this is often due to battles for power and status during the storming stage. Youth workers are in the position of being able to facilitate groups going through the difficult and often stressful process of deciding 'who's who' and 'who's doing what', so that the group can achieve the satisfaction of performing the task. The process is developmental and educational, young people learn much about the way they relate to others, and the way their peers relate to them through being members of both formal and informal groups. Youth workers facilitate this growth and development in young people via their ability to understand and interpret the patterns of interaction within groups, combined with their ability to build meaningful and purposeful relationships with young people.

Conclusion

Perceptions of the aims and work of the youth service by other bodies may differ from the way in which the service perceives itself. This incongruence has often been posed as a question: are youth workers agents of social control or agents of social change? This may be a dilemma for the service and its workers but, whether the scales tip on the side of control or of change, there is evidence to support the view that the process of working with young people through the forum of formal and informal groups, using sensitivity and an adherence to the belief in the right of self determination, helps young people to grow and mature into adults who are able to take charge of their lives.

References

Argyle, M. (1983) *The Psychology of Interpersonal Behaviour.* London: Penguin.

Batten, T.R. (1967) *The Non-Directive Approach in Group and Community Work.* Oxford: Oxford University Press.

Button, L. (1982) *Developmental Group Work with Adolescents.* London: Hodder and Stoughton.

Cartwright, D. and Zander, A. (1968) *Group Dynamics Research and Theory.* London: Tavistock.

Homans, G.C. (1968) *The Human Group.* London: Routledge and Kegan Paul.

Klein, J. (1970) *Working with Groups.* London: Hutchinson.

Leighton, J.P. (1972) *The Principles and Practice of Youth and Community Work.* London: Chester House.

Llewelyn, S. and Fielding, G. (1982) 'Forming, Storming, Norming and Performing'. *Nursing Mirror.* 155(3): 14–16.

Tuckman, B.W. (1965) 'Developmental Sequence in Small Groups'. *Psychological Bulletin.* 63 (6): 384–99.

CHAPTER 23

Group Work with Children and Adolescents in a Therapeutic Community

Jane Wright-Watson

Introduction

Therapeutic communities for children and adolescents can be thought of as the successors to many earlier experiments in educating or managing the circumstances and behaviours of destitute, orphaned or delinquent children. They date mainly from the beginning of the century, although several charities were founded during the last century which addressed the needs of this population. In the United States there was a system of schools known as the Junior Republics which were modelled on the US constitution, within a structure of self-government by the pupils. Homer Lane ran one of these schools and came to England in 1913 where he established a similarly self-governing school for adolescents in Dorset called The Little Commonwealth. He was particularly interested and influenced by the ideas of Freud.

Similarly influenced by the ideas of Freud and psychoanalysis was A.S. Neill who, in 1924, founded Summerhill. He believed the pupils should be allowed to decide for themselves what they considered to be in their best interests. Each child, said Neill, would be allowed 'to live according to his own deep impulses' (Bridgeland 1971). Both Homer Lane and A.S. Neill have been criticised for their particular ways of interpreting Freud's theories.

As with the development of therapeutic communities for adults, World War II and post-war legislations were to have considerable influence on the development of provision for disturbed and deprived children and adolescents, where psychotherapy and education were to be combined within a more flexible framework. The Caldedott Community, which had been in existence since

1911, Finchden Manor founded in 1930, and the Mulberry Bush School are such examples. The Mulberry Bush School, founded by Barbara Dockar-Drysdale during the war years, was very much influenced by the work of the founder's mentor, D.W. Winnicott, and the theories of Anna Freud and Melanie Klein. These were a vast improvement on the bleak and harshly disciplined system which by 1914 housed over 25,000 children in some 223 industrial and reformatory schools.

In 1933 approved schools came into being. These, too, meted out severe discipline in harsh conditions and focused on the application of 'training'. In 1969 they were abolished under the Children and Young Person Act, which held evidence that the approved schools actually increased the likelihood of delinquent and criminal behaviour. Some were abolished completely and others were converted into children's homes with education, (CHEs). In a few instances they were reopened as therapeutic communities, Two examples of these were the Cotswolds and Peper Harow.

Peper Harow was founded as a therapeutic community in 1970. The founding Director, Melvyn Rose, had been a member of staff at Finchden Manor under George Lyward and was a housemaster at Park House school, the approved school which Peper Harow replaced. Dr Nora Murrow, the consultant psychiatrist, had been a junior staff member at the hospital under Maxwell Jones. Their combined experiences and personal qualities were central to the evolution of Peper Harow as a therapeutic community which emphasised daily community meetings, small psychotherapy groups and the creation of a nurturing physical environment as central to the treatment of its residents (Worthington 1992).

Thornby Hall was established as a therapeutic community and special school by the Peper Harow Organisation in 1985. Since the group work material I describe in this chapter occurred at Thornby Hall I shall describe more fully the environment and context.

The context of groups

Thornby Hall is a large 16th century manor house, built of yellowing Northamptonshire stone. It was opened as a therapeutic community in 1986 with the intention of treating up to 35 seriously disturbed children and adolescents aged between 10 and 17. The community comprises children from many different local authorities and the geographical and racial mix adds a richness, both of experience and culture. Thornby Hall stands in its own 17 acres of land, comprising fields, woodland and lake, in addition to a renovated stable block which now houses educational facilities and creative arts studios. Approximately one fourth of the staff group live on site or within the village of Thornby; many others live in local villages and small towns nearby.

Many of the children have been in the care of local authorities for much of their young lives and some have had as many as 17 moves or placements prior to arriving at Thornby. About 70 per cent of the children have suffered severe physical, emotional and sexual abuse and, when there has been family involvement, it would be fair to say all the families are in some way dysfunctional. The ability to foster trust, dependency and hope within these children is the primary task of staff. Challenging existing belief systems, including issues of extremely low self-esteem or fear around the very notion of 'belonging' anywhere are the very difficult first stages of the treatment program.

Every child arriving at Thornby Hall will have gone through a referral process with their social worker and sometimes parents and the minimum commitment expected from the child at the outset is that he or she wishes to come to Thornby. Children are selected who, it is felt, can respond to the notion of joining in with a process whereby ultimately they will take some responsibility for their right to a good life and some responsibility for looking at their own behaviours, both intrapsychically and in terms of the community group.

The complexities of groups and sub-groups may become clearer as I describe the staff group, both as a whole and in terms of tasks. Every member of staff joins the community, regardless of task, by a thorough application process which involves staff self-disclosure, informal interviews and panels plus a formal group interview. The value of this is apparent when one thinks 'community' for in addition to weeding out potentially inappropriate appointments (those persons, for example, unable to function within a team) the self-disclosive element of the application process enables both interviewer and interviewee to focus most specifically on what motivates to join a community and whether that motivation is self-serving or community-oriented. For the purposes of description, the most easily identifiable staff groups at Thornby comprise the following:

- Director and two assistant directors
- Senior staff
- Multi-disciplinary residential staff
- Assistant staff
- Teachers
- Administrative staff
- Domestic staff
- Maintenance staff
- Garden and grounds staff

One of the significant features in the historical delineation of therapeutic communities from the institutions they replaced and challenged was the relative absence of clear role boundaries between different groups. In the very early therapeutic communities for adults in Britain – The Northfield Military Hospital (W.R. Bion), The Henderson Hospital (Maxwell Jones) and the Cassel

Hospital (Tom Main) – a key factor included the blurring and changing of traditional boundaries with greater degrees of flexibility and integration between staff roles and, moreover, between the staff and residents. Most particularly, they underlined the active engagement of patients in the management of the communities and in the process of each other's treatment. Similar role boundary diffusion existed within and between staff teams – for example between doctors and nurses at the Cassel Hospital, all of whom undertook psychoanalytic training and ran small therapy groups with patients (Kennard 1983).

At Thornby Hall, given the age group of the client group, a clear delineation exists between staff and residents, of course, but the input of peers in group situations at any age is central to the ethos of a psychodynamic process. Within the overall staff group, however, there is a considerable degree of flexibility and overlap in role boundaries, although it is interesting to note that as we have developed we have moved towards a greater clarity of role boundary between different staff groups than the very multi-functional model with which we began. Various factors have influenced this shift, but at the core of the staff team lies a multi-disciplinary staff group which is involved in all aspects of the residents' lives: care, treatment, and education, as well as the social programme. These staff are both supported by and supportive of the other staff groups in maintaining the integration of the whole.

The children's group is clearly most easily defined by whether residents belong to the boy's or the girl's group. The children have a 'Senior' group, which usually comprises the older children who might be somewhat more integrated (although this is often questionable!). Staff, however, might further divide the residents' groups in terms of the developmental tasks being undertaken, levels of dependency or autonomy, college groupings or home-based educational groups, groups of children gearing up for examination work and groups considering departure from the community. In addition, groups are formed by the sharing of bedrooms, small therapy groups and social activities. As within the staff group, there are other areas where there is a fluidity and overlap of memberships of different groups, both formal and informal. Within the constellation of group memberships, therefore, each child will belong to several groups at once. It is thus imperative that any psychodynamic model of treatment and understanding which might be applied must have at its core a systemic view of community. That each child be held in the awareness of where he or she is for the moment is fundamentally important to the overall task of treatment and that there be understanding that progress is not necessarily always forward-moving central to the understanding of working with this disturbed, and disturbing population.

Whilst I shall attempt to discuss 'group work' at Thornby Hall I must preface this with the statement that any group within a well-functioning therapeutic community is essentially a group where the conscious and unconscious material of all its members, both adult (staff) and children, are in play at all times. So whilst one may focus on the observable phenomena of the children's group – in order to make sense of the behaviours and observations – much of the internal process of the adult 'in empathy' forms the clarifying tool which allows such observations and interpretations to be described. Indeed, it is the absolute willingness to trust the intrapsychic mechanisms of the adults working with these children, and to trust that the holding of awareness of their feelings means to hold an awareness of the whole child, and to 'contain' all this material which is central to the ethos of the Therapeutic Community.

The community meeting

The community meeting is a daily meeting which has undergone considerable change within Thornby Hall over the past several years. Initially, our community meeting involved attendance by all the children and all the senior and multi-disciplinary residential staff on duty. Latterly, this meeting has included assistant staff as they have been added to the staff team and those teachers who were available to participate (by teachers, I mean full or part-time teaching members of staff who were added to the staff group rather than to multi-disciplinary residential staff, who teach as part of their role within the community).

As our population has grown we have noticed a great difficulty among the older children to perceive the acting-out behaviours demonstrated by the younger children as similar to their own acting-out behaviours. It has become more difficult to focus the delinquent content of the older children's group as the younger children's group so frequently act it out on their behalf. Worthington (1990) succinctly describes the need to be open to the various languages that disturbed children use in communicating their personal history and predicament and that to set out to control this is, in essence, a message to these children to 'shut up'. Whilst we as adults can understand this concept, the older children's group find it a convenient foil to reflect their own disturbance onto the younger, less integrated members of the community. Thus, as time has gone by, the older children sometimes avoid looking at their own misbehaviours by focusing on the disruptions to the community meeting enacted (often on their behalf, or for their approval) by the younger members. It is a difficult task and requires a delicate balance to remain considerate of the differing levels of dependency and differing developmental tasks of children with chronological ages of between 10 and 17. The task is made more complex by the frequency with which an older child in fact enacts needs at a much earlier level of human development.

Once a week we divide the community meeting into a boy's Group and a girl's Group. Because of time constraints and rota changes, we have also scheduled small therapy groups to happen simultaneously at a time which had previously been a community meeting space. One of the considerations for this has to do with incorporating expectations from external bodies such as the

Department of Education that there be a certain number of specific hours of education provided to the children at Thornby. This provides interesting dialogue between sub-groups of staff at Thornby Hall and elicits feelings within groups that one focus of the treatment plan may be more important or valuable than another. Ultimately, we and the Department of Education must come to a real as opposed to a minimalist understanding of what we hope to achieve within therapeutic communities. Any 'examiner' coming into the 'madness' of the children's chaos must somehow be enabled to understand the chaos as 'work in progress' which is not contrary to the development of good educational practice. This must be considered an important next step if we are to avoid the dichotomy between complying with external demands without the flexibility needed within therapeutic organisations to adjust foci with uncomfortable regularity.

The community meeting might be an open invitation for the children to name their own agenda, or for discussion about anything which affects the community, such as visitors, building work, or an incident from the day before. There might be an issue about trips out of the community – who should go, for instance, or conditions under which another resident may be considered for a trip out. Bedroom changes must be discussed within the community meeting forum and the dynamic issues around the various bedroom groupings form interesting material which is easily related to by other children within the community. Frequently, there will be the need to address behaviours of some, or all of the children and to think together about the meaning within the whole group of the acting-out of some of its members. Different meetings have a different 'feel' or quality to them. An observer would notice the quiet attentiveness of some, and the obvious disruptions of others. Sometimes the community goes through a spate of helpful meetings where issues are discussed and resolved; at other times there may be several consecutive meetings where children seem unable to share either the physical space or are triggered by forces which can only be acted out disruptively.

Description of community meeting

Recently, one of the girls, Sally, revealed to an assistant director that one of the girls with whom Sally shared a room was involved in a sexual relationship with another of the residents. This second girl, Carole, and the boy involved, Dennis, were part of the community meeting the next day.

By the time the meeting had begun, there had been a considerable amount of gossip about Carole and Dennis amongst the children's group. One of the younger boys within the community asked very directly as the meeting started 'Is it true that Carole's pregnant?' Carole immediately curled up in the corner seat of the meeting and hid her head in her arms. She looked embarrassed, as did Dennis who was seated at the other end of the room, and who was very rarely able to verbalise his thoughts within the meeting. Carole was invited to respond to the question but remained silent, as did Dennis.

The larger group made attempts to involve both in a conversation and appeared angry that Carole and Dennis would not respond to them. 'I think you should say something Carole, – you did last night' invited one of the girls. 'Leave her alone – you know she's not going to say anything – she never does' responded another girl. There were other interventions – the suggestion that this was something Carole might prefer to discuss privately with her personal counsellor was one.

The meeting then moved on to thinking about the meaning of Sally's having 'protected' Carole from herself when, in fact, many members of the group were fantasising that Sally might be similarly involved with another of the residents. 'You staff never let us even have friendships!' was another theme of the meeting. 'If we went to a local comprehensive school, we wouldn't have any problems and no one would hassle us about going out together'.

The community meeting went on to consider how special 'friendships' often ended in the hurtful rejection by one child, or group of children of another. There was discussion that within the context of a therapeutic community such relationships inevitably led to jealousy, scapegoating, or someone, like Carole being the 'carrier' of a community issue.

In a large community meeting we try to involve the children in discussions which may appear localised to one specific child or group at the outset, but which are pertinent to the whole group. A successful meeting includes listening to and exploring the views of as many children as possible. It is possible within this forum to refer sensitively to one of the children's family history to link the children's understanding of the process evolving.

An example of this might be a child being confronted because of his or her stealing. If another resident has successfully managed to stop stealing, he might be encouraged to describe what had happened to him that now made it possible for him not to steal any more. That child may make the interpretation to the group that he didn't 'need' to steal because he felt happier than he felt when he left his family where the only way to claim attention might have been to steal. This kind of interaction affords the younger or less integrated child much hope. When a peer is able to say, and perhaps even be praised for, his ability to share the information that he used to steal, the child still stealing might then be able to think 'maybe I can stop too'.

Sometimes the content of the large community meeting is better able to be discussed within the smaller therapy group where it is possible to focus more intently on the individuals in a way which, within the community meeting might have the effect of leaving some children feeling excluded.

Small therapy groups

These are weekly groups of five or six children with two staff facilitators. Children allocated to small groups are generally thought to be open to verbal interventions and at a point in their treatment where this would make sense, as opposed to non-verbal therapy which occurs within the play studio and art therapy arenas (Wright-Watson 1990). The primary requisite for being a member of a small group is the child's ability to function as part of a group. We have children who, in the initial stages of their stay in the community, are completely 'ungroupable' and most intervention with them has to be conducted one-to-one by adults.

Description of small therapy group

I shall try to illustrate the longitudinal importance of crises within the community in the context of small group work undertaken over a period of almost one year. At the beginning of the year in question, two of the residents had formed a partnership and the young woman became pregnant. Patti, the young woman carrying the child, was present within the Community for seven of her eight-and-a-half months of pregnancy, the first five having been kept 'secret' from the adult group, but known by many of the children, especially within the girl's group. One issue was whether Patti could remain in the community once her pregnancy was known. John, the father of this baby, was a member of a small group which addressed this issue and had present amongst its membership two other children who periodically and in response to their very abusive backgrounds, became involved in inappropriate sexual activity. Another young member of this therapy group, Ellen, was currently enamoured of John and found it impossible to see that their 'relationship' was a dysfunctional pairing relating to her need to be a 'good mother' to John. Ellen could not see that John had a long series of relationships of this kind during his time within the community which related to John's need for warmth and his confusing warmth and sexuality. Once the reality of Patti's pregnancy was known, a collective defensiveness and denial came to the fore which took the form of questioning who was the father, thus protecting John from the full impact of the group's true response to the situation regarding his paternity. Within the group, then, were constellated forces which, even though apparently addressing the issue openly, somehow became enacting of a sympathetic, non-judgmental, allowing and therefore 'boundary-less' parent. Feelings were described and explored and on the surface; the group was paying attention to this serious event. It was not until John left the community and nine months after the pregnancy was announced that the same small group could identify their true feelings around this.

It was, in fact, the girl previously enamoured of John who raised the issue about some gossip which had reached the community about Patti's purported abuse of her infant daughter. At this point, in the absence of the father, the children were better able to share genuine feelings about the awfulness of being unwanted or abused, growing up in one-parent families, being abandoned at birth, and, an important point, discuss the 'secret' behaviours of the two members of the group currently acting-out sexually. It is not surprising that, given the high proportion of children who have been sexually abused within the community, their acting-out behaviours would address the serious distortion of boundaries from their histories. Thornby Hall has very clear boundaries around the inappropriateness of sexual activities between residents.

To illustrate further the complexities of community living, there must also have been a huge unconscious fantasy regarding one of the small group leaders who had been Patti's personal counsellor. What did it mean to the group that Patti chose the same name for her daughter as the daughter of their group-worker?

Group location

There are many factors which affect children and adolescents undergoing small group therapy within a community such as ours. For example, when several small groups are being conducted within the same time period, there may be issues arising from competition between different groups around the location. Who has the 'best', 'most comfortable', or the room with associations of 'warmth' or 'authority?' If the room is multi-functional, there may be distractions such as paintings or books which offer a way out of the group processes being enacted there. Useful group material can be salvaged from such complaints, however. Recently, the boy's group complained that the girl's group got the 'best' lounge, while they were relegated to an untidier and more worn community lounge. Had we become bogged down in the argument, we would not have been able to discuss the rivalry and competition, or the sexual tensions which existed more profoundly than usually during this period in the community's life. Using the director's room for children's meetings, even when the director is absent, always brings a kind of weightiness to proceedings. It is as though the authority of the room itself and the children's (and perhaps staff's) associations with that room change the dynamic.

The boy who would be Director

Due to building work being undertaken within the community, we were forced to hold a meeting of the boy's group in the Director's office. The director was away from the community at a meeting. Staff present had placed themselves in different areas of the room which is furnished with comfortable sofas, plus an office arm chair (the Director's). One boy of 16, Dan, has a history which leads him to act out intrusively and with dangerous levels of aggression. He constantly challenges adult authority.

Dan arrived slightly late to the meeting, and sat in the Director's chair. He had arrived in the frame of mind where to 'belong' to the group would be to belong delinquently and Dan set out to sabotage the group by entertaining its members. This took the form, initially, of discovering a most impressive squeak when he rocked the chair and adopting postures similar to those of our Director. Dan then swivelled the chair, turning his back to the group and proceeded to 'intrude' into the desk drawers. As he was making these attempts, the rest of the group were addressing one of its members who had been cruelly bullying another of the younger boys. The meeting was progressing in a satisfying way – the children concerned were describing recent events and the listening children were offering confrontive but supportive encouragement to the child who had been bullying. Twice this process was interrupted to invite Dan to 'join' the meeting. The rest of the children were not buying into the disruption, but nor were they able to join in staff efforts to manage Dan, who was, essentially, 'bullying' the meeting. Consequently Dan escalated his attempts by displaying objects from within the drawers and reading through a booklet about Child Protection Procedures. (This was a deliberate and highly manipulative effort to derail the meeting to readdress an old agenda of his own about accusations of abuse by staff which he had used in the past to activate enormous anxiety and fear within the children's group.) He then tore several sheets of 'Post-It' memos and proceeded to write obscene notes which he placed on the board above the Director's desk. The meeting was halted briefly to invite Dan to sit elsewhere, to reinvite him back into the meeting differently and to find out whether his own needs were not being addressed. The group reminded him that there was still plenty of time.

Staff within the room were well aware that Dan was a boy who sought holding and containment at around the level of a four-year-old, but who responded to such holding as if he were being attacked and threatened and who could seduce other children into a mad belief that he was being hurt when he was being contained following one of his own assaults. It was important not to confront Dan in such a way that there would be physical contact. It also seemed important to staff running this meeting that Dan not be successful in intimidating the meeting into moving away from its important work by receiving too much attention for his behaviours.

Towards the end of the meeting one of the senior boys who had earlier attempted to 'excuse' Dan's behaviours, rose to remove matches from Dan which he had begun to strike as an ultimate threat to the meeting. The meeting continued; participants managed their anxieties around what would happen next and the children left the room, except for Dan! The tension and anxiety which he had imported late to the meeting exploded immediately the meeting finished, and he deliberately smashed a vase, and a large filing tool which he had removed from the desk and was waving around in a threatening manner had to be forcibly removed by staff.

The meeting I describe afforded no visible relief or understanding for Dan (unless it was to be 'held' at the end of it) – yet we would describe this kind of meeting as staying on task and good for the majority. Having said that, staff discussing this meeting afterwards had several thoughts about what they were containing on behalf of the children and within their own reactiveness to it. There was always the risk of unmanageable escalation, fear of physical violence, anger towards the disruptive child who could not see how his omnipotence threatened the insight gained by the children who were working. It can be very painful, as well as frustrating for staff to manage their own responses as they are triggered by such overt threat, but how much more we understood the theme of the working part of the meeting – that of being 'bullied'.

To work with groups within a therapeutic community requires a high level of tolerance, an ability to constantly monitor one's own, as well as the children's responses, flexibility, an ability to withstand personal attack and be able to reflect upon this as the child's own sense of being attacked. In addition to these qualities, humour in the face of being encouraged to feel helpless or stupid, but overall an ability to manage to hold a myriad of often conflicting and confusing responses until such time as, through discussion afterwards, sense can be made of the chaos!

Conveying understanding to other groups

Consideration must be given to members of the community who sometimes function outside of the groups I have described. For example, after Dan's experience in the boy's group it was important that the group workers took responsibility for informing other staff groups and members. Teachers who were working with him needed to be informed, as did cleaning and maintenance staff who were likely to see Dan continuing to interfere in their work that morning. The assistant director responsible for an on-going liaison with Dan's local authority needed to know, as did his personal counsellor when he came on duty later that day.

Dan's behaviours were likely to have an impact on several groups this day, including secretarial and administrative staff. Some of these staff would be present at the next staff meeting and some would not. Nor would it be sufficient to feel one had discharged one's responsibility by entering something into a daily log. The need to impart this crisis within Dan might make the difference between someone outside the small group inadvertently 'setting him off' or being more at risk of Dan's aggression and violence.

Support and supervision

Thornby Hall places great emphasis on the need for external consultancy to help staff differentiate their own responses from the material which belongs uniquely to the children. Whilst it becomes 'our' material in context of working within a community and the material is a communiqué of some distress, perhaps, real understanding for the child is achieved by enabling the child to reclaim the split-off parts of himself, often projected into the staff group. We can often use counter-transference material successfully to enable this process, but without the ability to non-defensively describe some of this to a consultant who is potentially less caught up in the Community dynamics, I fear we would be far less successful in working within such a complicated environment.

Summary

I have attempted to describe the complexity of group work with children and adolescents in a therapeutic community, to show the considerable overlap of many groups and group functions and to include the multi-disciplinary role of the staff group and its impact. The illustrative groups will, I hope, give a flavour to the reader of children's ability to use this psychodynamically-oriented model well. Interpretative comments added to the body of the text should be read as explanatory to the reader rather than part of the content of the groups themselves. We do not pretend that to participate in this kind of group process is, for the child, the same as to understand the process as part of the adult group. It has been necessary to omit several important factors which also influence groups – for example issues of loss when group leaders leave the community or are ill, 'charismatic' leadership (Rose 1990), competitive or rivalrous feelings, as they are both part of group processes and personal material within both children and adults, to name but a few.

Thornby Hall is alive to the notion of a community-in-evolution. Changes are and must be made to reflect the changing needs of its residents. Consideration of groups and their impact on the whole community continues to be both central and a priority within the notion of psychodynamic thinking and functioning.

References

Bridgeland, M. (1971) *Pioneer Work With Maladjusted Children*. London: Staples Press.

Kennard, D. (1983) *An Introduction to Therapeutic Communities*. London: Routledge and Kegan Paul.

Rose, M. (1990) *Healing Hurt Minds: The Peper Harow Experience*. London: Tavistock/Routledge.

Worthington, A. (1990) 'The Establishment of a New Therapeutic Community'. *International Journal of Therapeutic Communities*. 11(2): 95–102.

Worthington, A. (1992) The Therapeutic Community. (unpublished paper, personal communication).

Wright-Watson, J. (1990) 'The Function of Play in a Therapeutic Community for Children and Adolescents'. *International Journal of Therapeutic Communities.* 11(2): 77–86.

About the Authors

Janet Adams, (Cert. Comm. Youth Work) is a Trainer in Northamptonshire Youth Service and has 18 years experience of face-to-face youth work in a variety of places as a volunteer, part time and full time professional worker. As a Trainer, she contributes to the design, development, delivery and evaluation of the in-service training programme for full and part time youth workers. She is currently doing her M.Ed. (Human Relations) at Nottingham University.

Susan Bell, (RMN, ENB 603), Clinical Nurse Specialist in the Child and Adolescent Service of the Milton Keynes Community Mental Health Trust has, over the past 20 years, worked in various capacities within both the private and state sectors of psychiatric nursing. She moved into the Child and Adolescent field in 1985 in Northampton and then to Milton Keynes in 1988. She is also a member of the Regional Committee of A.P.S.A. and the Committee of the Association of Community Nurses (Child and Adolescent Psychiatry).

Paul Cook, Unit Manager, St John's Centre, Northampton, has worked in Child Care for nearly a decade and has developed and managed a 'High Supervision Unit' for those young people who may otherwise require secure provision. He has extensive experience of working with adolescents who exhibit severe behavioural problems, high tarrif offences, remands and those young people on Section 536 sentences.

Carol Coppock, is Special Needs Co-ordinator and the Head of Learning Support at Weston Favell Upper School, Northampton, where she has taught since 1974. She qualified as a mathematics teacher in 1973, but her rapidly developing interest in pupils with learning difficulties directed her career towards the field of Special Needs. Most recently she has gained the RSA Diploma of Teachers of Pupils with Specific Learning Difficulties.

Barbara Coward, SEN, BA (Hons), CQSW, has been a Development Officer (African Caribbean communities) for four years and is now a Planning and Development Officer for the Social Services Department, Coventry. She began her career in the caring professions first as a nurse and then in Social Services. She has presented Coventry Social Services Department with various models on how practices and services could be improved as well as confronting and challenging oppressive professional practices.

Tessa Dalley, BA (Hons), Dip Psych, RAth, is Senior Art Therapist in the Child and Parent Department at Parkside Clinic, London. This is a consultation and therapeutic centre for children and adults. She also works as a supervisor with other practising art therapists and in private practice. Tessa is on the teaching staff on the Postgraduate Diploma Course in Art Psychotherapy, Goldsmiths College and has written several books on art therapy.

Pratima Dattani, BA (Hons), CQSW, is Community Care Planning Officer, Social Services Department, Northampton. She also worked as a Development Officer (Asian Communities) in the Ethnic Minority Development Unit, Coventry, where she advised on race equality strategies, policies and practices.

Dr Kedar Nath Dwivedi, MBBS, MD, DPM, FRC Psych is a Consultant Child, Adolescent and Family Psychiatrist at the Child and Family Consultation Service and the Ken Stewart Family Centre, Northampton. He graduated in medicine from the institute of Medical Sciences, Banaras Hindu University, Varanasi, India and served as Assistant Professor in Preventive and Social Medicine in Simla before coming to the UK in 1974. Since then he has worked in Psychiatry. He is a member of more than a dozen Professional Associations, including the Group Analytic Society, and has contributed extensively to the literature (nearly 30 publications), teaches on the Midland Course on Group Work and Family Therapy and is the Course Director of the Introductory Course on Group Work with Children and Adolescents in Northampton. He is interested in Eastern, particularly Buddhist, approaches to mental health.

Bernie Evans, CSS., is Social Worker in the Adolescent Response Team, Broadlands Childrens Centre, Northamptonshire. Bernie has also worked as a residential Social Worker in child care and a Deputy Unit

Peter Harper, BSocSC, BA (Hons), MSc (Clinical Psychology), AFBPsS is a Consultant Clinical Psychologist working in the Child Health Directorate, Northampton. He has extensive experience as a clinician, therapist, trainer and supervisor both in the United Kingdom and abroad. He is a member of several professional organisations and is on the Editorial Board of *The Child Care Worker,* a journal to which he has made a number of contributions on working therapeutically with children.

Fredi Harrison, Group Facilitator, Personal Counsellor and Trainer, has worked with groups which were designed to teach very young children how to protect themselves from abuse or attack and has counselled with children and adolescents for problems such as sexual abuse, bullying, stress, family relationships and assertion skills. She also worked as a Training Officer for a youth counselling service in Northampton and supervised the trained volunteer counsellors. She spends much of her professional time working with groups of people who are mentally ill.

Julie Harrower, BA, MA, CQSW, Dip App Soc Studies, Cert Ed is a Lecturer in Psychology at Nene College, Northampton. She has also worked as a Probation Officer, a Divorce Court Welfare Officer and a Child Protection Officer (NSPCC) over a period of ten years. For the last four years she has been teaching social work students and undergraduate psychology students, specialising in the areas of Criminological Psychology, Violence and Aggression.

Sarah Hogan, RMN, SRN, is Senior Nurse and Manager for the Ken Stewart Family Centre. This is a day resource for the Northampton Child and Family Consultation Service, Northampton, offering primarily group therapy for children and families, but also individual and family therapy. Her interest in group work developed after working with Dr Harry Tough at the Mayfair Centre, Kettering. She also contributes to the training of nursing students and acts as supervisor for Lowdown, the local Youth Counselling and Information Service.

Andy Howard, BA (Hons), MA, RMN, CQSW is Unit Manager based at the Lindfield Community Mental Health Centre. He was formerly Principal Social Worker in the Child and Family Consultation Service, Northampton. Following the completion of an Honours Degree course in Social Administration at Leicester University he trained and worked as a registered psychiatric nurse, specialising in Children and Adolescent Services. After completing a Master's Degree in Applied Social Studies, combined with a Certificate of Qualification in Social Work at Warwick University, he worked as a Social Worker in the Northampton Social Services Department and then in the NSPCC.

Suzanne Lawton, CQSW, Social Worker in the Child and Family Consultation Service, Northampton, has previously been an infant teacher in Berkshire and Warwickshire. She worked as a generic Social Worker in Warwickshire before taking up her present post, She is interested in women's issues and in preventive work in the field of Child Sexual Abuse. She was co-worker in an adolescent group at the Ken Stewart Family Centre from 1989–1992.

Patrick McGrath, BA (Hons), HDipinEd, DipSoc, MInstGA is Care Manager Co-ordinator for Mental Health, Hospital Social Work and the Emergency Duty Services and the Disaster Counselling Service for the Northern Division of Buckinghamshire Social Services. He was born and grew up in Ireland where he obtained his BA Degree and Higher Diploma in Education and Diploma in Social Studies. Having taught for a short time he worked as Chaplain at a Reformatory School for boys and then came to England and worked with the homeless in the West End of London. Since then he has been working for Buckinghamshire Social Services in various managerial capacities. He completed the Human Relations Course at the Richmond Fellowship in London and graduated in 1986 from the Institute of Group Analysis.

Diddy Mymin, BA (Jer) is a psychologist in Northampton. She has completed her training toward an MA in Clinical Child Psychology at Bar Ilan University, Israel. She has had experience working with adolescents in various capacities since 1983. Specific group related experience includes design and implementation of leadership training programmes for youth workers, facilitating social skills training groups for learning disabled adolescents, creative group work with autistics and cognitive-behavioural groups with adults.

Sister Margaret Pennells, CQSW, MA (Social & Comm Work), has been Social Worker in Child and Family Consultation Service, Northampton for five years, before which she worked as a Psychiatric Social Worker in Merseyside Child Guidance Clinic. Along with Sue Smith, Sister Margaret has pioneered a structured group work programme for bereaved children and adolescents and has developed a training package with videos, for which they received the Social Work Today Award for 1991. She also works for CRUSE as a voluntary Bereavement Counsellor and has been involved extensively in training professionals in this work both locally and nationally.

Susan C. Smith, CQSW, has been Social Worker, General Hospital, Northampton for three years, before which she worked in the Child Care Team as the Social Worker for two years. Along with Sister Margaret, she has been involved in pioneering the group work programme for bereaved children and adolescents and in developing the training package with videos, for which they obtained the Social Work Today Award for 1991. She has also been involved in training professionals both locally and nationally, is the Co-ordinator for GAP, a local counselling service, and a Volunteer Counsellor for the in-service counselling provision at Northampton General Hospital.

Cherry Stephenson, BPhil (Educ), CertEd, ADBEd (Associate of the Drama Board), FRSA (Fellow of the Royal Society for the Arts), Acting Head of the Drama and Dance Advisory Service in Leicestershire, started her professional career as a Drama Teacher in Secondary Education and then as a Drama Therapist in psychiatric units for children and adolescents. She spent several years as an advisory teacher, covering a wide range of areas related to drama in both mainstream and special education and has always maintained a strong interest in therapeutic group work, particularly psychodrama. She is also keenly interested in counselling techniques and in Buddhism.

Dr Malcolm R. Walley, C Psychol, PhD, Dip Counselling, is a Principal Lecturer in Psychology and Counsellor at Nene College, Northampton where he also worked as the Head of Studies in Psychology. He has a long standing interest in the application of Buddhist Psychology to Western psychology and therapeutic work, having run workshops and contributed articles in this area. Malcolm is joint-convener of the 'Buddhism, Psychology, Psychiatry Group'. His other academic and research interests include the nature of consciousness, psychological wellbeing, empathy, anger management, counselling and sports psychology.

Jane Wright-Watson, MA, has worked as both a multi-disciplinary residential staff member, and a Senior Member of Staff at Thornby Hall, Northamptonshire, since 1987. Her particular responsibilities included designing and overseeing the functioning of the Play Studio, supervision of casework material and the running of groups, including children's groups. She is also involved in private counselling and consultancy.

Subject Index

Author Index

Chain Reaction
Children and Divorce
Ofra Ayalon and Adina Flasher
ISBN 1 85302 136 9

'This is a truly excellent book, easy to read and instantly useable… The healing structure offered and the sensible yet tender approach to helping children overcome disastrous life events is secure and workable… The light touch, the many experiences, the creative responses and the absolute respect shown to all parties involved will make this an essential and frequently used handbook to use in a wide variety of situations.'   *– Counselling*

'After discussing the implications of divorce on families, including the adult games in which children may be unwilling participants, the text develops into a refreshingly creative approach to group and individual therapy for such children. The techniques include literature therapy, play and art therapy as well as problem-solving techniques. The text is replete with child-friendly exercises and questionnaires enhanced by cartoons. There is much for the therapist to dip into. Nurses attached to child psychology or psychiatry services will find this book helpful.'   *– Nursing Times*

'The ideas and techniques are explained in a simple, direct way, and are well illustrated by case examples… The ideas and methods described could easily be used in individual and family work, as well as group work, and overall I felt that the book would be invaluable as a source book of techniques and ideas.'
                              – Association for Child Psychology and Psychiatry Newsletter

'…Dr Ofra Ayalon and Dr Adina Flasher speak authoritatively about the effects of divorce. They measure the stress involved in drastic changes in lifestyle, pointing out that these are potentially very dangerous to the psychological and the physical well-being of everyone involved. They give moving examples of some of the ways in which children may react.'   *– The Tablet*

'This book is clear and straightforward in its approach, offering practical ideas for face to face work with children. The emphasis is on group work which the authors argue provides an important source of support and strength to children who can share experiences.'   *– The Clarion*

'Unlike similar books it does not latch on to one particular 'therapy' or school of thought, but suggests a variety of approaches from physical activities and relaxation to emotional expression of the full range of feelings.'   *– Scottish Baptist*

'The book is an excellent one of its kind… Those who want to turn 'learned helplessness into resourcefulness' could well begin by dipping into this carefully documented book.'   *– ISIS Magazine*

Jessica Kingsley Publishers
116 Pentonville Road, London N1 9JB

Parenting Teenagers
Bob Myers
ISBN 1 85302 366 3 pb

'Based on more than twenty years' experience, this very level-headed text is intended for all who have to deal with the needs of adolescents. There are no quick-fix solutions here but rather an examination of often complex relationships. Strategies are developed for problem solving and helping the teenager build self-esteem, responsibility and independence while at the same time keeping the carer's sanity. In a friendly, supportive voice and while not minimising difficulties, Myers recommends that patience and perseverance in applying them will gain the desired results in the end.'

Interventions with Bereaved Children
Susan C Smith and Sister Margaret Pennells
ISBN 1 85302 285 3 pb

'The editors have chosen their contributors from many different contexts with great care and should be congratulated for producing a book as touching and moving as it is informative and professional.'   *– Stillbirth and NeoNatal Death Society*

Grief in Children
A Handbook for Adults
Atle Dyrerov
ISBN 1 85302 113 X pb

'An invaluable resource for parents, pastoral workers and those in caring professions.'
    – Methodist Recorder

'A handy, small book ideal for teachers, social workers, counsellors, parents and others faced with the task of understanding children in grief and trying to help them.'   *– Association for Child Psychology and Psychiatry Newsletter*

Art Therapy in Practice
Edited by Marian Liebmann
ISBN 1 85302 057 5 hb ISBN 1 85302 058 3 pb

'This book offer(s) a valuable contribution to the dissemination of information about the practice of art therapy...fascinating reading.'   *–Counselling Psychology Quarterly*

Project Based Group Work Facilitator's Manual
Participation in Practice
Andy Gibson
ISBN 1 85302 169 5 pb

'this very practical manual provides a basis for project work of all kinds.'
    Aslib Book Guide

Jessica Kingsley Publishers
116 Pentonville Road, London N1 9JB

Symbols of the Soul
Therapy and Guidance Through Fairy Tales
Birgitte Brun, Ernst W Pedersen and Marianne Runberg
Foreword by Murray Cox
ISBN 1 85302 107 5 hb

'The book...has many of the best qualities of fairy tales. Its descriptive style is lucid and simple. It contains many pointers and signposts which provoke the reader's curiosity. '

–from the foreword

Good Practice in Child Protection
A Manual for Professionals
Edited by Hilary Owen and Jacki Pritchard
ISBN 1 85302 205 5 pb

'A distinguishing feature of the book is its strong practice and training orientation. The majority of chapters contain experiential exercises which can be used by teams or incorporated into training courses, many of which are focused on multi-disciplinary working...practitioners and trainers will find much in this collection which is of value'

– British Journal of Social Work

'Each chapter is fully referenced, and some include case studies and exercises. I found *Good Practice in Child Protection* not only interesting but educational. It was harrowing to read the case studies and descriptions, and this shows the vital need of good training, supervision and support for workers in this field or for those who come into situations in which a child may be being abused in any way.'

– Nursing Standard

'will delight trainers. They could use the text as a pattern to mount immediate courses with stimulating exercises.'

– Community Care

'This text would be very useful for any doctor involved in the care of children.'

– Australian Family Physician

Storymaking in Education and Therapy
Alida Gersie and Nancy King
ISBN 1 85302 520 8 pb

'The myths themselves are veritable jewels that evoke an immediate response in the reader, and they stand on their own as a valuable asset to any library.'

–The Arts in Psychotherapy

'For the dramatherapist this book contains a rich variety of thought provoking and inspiring material...a core text for dramatherapists to acquire.'

–Dramatherapy

Jessica Kingsley Publishers
116 Pentonville Road, London N1 9JB

Working with Children in Need
Studies in Complexity and Challenge
Edited by Eric Sainsbury
Foreword by Tom White
ISBN 1 85302 275 6 pb

'…gives detailed accounts of what is often know as 'direct work' with children allowing readers to see for themselves what this intensive work with abused children requires…we are privy to the content of sessions and the thoughts and judgements of the social workers as they unfold. Because of this the instructional value of these contemporaneous accounts is immense.'   *– Community Care*

Music Therapy in Health and Education
Edited by Margaret Heal and Tony Wigram
Foreword by Anthony Storr
ISBN 1 85302 175 X pb

'music therapy is now flourishing in many parts of the world, as the various chapters of this book amply demonstrate… Everyone who plays an instrument or who listens to music for pleasure knows that music has potent effects upon mind and body. Music can alter our moods, reduce fatigue, facilitate muscular movement, stir our memories… Today, when at last more attention is being given to the effects of music upon human beings, we have almost reached the depth of insight displayed by the Greeks in the 5th century B.C.'   *–from the foreword*

Play Therapy
Where the Sky Meets the Underworld
Ann Cattanach
ISBN 1 85302 211 X pb

'…an excellent, stimulating read with a manageable style and numerous sensitive insights into the world of play for the child and how it can become a therapeutic process where children 'play out' their perception of their own experiences…uses clear, straightforward language to discuss the theoretical basis for play therapy… The book does not make great claims as to its powers of healing, but it seems to offer a means towards constructively working through traumatic experiences for children.'
     – Nursery World

'Cattanach packs a large amount of theory into this easy-to-read volume, together with practical guidelines on how to be a safe companion for the child's journey.'
     – Professional Social Work

'This is an excellent introduction to an activity whose relevance is increasingly recognised and used, not least in the communication of good health practices.'
     – Institute of Health Education

Jessica Kingsley Publishers
116 Pentonville Road, London N1 9JB

Play Therapy with Abused Children
Ann Cattanach
ISBN 1 85302 120 2 hb ISBN 1 85302 193 8 pb

'Her accounts of the ways in which play is used to made sense of traumatic experiences are full of insight and often moving. All aspects of the work are covered, including preparation for play, starting play, boundary testing and the play therapy process. There is a good book list. The effects on the therapist of working with these problems and the type of support and supervision needed are described. This exceptional volume...goes far beyond a mere text book.' *–Therapy Weekly*

Dramatherapy with Families, Groups and Individuals
Waiting in the Wings
Sue Jennings
ISBN 1 85302 014 1 hb ISBN 1 85302 144 X pb

'This is a clear, well-written text that reflects a drama therapist who is clinically astute and well-grounded in drama, theatre, and ritual processes.'
–The Arts in Psychotherapy

How and Why Children Hate
A Study of Conscious and Unconscious Sources
Edited by Ved Varma
Foreword by Martin Herbert
ISBN 1 85302 116 4 hb ISBN 1 85302 185 7 pb

'The roots of hatred, sad to say, can often be traced to infancy and childhood. It seems a sacrilege to suggest that the children we love, the children who can be so loving, should have in them the seeds of the indifference, cruelty and violence which are the accompaniments of hatred... This is a worthy project indeed; its insights into the human conditions of love and its relative, hate, will be of value to a wide audience. *–from the Foreword*

'The authors suggest worthwhile methods of exploring the roots of hatred, demonstrating how class, society, family, and peer relationships form the foundation for a hatred that is sometimes later acted out against society or the self.'
– Contemporary Psychology

'...this collection of essays on the subject from psychiatrists, psychologists and psychotherapists as well as a sociologist and an educationalist is most welcome... [a] scholarly, well-researched and brilliant book on such a difficult subject.'
– Counselling News

'...a detailed and extensive study with lists of useful references. It is a must for studying children's hatred or its relative, love.' *– Nursery World*

Jessica Kingsley Publishers
116 Pentonville Road, London N1 9JB

How and Why Children Fail

Edited by Ved Varma
Foreword by James Hemming

ISBN 1 85302 108 3 hb ISBN 1 85302 186 5 pb

'will bring new insights, as well as the confirmation of good practice, to those engaged in the hugely important task of making sure that no child suffers unnecessary diminution of effectiveness and self-esteem at home or at school.

—from the Foreword

'The problems experienced within the school environment by children with a variety of challenges, (social, emotional, cultural and specifically educational) are well explored, as are compounding factors inherent in the education system of Great Britain.'

The Canadian Child Psychiatric Bulletin

'Ved Varma has compiled a book with a wide breadth of topic discussions that reveals an extensive and consistent trend in childhood failure… Through their discussions, the reader is led to rethink the ways in which success and failure for children are defined and assessed…this book is an excellent source of stimulation for discussion on several domains that affect childhood failure. The discussions and points raised are compelling and interesting; they left me knowledgeable about what can contribute to childhood failure. This text would be suitable for graduate student use within the fields of psychology and education.'

– Contemporary Psychology

'The scope is wide-ranging and includes, from the child psychiatrists, an object-relations approach to creativity, a broad-based chapter on anxiety, an interesting integration of object relations and systemic family approaches to underfunctioning in children, and chapters on the effects of physical illness, child abuse and the chaotic family. From the psychologists there is a useful discussion of the concept of intelligence, an excellent on dyslexia which suggests a simple way in which teacher might prevent this important diagnosis being missed.'

– British Journal of Psychiatry

'…a well documented, research based analysis of etiological factors that hinder optimal realisation of human potential in general and in the childhood in particular. The empirical cases cited by the authors, to substantiate their theses, have made the publication a practical reference book for parents of growing children, adults interested in child welfare, teachers, teacher educators, curriculum framers, and all those who are charged with the responsibility of nurturing human personality during the developmental period.'

– Journal of Educational Planning and Administration

Jessica Kingsley Publishers
116 Pentonville Road, London N1 9JB

Lifegames

Yvonne Searle and Isabelle Streng

Lifegames is a new series of therapeutic board games for children and adolescents, devised to facilitate the understanding and disclosure of the complex feelings experienced by children and adolescents when they are confronted with traumatic life events. Each game has been carefully developed utilising an integrative psychotherapy model which incorporates systemic, cognitive–behavioural, humanistic and psychodynamic orientations. The games address factual issues and focus on emotional expression, belief systems, cognitive processes, behavioural responses, relationships, fantasies, memories and dreams. They provide a safe, boundaried space where children and adolescents may explore their inner feelings, and can be used to answer questions which children may have been afraid to ask.

Designed to be flexible, the games can be tailored towards the pace of the therapeutic process. They may be used with groups and with individuals and they should always be played with a therapist. The recommended age range for participants is 6–16 years, although it is possible for the clinician to adapt games for working with younger or older children. Where appropriate, the therapist may participate as a co-player or remain solely in the role of facilitator.

Dr Yvonne Searle, BSc, MPhil, CertBehPsych, is a clinical psychologist and in the latter stages of training as a psychodrama psychotherapist (UKCP reg). She is also a lecturer at the Institute of Dramatherapy, Roehampton. Drs Isabelle Streng is a Chartered Clinical Psychologist and works with the Children's Disability Team and the Child and Family Psychiatry Services, Cambridge.

The Grief Game

ISBN 1 85302 333 7

The Grief Game is for children and adolescents who have experienced bereavement and is particularly useful for those struggling to come to terms with their loss. Intended for group work, it may also be played with individuals and can be used to facilitate intra-familial communication when played with families. The game can help to remove some of the taboo surrounding death and can help children to realise that other children – and adults – experience similar reactions. It can be played over several consecutive sessions or tailored to the pace of the treatment. The game comprises a game board, counters, dice and four sets of colour-coded cards arranged in categories corresponding to coloured shapes on the board: *Facts, Thoughts, Wishes and Dreams, Memories* and *Emotions*.

Jessica Kingsley Publishers
116 Pentonville Road, London N1 9JB

The Social Skills Game

ISBN 1 85302 336 1

The Social Skills Game is a lively and exciting therapeutic board game for children and adolescents who experience difficulties with relationships, and enables them to explore and reflect upon adaptive interaction styles. The game addresses behavioural responses, cognitive processes, belief systems, interactive processes, belief systems, verbal and nonverbal communication, and assertiveness. The focus of the game is on a *positive* group experience and is non-threatening.

The game will allow children to explore adaptive interaction styles within a safe group and helps them to improve self-concept, whilst encouraging the generalisation of behaviour into other settings. The game comprises game board, counters, dice and four sets of colour-coded cards arranged in categories corresponding to coloured shapes on the board.

The Anti-Bullying Game

ISBN 18302 335 3

Desig ed for children and adolescents who experience difficulties with peer relationships, *The Anti-Bullying Game* enables both victims and bullies to understand the dynamics underlying bullying behaviour and helps them to explore more adaptive interaction styles. Exploring the mechanisms behind passive and provocative behaviour, the game focuses on interactive processes, communication, belief systems and assertiveness.

Providing an opportunity for exploration within a safe group, the game helps young people to understand the dynamics of the power differential between victim and bully. It promotes positive self-esteem and encourages behaviour to be taken over into other settings.

The game comprises game board, counters, dice and four sets of colour-coded cards arranged in categories corresponding to coloured shapes on the board.

The Divorced and Separated Game

ISBN 1 85302 334 5

Developed for children and adolescents whose parents are separated or divorced, *The Divorced & Separated Game* is of especial use for those who are finding it difficult to cope with or understand the pain and upheaval surrounding separation. The game can be played with groups of siblings, peers or children from reconstituted families, and is also suitable for working with individuals. It may be played over consecutive sessions or adapted to the pace of the treatment. The game comprises a game board, counters, dice and four sets of colour-coded cards arranged in categories corresponding to coloured shapes on the board: *Facts, Changes, Emotions* and *Wishes, Dreams, Memories.*

Jessica Kingsley Publishers
116 Pentonville Road, London N1 9JB